Working Memory

Working memory—the conscious processing of information—is increasingly recognized as one of the most important aspects of intelligence. This fundamental cognitive skill is deeply connected to a great variety of human experience—from our childhood, to our old age, from our evolutionary past, to our digital future.

In this volume, leading psychologists review the latest research on working memory and consider what role it plays in development and over the lifespan. It is revealed how a strong working memory is connected with success (academically and acquiring expertise) and a poor working memory is connected with failure (addictive behavior and poor decision-making). The contributions also show how working memory played a role in our cognitive evolution and how the everyday things we do, like what we eat and how much we sleep, can have an impact on how well working memory functions. Finally, evidence on the benefits of working memory training is explored.

This volume is essential reading for students, researchers, and professionals with an interest in human memory and its improvement, including those working in cognitive psychology, cognitive neuroscience, developmental psychology, gerontology, education, health, and clinical psychology.

Tracy Packiam Alloway is interested in the role of working memory in education, particularly in individuals with learning disorders. Her research has received widespread media attention and appeared in over 250 news articles. She has also been invited to comment on television and radio as an expert on working memory.

Ross G. Alloway is involved in cutting-edge research on the impact of a highly saturated technological environment on the brain. He has co-published work on the growth and decline of working memory over the lifespan, as well as the importance of working memory in education, which was featured on BBC radio and in the UK *Sunday Times*.

FRONTIERS OF COGNITIVE PSYCHOLOGY

Series Editors
Nelson Cowan, *University of Missouri-Columbia*
David Balota, *Washington University in St. Louis*

Frontiers of Cognitive Psychology is a new series of cognitive psychology books, which aims to bring together the very latest research in the discipline, providing a comprehensive and up-to-date review of the latest empirical, theoretical and practical issues in the field. Each volume concentrates on a traditional core area of cognitive psychology, or an area which is emerging as a new core area for the future, and may include interdisciplinary perspectives from areas such as developmental psychology, neuroscience, evolutionary psychology, forensic psychology, social psychology, and the health sciences.

Published

Working Memory: The Connected Intelligence, Tracy Packiam Alloway & Ross G. Alloway (Eds)

Forthcoming

New Methods in Cognitive Psychology, Daniel H. Spieler & Eric Schumacher (Eds)

Neuroeconomics and Decision Making, Valerie F. Reyna & Evan Wilhelms (Eds)

Motivation and Cognitive Control, Todd S. Braver (Eds)

Working Memory

The Connected Intelligence

Edited by

Tracy Packiam Alloway

and

Ross G. Alloway

ΨP Psychology Press
Taylor & Francis Group

NEW YORK AND LONDON

First published 2013
by Psychology Press
711 Third Avenue, New York, NY 10017

Simultaneously published in the UK
by Psychology Press
27 Church Road, Hove, East Sussex BN3 2FA

Psychology Press is an imprint of the Taylor & Francis Group, an informa business

Library of Congress Cataloging-in-Publication Data
A catalog record for this book has been requested

ISBN: 978–1–84872–614–7 (hbk)
ISBN: 978–1–84872–618–5 (pbk)
ISBN: 978–0–203–09460–0 (ebk)

Typeset in New Caledonia LT Std
by Keystroke, Station Road, Codsall, Wolverhampton

Certified Sourcing
www.sfiprogram.org
SFI-00453

Printed and bound in the United States of America
by Edwards Brothers, Inc.

Contents

Contributors

Ross G. Alloway
University of Edinburgh
Edinburgh, UK

Tracy Packiam Alloway
Department of Psychology
University of North Florida
Jacksonville, FL, USA

Chandramallika Basak
The Center for Vital Longevity
University of Texas
Dallas, TX, USA

Sian L. Beilock
Department of Psychology
University of Chicago
Chicago, IL, USA

Martin Buschkuehl
Department of Psychology
The University of Michigan
Ann Arbor, MI, USA

Lavinia Cheie
Developmental Psychology Lab
Department of Psychology
Babeş-Bolyai University
Romania

Andrew R. A. Conway
Department of Psychology
Princeton University
Princeton, NJ, USA

Fred L. Coolidge
Department of Psychology
University of Colorado
Colorado Springs, CO, USA

Anita Cservenka
Department of Behavioral
    Neuroscience
Oregon Health and Science University
Portland, OR, USA

Pascale M. J. Engel de Abreu
University of Luxembourg
Luxembourg

K. Anders Ericsson
Department of Psychology
Florida State University
Tallahassee, FL, USA

J. M. Fuster
Semel Institute for Neuroscience and
    Human Behavior
University of California
Los Angeles, CA, USA

David Z. Hambrick
Department of Psychology
Michigan State University
East Lansing, MI, USA

Megan M. Herting
Department of Behavioral
    Neuroscience
Oregon Health and Science University
Portland, OR, USA

Susanne M. Jaeggi
Department of Psychology
University of Maryland
College Park, MD, USA

Scott E. Kanoski
Department of Biological Sciences
University of Southern California
Los Angeles, CA, USA

Cindy Lustig
Department of Psychology
University of Michigan
Ann Arbor, MI, USA

Brooke N. Macnamara
Department of Psychology
Princeton University
Princeton, NJ, USA

Andrew Mattarella-Micke
Department of Psychology
University of Chicago
Chicago, IL, USA

Elizabeth J. Meinz
Department of Psychology
Southern Illinois University
Edwardsville, IL, USA

Andrei C. Miu
Cognitive Neuroscience Laboratory
Department of Psychology
Babeş-Bolyai University
Romania

Daniel A. Monti
Jefferson-Myrna Brind Center of
    Integrative Medicine
Thomas Jefferson University
Philadelphia, PA, USA

Aleezé Sattar Moss
Jefferson-Myrna Brind Center of
    Integrative Medicine
Thomas Jefferson University
Philadelphia, PA, USA

Jerad H. Moxley
Department of Psychology
Florida State University
Tallahassee, FL, USA

Bonnie J. Nagel
Department of Psychiatry and
    Behavioral Neuroscience
Oregon Health and Science University
Portland, OR, USA

Andrew Newberg
Jefferson-Myrna Brind Center of
    Integrative Medicine
Thomas Jefferson University
Philadelphia, PA, USA

Karenleigh A. Overmann
Department of Psychology
University of Colorado
Colorado Springs, CO, USA

Patricia A. Reuter-Lorenz
Department of Psychology
University of Michigan
Ann Arbor, MI, USA

Peter J. Rosen
Department of Psychology
Washington State University
Pullman, WA, USA

Laura Visu-Petra
Developmental Psychology Lab
Department of Psychology
Babeş-Bolyai University
Romania

Paul Whitney
Department of Psychology
Washington State University
Pullman, WA, USA

Thomas Wynn
Department of Anthropology
University of Colorado
Colorado Springs, CO, USA

Elizabeth M. Zelinski
Leonard Davis School of Gerontology
University of Southern California
Los Angeles, CA, USA

Foreword

J. M. FUSTER

The concept of working memory has evolved considerably since Baddeley proposed it in the early 1980s. This conceptual evolution actually began one decade before his proposal with the discovery of so-called "memory cells" in the prefrontal cortex of monkeys performing short-term memory tasks—now called working-memory tasks. Memory cells are neurons that exhibit sustained activation while the animal retains an item of information for a correct and rewarded choice a few seconds or minutes later.

Subsequently, memory cells were found in other cortical locations, depending on the item in memory (the "memorandum"). It was further found that one given memorandum (visual, auditory or tactile) would activate cells in several non-contiguous areas of the cortex. Conversely, several memoranda would activate the cells of one given area. Memory-cell activations could be blocked by the reversible inactivation of a given cortical area, notably the lateral prefrontal cortex; this induced a working-memory deficit. The aggregate of these findings led this writer to postulate that working memory consisted in the temporary activation of a widely distributed network of cortical cell assemblies linked together by experience (in learning the task). The synaptic linkage between cell assemblies in the formation of those networks—which he called *cognits*—would result from the temporal coincidence of external stimuli, in accordance with the principles proposed by the Canadian psychologist Donald Hebb.

The functional neuroimaging in the human confirms the wide distribution, the overlap, and the hierarchical organization of the cortical memory networks or cognits activated in working memory. When viewed in the light of the clinical manifestations and symptoms of patients with cortical lesions, many neuroscientists, this writer included, have reached the conclusion that the cortical networks representing long-term memory are the same as those activated in working memory. It is now becoming increasingly accepted that working memory and long-term memory share the same cortical networks, and that working memory consists in the temporary activation of a long-term memory network updated *for* reaching a goal or solving a problem. This prospective, purposive, aspect of working memory, which was already in Baddeley's definition, is what distinguishes working memory from all other forms of short-term memory.

That prospective aspect of working memory, together with its temporal integrative function, is also what makes of it an executive function and puts it under the purview of the cortex of the frontal lobe. Indeed, it is by the dynamic co-operation of the prefrontal cortex with associative posterior cortices that working memory integrates percepts and acts across time in goal-directed behavior, reasoning and language. The latest computational models, based mainly on electrophysiological data, contend that working memory retains and integrates information across time by reentry (reverberation) between frontal and posterior cognits.

The cognit is a unit of memory and knowledge—which is semantic memory—in the form of a cortical network that, in the active state, serves not only working memory but also every other cognitive function: attention, perception, language and intelligence. In fact, it is largely by its role in working memory that the cognit serves those other cognitive functions, notably intelligence.

Intelligence is a complex cognitive function that feeds on all the others (especially attention and memory). It has almost as many definitions as the measures of performance to test it. At the beginning of the last century, Spearman named *general intelligence* the faculty needed to perform well on a variety of psychological tests (visual, spatial, sensory-motor) and devised the g-factor as a global measure of it. In modern times, John Duncan, on the basis of neuroimaging data, has identified the lateral prefrontal cortex as the cortical region whose level of activity is best correlated with general intelligence.

On close examination, most of the tests that go into the measure of general intelligence have one feature in common, namely, the requirement to bridge time with working memory—at least the memory of the instructions from the tester before the test. Thus, general intelligence and working memory appear to be based in the prefrontal cortex. Two caveats, however, are in order here: first, correlation is not causality, and second, the prefrontal cortex does not perform its role in isolation, but in close cooperation with other cortical and sub-cortical structures. With respect to the first caveat, it has been successfully argued that temporal correlation actually facilitates the inference of causality. The second caveat is resolved by taking away from the prefrontal cortex the designation of "central executive" and instead adopting that of "enabler" (the former epithet leads inevitably to an infinite regress).

What does the prefrontal cortex enable with working memory? Above all, at the top of the perception/action cycle, the prefrontal cortex enables the mediation of cross-temporal contingencies (*if* now this, later that; *if* earlier that, now this). To understand it, we have to descend to elementary biology. The organism of lower animals adapts to the environment via the limbic brain, by reflexes and conditioned responses, in essence automatically. Instead, in the human and higher primates, the organism adapts to its environment via the cerebral cortex, by using cognition and experience, that is, the fund of memory and knowledge that the individual has acquired in life; in other words, the enormous array of perceptual and executive cognits that life experience has formed in the individual cortex.

The perception/action cycle is the circular cybernetic process of information between the human organism and its environment, the cortical expansion of the reflex adaptation of lower organisms. Sensory signals from the environment are processed through the posterior (perceptual) cortex, which informs adaptive actions in the frontal (executive) cortex, which generate new signals processed through the posterior and frontal cortices, which leads to new actions and new signals, and so on, until the cycle reaches its adaptive goal. A beautiful example of the perception/action cycle at work is the dialogue between two individuals, where each interlocutor's speech leads to the response of the other, and that response leads to further speech by the first speaker. And so on. In reality, the dialog consists of two interlinked cycles, where each interlocutor constitutes the environment of the other.

The same process ties an individual to his physical and social environment. Although some activity in the cycle is purely reflex and integrated at lower cortical and sub-cortical levels of the hierarchies of percepts and actions, high-level integration involves higher cortex, perceptual and executive. Indeed, the posterior associative and prefrontal cortices enter the cycle when there is complexity, ambiguity, and uncertainty in the process. Further, when for whatever reason the cycle is discontinuous between perception and action, working memory becomes essential and, with it, the prefrontal cortex.

There is another property of the human cycle and cortical dynamics that transcends those of the nonhuman primates and lower organisms: The perception/action cycle and the prefrontal cortex of the human are not only adaptive but also *pre-adaptive*. That means that the human can predict and prepare for anticipated action in the integration of goal-directed (purposive) behavior, reasoning and language.

From these considerations it follows that the prefrontal cortex of the human enables the mediation of cross-temporal contingencies, to connect the past with the future. At the same time, it enables the subject to make that future by decisions, plans and creativity, all the product of new connections between existing cognits, and all aided by working memory. This is the way I view working memory as the foundation of a *connected intelligence*.

Part I

Working Memory
The Connected Intelligence

1

Working Memory

An Introduction

ROSS G. ALLOWAY

University of Edinburgh, Edinburgh, UK

TRACY PACKIAM ALLOWAY

Department of Psychology, University of North Florida, Jacksonville, FL, USA

THE CASE OF PHINEAS GAGE

*I*n 1848, a three-and-a-half-foot iron rod shot through the brain of Phineas Gage, and didn't instantly kill him. After a few moments on his back, he got up, climbed into a horse cart, and went home. When the doctor arrived, he found Phineas sitting in a chair, able to discuss rationally what happened to him. The story caused a sensation in the papers, as well as in the medical community, and no one expected him to survive for long.

Phineas was a railway foreman, and the accident happened when he was setting explosives for a new rail line. His tamping rod, used to pack in the charges, sparked on a rock and detonated the blasting powder, sending the rod up through his left cheek, through the frontal region of his brain, and out the top of his skull. For a number of days following the accident, his head bled, and bone and pieces of brain fell out or were removed. But, amazingly, he survived.

What happened after the incident shocked doctors as much as his survival. They found that Phineas was profoundly altered by the damage; he had become a totally different man. Before the accident, Phineas was described as polite and hard working, the "most efficient" foreman in the company. After the accident, he became short-tempered, childish, and profane. He would constantly make new plans, invent new ideas, but never execute any of them. He was soon fired, and was eventually found begging on the street, with the iron rod from his accident.

Before Phineas, there was still considerable debate on the nature of the brain and how it influenced behavior, if at all. Because Phineas survived and because his doctor was able to document the dramatic change, scientists now had powerful confirmation that human behavior is directly related to the brain. But we would suggest that Phineas has even more to offer the world. By damaging his brain, Phineas damaged something so crucial, so intricately tied up in who he was and how he related to the world, that he was unrecognizable to those who knew him. But his loss has become our gain. We now know that the rod likely damaged his *working memory* when it shot through his brain (for more on Phineas Gage, see Chapter 3 by Coolidge, Wynn, & Overmann).

Working memory is the brain's conductor. Like a conductor, it brings together all of the different areas and functions of the brain into harmony. In the same way, the brain is like an orchestra, with each area like a different section. The language center, Broca's area, is like the articulate expressiveness of the string section. The intraparietal sulcus, the math area, is like the precise keyboard section. The amygdala, the heart of our emotions, is like the thundering percussion section that must be brought under control or it will overpower the whole orchestra. Without its conductor, the orchestra makes the jarring sounds of a cacophony. It is not until working memory walks out on stage that all instruments are brought under control, and the symphony can begin.

The ability to moderate our emotions, to control what we say and do, to form a plan and execute it, to do mental math, to perceive the needs of others, to focus on the positive and disregard the negative, to quickly shift between tasks, to write and carry on a conversation, to put names together with faces, all would be impossible without working memory. No wonder Phineas changed.

TRACES OF WORKING MEMORY

Though the term "working memory" is a twentieth-century invention, concepts linked with working memory have been explored throughout Western thought. A sampling of key historical figures shows that the notion of a conductor or controller moderating, organizing, and giving attention to behavior and emotions can be traced from Socrates through to René Descartes and beyond.

Socrates was interested in the rational control of human behavior, an ability we now associate with working memory. At the center of his enquiries was the concept of the "Soul." In fact, "psychology" is a term with Greek roots that literally means "the study of the soul." The concept of the Soul encompassed much of the behavior we now know is based in the brain. Socrates divided the Soul into three parts: Appetite, Spirit, and Rationality. Appetite gives us our basic drives like hunger, sex, and survival. Spirit is responsible for our virtuous qualities and emotions, including our desire for love and happiness, and is also associated with emotions like anger. The last part, Rationality, is given pride of place. It directs the other two. Like working memory, it controls our urges, harmonizes our emotions, and helps us to act in a planned and appropriate manner. In much the same way that Phineas was seen to be a different person when he damaged his working memory, how rational you are defines who you are.

Working memory also helps us categorize and make connections between things around us. We can see this process in the work of Aristotle, who wanted to understand how Rationality related to the world around him. Aristotle's brain worked like an ancient version of Google. If you search Google for seemingly unconnected words like "baseball" and "humming bird," you will find over a million and a half hits ranked from the most to the least relevant. In the same way, working memory allows you to search through information and to perceive connections. Aristotle didn't have the computing power of the World Wide Web, but, like Google, he was able to perceive an order everywhere he looked. Not only was he a philosopher, he was one of the world's first scientists to generate a taxonomy of the animal kingdom, which had a huge influence on the way we understand the natural world.

Perhaps the most memorable line from an introductory philosophy class is "Cogito ergo sum": *I think therefore I am*. By writing these lines, the French philosopher René Descartes unwittingly implicated working memory in the emergence of modern philosophy, and its focus on consciousness. Descartes reasoned that the only things he could believe in were those that could not be doubted. Descartes soon realized that even his senses could be doubted because he might be dreaming, which meant that he couldn't know for certain that he had a body. The only thing he couldn't doubt was the fact that he was doubting. To doubt, he had to have a consciousness, and to have a consciousness, he had to exist. *Cogito ergo Sum*.

Consciousness is an important feature of working memory. Working memory is the space where we give our *attention* to information. Neuroscientists, such as Joaquin Fuster, argue that attention, or awareness, is related to consciousness and that this is deeply connected to working memory (Fuster, 1997). By working with information—for example, by processing a list of instructions or performing a multi-step mental math problem—we are giving attention to it, and therefore we are conscious of it. Of course, we use other cognitive resources when we are feeling emotions, hunger, or listening to music. But when we *think* about how we feel, we are giving our attention to our emotions and we are recruiting our working memory in the process. When we use our working memory, we are conscious of the task at hand. Echoing Descartes, working memory therefore consciousness.

WORKING MEMORY AND THE PREFRONTAL CORTEX (PFC)

The conversation that began in philosophy was taken in a different direction by scientists who wanted to understand how the brain influences who we are. In the 1870s, the Scottish brain scientist David Ferrier discovered where working memory was located in the brain. This discovery was made possible by the concept of *localization*. Localization means that we can map the brain according to what it does. It was in the nineteenth century that the medulla oblongata was linked to respiration, the cerebellum was linked to equilibrium, and the language centers of the brain were discovered.

Many of the advances in nineteenth-century brain science were made possible by the use of techniques like *ablation*—cutting a piece of brain out to see what ability would be affected—and *galvanic stimulation*—attaching an electrical conductor to an exposed section of brain to stimulate it. Ferrier made huge leaps forward in understanding the motor cortex by using these methods on monkeys. Ferrier found that when he electrically stimulated the top and side of a monkey's brain, he could make certain muscles move, but when he stimulated the front of the brain, nothing happened: No muscles moved. It wasn't until he ablated the front of the brain that he saw something that he didn't expect. Monkeys that had taken an interest in their surroundings before the ablation now became apathetic and lazy, they had suffered a "mental degradation," and lost the ability to focus their attention. Ferrier argued that he had removed a center of the brain responsible for what he called *inhibitory function*. According to Ferrier, these centers allow us to inhibit muscle movements, focus attention, and form an idea (Macmillan, 2000).

Ferrier's importance is not so much that he crudely conceptualized functions we now associate with working memory—this had been done since Socrates—but that he accurately associated these functions with a *region* of the brain. By doing so, Ferrier had discovered the seat of working memory.

We now know that working memory is located in the prefrontal cortex, also called the PFC. The PFC is located in the front of the brain, around the same area that Ferrier cut out from his monkeys. Because the monkeys had a similar brain structure to humans, Ferrier believed that his map of the monkey brain would also hold true for humans. But he wanted to know for sure that the frontal region in monkeys was also responsible for inhibition in humans. Ferrier didn't have an fMRI scanner, so he couldn't see what was happening in the human brain, and he couldn't cut into the brains of live human subjects without going to jail.

Fortunately for Ferrier, he heard how Phineas' behavior was similar to his ablated monkeys, and he wondered if Phineas' injuries would match up. When he looked at photographs of Phineas' skull it was a true Eureka moment. Ferrier believed that the damage to Phineas matched the same region as his monkeys, and wasted no time in publicizing his discovery in a series of sensational lectures.

Phineas is so important to the story of working memory because he demonstrated that when the PFC is damaged, so is working memory. After the rod shot through the front of Phineas' brain, he became unable to inhibit his anger, he acted impulsively, he was unable to execute his plans, he swore excessively, he acted in a socially inappropriate manner, and appeared unintelligent for his age and experience. His behavior matches up with those who have severely impaired working memory. The behavioral evidence combined with analysis of the probable trajectory of the steel rod strongly suggests that his PFC was injured and that this had seriously degraded his working memory. When his working memory changed, so too did Phineas (see Damasio, Grabowski, Frank, Galaburda, & Damasio, 1994). Unfortunately, Ferrier neglected his thesis, and the study of what came to be known as working memory lay dormant for over eighty years.

THE MODERN-DAY PHINEAS

In the 1960s, psychologists believed that short-term memory was responsible for helping us to learn new information. The prevailing idea was that we learn and store new information with short-term memory and it is transferred to long-term memory.

Then, in a remarkable repeat of history, a modern-day Phineas emerged. When KF drove his motorcycle into a tree in the 1960s, psychologists were once again offered a clue to how the brain works. Although KF walked away alive, he sustained serious brain injuries. His memory, in particular, was severely affected. For example, in a gold standard test of short-term memory—remembering a string of numbers in the correct sequence—KF could usually remember only two numbers. As a result, he was diagnosed with having a short-term memory deficit.

The prevailing view of the time was that short-term memory functioned like working memory: it was a mental workspace to remember and process information. It also served as a gateway to transfer new information into long-term memory. A major problem with this view soon became apparent. Patient KF continued to function well in other areas of his life. He could even learn new information, sometimes even faster than normal controls, and could still remember this information months later. How could this be if his short-term memory (which was supposed to be his gateway to learning new information) was impaired?

TOUCHDOWN MOMENT

This is the question that two British psychologists, Alan Baddeley and Graham Hitch, came to ask. In the early 1970s in the UK, American football was unfamiliar, and very few people knew about a linebacker, Hail Mary, or running back. Though football fascinated him, Baddeley hadn't grown up playing it or watching it on television. It took him some time to understand the different plays and terminology, in part because he could only find his games on the radio. He describes how listening to the commentator and reconstructing the plays in his head was a very mentally demanding task (A. Baddeley, personal communication, February 10, 2011).

One day, while driving, he was so engrossed with listening and imagining the game on the radio that he hadn't realized his car was weaving around the road! But he didn't crash. He was able to recover and realized that something more than his short-term memory was at work. When he was driving and listening to the game, he was doing more than remembering information; he was switching between two different tasks. There had to be something else—another brain function that could let him jump between two different things.

That was the "touchdown moment" for Baddeley. He realized that we need a "controller," something that can keep a goal in mind, bring in cognitive resources from different parts of the brain, and also manage incoming information. So Baddeley and Hitch started formulating their view of working memory as the controller that allows us to do all these things.

But Baddeley and Hitch couldn't write a paper about listening to the radio while driving. To prove that short-term memory couldn't account for his experience, he would have to demonstrate it in an experiment. The only problem was that brain injury patients who had damaged their short-term memory were so few and far between that it would be hard to prove they had a controller. So they came up with an innovative plan to "create" short-term memory deficits in undergraduate psychology students. Using the same number task that patient KF did, Baddeley and Hitch gave the students increasingly long number sequences until their memory failed them and their performance looked very much like a patient with a short-term memory deficit. At the same time, they gave students logic and reasoning problems. If they could do the problems with their overloaded short-term memories, it would prove that something else was at work. Baddeley and Hitch discovered that the students could still do the problems (Baddeley& Hitch, 1974).

Baddeley and Hitch's framework for working memory was almost not published. Scientific journals typically accept well-established and empirically solid results, not speculative models. But Baddeley and Hitch were optimistic about the results they had seen in their lab work and were convinced that they should go ahead and try to publish it. As Hitch said, "The concept was out there but the model was new" (G. Hitch, personal communication, February 11, 2011). Their working memory model view first appeared as a book chapter. Since then, hundreds of research papers have tested this model.

WORKING MEMORY CONNECTIONS

Almost forty years on from that first publication by Baddeley and Hitch, there has been an explosion of research on working memory. This edited volume picks up the journey of working memory. We, the editors, see working memory as a "cognitive controller"—the ability to plan actions and thought processes, and direct behavior toward a desired goal. Thanks to breakthroughs in brain imaging and neuroscience, we see how areas in the PFC are associated with working memory. Joaquin Fuster's groundbreaking discoveries have expanded the notion of working memory to include a range of executive skills, from attentional focus to goal-directed behavior (Fuster, 1997). Working memory has since become associated with more than a simple process of maintaining and manipulating information.

This volume has benefitted immensely from contributions from psychologists opening new frontiers in research on working memory. Throughout this volume, we see how working memory is connected to a great variety of human experience, from our learning (Chapter 4) to our diet (Chapter 8), from adapting in our evolutionary past (Chapter 3) to training to achieve our cognitive potential (Chapters 14 and 15).

Part I explores the history of working memory from its theoretical background to its pivotal role in human evolution. Conway, Macnamara, and Engel de Abreu provide an excellent discussion of how working memory differs from traditional notions of intelligence, as measured by IQ tests. Beginning with a historical perspective of intelligence testing, the authors reveal how the focus of psychometric testing of intelligence has shifted over the last 100 years and what this shift means for working memory.

How can the action of striking a rock against another while holding the idea of a shape in mind millions of years ago inform modern life? Coolidge, Wynn, and Overmann take us on a journey through time to discover how we developed the ability to conceive and execute complex plans of action. They argue that this ability—working memory—is "fundamental to human thinking and one that underpins much of our success."

In Part II, we learn more about the development and decline of working memory. Alloway and Alloway discuss individual differences in working memory and the implications of this during childhood. Why do some students struggle, while others don't? We learn how working memory is the "engine of learning." Like the engine of a car, working memory drives learning forward while working with different parts of the brain when we use language or solve mathematical problems. We also discover the implications of poor working memory in education—without adequate support, students find it difficult to acquire key learning skills and concepts. However, with the growing availability of standardized diagnostic tests and evidence-based training programs, such students can receive the necessary intervention.

Basak and Zelinski extend the discussion of working memory to detail what is known about changes and differences as people grow older. They begin with a historical perspective of observations of age-related decline in working memory, including how individual differences in older adults' working memory affects performance on other cognitive abilities. They review the specific processes that change with aging and examine how we use working memory in goal maintenance and attentional focus. They also demonstrate how working memory pervades many higher-level processes that are relevant to everyday activities, such as driving, and how this relationship changes as we age.

Part III examines the role of working memory in expertise. Ericsson and Moxley provide a comprehensive overview of highly specialized skills, like chess, to everyday skills, such as typing and driving. The authors evaluate different theories of how working memory interacts with long-term memory to direct expertise in these areas. We find out whether practicing long hours makes a difference, and whether we can transfer our expertise in one domain to another, unrelated, domain.

Hambrick and Meinz focus the discussion of working memory in expertise on the fascinating topic of music. They tackle the two opposing views of musical skill. One view is that experts are "born" (the *talent view*), and the other is that they are "made" (the *acquired characteristics* view). Looking at evidence from unskilled and skilled musicians, children and adults, the authors discuss possible reasons for the popularity of music as a domain for expertise research, as well as an approach to the scientific investigation of music skill. They also review evidence for the role of acquired characteristics and basic capacities—especially working memory capacity—in music skill.

In Part IV, we learn about the interaction between working memory and the body. The first chapter in this section deals with working memory and diet. Kanoski points to how the sharp rise in obesity rates in the USA since the early 1980s has spurred on researchers to discover the effects on cognition and neuropsychological function of being overweight, obese, and consuming unhealthy high-calorie foods. The emerging picture is that there is a two-way street between working memory and dietary choice. Kanoski suggests that the Western diet includes saturated fat and simple carbohydrates (e.g., sugars) that can have detrimental effects on working memory, which in turn hinders our ability to make good dietary choices.

Whitney and Rosen bring us up-to-date research on how not all aspects of cognition are equally affected by sleep loss. The authors describe working memory as "a hub of activity in almost any interesting cognitive task," and thus fatigue effects on working memory are especially interesting to consider. Just as brain lesions and damage have informed our understanding of working memory, Whitney and Rosen discuss how we are beginning to see evidence that sleep deprivation produces dissociations among different working memory-related processes. The benefit, as the authors point out, is that research on "fatigue effects enjoy a particular advantage in comparison to lesion studies in that the compromised brain functions can be manipulated experimentally and the effects reversed."

What leads to addictive behavior patterns? Nagel, Herting, and Cservenka review evidence highlighting the contribution of working memory in decisions involving alcohol dependence, substance abuse, and gambling addiction. The authors include evidence from brain research, using functional magnetic resonance imaging (fMRI), to understand how addiction is associated with various abnormalities in working memory-related brain response.

Part V shifts focus to consider the interaction between working memory and the mind, specifically the dynamic role it plays in anxiety and stress. Visu-Petra, Cheie, and Miu discuss the interaction between working memory and anxiety in developmental populations. They provide an excellent review of different theoretical positions, including the influential Processing Efficiency Theory.

Mattarella-Micke and Beilock look at how working memory in adults affects performance in everyday, high-stress situations, whether fumbling during an important speech or staring nervously at a blank test. They argue that working memory is "studied not simply because it relates to elementary cognitive tasks measured in the lab, but because it is extremely good at predicting how people will perform on a wide range of real world tasks."

Moss, Monti, and Newberg review cutting-edge research on how to manage anxiety and stress with mindfulness meditation. They review findings that even short periods of meditation can alter brain structure and function, leading to improved working memory. From research on first-time meditators, expert meditators, and Buddhist monks, we learn how increased focused attention can train and develop other cognitive skills, as well as preserve working memory functioning during high-stress moments.

In Part VI we review whether we can increase working memory capacity. What works and what doesn't? Interest in brain training programs has skyrocketed over the last few years. This section of the book examines research on whether reported gains are simply practice effects or transfer to other tasks, and explores whether all age groups and both typical and clinical populations can benefit from working memory training.

Jaeggi and Buschkuehl review the "state of the art of working memory training and transfer," and discuss the underlying mechanisms that could be driving transfer effects. To date, there is some evidence for the efficacy of working memory training in typically developing preschoolers, school-aged children, young adults, older adults, as well as special needs populations with pre-existing working memory deficits, such as ADHD and schizophrenia. While initial research on working memory is promising in that near transfer effects are evident, the authors describe how far transfer effects may be more elusive.

Lustig and Reuter-Lorenz extend this discussion to review the neuroimaging evidence from working memory training. The authors demonstrate how this process "can provide insights about underlying mechanisms of training-related change difficult to ascertain through behavior alone." The authors describe CRUNCH (Compensation-Related Utilization of Neural Circuits Hypothesis) as a way to evaluate an increase or decrease in brain activation across a range of task demands.

As these chapters demonstrate, working memory is a key cognitive skill that connects a wide range of human behavior and abilities. We believe that this research is just the tip of the iceberg of what may be discovered. As the various roles of working memory are more deeply understood and investigated, we may find new evidence and research avenues that further demonstrate that working memory is indeed the Connected Intelligence.

REFERENCES

Baddeley, A. D., & Hitch, G. J. (1974). Working Memory, In G.A. Bower (Ed.), *The Psychology of Learning and Motivation: Advances in Research and Theory* (Vol. 8, pp. 47–89), New York: Academic Press.

Damasio, H., Grabowski, T., Frank, R., Galaburda, A. M., Damasio, A. R. (1994). "The return of Phineas Gage: clues about the brain from the skull of a famous patient." *Science* 264, 1102–1105.

Fuster, J. M. (1997). *The Prefrontal Cortex* (third edition).New York: Raven Press.

Macmillan, M. (2000). *An Odd Kind of Fame: Stories of Phineas Gage*. Cambridge, MA: MIT Press.

2

Working Memory and Intelligence

An Overview

ANDREW R. A. CONWAY
Department of Psychology, Princeton University, Princeton, NJ

BROOKE N. MACNAMARA
Department of Psychology, Princeton University, Princeton, NJ

PASCALE M. J. ENGEL DE ABREU
University of Luxembourg, Luxembourg

BACKGROUND INFORMATION

The terms working memory and intelligence are generally used to refer to two very different psychological constructs, yet measures of working memory capacity are strongly related to scores on most intelligence tests. Behavioral scientists don't normally get very excited about correlations because they are reminded more often than most that correlation does not imply causation. However, when it comes to the correlation between working memory capacity and intelligence, there is quite a bit of excitement. The reason is simple: If two psychological constructs are strongly correlated then in most applied settings, either construct can be used to predict future behavior. Assessment of one construct is sufficient; assessment of both constructs is redundant. For example, either working memory capacity or intelligence can be used to predict academic achievement in children (Alloway & Alloway, 2010). With respect to the behavioral sciences, this is more than a convenience. It presents the opportunity for a revolution in the assessment of cognitive ability. A century has passed since the first intelligence tests were developed, yet to this day no one can agree on what intelligence really means. In the twentieth century the Intelligence Quotient (IQ) emerged as the default marker of one's intellectual ability, yet the design of IQ tests was at first subjective and later motivated by data, not theory. In contrast, working memory is a well-defined construct and tasks designed to measure working memory capacity are motivated by psychological and biological theories, developed to account for what is known about the mind and brain and, more importantly, amenable to change as more knowledge is accumulated.

The goal of the current chapter is to review empirical evidence demonstrating a strong correlation between working memory capacity and intelligence. The chapter will also provide the reader with an introduction to *psychometrics*, which is a scientific approach to the measurement of psychological constructs that has largely dominated research on cognitive abilities for over 100 years, and informs current thinking on the relationship between working memory capacity, intelligence, and their many correlates.

The chapter begins with a brief and selective historical review of research on intelligence, includes descriptions of popular measures of intelligence, and introduces the notion of IQ. This is followed by, in similar fashion, a review of research on working memory and a discussion of measures of working memory capacity. These introductory sections set the stage for a review of empirical evidence illustrating strong correlations between working memory capacity and intelligence. Finally, to put this work into perspective, the chapter concludes with a critical analysis of the psychometric approach to the investigation of cognitive ability.

CURRENT EVIDENCE

Intelligence

Intelligence is a construct used by scientists and laypeople alike to describe and predict individual differences in cognitive abilities. An individual is typically described as "highly intelligent" if he or she consistently performs well above average on various cognitive tasks, or tests, for example, by achieving high marks in school or by scoring well on standardized tests or entrance exams. (Assessments of intelligence are typically referred to as "tests" while measures of working memory capacity are referred to as "tasks.") As mentioned, no one consensus definition of intelligence exists, so it's hard to find one that will satisfy every reader. In his recent compendium, *IQ and Human Intelligence*, Nick Mackintosh (1998) successfully sidestepped this problem, so we will follow suit, and cite the *Oxford English Dictionary*, which defines an "intelligent" person as, "Having a high degree or full measure of understanding; quick to understand; knowing, sensible, sagacious."

It's fair to say that most contemporary scholars would accept this definition of "intelligent," albeit to varying degrees. Indeed, it bears some resemblance to a definition of intelligence provided in a 1994 editorial statement to *The Wall Street Journal*, signed by 52 academic researchers:

> A very general mental capability that, among other things, involves the ability to reason, plan, solve problems, think abstractly, comprehend complex ideas, learn quickly and learn from experience. It is not merely book learning, a narrow academic skill, or test-taking

smarts. Rather, it reflects a broader and deeper capability for comprehending our surroundings—"catching on," "making sense" of things, or "figuring out" what to do.

(Gottfredson, 1994)

Where did this general notion of intelligence come from? Historical analyses of both literature and linguistics suggest that the basic idea that some people are "smarter" than others has been around for quite some time, dating back at least to early Greek philosophers (Sternberg, 1990). More contemporary definitions of intelligence stem from systematic research conducted in Psychology and Education in the late nineteenth and early twentieth century. Two men in particular, Charles Spearman and Alfred Binet, had significant effects on theories of intelligence and IQ testing respectively. We start here with Spearman and then discuss Binet in the following section on intelligence tests.

British psychologist Charles Spearman (1904) was the first to demonstrate an empirical phenomenon known as the "positive manifold," which refers to the commonly observed pattern of positive correlations among a wide variety of measures of cognitive performance. For example, high school grades, standardized test scores, and scores on working memory tasks all tend to be positively correlated, yet they are all very different assessment tools (for instance, some are computerized and some are "paper and pencil," some use verbal material and some use spatial material, etc.). Spearman demonstrated the positive manifold by calculating correlations among children's grades in six different disciplines: Classics, French, English, Math, Pitch, and Music. Correlations are typically presented in a matrix, so in Spearman's case it was a 6×6 matrix. Spearman observed that all the correlations in the matrix were positive and strong. He then conducted a statistical procedure called factor analysis and found that one single factor accounted for the majority of variance in all the measures. In other words, the six different measures could be reduced to one, and the variance among children could still, largely, be explained. This general factor is now known as Spearman's g.

Of course, debate still rages as to what g really means, if anything. Broadly speaking, three main camps exist: (1) it reflects a general cognitive ability; (2) it reflects the correlation among several different but related abilities; and (3) it is merely a statistical artifact. We will have more to say about these opposing views later in the section on psychometrics. Here, we will consider just a few of the most influential theories that have been proposed since Spearman's initial findings.

Spearman belonged to the first camp and argued that g corresponds to a single mental ability. He used energy and resources as metaphors to argue that some people simply have greater mental energy or more cognitive resources and will therefore perform above average on any cognitive task, regardless of domain. This theory has intuitive appeal and was supported by his factor analysis on children's grades in different classes. For instance, in school settings Mathematics and English are very different subjects, with a different curriculum and different instruction and testing formats, yet among the children that Spearman observed, those who did well in Mathematics also tended to do well in English. Similar patterns of correlations are still being observed and have serious implications in modern society. In the United States, for example, most young adults planning to attend college take the SAT test (formerly known as the Scholastic Aptitude Test), which is used by universities to make admissions decisions. In short, if one does well on the SAT then chances of being admitted to a prestigious university increase. Two subtests of the SAT are the Quantitative SAT (QSAT), which measures mathematical knowledge and reasoning, and the Verbal SAT (VSAT), which measures language-based knowledge and reasoning. The subtests, at face value, look very different from one another, and they are obviously designed to test different aptitudes. The implicit assumption is that the QSAT will have greater predictive validity with respect to the sciences, whereas the VSAT will have greater predictive validity with respect to the humanities. There is some support for this differential validity. However, the correlation between the QSAT and VSAT is strong, typically around $r = .70$ (e.g., Frey & Detterman, 2004). This strong positive correlation is consistent with Spearman's notion that there must be a general ability that accounts for consistent variation among such different tests. Moreover, the theory of a general ability is anecdotally supported by real-life experiences, which are admittedly subjective, yet seem consistent enough to support the notion that some people are simply smarter than others, in a very general sense.

Other researchers were quick to critique Spearman's theory of g. One early influential approach was the bi-factor theory of g, which is really just an extension of Spearman's theory (Holzinger & Swineford, 1937). According to bi-factor theory, g refers to a general mental ability that accounts for the majority of variation in test performance, but the total variance in any one test must be accounted for by two factors, one general, and the other specific to the particular test. In contemporary terms, the two factors in the original bi-factor model map onto domain-general sources of variance and test-specific sources of variance. In other words, individual differences in cognitive ability can be explained by cognitive and neural mechanisms that are general and exert their influence on all tests, yet some variance in individual tests is accounted for by mechanisms specific to the particular test. Formally incorporating a second factor to account for test-specific variance allowed the bi-factor model to account for patterns of correlations better than the one-factor general ability model (Holzinger & Swineford, 1937).

The second camp of theories argues that g reflects the correlation of several, separable primary mental abilities (e.g., Thurstone, 1938). In his primary mental abilities model, Louis Leon Thurstone argued that domain-specific abilities were more integral to individual differences than a general factor. He identified several primary abilities, such as verbal comprehension, inductive reasoning, perceptual speed, numerical ability, verbal fluency, associative memory, and spatial visualization. The primary mental abilities model is supported by the fact that tasks designed to test the same mental ability tend to be correlated more strongly with each other than with tasks designed to measure a different ability, even though the positive manifold is still observed. Thus, a general factor still plays a role but Thurstone placed greater emphasis on more specific, primary abilities. (For an even more elaborate primary ability model, see the work of Guilford, 1988).

Thurstone and Guilford, and many others, proposed several different mental abilities that are defined by the content of test materials. For example, verbal ability is operationally defined by tests that primarily consist of verbal material. Another way to categorize tests of intelligence is to consider the extent to which a particular test requires previously learned information, or acquired knowledge, versus novel problem-solving techniques. For example, Cattell and Horn (1978) distinguished crystallized intelligence from fluid intelligence. Crystallized intelligence refers to the ability to access and use knowledge, experience, and skills stored in long-term memory and is measured by tests that are designed to assess a person's depth and breadth of knowledge of particular topics, such as general knowledge, vocabulary, and mathematics. In contrast, fluid intelligence refers to inductive and deductive reasoning in situations that don't allow for the use of prior experience but instead challenge the individual to adapt and develop novel ideas and strategies to succeed. The distinction between crystallized and fluid intelligence is supported by psychometric studies as well as neuropsychological and developmental investigations of cognitive ability. For example, certain types of brain damage or disease cause a deficit in fluid intelligence but not crystallized intelligence, and fluid intelligence declines in later years of life while crystallized intelligence accumulates over the lifetime (Cattell, 1987).

Thurstone, Guilford, Horn, Cattell, and many others all struggled with the problem of determining how many primary abilities exist, and how they should be categorized. The best one could do is conduct an exhaustive analysis of all the correlational studies ever reported on cognitive ability and attempt to organize specific tasks by primary abilities in a manner that is consistent with all the empirical evidence. John Carroll (1993) accomplished this remarkable feat. His book, *Human Cognitive Abilities: A Survey of Factor-Analytic Studies*, is staggering in its scope. Based on 461 independent data sets on individual differences in cognitive abilities, Carroll proposed a three-stratum theory of cognitive ability. The three strata are "narrow," "broad," and "general." Narrow abilities are specific to particular tasks, broad abilities reveal their influence in broader classes of tasks, and the general factor permeates all cognitive tasks.

In contrast to Carroll and other psychometricians who preceded him, the third camp of theorists argues that g is merely a statistical artifact and has no direct cognitive or biological basis. Theorists in this camp are quick to point to a fundamental error in the interpretation of factors in the statistical procedure called factor analysis. Most behavioral scientists interpret factors from a factor analysis as reflecting a unitary construct that can be linked to specific cognitive and neural mechanisms. However, early critics of Spearman's work demonstrated that a general factor could emerge from a factor analysis even when there is no single underlying source of variance permeating all tasks (see Thomson, 1916). In short, if a battery of tasks all tap a common set of cognitive processes, in an overlapping manner, such that each task shares at least one process with another, then a general factor can emerge despite the fact that no one cognitive process is required by all tasks. Thomson's theory, and others that followed, have become known as "sampling theories" of g because the battery of tasks that reveal g all "sample" from a large number of cognitive processes. According to proponents of this view, the notion of *general* cognitive ability is not necessary to account for g.

Historically, sampling theories of g have garnered much less attention than general ability theories. However, Thomson's simple framework, first illustrated in

1916, has recently been resurrected and interest in sampling theories of g is on the rise (Bartholomew, Deary, & Lawn, 2009; Conway et al., 2011; Kovacs, 2010; van der Maas et al., 2006). We will return to a discussion of sampling theories later in the chapter but we will conclude here with a few important points: (1) Sampling theories are not the same as the idea of multiple intelligences (cf., Gardner, 1983); (2) Sampling theories do not deny the importance of g (cf., Gould, 1981); (3) The stumbling block for sampling theories of g is how to identify the underlying cognitive and neural processes, or mechanisms, that are being sampled by a battery of tests.

Intelligence Tests

Spearman can be credited with launching the debate about theories of intelligence but his primary work on the topic was pre-dated by the work of French psychologist Alfred Binet. Binet was charged with developing a test that determined which children would most benefit from special schools devoted to teaching those who could not keep pace with a normal curriculum. Having two daughters, Binet had been observing tasks the elder daughter could perform that the younger still could not. This lead him to the idea of "mental age," which refers to an individual child's cognitive ability relative to his or her peers of the same age, as well as to younger and older children. Binet tested children in various age groups on various tasks to develop "benchmarks" of performance for each age group, which allowed him to determine whether an individual child was advanced, average, or behind relative to his or her peers of the same chronological age. For example, if a four-year-old child could complete most of the tasks that an average six-year-old child could perform, then s/he was considered advanced, and would be described as having a mental age of six. If an eight-year-old child could not complete the majority of tasks completed by other children of the same age but could only complete tasks that an average six-year-old could, then s/he was classified as behind, and so too would be described as having a mental age of six.

The Binet-Simon Scale (commonly referred to as the Binet Scale) was first published in 1911 (Binet & Simon, 1911) and included tasks such as defining words, pointing to parts of the body, naming objects in a picture, repeating digits, completing sentences, describing differences between similar items, saying as many words that rhymed with another word as one could in a minute, telling time and figuring out the time if the hands of a clock were reversed, and cutting a shape in a folded piece of paper and determining what the shape would be once unfolded. Binet was the first researcher to systematically study average cognitive abilities by age and his scales are the basis of modern IQ tests.

Lewis Terman, a psychologist at Stanford University, translated the French test into English and administered it to groups of children in the United States. After confirming a high correlation with teachers' rating of students' cognitive abilities, Terman began adapting the tests for broader use in American schools. Terman tested a larger group, approximately 1,000 children between the ages of four and fourteen in communities with average socio-economic statuses, and found that many of the benchmarks established by Binet had to be shifted. For example, if a test item was too hard for children of a particular age group then it was shifted down and used as a benchmark for a younger age group. This is a clever approach to testing but as noted at the outset of the chapter, it is completely data-driven, and not motivated by any theoretical account of cognitive development. Terman also standardized the number of test items per age, and removed items that did not test satisfactorily. In 1916, Terman published the Stanford Revision of the Binet–Simon Scale (Terman, 1916), which became known as the Stanford-Binet. The scoring procedure differed from the original Binet-Simon Scale and followed an idea first proposed by Stern (1912), that IQ should be quantified as mental age divided by chronological age multiplied by 100. For example, in our example above, a four-year-old with a mental age of six would have an IQ of 150 (i.e., $6/4°100 = 150$), which is extremely high, and an eight-year-old with a mental age of six would have an IQ of 75 (i.e., $6/8°100 = 75$), and would be classified as having a borderline deficiency. The Stanford-Binet Scales are still used to calculate the IQs of children and adults. The scales, currently in their fifth edition, produce scores that approximate a normal distribution in which 100 is the mean, and the standard deviation is 16 (most IQ tests use a mean of 100 with standard deviations of 15 or 16).

These standardized scales allowed for the formal assessment of children's intellectual abilities, and were used to provide appropriate education and other services. IQ tests became used for both placement into special education programs for those who scored below average and for placement into gifted education programs for those who scored above average. Soon, classification of adults' intellectual abilities for predicting future performance was also sought. The United States Army conducted the first large-scale effort to this end.

At the start of U.S. involvement in World War I, the year after the Stanford-Binet was published, the U.S. Army needed to quickly screen a large number of men for military service, place recruits into military jobs, and select those to be assigned to leadership training. Testing one individual at a time, as was done with the Stanford-Binet, was considered too time-consuming. The U.S. Army wanted a multiple-choice test that could be administered to large groups of test-takers. Lewis Terman, the developer of the Stanford-Binet, with Henry Goddard, Carl C. Brigham and led by Robert Yerkes, developed two tests to aid the U.S. Army in quickly assessing a large number of potential soldiers. The Army Alpha battery included tasks such as sentence unscrambling, mathematical word problems, and pattern completion. The Army Beta battery was created for illiterate men and for those who failed the Army Alpha. The Army Beta did not rely on reading ability, but used pictures and other visual stimuli. Tasks included filling in missing components of pictures (e.g., a face without a mouth, a rabbit missing an ear), visual search, and recoding.

One particular army recruit, David Wechsler, had a Master's degree in Psychology and volunteered to score the Army Alpha as he was waiting for induction. Based on his education and experience with the Army Alpha, the Army later tasked Wechsler with administering the Stanford-Binet to recruits who had performed poorly on the Army Beta. Wechsler felt that the Stanford-Binet emphasized verbal abilities too much and in 1939 developed the Weschler-Bellevue test (Wechsler, 1939), which in 1955 became the Wechsler Adult Intelligence Scale (WAIS; Wechsler, 1955). As an individually administered IQ test for adults, the scoring problem of the original Binet scale was apparent: adults' mental ages do not increase substantially like children's. In other words, an average 34-year-old and an average 36-year-old are more alike than an average four-year-old and an average six-year-old in cognitive abilities, so therefore the mental age divided by chronological age times 100 formula was not appropriate. Wechsler instead compared scores with the average score of someone of the same age. Wechsler also developed the Wechsler Intelligence Scale for Children (WISC; Wechsler, 1949). The WAIS and the WISC yield a verbal IQ score (which highly correlates with the Stanford-Binet [for a review see Arnold & Wagner, 1955]), a performance IQ score, and an overall IQ score (the average of the verbal and performance IQ scores). The current versions of the WAIS and WISC yield an aggregate IQ score from four factor indices: verbal comprehension, perceptual reasoning, processing speed, and working memory.

Following World War I, the Army Alpha was released as an unclassified document and immediately became popular within businesses and educational institutions. Brigham, who helped develop the Army Alpha and Beta, administered his own version of the Army Alpha test to Princeton University freshmen and students at a technical college in New York City. Soon after, the College Board asked Brigham to lead a group in developing a standardized admissions test to be used around the country. The first SAT, then named the Scholastic Aptitude Test, was administered to high school students in 1926. The 1926 SAT included vocabulary, arithmetic, number series, classification, artificial language learning, analogies, logical inference, and reading comprehension. The SAT has been revised many times since 1926 and is currently the most widely used college entrance exam. It is important to note, however, that the revisions are largely data driven, in the same manner that Terman revised the Stanford-Binet tests.

John C. Raven, a British psychologist, strove to develop a measure of intelligence that was based on a theoretical framework as opposed to data driven. To this end, he created a test to capture the eductive ability (the ability to find meaning) component of Spearman's g. Raven also believed that many of the available IQ tests were too difficult to interpret so created a test that was simple to administer and score. The takers of his test are presented with matrices in which a piece of the pattern is removed and multiple options for the missing piece are presented, with only one correct option among them. The matrices are progressively more difficult to solve, so are typically scored simply as the number of correct responses. The test is non-verbal and very little prior knowledge is necessary. For these reasons, the Raven's Progressive Matrices (Penrose & Raven, 1936; Raven, 1938) is now one of the most popular tests of intelligence and is used around the world among people who speak different languages.

Performance on intelligence test has considerable impact on individuals' lives. At a young age, children are classified as normal, gifted, or deficient. Their education and the peers with whom they are grouped to interact are decided primarily on these tests. For those who score below average, as they approach adulthood the amount of government funding and non-profit service received for having a cognitive disability is contingent upon intelligence test scores. For those who score normal or above average, as they approach adulthood, those wishing to attend college have different opportunities for admission and funding (in the United States) based on their performance on college entrance exams. One's college education again has a considerable effect on the peers with whom one interacts and one's future career.

We have discussed just a few of the large number of standardized intelligence tests that have been developed over the last 100 years (for a more comprehensive review, see Urbina, 2011). We conclude this section with two main points: (1) the majority of standardized intelligence tests are revised in a data-driven manner, and are therefore difficult to explain in terms of psychological theory; and (2) the impact that these tests have had on modern society is enormous. While the consequences can be negative, for example, a student not being admitted to the school of her choice even though she perhaps could have succeeded, the enterprise is not all bad. For instance, before the SAT was developed, wealth, class, and ethnic background largely determined acceptance to a prestigious university in the United States. For many people, standardized tests created opportunities that otherwise would not have been possible. That said, new research on working memory might offer an even more promising way forward.

Working Memory

Working memory (WM) is a construct developed by cognitive psychologists to characterize and help further investigate how human beings maintain access to goal-relevant information in the face of concurrent processing and/or distraction. For example, suppose you are attempting to schedule an airline reservation using the Internet. To search for flights you must mentally maintain the departure city, the arrival city, and the dates of travel while you scan the multiple options presented and ignore potentially distracting information, such as pop-up advertisements, or incoming email. Working memory is required to remember the critical travel information while concurrently searching potential flights and ignoring irrelevant information. Many important cognitive abilities, the same ones that fall under the umbrella of intelligence, such as academic achievement, learning, problem-solving, reading comprehension, and reasoning require WM because for each of these activities, some information must be maintained in an accessible state while new information is processed and potentially distracting information is ignored.

Working memory is considered to be a limited-capacity system and according to most contemporary theoretical accounts of WM, this capacity constrains intelligence, evidenced by the fact that individuals with lesser capacity tend to perform worse on most intelligence tests than individuals with greater capacity. For example, older children have greater working memory capacity (WMC) than younger children, the elderly tend to have lesser WMC than younger adults, and patients with certain types of neural damage or disease have lesser WMC than healthy adults. There is even a large amount of variation in WMC within samples of healthy young adults, for example, in samples of college students. In all these cases, individuals with greater WMC almost always perform better on intelligence tests than individuals with lesser WMC.

Research on the specific nature of the cognitive and neural mechanisms that constitute WM is extremely active in both Psychology and Neuroscience. For example, a search of Google Scholar using the exact phrase "working memory," constrained to 2006–2010, yields 142,000 links. If we go back 20 years and conduct the same search, constrained to articles published between 1986 and 1990, it yields 6,670 links. Step back another 20 years, 1966 to 1970, and the search yields 243 links and most of these don't use the phrase working memory as it is used today. It is therefore safe to say that research on WM is relatively new, compared to research on intelligence.

Given the fervent activity of research on WM, it is impossible to summarize all current work here. Instead, we describe just one of the more influential theoretical models of WM and provide references to other influential models and/or frameworks. Our apologies in advance to any colleagues not cited. There's simply too much contemporary work for any one chapter to cite.

The most influential model of WM over the last few decades is the multi-component model of Baddeley and Hitch (1974, revised subsequently by Baddeley in 2000 and by Baddeley, Allen, & Hitch in 2011). Historically, the multi-component model has evolved from the concept of a unitary short-term memory (STM) system. According to a dominant view of memory in psychology in the mid-twentieth century, information has to pass through a single STM store to enter or exit long-term memory (Atkinson & Shiffrin, 1968). In other words, STM serves as a gateway to further information processing and consequently plays a key role in higher-order cognitive abilities such as reasoning, planning, and problem solving. It soon became clear that things were more complex than originally thought. Experiments showed that disrupting the functioning of STM had little impact on complex cognitive task performance (Baddeley & Hitch, 1974). Furthermore, the existence of patients with normal long-term learning but impaired STM capacity could not be explained by the unitary account of STM (Shallice & Warrington, 1970).

Largely motivated by these patient data, British psychologists Alan Baddeley and Graham Hitch proposed a new model of WM that replaced the concept of a unitary STM with a more dynamic system involving the interplay of attention and multiple short-term storage buffers (Baddeley & Hitch 1974). The model was called the "multi-component model of working memory" and has had a major influence on memory research ever since it was first proposed. The model originally consisted of three major components: the "central executive," which is an attentional control system that is supplemented by two passive storage buffers namely the "phono-logical loop," which stores and processes verbal information and the "visuo-spatial sketchpad," which stores and manipulates visual and spatial information. In a more recent update of the model, Baddeley added a fourth component to the tripartite system—the "episodic buffer," which serves as an interface between the executive, the buffers, and long-term memory (Baddeley, 2000; Baddeley et al., 2011).

The model's structure (see Figure 2.1) is largely based on the study of neuro-psychological patients and the so-called dual-task methodology, in which subjects have to complete several memory-taxing tasks at the same time. Experiments of this kind showed that some pairs of tasks interfered with each other more so than

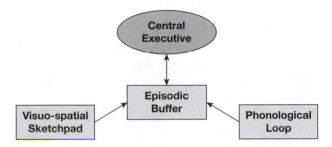

Figure 2.1   Simplified representation of the multi-component WM model based on Baddeley et al. (2011)

other pairs of tasks. For example, if you are asked to repeatedly utter the word "the" and also remember a list of spoken digits or visually presented colors, you will most likely find it easier to remember the colors than the digits. According to Baddeley and Hitch, this demonstrates separability of storage buffers, with words being stored in the loop (which causes interference) and visual information being stored in the sketchpad.

The most extensively investigated WM component is the phonological loop. It is assumed to consist of a passive phonological store that can hold speech-based information for up to two seconds coupled with an articulatory control process that prevents decay in the store by reactivating the fading phonological representations via subvocal rehearsal (Baddeley, 1986). Importantly, it has been proposed that the phonological loop might have evolved in humans as a "language learning device," in other words, as a system to facilitate the process of learning languages (Baddeley, Gathercole, & Papagno, 1998). Just imagine having to thank a Quechua speaker in Bolivia. You will need to be able to keep the sound sequence *"diuspagarapusunki"* in your phonological loop in order to repeat it correctly. Most Anglo-Saxon speakers will face difficulties in repeating this new word after having heard it only once, simply because it might exceed the limits of their phonological loop. Without an adequate temporary representation of the phonological sequence of this new word in the phonological loop, a robust long-term-memory representation will not be constructed and so the unfamiliar word will most likely not become part of your vocabulary after being exposed to it only once.

The second short-term storage system featured by the model is the visuo-spatial sketchpad. The current model of this subcomponent is less well advanced than for the phonological loop. The visuo-spatial sketchpad is responsible for the limited short-term storage and possibly the binding of visual and spatial information and is thought to be fractionable into separate visual, spatial, and haptic components (Baddeley, 1997; Baddeley et al., 2011). Like the phonological loop, it might consist of a passive temporary store and a more active rehearsal process (Logie, 1995). The visuo-spatial sketchpad is involved in tasks that require the recall of spatial or visual features such as finding your way through a supermarket or remembering the faces of your students after the first lecture.

The third temporary storage system is the episodic buffer (Baddeley, 2000; Baddeley, Allen, & Hitch, 2010, 2011). It is the most recently developed subcomponent of the model and was added in response to the increasing problems that the tripartite model encountered in explaining the way in which the visuo-spatial and phonological systems interact and how WM communicates with long-term memory (see Baddeley, 2000 for a review). Despite intense research efforts over the last ten years, the episodic buffer "remains a somewhat shadowy concept" (Baddeley et al., 2010, p. 240). According to the most recent position (Baddeley et al., 2011), it represents a capacity-limited passive store that is capable of storing integrated chunks of information (i.e., episodes). In contrast to the loop and the sketchpad it can be considered as a "higher-level" storage buffer in that it links both of these to long-term memory and is assumed to be accessible through conscious awareness.

The most essential component of the WM system is the central executive (Baddeley et al., 2010; Vandierendonck, De Vooght & Van der Goten, 1998). In contrast to the buffers it does not encompass a storage function but instead represents a purely attentional subsystem that controls the subsystems in a domain-free manner (Baddeley & Logie, 1999). The initial specification of the central executive was largely based on the Norman and Shallice (1986) model of executive control. It has been described as a homunculus that enables the WM system to focus, divide, and switch attention in order to process, access, and store more information than would be possible by the relatively passive, limited-capacity short-term storage buffers alone (Baddeley, 1996). Whether or not it is a unitary system or is composed of different subcomponents, is open to debate (Baddeley, 1996, 2006).

We believe it is fair to say that the multi-component model of working memory has stood the test of time. It has stimulated a great deal of investigation over the last 35 years, and although far from being embraced by everybody, continues as one of the leading models in the field. The popularity of the model is partially related to its simple structural approach, which is particularly useful in describing and understanding a range of neuropsychological deficits in adults as well as in children (Baddeley, 1990, 2003; Gathercole & Baddeley, 1990; Gathercole, Alloway, Willis, & Adams, 2006; Papagno, Cecchetto, Reati, & Bello, 2007).

Alternative models have, however, been developed in recent years and they provide a slightly different view of the WM system. Whereas the multi-component model has a strong structural focus, separating WM into distinct components with different features, alternative WM theories emphasize functions and processes over structure (see Cowan, 2005; Engle & Kane, 2004; Jonides et al., 2008, Nairne, 2002).

Tests of Working Memory Capacity

One of the core features of the Baddeley model of WM, and one that is not disputed by other theories, is that WM consists of multiple interacting mechanisms. At a general level, there are separable components for different kinds of information (for example, verbal vs. spatial) and for different types of processes (for example, memory vs. attention). At a more specific level, there are different mechanisms for particular processes, such as encoding, stimulus representation, maintenance, manipulation, and retrieval. Evidence for separable components and for different mechanisms comes from a variety of sources including dual-task behavioral experiments, neuropsychological case studies, and more recently, neuroimaging experiments. This is a critical point to remember when considering the measurement of WMC. A spatial WM task that requires the manipulation of information is very different from a verbal task that doesn't require manipulation but does require encoding, maintenance, and retrieval, yet each is dependent upon WM and can therefore fairly be considered a test of WMC.

We therefore define WMC as the maximum amount of information an individual can maintain in a particular task that is designed to measure some aspect(s) of the WM system. This has caused some confusion in the scientific community because different researchers often use different tasks to measure WMC, and this can lead to different conclusions regarding the nature of individual differences in WMC. We will have more to say about this dilemma in our discussion of psychometrics. Here we describe some of the more popular measures of WMC.

Complex Span Tasks   Complex span tasks were designed from the perspective of the original WM model, discussed above (Baddeley & Hitch, 1974). There are many different versions of complex span tasks, including reading span (Daneman & Carpenter, 1980), operation span (Turner & Engle, 1989), counting span (Case, Kurland, & Goldberg, 1982), as well as various spatial versions (Kane et al., 2004; Shah & Miyake, 1996). Complex span tasks are essentially "dual tasks"; the subject is required to engage in a relatively simple secondary task in between the presentation of to-be-remembered stimuli. For example, in the counting span task, the subject is presented with an array of objects on a computer screen. The objects typically differ from one another in both shape and color, for example, circles and squares colored either red or blue. The subject is instructed to count a particular type of object, such as blue squares. After counting aloud, the subject is required to remember the total and is then presented with another array of objects. The subject again counts the number of blue squares aloud and attempts to remember the total. After a series of arrays has been presented the subject is required to recall all the totals in correct serial order. Thus, maintaining access to the to-be-remembered digits is disrupted by the requirement of counting the number of objects in each array, which demands attention because multiple features (shape and color) have to be bound together to form each object representation (Treisman & Gelade, 1980). Indeed, the point of the secondary task is to engage attention and therefore disrupt active maintenance of the digits. This process is thought to create an ecologically valid measure of WM, as proposed by Baddeley and Hitch (1974), because it requires access to information (the to-be-remembered digits) in the face of concurrent processing (counting).

Several different versions of complex span tasks have been developed over the last 30 years. The different versions all have the same basic structure but differ in terms of the type of stimuli that are presented for recall (digits, letters, words, spatial locations) and the type of secondary task that is used to engage attention and disrupt maintenance (counting the number of objects in an array, reading sentences aloud, solving simple math problems, judging whether a figure is symmetrical or not). In most complex span tasks the number of stimuli presented for recall varies from trial to trial, typically from two to seven, and average recall performance among college students is about four to five (for more details, see Conway, Kane, Bunting, Hambrick, Wilhelm, & Engle, 2005).

A battery of complex span tasks is defined as a group of several tasks, and typically the tasks in the battery differ with respect to the type of stimuli to be remembered and/or the type of secondary task. When a battery is administered to a large group of subjects, a positive manifold emerges, just as Spearman (1904) observed when looking at children's grades. That is, different versions of complex span tasks correlate strongly with each other and typically account for the same variance in other measures of cognitive ability, such as the SAT (Turner & Engle, 1989). For example, Kane et al. (2004) administered several verbal and several spatial complex span tasks and the range of correlation among all the tasks ranged from $r = .39$ to $r = .51$. After statistically removing variance specific to each individual task, the correlation between "latent" variables representing spatial complex span and verbal complex span was $r = .84$. These results suggest that individual differences in complex span are largely determined by cognitive and neural mechanisms that are domain-general, akin to the measures that gave rise to Spearman's g.

Simple Span Tasks   Simple span tasks, for example, digit span or letter span, in contrast to complex span, do not include an interleaved secondary task between each presentation of to-be-remembered stimuli. For example, in digit span, one digit is presented at a time, typically one per second, and after a series of digits the subject is asked to recall the digits in correct serial order. Simple span tasks are among the oldest tasks used in memory research. Digit span was included in the first intelligence test (Binet, 1903) and is still included in two popular tests of intelligence, the WAIS (Wechsler, 1955) and the WISC (Wechsler, 1949).

However, simple span typically does not reveal very strong correlations with other measures of cognitive ability (Conway, Cowan, Bunting, Therriault, & Minkoff, 2002; Daneman & Carpenter, 1980; Daneman & Merikle, 1996; Engle, Tuholski, Laughlin, & Conway, 1999; Kane et al., 2004). Also, individual differences in simple span tasks are largely determined by domain-specific cognitive and neural mechanisms. We know this because within-domain correlations among simple span tasks are higher than cross-domain correlations among simple span tasks (Kane et al., 2004). Moreover, this domain-specific dominance is greater in simple span tasks than in complex span tasks (Kane et al., 2004). Also, patients with localized neurological damage or disease may exhibit normal performance on a simple span task with spatial materials yet exhibit a severe decrement on a simple span task with verbal materials, and vice versa. These results suggest that individual differences in simple span are largely determined by cognitive and neural mechanisms that are domain-specific, unlike the measures that gave rise to Spearman's g. Therefore, when we consider the link between WMC and intelligence, we will focus on complex span tasks, not simple span tasks.

Visual Array Comparison Tasks   Memory span tasks, both simple and complex, have a long tradition in cognitive psychology. However, they are not ideal measures of the amount of information a person can "keep active" at one moment in time because the to-be-remembered stimuli must each be recalled, one at a time, and therefore performance is susceptible to output interference. In other words, a subject might get a score of four on a memory span task but it's possible that more than four items were actively maintained. Some representations might be lost during recall (Cowan et al., 1992).

For this reason, the visual array comparison task (Luck & Vogel, 1997) was developed as a measure of memory capacity. There are several variants of the visual array comparison task but in a typical version subjects are presented with an array of several items that vary in shape and color and the presentation is extremely brief, for example, a fraction of a second. After a short retention interval, perhaps just a second, the subject is then presented with another array and asked to judge whether the two arrays were the same or different. On half the trials the two arrays are the same and on the other half one item in the second array is different. Thus, if all items in the initial array are maintained then subjects will be able to detect the change. Most subjects achieve 100% accuracy on the task when the number of items is fewer than four but performance begins to drop as the number of items in the array increases beyond four.

Visual array comparison tasks have not been used as often as memory span tasks to investigate individual differences in cognitive ability. However, recent research shows that array comparison tasks account for nearly as much variance in cognitive ability as complex span tasks (Cowan et al., 2005; Cowan, Fristoe, Elliott, Brunner, & Saults, 2006; Fukuda, Vogel, Mayr, & Awh, 2010). The precise relationship between visual array comparison tasks, complex span tasks, and measures of intelligence remains unclear and is an active topic of research.

N-back Tasks   The process of *updating* working memory is considered to be one of the most fundamental characteristics of the system. Information that is relevant to a current goal needs to be represented in a readily accessible state and must continuously be updated in accordance with changes in the environment. One popular updating task is called the n-back. In an n-back task, the subject is presented with a continuous stream of stimuli, one at a time, typically one every two to three seconds. The subject's goal is to determine if the current stimulus matches the one presented n-back. The stimuli are often verbal, for example, letters or words, but they can also be non-verbal, for example, visual objects, or spatial locations.

N-back tasks have been used extensively in neuroimaging experiments because the timing of stimulus presentation is easily controlled and the response requirements are simple. Numerous imaging experiments have demonstrated that the brain regions recruited to perform an n-back task are also recruited when performing intelligence tests (see Kane & Engle, 2002 for a review). Moreover, accuracy on an n-back task is correlated with scores on a test of intelligence and this correlation is partially mediated by neural activity in these common brain regions (Burgess, Gray, Conway, & Braver, 2011).

Coordination and Transformation Tasks   All of the above-mentioned WM tasks require subjects to recall or recognize information that was explicitly presented. There is another type of WM task, which we label "coordination and transformation," because subjects are presented with information and required to manipulate and/or transform that information to arrive at a correct response. For example, consider "backward span" tasks. Backward span tasks are similar to simple span tasks except that the subject is required to recall the stimuli in reverse order. Thus, the internal representation of the list must be transformed for successful performance. Another example is the letter–number sequencing task. The subject is presented with a sequence of letters and numbers and required to recall first the letters in alphabetical order and then the numbers in chronological order. Another example is the alphabet-recoding task. The subject is required to perform addition and subtraction using the alphabet, for example, C – 2 = A. On each trial, the subject is presented with a problem, C – 2, and required to generate the answer, A. Difficulty is manipulated by varying the number of letters presented, for example, CD – 2 = AB.

Kyllonen and Christal (1990) found very strong correlations between WMC and reasoning ability, using a variety of WM tasks that can all be considered "coordination and transformation" tasks (rs between .79 and .91). Also, Oberauer and colleagues demonstrated that the correlation between WMC and fluid intelligence does not depend upon whether WM is measured using complex span tasks or transformation tasks, suggesting that coordination and transformation tasks tap the same mechanisms as complex span tasks, meaning that they too are domain-general (Suß, Oberauer, Wittman, Wilhelm, & Schulze, 2002).

The Link between Intelligence and Working Memory Capacity

Now that we have considered the various ways in which intelligence and WMC are measured, we are ready to evaluate the empirical evidence linking WMC and intelligence. The number of published papers reporting a significant correlation between WMC and intelligence is enormous, so to make this discussion tractable we start with two meta-analyses, both focused more specifically on the relationship between WMC and fluid intelligence. The two analyses were conducted by two different groups of researchers; one estimated the correlation between WMC and fluid intelligence to be r = .72 (Kane, Hambrick, & Conway, 2005) and the other estimated it to be r = .85 (Oberauer, Schulze, Wilhelm, & Süß, 2005). More recent studies also demonstrate correlations in this range, and most scholars agree that the relationship between WMC and fluid intelligence is very strong. Kane et al. (2005) summarized the studies included in their meta-analysis in a table, which is reproduced here (see Table 2.1). Each of the studies included in the meta-analysis administered several tests of WMC and several tests of fluid intelligence, and factor analysis was used to determine the strength of the relationship between the two constructs. A variety of WM tasks were used in these studies, including complex span, simple span, and coordination and transformation tasks.

The studies referenced in Table 2.1 did not use either visual array comparison or n-back tasks and only involved adult participants. However, the more recent

Table 2.1   Correlations between WMC and gf/reasoning factors derived from confirmatory factor analyses of data from latent-variable studies with young adults

Study	WMC tasks	Gf/reasoning tasks	r(95% CI)
Kyllonen & Christal (1990) Study 2: N = 399	ABC numerical assignment, mental arithmetic, alphabet recoding	Arithmetic reasoning, AB grammatical reasoning, verbal analogies, arrow grammatical reasoning, number sets	.91 (.89, .93)
Study 3: N = 392	Alphabet recoding, ABC21	Arithmetic reasoning, AB grammatical reasoning, ABCD arrow, diagramming relations, following instructions, letter sets, necessary arithmetic operations, nonsense syllogisms	.79 (.75, .82)
Study 4: N = 562	Alphabet recoding, mental math	Arithmetic reasoning, verbal analogies, number sets, 123 symbol reduction, three term series, calendar test	.83 (.80, .85)
Engle, Tuholski, et al. (1999: N = 133)	Operation span, reading span, counting span, ABCD, keeping track, secondary memory/ immediate free recall	Raven, Cattell culture fair	.60 (.48, .70)
Miyake et al. (2001: N = 167)	Letter rotation, dot matrix	Tower of Hanoi, random generation, paper folding, space relations, cards, flags	.64 (.54, .72)
Ackerman et al. (2002: N = 135)	ABCD order, alpha span, backward digit span, computation span, figural-spatial span, spatial span, word-sentence span	Ravens, number series, problem solving. necessary facts, paper folding, spatial analogy, cube comparison	.66 (.55, .75)
Conway et al. (2002: N = 120)	Operation span, reading span, counting span	Raven. Cattell culture fair	.54 (.40, .66)
Süß et al. (2002: N = 121[a])	Reading span, computation span, alpha span, backward digit span, math span, verbal span, spatial working memory, spatial short-term memory, updating numerical, updating spatial, spatial coordination, verbal coordination	Number sequences, letter sequences, computational reasoning, verbal analogies, fact/opinion, senseless inferences, syllogisms, figural analogies, Charkow, Bongard, figure assembly, surface development	.86 (.81, .90)
Hambrick (2003: N = 171)	Computation span, reading span	Raven, Cattell culture fair, abstraction, letter sets	.71 (.63, .78)
Mackintosh & Bennett (2003: N = 138[b])	Mental counters, reading span, spatial span	Raven, mental rotations	1.00

Table 2.1   Continued

Study	WMC tasks	Gf/reasoning tasks	r(95% CI)
Colom et al. (2004)			
Study 1: N = 198	Mental counters, sentence verification, line formation	Raven, surface development	.86 (.82, .89)
Study 2: N = 203	Mental counters, sentence verification, line formation	Surface development, cards, figure classification	.73 (.66, .79)
Study 3: N = 193	Mental counters, sentence verification, line formation	Surface development, cards, figure classification	.41 (.29, .52)
Kane et al. (2004: N = 236)	Operation span, reading span, counting span, rotation span, symmetry span, navigation span	Raven, WASI matrix. BETA III matrix, reading comprehension, verbal analogies, inferences, nonsense syllogisms, remote associates, paper folding, surface development, form board, space relations, rotated blocks	.67 (.59, .73)

Note: WMC = working memory capacity; Gf = general fluid intelligence; 95% CI = the 95% confidence interval around the correlations; WASI = Wechsler Abbreviated Scale of Intelligence.

a N with the complete data set available (personal communication, K. Oberauer, July 7, 2004).
b N for each pairwise correlation ranged from 117 to 127.

studies referenced above have used these tasks and also found correlations of the same magnitude. For example, Fukuda, Vogel, Mayr, and Awh (2010) used visual array comparison tasks and the correlation between WMC and fluid intelligence was $r = .66$. Burgess et al. (2011) used measures from an n-back task and the correlation between WMC and intelligence was $r = .43$.

In contrast, Ackerman, Beier, and Boyle (2005) argued that the correlation between WMC and intelligence is weak, and moderate at best. Ackerman and colleagues chose to focus their meta-analysis on individual tasks, rather than factors from a factor analysis. The problem with this approach is that individual tasks are more susceptible to task-specific influences and are therefore less accurate assessments of the main construct under investigation, in terms of both reliability and validity. If multiple tasks are used then the common variance among tasks can be used to derive a "latent" variable required by all tasks. To better understand this argument, a more detailed discussion of latent variables, and psychometrics is necessary, so we turn to that topic now.

Psychometrics

Psychometrics is a field of study concerned with the theory and technique of measuring psychological constructs, including the measurement of intelligence and WMC, as well as personality traits. Generally speaking, a psychometric study involves administering a large battery of tasks to a large sample of individuals and then analyzing the correlations among the tasks to identify underlying factors, or latent variables, that can account for large portions of variance within and across tasks in the battery. The data from psychometric studies are analyzed using multivariate statistical procedures, such as factor analysis and structural equation modeling (SEM). SEM is also known as *causal modeling* because the psychometric theories under investigation imply causal relationships among variables, despite the correlational nature of the data.

This approach is powerful because competing theories about the structure of intelligence can be objectively compared with empirical tests. For example, it is possible to administer a battery of tests to a large group of students and test whether a one-factor model, like the one initially proposed by Spearman (1904), "fits" the data better or just as well as a two- or three-factor model. In SEM, if a one-factor model fits the data as well as a two-factor model then the one-factor model is preferable because it is more parsimonious.

As mentioned above, the most common interpretation of factors, or latent variables, in factor analyses and in causal models is that they represent a single source of variance that is common to all the tasks that "load" onto that factor. Furthermore, in causal models, a factor is purported to cause performance on the manifest variables, that is, the actual tests or tasks administered to people in the sample, such as intelligence tests or WM tasks. However, also mentioned above, many psychometricians dating back to Thomson (1916) have demonstrated that while this may be a valid interpretation of factors and the causal relationship between a construct and performance, it is not necessary to postulate a unitary source of variance from a factor. To reiterate, sampling theories of *g* can account for the emergence of *g* from a battery of tasks that taps a vast number of underlying cognitive processes in an overlapping fashion. This means that WMC and intelligence may be correlated because measures of each construct share multiple cognitive processes, not because they share one general factor. If sampling theories of *g* are correct then causal models of *g* that posit a causal link between a *g* factor and every single task in the model are wrong. This view, which implies the rather radical notion that there is no such thing as general cognitive ability, has recently gained traction (Bartholomew, Deary, & Lawn, 2009; Conway et al., 2011; Kovacs, 2010; van der Maas et al., 2006).

FUTURE DIRECTIONS

This chapter has shown that WM and intelligence are two psychological constructs that were developed for different purposes and have different histories and theoretical underpinnings. As a result, measurements of intelligence and measurements of WMC look very different from one another. However, scores on intelligence tests are strongly correlated with scores on WM tasks. Therefore, the enterprise of intelligence testing could be replaced by a new enterprise of WM tasking. In our opinion, this would be a welcome shift. However, the *g* dilemma remains.

REFERENCES

Ackerman, P. L., Beier, M. E., & Boyle, M. O. (2002). Individual differences in working memory within a nomological network of cognitive and perceptual speed abilities. *Journal of Experimental Psychology: General, 131*(4), 567–589.

Ackerman, P. L., Beier, M. E., & Boyle, M. O. (2005). Working memory and intelligence: The same or different constructs? *Psychological Bulletin, 131*, 30–60.

Alloway, T. P. & Alloway, R. G. (2010). Investigating the predictive roles of working memory and IQ in academic attainment. *Journal of Experimental Child Psychology, 106*, 20–29.

Arnold, F. C., & Wagner, W. K. (1955). A comparison of Wechsler Children's Scale and Stanford-Binet Scores for eight- and nine-year olds. *Journal of Experimental Education, 24*(1), 91–94.

Atkinson, R. C., & Shiffrin, R. M. (1968). Human memory: A proposed system and its control processes. In K. W. Spence & J. T. Spence (Eds.), *The psychology of learning and motivation: Advances in research and theory* (Vol. 2, pp. 742–775). New York: Academic Press.

Baddeley, A. D. (1986). *Working memory*. Oxford: Oxford University Press.

Baddeley, A. D. (1990). The development of the concept of working memory: Implications and contributions of neuropsychology. In G. Vallar & T. Shallice (Eds.), *Neuropsychological impairments of short-term memory*. Cambridge, UK: Cambridge University Press.

Baddeley, A. D. (1996). Exploring the central executive. *Quarterly Journal of Experimental Psychology Section A: Human Experimental Psychology, 49*(1), 5–28.

Baddeley, A. D. (1997). *Human memory: Theory and practice* (revised ed.). Hove: Psychology Press.

Baddeley, A. D. (2000). The episodic buffer: A new component of working memory? *Trends in Cognitive Sciences, 4*(11), 417–423.

Baddeley, A. D. (2003). Working memory: Looking back and looking forward. *Nature Reviews Neuroscience, 4*(10), 829–839.

Baddeley, A. D. (2006). Working memory: An overview. In S. J. Pickering (Ed.), *Working memory and education* (pp. 1–31). London: Elsevier.

Baddeley, A. D., Allen, R. J., & Hitch, G. J. (2010). Investigating the episodic buffer. *Psychologica Belgica, 50*, 223–243.

Baddeley, A. D., Allen, R. J., & Hitch, G. J. (2011). Binding in visual working memory: The role of the episodic buffer. *Neuropsychologia, 49*, 1393–1400.

Baddeley, A. D., Gathercole, S. E., & Papagno, C. (1998). The phonological loop as a language learning device. *Psychological Review, 105*(1), 158–173.

Baddeley, A. D., & Hitch, G. J. (1974). Working memory. In G. H. Bower (Ed.), *The psychology of learning and motivation* (Vol. 8, pp. 47–90). New York: Academic Press.

Baddeley, A. D., & Logie, R. H. (1999). The multiple-component model. In A. Miyake & P. Shah (Eds.), *Models of working memory: Mechanisms of active maintenance and executive control* (pp. 28–61). New York: University Press.

Bartholomew, D. J., Deary, I. J., & Lawn, M. (2009). A new lease of life for Thompson's bonds model of intelligence. *Psychological Review, 116*, 567–579.

Binet, A. (1903). *L'Etude Experimentale de l'Intelligence*. Paris: Schleicher.

Binet, A., and Simon, T. (1911). *A method of measuring the development of young children*. Lincoln, IL: Courier Company.

Burgess, G. C., Gray, J. R., Conway, A. R. A., & Braver, T. S. (2011). Neural mechanisms of interference control underlie the relationship between fluid intelligence and working memory span. *Journal of Experimental Psychology: General, 140*, 674–692.

Carroll, J. B. (1993). *Human cognitive abilities: A survey of factor-analytical studies*. New York: Cambridge University Press.

Case, R., Kurland, D. M., & Goldberg, J. (1982). Operational efficiency and the growth of short-term memory span. *Journal of Experimental Child Psychology, 33*(3), 386–404.

Cattell, R. B. (1987). *Intelligence: Its structure, growth, and action*. New York: Elsevier Science Pub. Co.

Cattell, R. B., & Horn, J. L. (1978). A check on the theory of fluid and crystallized intelligence with description of new subtest designs. *Journal of Educational Measurement, 15*, 139–164.

Colom, R., Rebollo, I., Palacios, A., Juan-Espinosa, M., & Kyllonen, P. C. (2004). *Intelligence, 32*, 277–296.

Conway, A. R. A., Cowan, N., Bunting, M. F., Therriault, D. J., & Minkoff, S. R. B. (2002). A latent variable analysis of working memory capacity, short-term memory capacity, processing speed, and general fluid intelligence. *Intelligence, 30*(2), 163–183.

Conway, A. R. A., Getz, S. J., Macnamara, B., & Engel de Abreu, P. M. J. (2011). Working memory and fluid intelligence. In R. J. Sternberg & S. B. Kaufman (Eds.), *The Cambridge handbook of intelligence*. Cambridge, UK: Cambridge University Press.

Conway, A. R. A., Kane, M. J., Bunting, M. F., Hambrick, D. Z., Wilhelm, O., & Engle, R. W. (2005). Working memory span tasks: A methodological review and user's guide. *Psychonomic Bulletin and Review, 12*(5), 769–786.

Cowan, N. (2005). *Working memory capacity*. New York: Psychology Press.

Cowan, N., Day, L., Saults, J. S., Keller, T. A., Johnson, T., & Flores, L. (1992). The role of verbal output time in the effects of word length on immediate memory. *Journal of Memory and Language, 31*, 1–17.

Cowan, N., Elliott, E. M., Saults, J. S., Morey, C. C., Matox, S., Hismjatullina, A., & Conway, A. R. A. (2005). On the capacity of attention: Its estimation and its role in working memory and cognitive aptitudes. *Cognitive Psychology, 51*(1), 42–100.

Cowan, N., Fristoe, N. M., Elliott, E. M., Brunner, R. P., & Saults, J. S. (2006). Scope of attention, control of attention, and intelligence in children and adults. *Memory and Cognition, 34*(8), 1754–1768.

Daneman, M., & Carpenter, P. A. (1980). Individual differences in working memory and reading. *Journal of Verbal Learning and Verbal Behavior, 19*(4), 450–466.

Daneman, M., & Merikle, P. M. (1996). Working memory and language comprehension: A meta-analysis. *Psychonomic Bulletin & Review, 3*(4), 422–433.

Engle, R. W., & Kane, M. J. (2004). Executive attention, working memory capacity, and a two-factor theory of cognitive control. In B. Ross (Ed.), *The psychology of learning and motivation* (pp. 145–199). New York: Academic Press.

Engle, R. W., Tuholski, S. W., Laughlin, J. E., & Conway, A. R. A. (1999). Working memory, short-term memory, and general fluid intelligence: A latent-variable approach. *Journal of Experimental Psychology: General, 128*(3), 309–331.

Frey, M. C., & Detterman, D. K. (2004). Scholastic assessment or g? The relationship between the SAT and general cognitive ability. *Psychological Science, 15*(6), 373–398.

Fukuda, K., Vogel, E. K., Mayr, U., & Awh, E. (2010). Quantity not quality: The relationship between fluid intelligence and working memory capacity. *Psychonomic Bulletin and Review, 17*, 673–679.

Gardner, H. (1983). *Frames of mind: The theory of multiple intelligences*. New York: Basic Books.

Gathercole, S. E., & Baddeley, A. D. (1990). Phonological memory deficits in language disordered children: Is there a causal connection? *Journal of Memory and Language, 29*(3), 336–360.

Gathercole, S. E., Alloway, T. P., Willis, C., & Adams, A. M. (2006). Working memory in children with reading disabilities. *Journal of Experimental Child Psychology, 93*(3), 265–281.

Gottfredson, L. S. (1994, December 13). Mainstream science on intelligence. *Wall Street Journal*, p. A18.

Gould, S. J. (1981). *The mismeasure of man*. New York: W.W. Norton & Co.

Guilford, J. P. (1988). Some changes in the structure of intellect model. *Educational and Psychological Measurement, 48*, 1–4.

Hambrick, D. Z. (2003). Why are some people more knowledgeable than others? A longitudinal study of real-world knowledge acquisition. *Memory & Cognition, 31*, 902–917.

Holzinger, K., & Swineford, F. (1937). The bi-factor method. *Psychometrika, 2*, 41–54.

Jonides, J., Lewis, R. L., Nee, D. E., Lustig, C. A., Berman, M. G., & Moore, K. S. (2008). The mind and brain of short-term memory. *Annual Review of Psychology, 59*, 193–224.

Kane, M. J., & Engle, R. W. (2002). The role of prefrontal cortex in working-memory capacity, executive attention, and general fluid intelligence: An individual differences perspective. *Psychonomic Bulletin and Review, 9*(4), 637–671.

Kane, M. J., Hambrick, D. Z., & Conway, A. R. A. (2005). Working memory capacity and fluid intelligence are strongly related constructs: Comment on Ackerman, Beier, and Boyle (2005). *Psychological Bulletin, 131*(1), 66–71.

Kane, M. J., Hambrick, D. Z., Tuholski, S. W., Wilhelm, O., Payne, T., & Engle, R. W. (2004). The generality of working memory capacity: A latent-variable approach to verbal and visuospatial memory span and reasoning. *Journal of Experimental Psychology: General, 133*(2), 189–217.

Kovacs, K. (2010). *A component process account of the general factor of intelligence*. Doctoral dissertation submitted to the University of Cambridge.

Kyllonen, P. C., & Christal, R. E. (1990). Reasoning ability is (little more than) working-memory capacity?! *Intelligence, 14*(4), 389–433.

Logie, R. H. (1995). *Visuo-spatial working memory*. Hove, UK: Lawrence Erlbaum Associates Ltd.

Luck, S. J., & Vogel, E. K. (1997). The capacity of visual working memory for features and conjunctions. *Nature, 390*(6657), 279–281.

Mackintosh, N. J. (1998). *IQ and human intelligence*. Oxford: Oxford University Press.

Mackintosh, N. J. & Bennett, E. S. (2003). The fractionation of working memory maps onto different components of intelligence. *Intelligence, 31*(6), 519–531.

Miyake, A., Friedman, N. P., Rettinger, D. A., Shah, P., & Hegarty, M. (2001). How are visuospatial working memory, executive functioning, and spatial abilities related? A latent-variable analysis. *Journal of Experimental Psychology: General, 130*(4), 621–640.

Nairne, J. S. (2002). Remembering over the short-term: The case against the standard model. *Annual Review of Psychology, 53*, 53–81.

Norman, D. A., & Shallice, T. (1986). Attention to action: Willed and automatic control of behaviour. In R. J. Davidson, G. E. Schwarts, & D. Shapiro (Eds.), *Consciousness and self-regulation: Advances in research and theory* (Vol. 4, pp. 1–18). New York: Plenum Press.

Oberauer, K., Schulze, R., Wilhelm, O., & Süß, H. (2005). Working memory and intelligence—Their correlation and their relation: Comment on Ackerman, Beier, and Boyle (2005). *Psychological Bulletin, 131*(1), 61–65.

Papagno, C., Cecchetto, C., Reati, F., & Bello, L. (2007). Processing of syntactically complex sentences relies on verbal short-term memory: Evidence from a short-term memory patient. *Cognitive Neuropsychology, 24*(3), 292–311.

Penrose, L. S., & Raven, J. C. (1936). A new series of perceptual tests: Preliminary communication. *British Journal of Medical Psychology, 16*, 97[104].

Raven, J. C. (1938). *Progressive Matrices: A perceptual test of intelligence*. London: H. K Lewis. Psychological Corporation.

Shah, P., & Miyake, A. (1996). The separability of working memory resources for spatial thinking and language processing: An individual differences approach. *Journal of Experimental Psychology: General, 125*(1), 4–27.

Shallice, T., & Warrington, E. K. (1970). Independent functioning of verbal memory stores:

A neuropsychological study. *Quarterly Journal of Experimental Psychology, 22*(2), 261–273.

Spearman, C. (1904). General intelligence, objectively determined and measured. *American Journal of Psychology, 15,* 201–293.

Stern, W. (1912). *Die Psychologische Methoden der Intelligenzprüfung.* Leipzig: Barth.

Sternberg, R. J. (1990). *Wisdom: Its nature, origins, and development.* New York: Cambridge University Press.

Süß, H. M., Oberauer, K., Wittman, W. W., Wilhelm, O., & Schulze, R. (2002). Working-memory capacity explains reasoning ability—and a little bit more. *Intelligence, 30,* 261–288.

Terman, L. M. (1916). *The measurement of intelligence.* Boston, MA: Houghton Mifflin.

Thomson, G. H. (1916). A hierarchy without a general factor. *British Journal of Psychology, 8,* 271–281.

Thurstone, L. L. (1938). *Primary mental abilities.* Chicago: University of Chicago Press.

Treisman, A. M., & Gelade, G. (1980). A feature-integration theory of attention. *Cognitive Psychology, 12*(1), 97–136.

Turner, M. L., & Engle, R. W. (1989). Is working memory capacity task dependent? *Journal of Memory and Language, 28*(2), 127–154.

Urbina, S. (2011). Tests of intelligence. In R. J. Sternberg & S. B. Kaufman (Eds.), *The Cambridge handbook of intelligence.* Cambridge, UK: Cambridge University Press.

Van Der Maas, H. L. J., Dolan, C. V., Grasman, R. P., Wicherts, J. M., Huizenga, H. M., & Raijmakers M. E. J. (2006). A dynamical model of general intelligence: The positive manifold of intelligence by mutualism. *Psychological Review, 113*(4), 842–861.

Vandierendonck, A., De Vooght, G., & Van der Goten, K. (1998). Interfering with the central executive by means of a random interval repetition task. *Quarterly Journal of Experimental Psychology, 51A,* 197–218.

Wechsler, D. (1939). *The measurement of adult intelligence.* Baltimore: Williams & Wilkins.

Wechsler, D. (1949). *Manual for the Wechsler intelligence scale for children.* New York: The Psychological Corporation.

Wechsler, D. (1955). *Manual for the Wechsler Adult Intelligence Scale.* New York: The Psychological Corporation.

3

The Evolution of Working Memory

FRED L. COOLIDGE

Department of Psychology, University of Colorado, Colorado Springs, CO, USA

THOMAS WYNN

Department of Anthropology, University of Colorado, Colorado Springs, CO, USA

KARENLEIGH A. OVERMANN

Department of Psychology, University of Colorado, Colorado Springs, CO, USA

Consider the following scenarios:

1. A modern chimpanzee pulls a plant out of the ground. She modifies the stem by removing the leaves with her fingers, and she pulverizes the end into fibers with her teeth. She then probes the simple tool into a termite mound, swishing it to antagonize the insects into biting the fibers and removing it carefully so that most of the termites are still holding on. She eats the termites off the tool, and once she has eaten her fill, she discards it.
2. About 2.5 million years ago, the hominid known today as *Homo habilis* hits one rock with another to produce sharp flakes. She discards everything but one or two of the flakes, which she then uses to butcher the remains of an antelope killed earlier by a large carnivore. Once the butchering is done, the hominid discards the flakes and carries off only the bits of carcass.
3. About 1.8 million years ago, another hominid, *Homo erectus*, strikes a rock against another while holding the idea of a shape in his mind. Through a series of skillful choices of angles and strikes, he imposes that shape to produce a biface handaxe (Figure 3.1). Once the handaxe is finished, he retains the handaxe, the larger flakes, and the remains of the original pieces of rock for his future use.
4. About 200,000 years ago, a *Homo sapiens neanderthalensis* (Neanderthal) hafts a sharp, symmetrical stone point onto a spruce shaft to produce a spear,

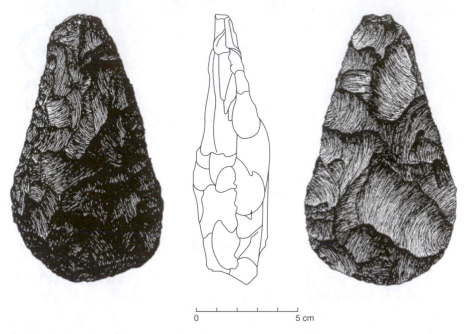

Figure 3.1   Bifacially symmetrical handaxe

to be used later in the close-range killing of the large, dangerous animals that are his prey. Producing the spear is laborious, effort that will hopefully be repaid with his later success in the hunt.

5. About 100,000 years ago, a *Homo sapiens*, whose anatomy we would recognize as modernly human, makes a projectile with a stone point. When the point breaks during the hunt, she resharpens it so she can continue to hunt with it, using other tools that she carries around with her just for this purpose.

6. Somewhere between 40,000 and 28,000 years ago, a *Homo sapiens sapiens*, whose behavior we would recognize as modernly human, carves a piece of mammoth ivory. He imposes on it the fantastic and highly imaginative shape of a female lion's head on a human body.

7. Just last week, another *Homo sapiens sapiens* working in an astrophysics laboratory runs a computerized analytical model to understand the gravitational influences of inhabitable planets on the stars they orbit. She enters observational data on stellar dynamics obtained by radio astronomy facilities contributing to the project, which is funded by a mixture of government, industrial, and private funding.

With the exception of the first and possibly the second scenarios, it is unlikely—impossible, really—that another species could conceive and execute the complex planning inherent in them. Not even another of the great apes can plan to the same extent, and their neuroanatomy and cognitive capabilities bear the closest similarities to our own. Moreover, even language appears to be insufficient to account for the ability to plan and carry out these scenarios. There is something else at play: an ability to construct and carry out increasingly elaborate plans of action. It is an ability that is fundamental to human thinking and one that underpins much of our success. Neuropsychologists and cognitive scientists use the terms *executive functions* (EFs) and *working memory* (WM) to refer to the high-level abilities to manipulate information, reason and solve problems, and plan courses of action. These abilities must have evolved during the course of human evolution, as the scenarios suggest. But when? And how?

In the argument that follows, we suggest that a specific cognitive ability, an enhancement to WM (*enhanced working memory*, EWM), was one of the key evolutionary acquisitions in human cognition, and indeed may even be the smoking gun of modernity. We hope to demonstrate that Baddeley's central executive, a key component of his WM model, is synonymous with the basic EFs that underlie the more complex ones such as planning. We then discuss the importance of WM to the modern mind, and how WM might be reflected in the archaeological record.

BADDELEY'S CENTRAL EXECUTIVE AND THE EXECUTIVE FUNCTIONS

The functions of the central executive described by Baddeley (1993, 2000, 2001, 2002, 2007) in his WM model appear to be synonymous with the key EFs described by Miyake et al. (2000). Baddeley's *attentional control* is identical to the EF of *shifting*: Both entail the transferring of attention from one cognitive task or mental operation to another, as well as the suppression of interference or priming, especially when the stimulus is constant but the operation is new. The idea that mental representations held in WM are maintained and manipulated by the central executive invokes *updating*, the monitoring of the mental representations held in WM and incorporating new information as needed on an ongoing basis. Finally, the notion that planning is the structuring of behavior based on the comparisons of actual and goal-state mental representations involves *inhibition*, the intentional blocking of automatic or dominant responses or behaviors in favor of less prepotent ones. These abilities, whether labeled EFs or the central executive of WM, are what enable us to shift our attention at will, make and adjust decisions based on new environmental input, and plan and achieve increasingly complex goals, and it is their increase, both gradual (as in scenarios 2 through 5) and dramatic (as in scenario 6), that we believe gave rise to the modern human mind.

Baddeley and others (e.g., Baddeley & Logie, 1999; Miyake & Shah, 1999; Miyake et al., 2000) currently view the central executive either as a unitary system or as multiple systems of varying functions including attention, active-inhibition, decision-making, planning, sequencing, temporal tagging, and the updating, maintenance, and integration of information from the two slave systems. Some brain function models have relegated WM (primarily phonological storage) to being simply a subcomponent of the various functions of the prefrontal cortex. However, with a raft of new evidence from empirical studies (for a review of contemporary WM models and empirical evidence, see D'Esposito, 2007), it may be more parsimonious to view Baddeley's WM model as having subsumed the traditionally defined aspects of EF. In most current models, WM not only serves to focus attention and make decisions but also serves as the chief liaison to long-term memory systems and to language comprehension and production. Indeed, Baddeley (1993) has noted that had he approached these systems from the perspective of attention instead of memory, it might have been equally appropriate to label them "working attention."

Differing conclusions from various studies show the highly complex yet highly interrelated nature of WM and its EF. As previously mentioned, in a factor analytic study of EF, Miyake et al. (2000) identified three factors as fundamental to executive functioning: mental set shifting, information updating, and the inhibition of prepotent responses. Oberauer, Suss, Wilhelm, and Wittman (2003) proposed that WM could be differentiated into two facets: one, the content domains (akin to Baddeley's phonological store and the visuo-spatial sketchpad) and the other related to its cognitive functions (Baddeley's EF). Oberauer et al., in a statistical analysis of 30 WM tasks, found three meta-WM functions: simultaneous storage and processing, supervision (i.e., EFs or the central executive), and coordination of elements into structures. Of course, all factor analytic studies' outcomes are completely dependent on the initial set of variables.

Whether the central executive is a unitary or nonunitary concept, we may still ask where, how, and why does it make its decisions? Miyake and Shah (1999) have proposed that the attention and decision-making qualities of the central executive may be an emergent property, that is, they arise as a function of the dynamic interplay of the multiple and interrelated systems associated with WM, including the two slave systems, the multiple long-term memory systems, and their cortical and subcortical connections. Support for the decision-making nature of the central executive also comes from Frankish (1998a, 1998b), who has speculated that it is an innate predisposition of human consciousness to accept, reject, or act on propositions. He postulates a "super mind" constituted by higher-order decision-making (as cited in Carruthers, 2002). These propositions are framed by language most often through inner speech or subvocalization, which are aspects of the WM component of phonological storage. We find it reasonable to assume that WM's ability to maintain appropriate attention and to make decisions would have been favored by natural selection. Certainly, the abilities to attend to relevant stimuli, filter out irrelevant stimuli, inhibit prepotent responses, and make quick and efficient decisions would have been favored over static processes. Further, it is these abilities that we believe characterize the modern human mind.

WM AND THE MODERN MIND

The importance of WM to the modern mind can be illustrated by the curious incident of one Phineas Gage, an apparently responsible, capable, and virile 25-year-old foreman of a railroad construction crew. On September 13, 1848, he accidentally dropped a 13¼ pound iron tamping rod, over three and a half feet long and more than an inch in diameter, onto a dynamite charge, which then exploded. The iron rod was driven through the left side of the young man's face to emerge from the top of the frontal portion of his cranium. He was taken to his nearby hotel, which was to serve as his hospital room until 32 days later, when he was able to leave his bed. At this point, the attending physician, J. M. Harlow, noted that his patient was eating and sleeping well, and that his long-term memories appeared to be intact. Seventy-four days after the accident, Phineas was able to return to his home, about 30 miles away. But there were discernible differences in his behavior, not related to his health, general intelligence, or memory. The original contractors who had hired him considered the "change in his mind" so great that they refused to rehire him. Phineas told Harlow that he could not decide whether to work or to travel. There were reports that Phineas was roaming the streets, purchasing items but without his usual concern about price. About this same time, Harlow (1868) noted that Phineas' mind seemed "childish" and that he would make plans and change them capriciously and then abandon them just as quickly. More importantly, Harlow wrote,

> Previous to his injury, though untrained in the schools, he possessed a well-balanced mind, and was looked upon by those who knew him as a shrewd, smart business man, very energetic and persistent in executing all his plans of operation. In this regard his mind was so radically changed, so decidedly that his friends and acquaintances said he was "no longer Gage."
>
> (Harlow, 1868, p. 340)

In the literature, the quote "no longer Gage" has famously become associated with Phineas' personality changes: his postmorbid use of profanity, his depression, his irritability and capriciousness. But this, however, misses what may be the most important point: Harlow associated his patient's most important change to the loss of the abilities that had once made him so valuable as a foreman: his once-shrewd business acumen and his former ability in "executing all of his plans of operation." Significantly, Harlow's description shows just how important to the modern human mind the EFs or central executive of WM are: Without them, it would be impossible to make decisions, form goals, plan, organize, devise strategies for attaining goals, and change and devise new strategies when the initial plans fail. Simply, without them modern human success would not be possible.

The Russian neuropsychologist Luria (1966) was the first to write extensively about the EFs, noting that in patients with frontal lobe damage, the abilities for speech, motor movements, and sensations are frequently intact, yet their complex psychological activities are tremendously impaired. Significantly, he observed that they were often unable to carry out complex, purposive, and goal-directed actions. Furthermore, he found that they could not accurately evaluate the success or failure of their behaviors, especially in terms of using the information to change their future behavior. Luria found these patients unconcerned with their failures, hesitant, indecisive, and indifferent to the loss of their critical awareness of their own behaviors. Lezak (1982), a contemporary American neuropsychologist, wrote that the EFs of the frontal lobes were:

> the heart of all socially useful, personally enhancing, constructive, and creative abilities. . . . Impairment or loss of these functions compromises a person's capacity to maintain an

independent, constructively self-serving, and socially productive life no matter how well he can see and hear, walk and talk, and perform tests.

(Lezak, 1982, p. 281)

In 2001, we proposed a hypothesis in which the evolution of the EFs was a key element in the evolution of modern human behavior and culture; we subsequently expanded this hypothesis by subsuming EFs under Baddeley's concept of WM (Coolidge & Wynn, 2001, 2005). We suggest that an enhancement of WM capacity (which we have labeled EWM) occurred in the relatively recent human past, most likely somewhere around the first appearance of the anatomically modern humans depicted in scenario 5, and that this development was the final piece—a final quantum leap in cognitive evolution, if you will—in the evolution of human executive reasoning ability, language, and culture.

WM/EWM IN THE ARCHAEOLOGICAL RECORD: METHODOLOGICAL CONSIDERATIONS

What might WM—and EWM, for that matter—look like in the archaeological record? And how might we tell, methodologically speaking? In general, we shall start by examining a candidate capability from the perspective of cognitive science. We will then identify archaeologically visible sequelae, specific actions or sets of actions that are enabled by the ability in question. Since the archaeological record consists of traces of action rather than direct traces of minds, the link between action and cognition must be explicit. Finally, we will define a set of criteria (attributes) by which these actions can be reliably identified in the archaeological record. These steps will make it possible to apply different standards of evaluation to the evidence.

The strict standard, which is the only one with real persuasive power, has the following two components:

1. Cognitive validity: The evidence must actually require the abilities attributed to it. The cognitive ability must be one recognized or defined by cognitive science; it must be required for the actions cited; and the archaeological traces must require those actions. A strict standard of parsimony must apply. If the archaeological traces could have been generated by simpler actions, or simpler cognition, then the simpler explanation must be favored.
2. Archaeological validity: The archaeological evidence must itself be credible. The traces in question must be reliably identified and placed appropriately in time and space.

Admittedly, archaeological validity is complicated, not merely by the indirect nature of cognitive traces or the challenge of formulating criteria for recognizing those traces in material remains. The archaeological record itself is an enormous jigsaw puzzle, consisting of bits and pieces that must be organized, interpreted, and interrelated to each other when many of them are missing and the few that are found may not easily cohere. What gets preserved is a matter of an unlikely combination of events that only starts with deposition. Until it is found (an unlikely event in itself), artifacts and features must successfully transition through a smorgasbord of human-initiated, animal-caused, or geological displacement processes that complicate interpretation (Villa, 1982). A demonstration of the latter is seen in the recent reinterpretation of the Châtelperron site at Grotte du Renne, central France (Gravina, Mellars, & Ramsey, 2005; Mellars, Gravina, & Ramsey, 2007), in which the re-attribution of artifacts from Neanderthals to modern humans "effectively collapsed" the evidentiary support for Neanderthal symbolic behavior (Mellars, 2010, p. 20148).

For the first step in the present analysis, we note that our cognitive candidate, WM, is the well-defined, voluminously documented component of the modern mind. Moreover, it is an ability that is highly heritable (perhaps as high as 77 percent; see Coolidge, Thede, & Young, 2000; also see Ando, Ono, & Wright, 2001; Hansell et al., 2001; Rijsdijk, Vernon, & Boomsma, 2002), and it is possessed by nonhuman primates at a comparatively reduced capacity, as reflected by the differences in human and nonhuman tool use (De la Torre, 2010). As we suggested with scenarios 1 and 2, the WM of our hominid ancestors appears to have differed little, either qualitatively or quantitatively, from that of modern apes. Hints at increasing capacity (that is, capacity beyond a modern ape's range) can be identified as far back as *Homo erectus* (1.8 million years ago), though unambiguous evidence of ubiquitous modern WM capacity might not emerge until as recently as 15,000 years ago (Coolidge & Wynn, 2009).

The second step in the present analysis is to identify activities that require not just WM, but EWM. This presents two related practical problems. First, WM capacity is typically measured in terms of numbers of discrete items (e.g., terminal words in a series of read sentences). We cannot apply such tests in prehistory, and thus a simple quantitative measure is unavailable. We must rely on behavioral correlates of WM capacity. Second, psychological tests of WM capacity rarely include activities that would leave an archaeological signature; it is necessary for the archaeologist to select the appropriate activities. In practice this requires that we, as researchers, make ordinal comparisons of everyday tasks. Because these judgments are ordinal (e.g., more versus less), they are by nature not fine-grained. For example, we will argue that planning months and years in advance is a feature of modern executive thinking enabled by modern WM. It is fairly easy to cite modern examples. But what would constitute archaic WM? We can argue that prehistoric groups who did not demonstrate appropriate activities did not have modern WM, but it is effectively impossible to assign a number. Moreover, there is always the danger of under-assessing WM if we rely on only a few kinds of activities. We must therefore use a variety of different activities if we wish to have reasonable confidence in our assessment. Below we will identify technological activities, subsistence activities, and information processing activities that we suggest are reliable indicators of EWM.

The final step in the analysis is to scour the archaeological record for the earliest credible evidence for the activity in question. There are several inherent pitfalls in this step. One is the problem of equifinality, the idea that any given end state can be reached by a variety of potential means. A second is simple serendipity. Much of the evidence we seek requires good preservation—a rarity in Paleolithic sites—but we also need the good fortune to find such sites. Archaeologists have little control over these factors. However, we need not kowtow to the dictum "absence of evidence is not evidence of absence." Absence of evidence is often evidence of absence. Nevertheless, it is always dangerous to conclude that evidence from one site will always be the oldest, or to adhere to too strict a chronology. As a corollary, it is important to use as many different kinds of archaeological evidence as possible. If the archaeological evidence for many different activities all point to the same chronological conclusion, then confidence in the conclusion improves. Finally, some archaeological evidence is direct—archeologists find physical remains of the activity. But some is indirect; the archaeological remains strongly imply the presence of the activity. For example, archaeologists have occasionally found actual traps made of wood and fiber. As you might suppose, these are very rare because the constituent materials rarely survive the ravages of time. The oldest such examples are only about 8,000 years old. So, was the first use of traps only 8,000 years ago? Archaeologists think not, but the evidence is indirect, primarily in the form of animals that could not be effectively killed or captured without the use of traps. This indirect evidence pushes traps back to perhaps 70,000 years ago (Wadley, 2010), a considerable difference.

EVIDENCE OF WM/EWM IN TECHNOLOGY

The irony for archaeologists is that technology is the most visible activity in the archaeological record, but one of the least likely to require the resources of EWM or even WM. Most tool making and tool use relies, often exclusively, on a style of thinking known as expertise or expert performance (Ericsson & Delaney, 1999; Keller & Keller, 1996; Wynn & Coolidge, 2004). This kind of thinking relies on procedural cognition and long-term memory—motor action patterns learned over years of practice and/or apprenticeship. It is also largely nonverbal. Very little of the problem solving ability of EWM is ever devoted to tool use. Instead, flexibility in tool use comes from the large range of procedures and solutions learned over years. The millions of stone tools produced over human evolution tell us mostly about this other cognitive system, not WM. It is not that WM was never used, just that it is almost impossible to eliminate procedural cognition as a candidate for the cognition behind the tool or use in question (e.g., equifinality and parsimony). Nevertheless, there are technical systems that do require EWM, and which cannot be reduced to procedural cognition. Most of the good examples (e.g., alloyed metals and kiln-fired ceramics) appeared so late in human evolution as to engender little controversy or interest (ca. 6,000 years ago). There are just a few that extend much further back.

The further possible enhancement of WM appears to have been marked by several types of technological development, including traps and snares, reliable and maintainable technologies, and hafting.

Traps and Snares

"Facility" is an archaeological term for relatively permanent immobile constructions built onto or into the landscape (Oswalt, 1976). Perhaps the most common facilities used by hunters and gatherers are traps and snares, which are facilities designed to capture or kill animals (including fish; an example is the fishing weir in Figure 3.2). Facilities, including traps and snares, are often multicomponent gadgets, occasionally very heavy, that are time-consuming to build, and which operate remotely, occasionally in the absence of direct human engagement. It is the remote action that implicates EFs and EWM. To make a trap one must project present action toward a future, uncertain result. This requires the long-range planning in space and time of modern EFs, and relies significantly on the response inhibition of the central executive of WM (delayed gratification).

Direct archaeological evidence for traps and snares, as mentioned above, have a relatively shallow antiquity. Actual wooden fish traps date back 4,500 years in North America, and a few thousand years earlier in Europe, that is, not much earlier than the alloyed metals passed over above. The oldest direct evidence of a kind of trap appears to be the "desert kites" of the Middle East (Moore, Hillman, & Legge, 2000). These are lines of piled stone cairns, often hundreds of meters

Figure 3.2   Fishing with a stone weir. Reproduced from original paintings and drawings by Monte Crews and Kenneth Phillips in the collection of the New Jersey State Museum

long, converging on a stone enclosure. They were used to hunt gazelle, and the oldest are about 12,000 years old.

Indirect evidence pushes traps and snares back to about 35,000 and perhaps 75,000 years ago. At Niah cave on Borneo, Barker et al. (2007) have evidence of extensive remains of bush pigs from about 35,000 years ago, an animal best hunted using nets or snares. Similarly, Wadley (2010) has recently argued that extensive blue duiker remains at Sibudu are indirect evidence for using traps by 75,000-year-old Middle Stone Age people in South Africa. In sum, traps and snares supply direct evidence for modern WM back to 12,000 years ago, and indirect evidence back to 75,000 years ago.

Reliable Weapons

Twenty-five years ago, Bleed (1986) introduced a distinction in technical systems that has important cognitive implications, that between "maintainable" and "reliable" weapons. The former require comparatively less effort to produce but are easier to fix ("maintain") when necessary, for example, when damaged through use. Most stone tools, even from recent time periods, qualify as maintainable. Reliable weapons, on the other hand, are designed to assure function, that is, to reduce as far as possible the chances for failure. As such they tend to be over-designed, complex in the sense of having several interrelated parts, hard to maintain, and often heavy. They often require long periods of "downtime" for their construction and maintenance, and are most often intended to be deployed over short time-spans of heavy use. Bleed developed this distinction as a way to understand the difference between simple stone-tipped thrusting spears and the sophisticated projectile systems of North American Paleoindians, which included spear throwers, flexible aerodynamic shafts, replaceable foreshafts, and thin, fluted stone points. However, the distinction between maintainable and reliable applies generally to all technologies, not just weapons. The guiding principle behind reliable systems is that the investment of time and labor well in advance of need will maximize future success. More recently, Shea and Sisk (2010) have taken a related but narrower focus and argued that the use of complex projectile weaponry (spear throwers and bows and arrows) is a good marker of modern technical prowess.

> We use the term "complex projectile technology" to refer to weapons systems that use energy stored exosomatically to propel relatively low mass projectiles at delivery speeds that are high enough to allow their user to inflict a lethal puncture wound on a target from a "safe" distance.
>
> (p. 102)

They consider this development significant enough to qualify as a derived feature of modern behavior.

The archaeological record in North America clearly places reliable weapons back to Paleoindian times, at least 11,500 years ago (roughly the same age as the earliest desert kites in the Near East, which were also reliable technical systems).

Earlier examples rest on our ability to judge time investment and effectiveness of technical systems. Following Pike-Tay and Bricker (1993), we believe that one earlier type of Paleolithic artifact qualifies as being a component of a reliable system, and certainly an element of complex projectile technology—the bone and antler projectile points (aka sagaies) of the European Upper Paleolithic. To make these artifacts, artisans used stone tools to remove appropriately sized blanks from a piece of bone or antler, often after soaking the raw material, and then carved the blanks into specific shapes (split-based, barbed, etc.). Most were spear points hafted directly onto shafts, but others were harpoon heads, designed to come off the shaft while attached to a line. There are many examples of reworked points, attesting to the time required to make one from scratch. The most spectacular examples of such projectile points, which include the harpoons, date from the late Upper Paleolithic, about 14,000–18,000 years ago, with slightly simpler systems extending back to 30,000 years ago. In Africa, bone points date back even earlier, perhaps as early as 90,000 years ago in the Congolese site of Katanda (Shea & Sisk, 2010; Yellen, Brooks, Cornelissen, Mehlman, & Stewart, 1995). The European evidence is more compelling because of the contemporary evidence for managed foraging, and evidence for spear throwers and harpoons, which imply systems of gear. As yet the early African evidence consists of just the bone points, but it is provocative nonetheless.

Hafting

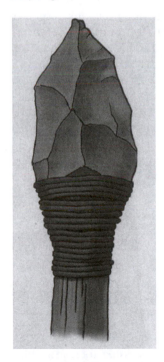

Figure 3.3   Hafted point

Hafting—attaching a stone tool to a shaft—has itself often been touted as a technological and even cognitive watershed in human evolution (Ambrose, 2001, 2010). Hafted tools represent the first time Paleolithic people united separate elements into a single tool (Figure 3.3). These compound tools consist of three distinct elements: the stone tool (usually a spear point), the shaft, and the haft itself. It was the haft that was the challenge because it had to withstand significant impact forces when the tool was used. Spears with hafted stone points represent a clear escalation in the human-prey arms race, and it is fair to emphasize their importance in technological history. But their cognitive significance is harder to assess. Much hinges on how the hafting was done. A simple haft using a naturally available glue has different implications than a haft requiring days of soaking animal tendons followed by controlled, heated drying of the lashings on the shaft. The former is a straightforward, single-sitting task, while the latter is a multiday procedure. In a sense, the former leans towards maintainable, the latter toward reliable on the maintainable–reliable continuum. It is only the latter that carries clear implications for EWM capacity. Hafting also calls out for a discussion of invention, the conscious design of an innovative technology. Someone had to design the first haft; it could not have occurred by accident. And it would be very informative, from a cognitive perspective, to know just how that person came up with the idea. The frustrating answer is that we just do not know. We can speculate, but our speculations cannot then be used as data for a cognitive interpretation.

The earliest evidence for hafting extends back probably 200,000 years in Europe, the Middle East, and Africa (Mazza et al., 2006; Rots & Van Peer, 2006; Shea, Fleagle, & Assefa, 2007; Villa, Boscato, Ranaldo, & Ronchitelli, 2009), and includes examples by Neanderthals and modern humans. Thus far, at least, these early hafts seem to be of the simpler, single-sitting task variety, though certainly collection of natural adhesives adds a component of complexity to the task, and Grünberg (2002) and Koller, Baumer, and Mania (2001) have argued that the production of birch pitch required sophisticated knowledge of heating temperatures. It was only after 100,000 years ago that there is evidence for multiday hafting procedures. The best evidence comes from Sibudu in South Africa (the same site as the indirect evidence hunting blue duikers with snares) at about 70,000 years ago. Here hunters used a mixture of acacia gum, a little beeswax, and powdered ocher to produce an adhesive that had to be carefully dried using fire (Wadley, Hodgskiss, & Grant, 2009). Although in theory such hafting could be accomplished by procedural cognition, the variety of constituents required for the adhesives, and the multiday procedure itself, imply the use of modern WM, particularly the EFs of projecting future action, anticipating problems, response inhibition, and contingency planning (Wadley, 2010). Interestingly, however, Wadley notes that despite the steps in making compound adhesives for hafting (for example, abstraction, recursion, and cognitive fluidity), that it does not necessarily imply the use of symbolic behavior.

To summarize, three lines of technical evidence are in broad agreement. Convincing archaeological evidence extends easily back to 18,000 years ago or so, but there are strong examples going back as far as 70,000 years ago in Africa. Earlier than that there is only the single example of simple hafts, which cannot alone bear the weight of assigning modern WM or EWM. It is important to reiterate that technology is not a domain of activity that easily documents WM capacity. Procedural cognition can be effective and flexible, and can encompass almost all technical activity. Certainly hafting, or even complex projectile technology, could not alone stand as evidence for fully modern EFs. Of the examples we cite, the only one that might stand alone as an argument for modern cognition is the example of traps.

EVIDENCE OF WM/EWM IN FORAGING AND LABOR SYSTEMS

Technical evidence works better when it supports or corroborates evidence from other domains, and next to technology, the domain of activity most visible in the archaeological record is subsistence—acquiring and processing food. And like technology, archaeologists' arguments for modern subsistence systems have been heavily distorted by the record of the European Upper Paleolithic, especially its later phases, which included examples of specialized hunting of single species such as reindeer or mammoth. These were no doubt impressive subsistence systems but specialization per se does not actually require the planning resources of modern EFs and EWM. It can easily be organized and executed by expert procedural cognition. In fact this is arguably a more appropriate cognitive strategy because it consists of well-learned, automatic responses that can be selected and deployed quickly in dangerous situations. Neanderthals were very good at this kind of thinking and, no surprise, we have extensive evidence for their specialized hunting (Callow & Cornford, 1986; Gaudzinski & Roebroeks, 2000). Thus, it is necessary to eschew this war-horse of modernity and identify subsistence activities that actually do require modern EFs and EWM.

Modern people manage their food supply. This is obvious in agricultural economies, where activities must be planned on a yearly scale (for nontropical systems). It clearly relies on the long-range planning of EFs and, more specifically, the response inhibition that is a key component of modern WM (e.g., retaining a portion of the harvest for replanting even in the presence of extreme want). But agriculture is not the only form of managed foraging. Most of the hunting and gathering systems archaeologists have recognized as "complex" also qualify (Price & Brown, 1985). Good recent ethnographic examples include foragers of the Northwest Coast of America, the Arctic, and Australia. In Northern and Western Australia, hunter-gatherers systematically burn tracts of land in order to encourage a second green-up of grass, which attracts herbivores. They rotate the tract to be burned every year, and do not return to a tract for at least a decade (Lewis, 1982). This is a managed system, with planning over long periods, as well as response inhibition.

Another component of modern hunting and gathering systems is a marked division of labor by age and gender (Kuhn & Stiner, 2006). Kuhn and Stiner have proposed that the division of economic labor by age and gender is a salient feature of the recent human condition and that it emerged relatively late in human evolutionary history. We note that complementary economic roles and food sharing implies the ability to negotiate these roles and to penalize those who deviate from these norms. We note that gendered division of labor requires coordination of separate labor pools, but more importantly is manifested in the tropics by increased reliance on small, seasonal resources (plants and small animals) that require scheduled harvesting, typically by women and children. We believe that the functions of organization, delegation, disputation resolution, and so on weakly implicate WM and its EFs.

Archaeological evidence for agriculture extends back to 10,000 years on several continents, and evidence for managed forms of hunting and gathering back another several thousand years in the guise of late Paleolithic cultures all over the world. An especially good example is that of the Epipaleolithic site of Abu Hureyra in Syria (Moore, Hillman, & Legge, 2000). Here a group of hunters and gatherers established a sedentary community based on hunting gazelle and gathering a wide variety of local plants. When the local conditions became much drier 11,000 to 10,000 years ago, these people did not simply shift the focus of their hunting and gathering; they changed its very basis by beginning to cultivate rye. The interesting point is not so much the broad spectrum hunting and gathering but the inventive response to changing conditions. These people were clearly using the planning abilities enabled by EWM.

Finding evidence for managed foraging that is earlier than about 10,000 years ago is fraught with problems, mostly linked to preservation, but also to mobility patterns of earlier hunter-gatherers who rarely settled in permanent sites like Abu Hureyra. The amount of refuse is much less, and harder to characterize. Nevertheless, there are several provocative earlier examples. A well-known example is that of late Upper Paleolithic reindeer hunters (Straus, 1996) of southwestern Europe (ca. 18,000 years ago). Here it is not the specialization that is telling (see above), but the evidence for a tightly scheduled hunting system in which herds were intercepted and slaughtered in the fall at specific locations during migrations, but at other times of the year were hunted individually using a different set of tactics. Though other resources were used, reindeer were the clear focus year-round, using a seasonally adjusted strategy that included periods of down-time during which the hunters made and maintained their complex technical gear (see above). At about the same time, hunters on the Russian Plain used a system in which they killed large numbers of animals during late summer/early fall and then cached large quantities of meat in underground storage pits for freezing and future consumption (Soffer, 1989). Storage and delayed consumption are strong evidence for modern WM, without necessarily invoking symbolic behavior or EWM.

Earlier evidence is largely indirect. At Niah Cave on the island of Borneo (Barker et al., 2007), archaeologists have recovered large quantities of pollen from plants that flourish on recently burned areas. The local tropical conditions are quite wet, and the pollen far exceeds what one would normally expect to find, suggesting extensive human-induced burning. This evidence dates to sometime between 42,000 and 28,000 years ago. Earlier still is the evidence for hunting blue duiker in South Africa using snares or traps (70,000 years ago). Of similar antiquity is evidence from other South African sites for extensive use of corms (fleshy, semisubterranean stems), which are features of plants that flourish on burned landscapes, suggesting as at Niah human use of fire as an ecology altering tool (Deacon, 1993). Kuhn and Stiner (2006) argue that this broadening of the subsistence base in South Africa is an indication of division of labor by age and sex. In sum, the archaeological evidence for managed foraging parallels the evidence of technology. There is a strong signature going back 18,000 years or so, and a weaker, but still provocative, set of isolated examples going back 70,000 years.

EVIDENCE OF WM/EWM IN INFORMATION PROCESSING

Thus far in our discussion we have focused primarily on the long-range planning and response inhibition components of modern EFs and EWM and have traced them archaeologically through the technological and subsistence records. We now shift focus to problem solving, another of the EFs enhanced through an increase in WM capacity. WM is the active problem solving "space" of the modern mind. We use WM to construct analogies, perform thought experiments, make contingency plans, and even make metaphors. It is how and where we bring things together in thought; however, even modern WM has a limited capacity, because the episodic buffer is a limited capacity store. If the capacity of this store is depleted by holding raw information, little comparison and processing can also occur (try multiplying two four-digit numbers in your head). One solution to the problem that modern humans regularly use is externalization of some of this information, that is, holding the information outside of the mind itself. This is an aspect of extended cognition, which has recently received significant attention in cognitive science (Wilson & Clark, 2009) and even archaeology (Malafouris, 2008, 2010). Our interest is in the implications that extended cognition holds for WM, and the primary effect is to extend WM capacity by relieving the necessity to hold information in the episodic buffer, thereby freeing capacity for the processing components of the central executive. Examples of such externalized storage systems abound in the modern world—writing, numbers, calculators, and so on. External systems need not be artifactual—one can, for example, count on one's fingers—but they often are artifactual, which gives us an avenue to follow into the prehistoric past.

It is uncontroversial to assert that early writing and accounting systems, which date back at least 5,000 years, were external information storage. Systems of clay tokens, used for accounting purposes, extend the record back several thousand years into the early Neolithic (Malafouris, 2010; Schmandt-Besserat, 1992). We pick up the trail about 12,000 years ago at the site of Grotte du Tai in western France (Marshack, 1991b). The plaque (Figure 3.4a) appears to have been a record-keeping device. Someone engraved a series of long lines crossed by groups of slashes on a piece of flat bone. Marshack, and later d'Errico (2001), examined the markings microscopically and determined that they were produced by different tools, probably in different episodes. Marshack argued that the marks were produced by different techniques that corresponded to lunar phases, while d'Errico concluded simply that it was an external memory device. We do not know what the engraver was tracking, but it was clearly something, attesting to a desire to externalize information, thereby freeing up WM capacity for processing. Similar objects, some more elaborate and others not as much so, date back in Europe to about 28,000 years ago (d'Errico et al., 2003). An example is the Abri Blanchard

Figure 3.4 (a) Tai counting device, ca. 14,000 (left); (b) Abri Blanchard lunar calendar, ca. 28,000 (right)

plaque (Figure 3.4b). Marshack (1991a) argued that the markings were iconic representations of the different phases of the moon, and thus the device was a lunar calendar; this supposition has been supported by recent field experiments in archaeoastronomy (Jègues-Wolkiewiez, 2005). Again, the device externalized the information, enabling its possessor to use his or her WM capacity for other tasks.

Earlier still and equally provocative are therianthropic figurines from Germany, the most famous of which is the Hohlenstein-Stadel figurine (Figure 3.5) referred to in scenario 6. This is an image of a lion-headed person (or human-bodied lion) carved in elephant ivory, roughly 28cm high and about 32,000 years old (Hahn, 1986). It is certainly an evocative piece, and has inspired much discussion about symbolism and Upper Paleolithic religious thinking. It also has a number of important implications for cognition (Wynn, Coolidge, & Bright, 2009), one of which concerns WM. The figurine is an externalized abstraction. Such a creature does not exist in the real world, and it may have been metaphorically glued together, initially at least, in the WM of some Upper Paleolithic person. The problems people need to solve are not always practical issues in day-to-day life. They are also social, and even metaphysical. The Hohlenstein-Stadel figurine may be the externalization of such a metaphysical problem, and its externalized presence frees up the WM of the artisan, and also observers, to ponder other related existential issues. So far, our discussion of externalized information processing has not yielded any surprises. Suggesting that Upper Paleolithic people in Europe 32,000 years ago exercised modern cognition is neither a novel nor a controversial conclusion. But what about earlier? Can we push externalized information back as far as the early evidence of traps, or managed foraging? The answer is yes, but it requires a slightly different take on a famous set of artifacts— the Blombos beads (Figure 3.6).

Blombos Cave is a site on the coast of South Africa whose Middle Stone Age levels date back at least 77,000 years. These MSA levels have famously yielded engraved bones, shaped and engraved pieces of ocher, bone awls, and marine shell beads (Henshilwood & Dubreuil, 2009; Henshilwood & Marean, 2003; d'Errico, Henshilwood, Vanhaeren, & van Niekerk, 2005). These are among the earliest putatively modern artifacts yet found, and make a strong case for extending many of the components of modern behavior and cognition back to this early period. But the initial enthusiasm has recently been tempered by more sober critiques. D'Errico, Henshilwood, and colleagues (2005), for example, argued that the presence of decorative beads indicates that the inhabitants had fully syntactical language. This conclusion was then elegantly challenged by Botha (2008), who pointed out that d'Errico and Henshilwood had not made explicit and convincing bridging arguments linking beads to language. Henshilwood and Dubreuil (2009) have replied, providing part of the linkage (a very nice example of a productive scholarly exchange), but the implications of the beads are still not entirely clear. We suggest that an alternative approach is to look at these artifacts not in their possible symbolic role, but as externalized information storage. Henshilwood and Botha agree that the shells with punched holes were beads, and that the beads were worn as ornaments. But why does one wear beads? One answer is that one wears beads to send information about oneself to another person. This could be an explicit

Figure 3.5   Hohlenstein-Stadel figurine, ca. 32,000

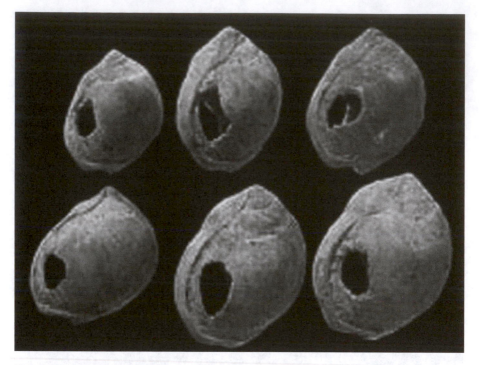

Figure 3.6   Six of the Blombos cave beads, ca. 77,000

message about social status ("I am an adult," "I am wealthy," "I am a surfer," and so on), or an implicit message ("I am a good mate prospect"), but by changing how others view the wearer, the wearer is externalizing information about him or herself.

Curiously, there is an alternative function for these beads that neither Henshilwood nor Botha have considered. They might have been tally devices, used to keep track of (remember) some sequential phenomena (much like modern rosary beads). The social implications of this option are different from the decorative bead interpretation, but the information implications are similar: Beads were an externalized store of information, freeing WM to devote space in the episodic buffer for processing information, rather than just holding it in attention.

This evidence of externalized information storage is provocative. We live in a modern world where externalized information has come to dominate, perhaps even overwhelm, our daily lives, and the thought that it had its roots far back in the Stone Age is certainly provocative. However, for our topic at hand—WM and EWM— external storage of information is actually an ambiguous signature. Externalization of information would release storage space for episodic buffers *of whatever capacity*, not just modern capacity. There need only be enough capacity to hold the external device as a token of some kind in the episodic buffer as one performs processes upon it. Because of this ambiguity, we suggest that evidence for the use of external storage devices cannot, on its own, provide compelling evidence for modern EWM, but perhaps they do argue for lower-level abstractive processes (that is, the maintenance and manipulation of mental representations with some kind of internal concept or referent) at the very least. It can, however, stand as corroborating evidence for assessments established by other means. As such, it supports the picture painted using technology and subsistence, that is, strong evidence in this case going back to perhaps 30,000 years, and weaker evidence extending further to 77,000 years ago.

CONCLUSION AND FUTURE DIRECTIONS

When we apply the strict standard to the EFs and their archaeological presence, the following picture emerges:

The ad hoc tool behavior seen in scenario 2, in which *Homo habilis* created, used, and discarded a stone tool about 2.5 million years ago, does not appear to differ greatly from that of modern apes. As suggested by scenario 1, in which a modern chimpanzee created an ad hoc tool for termite fishing, modern apes do not carry their tools around for future use; they discard them once they are done using them. However, the behavioral changes in scenario 3, in which *Homo erectus* created a handaxe about 1.8 million years ago, point to the development of important cognitive changes. The hominids in scenario 3 have begun to carry tools and tool materials around with them; we know this because both tools and tool material are found at great distances from the origins of the materials. A concurrent change in the archaeological record that signals a possible change in WM is the bifacial symmetry being imposed on handaxes (Figure 3.1), suggesting an emerging ability to hold mental representations in mind—in WM, that is. These changes in the archaeological record suggest that some improvement in WM has occurred, even if only a gradual increase in capacity concomitant with the increasing hominid brain volume that is also taking place.

In scenario 4, a Neanderthal produced a maintainable tool (a spear with a hafted point, Figure 3.3) about 200,000 years ago, and in scenario 5, a *Homo sapiens* produced a reliable tool (a projectile with a stone point) about 100,000 years ago. Maintainable and reliable tools are further archaeological indications of behavioral change pointing to cognitive change. The shift from ad hoc technologies to maintainable and reliable ones suggests that the hominids have acquired an increased awareness of time in the sense of episodic memory (Coolidge & Wynn, 2008; Tulving, 2002), as well as increased abilities for imagining contingencies, planning, and response inhibition. Reliable weapons, and in particular complex projectile weapons, rely on the EF ability to plan over long stretches of time, and especially the response inhibition of WM (i.e., do not hunt today, even if you are hungry, but instead invest your effort in producing tools more likely to succeed tomorrow), and contingency planning (if the foreshaft breaks, slip in a new one; it is quicker than making an entire spear). These changes in the archaeological record imply that a gradual but substantial improvement in WM has occurred, perhaps in WM capacity, the types of information accessible and manipulable by WM, or both.

In scenario 6, a *Homo sapiens sapiens* carved a piece of ivory into a fantastic shape approximately 40,000 to 28,000 years ago, and in doing so provides us with evidence of behavior that points to a quite dramatic change in cognition. The

Hohlenstein-Stadel figurine (Figure 3.5) suggests modern cognitive abilities of abstraction, cross-domain thinking (i.e., metaphor), and the ability to externalize a mental representation in a way that frees up WM for additional processing. The sophistication of this artifact, we suggest, implies EWM, a WM ability that resembles our own in its capacity and the information domains available for its manipulation. In many ways it also greatly resembles scenario 7, the present-day astrophysics example, in which things like technology and social organizations have expanded in complexity and scale, though modern WM remains on par with that seen in scenario 6.

The figurine and other archaeological evidence (technology, subsistence, and information processing devices) all suggest a relatively late emergence of modern EFs. Most of the evidence postdates 25,000 years ago, and it is not until 15,000 years ago that EFs appear to have been both unambiguous and ubiquitous.

There are four ways in which scholars could interpret this result:

1. Reject it entirely. Absence of evidence is not evidence of absence, or so the adage goes. The taphonomic threshold (Bednarik, 1994) and the serendipity of archaeological discovery have yielded a misleading signature. Moreover, the strict standard is too strict, and places unreasonable demands on archaeological inference.
2. This is the expected signature of the ratchet effect of culture change. EFs evolved long before 30,000 years ago and enabled modern innovation and culture change, but it required millennia before these changes accumulated to the point of archaeological visibility.
3. The mutation enabling EWM occurred long before 30,000 years ago but required millennia to increase in frequency to levels at which significant numbers of people expressed the EFs that are necessary for group planning (note that this interpretation is similar to #2, but here the emphasis is on biological process, not culture change).
4. The signature is accurate. EWM and EFs evolved late in a human population that was already anatomically modern. They then spread very rapidly because of their clear advantage in long-term planning, and innovative responses to challenge. Furthermore, modern empirical evidence supports the strong relationship between WM and fluid intelligence, i.e., novel problem solving.

A salient and long-known feature of the Paleolithic record would appear to favor option #4: About 50,000 to 30,000 years ago, the pace of culture change accelerated dramatically, beyond what seems explainable as the vagaries or biases of artifactual preservation, or as responses to the late Pleistocene climatic change. Yes, there were significant climatic events associated with late Pleistocene environments, but there had been significant environmental changes many times before without such a dramatic response. The pace is also different from the gradual increases in WM that appear with *Homo erectus* about 1.8 million years ago and which characterize hominid WM for well over the next million and a half years. The veritable explosion of behavioral changes that take place between 50,000 and 30,000 years ago is consistent with the idea that a cognitive "leap" has occurred, and one that we believe is consistent with an enhancement to WM through a genetic or epigenetic event. This time, the human response to late Pleistocene challenges was facilitated by modern EFs, and the long-term consequence was, ultimately, the modern world.

REFERENCES

Ambrose, S. H. (2001). Paleolithic technology and human evolution. *Science, 291*(5509), 1748–1753.

Ambrose, S. H. (2010). Coevolution of composite-tool technology, constructive memory, and language: Implications for the evolution of modern human behavior. In T. Wynn & F. L. Coolidge (Eds.), *Working memory: Beyond language and symbolism* (pp. S135–S147). Chicago, IL: University of Chicago Press.

Ando, J., Ono, Y., & Wright, M. J. (2001). Genetic structure of spatial and verbal working memory. *Behavior Genetics, 31*(6), 615–624.

Baddeley, A. D. (1993). Working memory or working attention? In A. D. Baddeley & L. Weiskrantz (Eds.), *Attention: Selection, awareness, and control: A tribute to Donald Broadbent* (pp. 152–170). Oxford, UK: Oxford University Press.

Baddeley, A. D. (2000). The episodic buffer: A new component of working memory? *Trends in Cognitive Sciences, 4*, 417–423.

Baddeley, A. D. (2001). Is working memory working? *American Psychologist, 11*, 851–864.

Baddeley, A. D. (2002). Is working memory still working? *European Psychologist, 7*(2), 85–97.

Baddeley, A. D. (2007). *Working memory, thought, and action.* Oxford, UK: Oxford University Press.

Baddeley, A., & Logie, R. (1999). Working memory: The multiple-component model. In A. Miyake & P. Shah (Eds.), *Models of working memory: Mechanisms of active maintenance and executive control* (pp. 28–61). New York, NY: Cambridge University Press.

Barker, G., Barton, H., Bird, M., Daly, P., Datan, I., Dykes, A. ... & Turney, C. (2007). The 'human revolution' in lowland tropical Southeast Asia: The antiquity and behavior of anatomically modern humans at Niah Cave (Sarawak, Borneo). *Journal of Human Evolution, 52*(3), 243–261.

Bednarik, R. G. (1994). A taphonomy of palaeoart. *Antiquity, 68*, 68–74.

Bleed, P. (1986). The optimal design of hunting weapons: Maintainability or reliability? *American Antiquity, 51*(4), 737–747.

Botha, R. (2008). Prehistoric shell beads as a window on language evolution. *Language and Communication, 28*(3), 197–212.

Callow, P., & Cornford, J. M. (1986). *La Cotte de St. Brelade 1961–1978: Excavations by C. B. M. McBurney.* Norwich, UK: Geo Books.

Carruthers, P. (2002). The cognitive functions of language. *Behavioral and Brain Sciences, 25*, 657–675.

Coolidge, F. L., Thede, L. L., & Young, S. E. (2000). Heritability and the comorbidity of ADHD with behavioral disorders and executive function deficits: A preliminary investigation. *Developmental Neuropsychology, 17*, 273–287.

Coolidge, F. L., & Wynn, T. (2001). Executive functions of the frontal lobes and the evolutionary ascendancy of *Homo sapiens. Cambridge Archaeological Journal, 11*(2), 255–260.

Coolidge, F. L., & Wynn, T. (2005). Working memory, its executive functions, and the emergence of modern thinking. *Cambridge Archaeological Journal, 15*(1), 5–26.

Coolidge, F. L., & Wynn, T. (2008). The role of episodic memory and autonoetic thought in Upper Paleolithic life. *PaleoAnthropology, 2008*, 212–217.

Coolidge, F. L., & Wynn, T. (2009). *The rise of* Homo sapiens: *The evolution of modern thinking*. Chichester, UK: Wiley-Blackwell.

d'Errico, F. (2001). Memories out of mind: The archaeology of the oldest memory systems. In A. Nowell (Ed.), *In the mind's eye: Multidisciplinary approaches to the evolution of human cognition* (pp. 33–49). Ann Arbor, MI: International Monographs in Prehistory.

d'Errico, F., Henshilwood, C., Lawson, G., Vanhaeren, M., Tillier, A.-M., Soressi, M. & Julien, M. (2003). Archaeological evidence for the emergence of language, symbolism, and music: An alternative multidisciplinary perspective. *Journal of World Prehistory*, *17*(1), 1–70.

d'Errico, F., Henshilwood, C., Vanhaeren, M., & van Niekerk, K. (2005). *Nassarius kraussianus* shell beads from Blombos Cave: Evidence for symbolic behaviour in the Middle Stone Age. *Journal of Human Evolution*, *48*(1), 3–24.

D'Esposito, M. (2007). From cognitive to neural models of working memory. *Philosophical Transactions of the Royal Society B, Biological Sciences*, *362*(1481), 761–772.

De la Torre, I. (2010). Insights on the technical competence of the early Oldowan. In A. Nowell & I. Davidson (Eds.), *Stone tools and the evolution of human cognition* (pp. 45–65). Boulder, CO: University Press of Colorado.

Deacon, H. (1993). Planting an idea: An archaeology of Stone Age gatherers in South Africa. *South African Archaeological Journal*, *48*, 86–93.

Ericsson, K., & Delaney, P. (1999). Long-term working memory as an alternative to capacity models of working memory in everyday skilled performance. In A. Miyake & P. Shah (Eds.), *Models of working memory: Mechanisms of active maintenance and executive control* (pp. 257–297). New York, NY: Cambridge University Press.

Frankish, K. (1998a) A matter of opinion. *Philosophical Psychology*, *11*, 423–442.

Frankish, K. (1998b) Natural language and virtual belief. In P. Carruthers & J. Boucher (Eds.), *Language and thought* (pp. 248–269). Cambridge, UK: Cambridge University Press.

Gaudzinski, S., & Roebroeks, W. (2000). Adults only: Reindeer hunting at the Middle Palaeolithic site Salzgitter Lebenstedt, northern Germany. *Journal of Human Evolution*, *38*(4), 497–521.

Gravina, B., Mellars, P., & Ramsey, C. B. (2005). Radiocarbon dating of interstratified Neanderthal and early modern human occupations at the Châtelperron type-site. *Nature*, *438*(3), 51–56.

Grünberg, J. (2002). Middle Palaeolithic birch-bark pitch. *Antiquity*, *76*(1), 15–16.

Hahn, J. (1986). *Kraft und aggression: Die botschaftder eiszeitkunstin Aurignacien suddeutschlands?* Vol. 7. Tubingen, Germany: Archaeological Venatoria.

Hansell, N. K., Wright, M. J., Smith, G. A., Geffen, G. M., Geffen, L. B., & Martin, N. G. (2001). Genetic influence on ERP slow wave measures of working memory. *Behavior Genetics*, *31*, 603–614.

Harlow, J. M. (1868). Recovery from the passage of an iron bar through the head. *Publications of the Massachusetts Medical Society*, *2*, 327–346.

Henshilwood, C., & Dubreuil, B. (2009). Reading the artefacts: Gleaning language skills from the Middle Stone Age in southern Africa. In R. Botha (Ed.), *The cradle of language* (pp. 41–63). Stellenbosch, South Africa: Stellenbosch University.

Henshilwood, C. S., & Marean, C. W. (2003). The origin of modern human behavior: Critique of the models and their test implications. *Current Anthropology*, *44*(5), 627–651.

Jègues-Wolkiewiez, C. (2005). Aux racines de l'astronomie, ou l'ordre caché d'une oeuvre paléolithique. *Antiquités Nationales*, *37*, 43–62.

Keller, C., & Keller, J. (1996). *Cognition and tool use: The blacksmith at work*. Cambridge, UK: Cambridge University Press.

Koller, J., Baumer, U., & Mania, D. (2001). High-tech in the Middle Palaeolithic: Neanderthal-manufactured pitch identified. *European Journal of Archaeology*, *4*(3), 385–397.

Kuhn, S. L., & Stiner, M. C. (2006). What's a mother to do? The division of labor among Neanderthals and modern humans in Eurasia. *Current Anthropology*, *47*(6), 953–980.

Lewis, H. (1982). Fire technology and resource management in aboriginal North America and Australia. In E. Hunn (Ed.), *Resource managers: North American and Australian hunter-gatherers* (pp. 45–68). Washington, DC: American Association for the Advancement of Science.

Lezak, M. (1982). The problem of assessing executive functions. *International Journal of Psychology*, *17*, 281–297.

Luria, A. R. (1966). *Higher cortical function in man*. New York, NY: Basic Books.

Malafouris, L. (2008). Beads for a plastic mind: The 'Blind Man's Stick' (BMS) hypothesis and the active nature of material culture. *Cambridge Archaeological Journal*, *18*(3), 401–414.

Malafouris, L. (2010). Grasping the concept of number: How did the sapient mind move beyond approximation? In C. Renfrew & I. Morley (Eds.), *The archaeology of measurement: Comprehending heaven, earth and time in ancient societies* (pp. 35–42). Cambridge, UK: Cambridge University Press.

Marshack, A. (1991a). *The roots of civilization: The cognitive beginnings of man's first art, symbol and notation*. Kingston, RI: Moyer Bell Ltd.

Marshack, A. (1991b). The Tai Plaque and calendrical notation in the Upper Palaeolithic. *Cambridge Archaeological Journal*, *1*(1), 25–61.

Mazza, P. P. A., Martini, F., Sala, B., Magi, M., Colombini, M. P., Giachi, G., ... & Ribechini, E. (2006). A new Palaeolithic discovery: Tar-hafted stone tools in a European Mid-Pleistocene bone-bearing bed. *Journal of Archaeological Science*, *33*(9), 1310–1318.

Mellars, P. (2010). Neanderthal symbolism and ornament manufacture: The bursting of a bubble? *Proceedings of the National Academy of Sciences*, *107*(47), 20147–20148.

Mellars, P., Gravina, B., & Ramsey, C. B. (2007). Confirmation of Neanderthal/modern human interstratification at the Chatelperronian type-site. *Proceedings of the National Academy of Sciences*, *104*(9), 3657–3662.

Miyake, A., Friedman, N. P., Emerson, M. J., Witzki, A. H., Howerter, A., & Wager, T. D. (2000). The unity and diversity of executive functions and their contributions to complex "frontal lobe" tasks: A latent variable analysis. *Cognitive Psychology*, *41*, 49–100.

Miyake, A., & Shah, P. (Eds.). (1999). *Models of working memory: Mechanisms of active maintenance and executive control*. New York, NY: Cambridge University Press.

Moore, A. M. T., Hillman, G. C., & Legge, A. J. (2000). *Village on the Euphrates: From foraging to farming at Abu Hureyra*. Oxford, UK: Oxford University Press.

Oberauer, K., Suss, H-M., Wilhelm, O., & Wittman, W. W. (2003). The multiple faces of working memory: Storage, processing, supervision, and coordination. *Intelligence*, *31*, 167–193.

Oswalt, W. (1976). *An anthropological analysis of food-getting technology*. New York, NY: John Wiley & Sons.

Pike-Tay, A., & Bricker, H. (1993). Hunting in the Gravettian: An examination of evidence from southwestern France. In H. Bricker, P. Mellar, & G. Peterkin (Eds.), *Hunting and animal exploitation in the Later Palaeolithic and Mesolithic of Eurasia* (pp. 127–144). Washington, DC: American Anthropological Association.

Price, T. D., & Brown, J. A. (1985). *Prehistoric hunter-gatherers: The emergence of cultural complexity*. New York, NY: Academic Press.

Rijsdijk, F. V., Vernon, P. A., & Boomsma, D. I. (2002). Application of hierarchical genetic models to Raven and WAIS subtests: A Dutch twin study. *Behavior Genetics*, *32*(3), 199–210.

Rots, V., & Van Peer, P. (2006). Early evidence of complexity in lithic economy: Core-axe production, hafting and use at late Middle Pleistocene site 8-B-11, Sai Island (Sudan). *Journal of Archaeological Science*, *33*(3), 360–371.

Schmandt-Besserat, D. (1992). *How writing came about*. Austin, TX: University of Texas Press.

Shea, J., & Sisk, M. (2010). Complex projectile technology and *Homo sapiens* dispersal into Western Eurasia. *PaleoAnthropology, 2010*, 100–122.

Shea, J., Fleagle, J., & Assefa, Z. (2007). Context and chronology of early *Homo sapiens* fossils from the Omo Kibish. In P. Mellars, K. Boyle, O. Bar-Yosef, & C. B. Stringer (Eds.), *Rethinking the human revolution* (pp. 153–164). Cambridge, UK: McDonald Institute for Archaeological Research.

Soffer, O. (1989). Storage, sedentism and the Eurasian Palaeolithic record. *Antiquity, 63*, 719–732.

Straus, L. G. (1996). Holocene transition in southwest Europe. In L. G. Straus, B. V. Eriksen, J. Erlandson, & D. Yesner (Eds.), *Humans at the end of the Ice Age: The archaeology of the Pleistocene–Holocene transition* (pp. 83–99). New York, NY: Plenum Press.

Tulving, E. (2002). Episodic memory: From mind to brain. *Annual Review of Psychology, 53*, 1–25.

Villa, P. (1982). Conjoinable pieces and site formation processes. *American Antiquity, 47*(2), 276–290.

Villa, P., Boscato, P., Ranaldo, F., & Ronchitelli, A. (2009). Stone tools for the hunt: Points with impact scars from a Middle Paleolithic site in southern Italy. *Journal of Archaeological Science, 36*(3), 850–859.

Wadley, L. (2010). Were snares & traps used in the Middle Stone Age and does it matter? A review and a case study from Sibudu, South Africa. *Journal of Human Evolution, 58*(2), 179–192.

Wadley, L., Hodgskiss, T., & Grant, M. (2009). Implications for complex cognition from the hafting of tools with compound adhesives in the Middle Stone Age, South Africa. *Proceedings of the National Academy of Sciences of the United States of America, 106*(24), 9590–9594.

Wilson, R., & Clark, A. (2009). How to situate cognition: Letting nature take its course. In P. Robbins & M. Aydede (Eds.), *The Cambridge handbook of situated cognition* (pp. 55–77). Cambridge, UK: Cambridge University Press.

Wynn, T., & Coolidge, F. L. (2004). The expert Neandertal mind. *Journal of Human Evolution, 46*(4), 467–487.

Wynn, T., Coolidge, F. L., & Bright, M. (2009). Hohlenstein-Stadel and the evolution of human conceptual thought. *Cambridge Archaeological Journal, 19*(1), 73–83.

Yellen, J. E., Brooks, A. S., Cornelissen, E., Mehlman, M. J., & Stewart, K. (1995). A Middle Stone age worked bone industry from Katanda, Upper Semliki Valley, Zaire. *Science, 268*(5210), 553–556.

Part II

Working Memory
Across the Lifespan

4

Working Memory in Development

TRACY PACKIAM ALLOWAY
Department of Psychology, University of North Florida, Jacksonville, FL, USA

ROSS G. ALLOWAY
University of Edinburgh, Edinburgh, UK

BACKGROUND INFORMATION

*T*he theoretical conceptualization of Working Memory has developed considerably from the early model proposed by Baddeley and Hitch (1974). A system whose function was once thought to focus primarily on the temporary storage and processing of information has been expanded to encompass a far larger cognitive role. Hints of such a role could be found in Fuster's work on physiological dynamics of working memory in the cerebral cortex (Fuster, 2005). His earlier work describes the discovery of the first "memory cells" found in the primate brain when cortical cells showed a greater and sustained discharge when memorizing a piece of information (Fuster & Alexander, 1971). Since then, his research has focused on the cognitive functions of the prefrontal cortex, the seat of Working Memory, and described the various roles from organizing behavior, goal-directed plans, and even encompassing aspects of controlled or focused attention (Fuster, 2008). His research has been instrumental in expanding what started off as a relatively small role for Working Memory, to a much larger part.

Indeed, psychologists have also picked up on his ideas, as Cowan has suggested that Working Memory operates in a role of controlled attention, highlighting key aspects from long-term memory and then translating these into action (Cowan, 2005). From an experimental perspective, Working Memory is related to a range of executive function skills, such as shifting between information, updating stimuli, and planning (see Miyake & Shah, 1999). We also know that the role of Working Memory is not restricted to a particular type of stimuli. In a large-scale study with a developmental population, various theoretical structures of Working Memory were investigated using statistical modeling techniques (Alloway, Gathercole, &

Pickering, 2006; also Alloway & Alloway, 2012). The best fitting model was one that included components for storing and processing both verbal and visuo-spatial information.

CURRENT EVIDENCE

Working Memory Capacity

How much information we can hold in the mind? In order to answer this question, we recently asked individuals aged from 5 to 80 years old to participate in a series of verbal and visuo-spatial working memory assessments (Alloway & Alloway, 2012). Working Memory was measured using an online version of a standardized memory assessment consisting of two verbal and one visuo-spatial Working Memory test (Alloway, 2007a). In the letter recall test, the individual saw a letter on the computer screen, immediately followed by another letter. They verified whether the letters were the same and then remembered the target letters in sequence. In the backwards digit recall test, the individual recalled a sequence of spoken digits in the reverse order. In the shape recall test, the individual saw a shape on a grid, immediately followed by another shape. They verified whether the shapes were the same and then remembered the target shape in the correct grid location.

Several patterns emerged (see Figure 4.1). First, Working Memory performance seems to experience tremendous change during development: between 5 and 19 years of age, there was a mean increase of 23 standard points. Contrast this growth to two other 20-year periods: between 20 to 39 years of age (a mean increase of four standard points); and between 50 to 69 years of age (a mean decline of one standard point). Another key pattern is that working memory scores were highest in 30-year-olds.

A surprising finding is that there was little decline in Working Memory capacity in the older adults: between 50 and 80 years old, there was a mean drop of six standard points. People in their sixties performed at a similar level to those in their twenties. The difference in Working Memory scores between age bands in the older adults was markedly less than that of the children. Contrast this with fluid IQ scores where decline in 80-year-olds was reported to be 15 standard points (1SD) below the average and reflected levels of cognitive impairments (Kaufman, 2001).

Finally, there were marked differences in the nature of Working Memory decline. Verbal Working Memory skills remained robust and individuals in their seventies to mid-eighties performed as well as those in their teenage years. In contrast, visuo-spatial working memory skills in the same age group (70–80 years) were at the same level as nine- and ten-year-olds (see Chapter 5 of this volume for more on Working Memory in older adults).

Each individual has a relatively fixed capacity that may be greater or lesser than that of others. So, a particular mental activity may be within the Working Memory capacity of one person, but exceed that of another (Alloway & Gathercole, 2006). Information is only stored in Working Memory for a few seconds. When information fades from Working Memory, it disappears because the space is

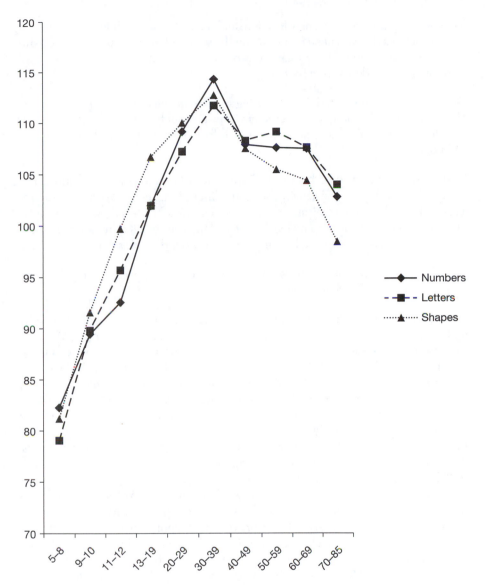

Figure 4.1   Working memory across the lifespan

occupied by other incoming information. This decay can be prevented by focusing attention on the information to-be-remembered, by constantly rehearsing it, or by transferring it to long-term memory.

A number of things can lead to loss of information in Working Memory. These are:

Trying To Hold In Mind Too Much Information   There is a limit to how much information can be held in Working Memory (Cowan, 2001). For example, trying to remember directions to a new location, and navigate there, while repeating your list of groceries that you need to pick up on the way, will likely result in failure. This is because the amount of information to-be-remembered exceeds the capacity of most people's Working Memory.

Distraction   An unrelated thought springing to mind, an interruption by someone else, or another distraction within the environment such as a telephone ringing or a child crying is often sufficient to cause information to be lost from Working Memory.

Doing Something Else at the Same Time   Activities that require attention to be switched to another mental activity use up the limited capacity of Working Memory. This reduces the amount of information that can also be stored. Some examples include trying to remember a recipe while checking your email or remembering the names of new classmates while learning your way around a new school.

What can account for the change in Working Memory capacity during development? Here are a few suggestions.

Knowledge   Although Working Memory is distinct from both short-term memory and long-term memory, information from these systems can help Working Memory. For example, our ability to rehearse information in short-term memory can boost recall (Gathercole, 1998). This is made easier when the list of words is distinct (e.g., '*bus, clock, spoon, fish, mouse*'), rather than similar sounding (e.g., '*man, cat, map, mat, can, cap*'): a phenomenon known as the phonological similarity effect. Long-term memory can also boost Working Memory capacity (Hulme, Maughan, & Brown, 1991). If a string of words are meaningful to us, such as a list of our favorite foods, we are more likely to remember them than a random combination of words. Also, highly frequent words, such as *party* and *average*, are easier to remember than less frequently used words like *barley* and *savage*.

As children get older, they acquire more information and so expand the contents of their long-term memory stores such as semantic and procedural knowledge. Increases in such knowledge stores provide an opportunity to boost working memory by allowing the child to group new information in meaningful ways (also known as "chunking"). For example, it is difficult to remember nine random letters such as BBCUSACNN. However, if we group these letters together to form a small, meaningful unit, it becomes much easier: BBC-USA-CNN. When we chunk information together, this counts as three units of information rather than nine. Placing items that have to be remembered in a common context or knowledge structure can also boost working memory capacity. For example, assigning a label of "birds" will make it easier to remember this list: *ostrich, parrot, sparrow, seagull*.

There is also evidence supporting the contribution of children's growing lexical knowledge to memory span (Gathercole, 2006). Ten-year-olds had better memory scores when remembering words rather than nonwords, compared to six-year-olds, even when other factors such as rehearsal rate were taken into account. This finding indicates that the ten-year-olds' greater word knowledge was able to boost their memory of word lists.

Knowledge and experience can also explain why our memory for words in sentences is almost twice as long as they are for unrelated word sequences (Alloway & Gathercole, 2005). We have the benefit of semantic and grammatical information in a sentence to assist recall that is not present in a word list. With respect to visual/spatial memory, shapes that look like letters are easier to remember than those that don't (Figure 4.2 and 4.3, respectively).

Figure 4.2   Example of unfamiliar shapes to test visual/spatial memory

Speed of Rehearsal   Researchers have suggested that the speed of rehearsal could account for memory span (e.g., Barrouillet, Bernardin, & Camos, 2004). We can remember as much information as we can rehearse in a short period, usually a few seconds. Information in verbal memory is lost if it is not refreshed soon enough through rehearsal. If we assume that everyone loses unrehearsed information at the same rate, then differences in rehearsal speed could explain differences in

Figure 4.3   Example of unfamiliar shapes to test visual/spatial memory

working memory capacity. Young children (for example, four-year-olds) speak more slowly and so can only rehearse a few items. The relationship between speed and memory can also be extended to how long it takes to produce a response. If the first item in the response is articulated too slowly or if there is a long pause after it, memory for the second and following items can fade during that time; and so on. This is illustrated in a test of digit recall between children in Wales and England (Ellis & Hennelly, 1980). Researchers found that the Welsh children had lower scores. They eventually realized that this was because Welsh numbers have more syllables in them and so it takes longer to say them aloud than it does in English. Once this difference was accounted for, the Welsh and English children's performance was equivalent.

Attentional Capacity   The ability of an individual to maintain focus on a particular task is linked to the development of the frontal lobes of the brain, which do not reach maturation until adolescence (Blakemore & Choudhury, 2006). Attentional capacity can affect children's ability to inhibit irrelevant information and to hold information for longer periods of time. Studies have found that when children are asked to remember information equivalent to their level of proficiency, the longer they have to remember the information the more likely they are to forget it (e.g., Astle, Nobre, & Scerif, 2010). Switching between processing and rehearsing information so they don't forget it requires attention. As children get older and their brain functions increase, their attentional capacity increases, which allows them to process information faster and more efficiently, leaving them more time available to rehearse memory items.

Interference   Another factor that affects working memory capacity is interference, which is when additional information forces existing information out of the memory store. There are two types of interference: proactive and retroactive. Proactive interference refers to when previous learning interferes with new learning. For example, you may be struggling to remember your new mobile phone number as you keep confusing it with your old one. In a classroom setting, a student learning about World War II might get the facts mixed up because of what they know about World War I. In one study of proactive interference, people were asked to remember short lists of words. If the words in the list were all from the same category (such as animals, e.g., cat, elephant, dog, crocodile, and so on), people had a much harder time remembering later words in the list. However, if the latter half of the words were from a different category (such as furniture, e.g., table, chair, bed, and so on), it was much easier for them to remember these words from the new category. The large amount of words from the same category (e.g., animals) caused proactive interference. However, words from a different category (e.g., furniture) were distinct enough and so not likely be to confused with the earlier words. *Retroactive interference* is when new information disrupts your previous learning. An example is when a student understood a concept the week before but now they can no longer discuss the concept correctly, because they have confused it with other concepts studied since that time.

Working Memory in the Classroom

We have previously referred to Working Memory as the "engine of learning." Like the engine of a car, Working Memory drives learning forward. However, it does not operate in isolation, but instead works together with different parts of the brain. For example, it works in concert with Broca's area when we use language (Rogalsky, Matchin, & Hickok, 2008), and the intraparietal sulcus (IPS) to complete mathematical problems (Silk et al., 2010).

Working memory is important in the classroom as children often have to hold information in mind while engaged in an effortful activity. Such activities include writing a sentence while trying to spell the individual words (Engle, Carullo, & Collins, 1991; Gathercole, Durling, & Evans, 2008). They could also be a set of instructions they have to remember while completing the individual steps in the task. Children with working memory deficits struggle in these activities because they are unable to hold enough information in mind to complete the task. Losing crucial information from working memory causes them to forget many things: instructions they have to follow, the details of a workbook activity and information they have to write down. Because children with poor working memory fail in many different activities on many occasions due to these kinds of forgetting, they will struggle to achieve normal rates of learning and so typically will make poor general academic progress. For this reason, we have described working memory as a "bottleneck" for learning (Alloway, 2009).

Working Memory and Learning

Traditionally, high scores on IQ tests have been associated with academic success. Yet in the last decade, there has been a growing body of research indicating that working memory is more strongly and consistently associated with learning out-comes. For example, in typically developing children, scores on working memory tasks predict reading achievement independently of measures of phonological skills, such as rhyming and initial consonant detection tasks (Alloway et al., 2004; Siegel & Ryan, 1989; Swanson, 2003). A study on poor comprehenders demon-strated a memory deficit specific to working memory in the verbal domain (Pimperton & Nation, 2010).

Working memory is also linked to math outcomes. For example, working memory scores were associated with teachers' math talk and the acquisition of number sense within kindergarten classrooms (Boonen, Kolkman, & Kroesbergen, 2011). Low working memory scores are also related to performance in arithmetic word problems and computational skills (Alloway & Passolunghi, 2011; Bull & Scerif, 2001; Geary, Hoard & Hamson, 1999; Gersten, Jordan & Flojo, 2005).

There are two key reasons that suggest that we should shift our attention from relying on IQ scores as a benchmark for academic success, and look instead to working memory. The first reason is that Working Memory assessments could provide a culturally fair measure of cognitive ability that is relatively impervious to a number of environmental factors. This is an important issue as IQ tests are sensitive to socioeconomic factors such as maternal education level (Groth, 1975), caregivers' attitude towards education (Reynolds, Willson & Ramsey, 1999) and cultural differences (Brody & Flor, 1998), which can disadvantage students from lower income backgrounds.

In contrast, working memory scores appear to be an "equal opportunities" measure, where the general pattern is that students from different income backgrounds perform similarly. In a study of over 600 kindergarteners, a child's working memory score was found to be unaffected by their mother's educational level (an index of socioeconomic background), the number of years they spent in pre-school education (Alloway et al., 2005), or even the area they lived (Alloway, Alloway, & Wooten, 2012). Additional support comes from various cultural groups. Children from low-income areas in South America did not differ significantly from their middle-income peers in working memory tests, although their vocabulary skills, reflecting crystallized abilities, were considerably worse (Engel, Heloisa Dos Santos, & Gathercole, 2008). Studies investigating differences between immigrant and native language speakers in the Netherlands demonstrated that immigrant children performed at the same level as their native language peers when they were tested in their own language on working memory tests (Messer, Leseman, Boom, & Mayo, 2010; also Leseman, Scheele, Mayo, & Messer, 2007). This indicates that immigrant children have the capacity to perform well in school; however, difficulties with learning a new language can result in learning difficulties. One explanation for why Working Memory appears to be relatively unaffected by such environmental factors is that it is a relatively pure measure of a child's learning potential, rather than a measure of acquired skills (Alloway et al., 2005; Campbell, Dollaghan, Needleman, Janosky, 1997; Weismer et al., 2000).

The second reason why we should look at Working Memory to explain scholastic attainment is based on a large number of research studies linking these scores to learning outcomes, independent of IQ scores. For example, in typically developing samples, Working Memory predicted attainment in reading, writing, and math in kindergarteners (Alloway et al., 2005). Working Memory scores also predict children's educational attainment in grade school. In a study of almost 100 school children aged seven to eight years, Working Memory scores were excellent predictors of a child's achievement (St Clair-Thompson & Sykes, 2010). Working Memory plays a role in college-aged students as well, such as in their performance in the Scholastic Aptitude Test (SAT; Turner & Engle, 1989).

Poor Working Memory can result in negative consequences in learning outcomes. In a government-funded project, 10% to 15% of children had working memory impairments that led to learning difficulties (Alloway, Gathercole, Kirkwood, & Elliott, 2009). In a large-scale study of over 3,000 children identified with Working Memory deficits, only 2 percent of them achieved scores in the average range (>96) in standardized assessments of reading and math. Working Memory scores uniquely predicted scores in these tests even after IQ was statistically accounted for.

Crucially, Working Memory also plays an important role in predicting subsequent academic achievement. In our own research, we investigated which would best predict learning outcomes over time: working memory or IQ scores. We tested typically developing children first at five years old and then again at 11 years old on standardized measures of working memory, IQ, and learning. The results demonstrate that children's working memory skills at five years of age were the best predictor of reading, spelling, and math outcomes six years later (Alloway & Alloway, 2010). This indicates that assessing working memory at the start of formal education is a more powerful predictor of subsequent academic success than IQ. A similar pattern was observed in students with learning difficulties. Working Memory scores were a better predictor than IQ scores, of subsequent learning outcomes measured by standardized assessments two years later (Alloway, 2009).

Working Memory and Anxiety

A common question is how stress and anxiety can affect working memory performance (see Chapter 10, this volume). This is an important one to consider as some children may feel anxious when confronted with difficult activities in the classroom. In fact, there are many studies confirming that anxiety levels affect a child's performance in many tasks. In a study investigating the relationship between trait anxiety and working memory in young children, high-anxiety children performed worse than low-anxiety children on verbal working memory tasks, but not on visuo-spatial working memory tasks (Visu-Petra, Cheie, Benga, & Alloway, 2011). Students with math anxiety can also demonstrate smaller Working Memory spans (Ashcraft & Kirk, 2001).

Anxiety can even affect performance in simple tasks such as searching for visual clues in the environment. In one study, participants had to drive through a motor racing track as fast as possible while using lights around the track to direct them (Janelle, Singer, & Williams, 1999). As anxiety levels increased, the participants took longer to notice the lights that guided them and as a result, their driving was slower. Anxious participants would look around more frequently and be distracted by anything along the track that they thought might be clues to direct them. Not only did they find it difficult to distinguish between clues that would lead them and information that was irrelevant, but they would also focus more on irrelevant or distracting information.

Why does anxiety affect working memory performance? Some researchers have suggested that when a person is anxious more effort is required to process information effectively and so reduces the processing and storage capacity of working memory (Owens, Stevenson, Norgate, & Hadwin, 2008). Usually, an increase in anxiety indicates that the task is important to the child and so they apply more effort in order to ensure that they succeed in it. Emotions such as worry and self-concern "use up" available processing resources and, consequently, reduce the resources available in working memory for the task at hand. This results in delays in responding to tasks and a greater likelihood of being distracted, as we have seen from the studies described above.

There is also a close relationship between the memory demands of a task and anxiety level. If a task places minimal demands on working memory, performance on a task won't suffer very much even if a child's anxiety levels increase. This is because they can compensate by adopting different strategies to help them manage the processing loads of the task. However, if a task places a heavy demand on working memory, high levels of anxiety will result in longer processing times and poorer performance. It is the combination of an excessive working memory load together with high levels of anxiety that overburden the cognitive resources available to perform the task. A study comparing the performance of low- and high-anxiety students on a grammatical reasoning task confirmed this (MacLeod & Donnellan, 1993). Both groups of students performed the task under low and heavy memory load conditions. Although both the low- and high-anxiety students were slow in completing the reasoning task in the heavy memory load condition, the high-anxiety group took a disproportionately longer time than the low-anxiety group. This confirms that while anxiety levels impact performance, the combination of a heavy memory load and anxiety can lead to a severe drop in classroom functioning.

Working Memory and Self-Esteem

The role of self-esteem in working memory also plays an important role in the classroom. For example, a more confident child is able to overcome their anxiety and still perform well. We investigated the role of working memory on self-esteem using the Insight Primary Test (Morris, 2002), which consists of a 36-item behavior checklist designed to assess three components of a child's self-esteem: sense of self (e.g., if this pupil is encouraged, does s/he respond positively?), sense of belonging (e.g., has this pupil always got plenty to say to other people?), and sense of personal power (e.g., can this pupil stand up for him/herself assertively rather than aggressively?). Each behavior is rated as characteristic of the child either most of the time, quite often, occasionally, or almost never. An overall self-esteem score is obtained by summing the three component scores, and is classified as high (87–108), good (64–86), vulnerable (40–63), or very low (0–39).

In a study of children with working memory deficits aged six to seven and nine to ten years old, both age groups scored lower on "sense of personal power" questions compared to the "sense of self" and "sense of belonging" ones (Alloway, Gathercole, Kirkwood, & Elliott, 2009). More than half of the sample was found to struggle with self-esteem: 60 percent had overall self-esteem scores classified as vulnerable or very low, rather than high or good. This suggests that the majority of children with working memory impairments will also have low self-esteem, particularly in areas requiring them to exercise some control over their environment. This can affect their confidence, which can result in further frustration and lack of motivation in the classroom.

Working Memory and Behavior

In observational studies, teachers often view children with working memory difficulties as having poor attention, making comments such as (Gathercole, Lamont, & Alloway, 2006):

1. He's in a world of his own.
2. He doesn't listen.
3. She's always day-dreaming.
4. It goes in one ear and out the other.

Yet, does this mean that children with low working memory have problems with attention, hyperactivity, or impulsivity? In order to answer this question, Alloway was part of a government-funded project to explore the profiles of classroom behavior of students with very poor working memory (Alloway, Gathercole, Holmes, Place, & Elliott, 2009). These children, aged five to six and nine to ten years old, were drawn from mainstream schools and did not have any clinical diagnoses of developmental disorders, including ADHD. All children had poor working memory skills. Their classroom teachers rated the students' behaviors using a diagnostic questionnaire designed to identify attentional failures and ADHD on the basis of classroom behaviors (the Conners' Rating Scale, Conners, 2005). Responses were scored as sums of values on four subscales: oppositional (e.g., spiteful or vindictive), cognitive problems/inattention (e.g., forgets things s/he has already learned), hyperactivity (e.g., is always "on the go" or acts as if driven by a motor), and ADHD index (e.g., restless, always up and on the go). The ADHD index is based on the best set of items for identifying children at risk of a diagnosis of ADHD.

In both age groups, the majority of the children obtained atypically high ratings of cognitive problems/inattentive symptoms, and were judged to have short attention spans, high levels of distractibility, problems in monitoring the quality of their work, and difficulties in generating new solutions to problems. In particular, they received high scores indicating a deficit in items such as:

1. forgets other things s/he has learned
2. poor in spelling
3. poor in arithmetic
4. not reading up to par

5. inattentive, easily distracted
6. distractibility or attention span a problem
7. short attention span
8. lacks interest in schoolwork
9. only pays attention to things s/he is really interested in.

The problem behaviors most commonly identified for this sample of children were therefore related to poor academic achievement in the areas of reading, writing, and arithmetic, and inattention associated with short attention spans. The hyperactive/impulsive symptoms that are typically present in children with a diagnosis of ADHD were not greatly elevated in this sample. This finding confirms other studies that children with a lower working memory capacity have more attentional difficulties at school such as difficulties in concentration and inability to sit still. It also suggests that poor working memory function is a factor contributing to the inattentive profiles of behavior present in many children with ADHD. Reduced working memory capacity played a critical role in the problem behaviors identified for these children.

Working Memory and Learning Disorders

The incidence of learning disorders is increasing. Currently, over five million schoolchildren in the US are classified as having a learning disability and receive special educational support, which translates to 13% of the school population (US Department of Education, 2010). It could be argued that the figure in the UK is much more than this, depending on how one defines learning disabilities.

As students with learning disabilities grow older, the gap between them and typically developing peers widens with respect to attainment levels. In a government-funded study, we looked at a group of 5- and 11-year-olds with working memory difficulties (Alloway, Gathercole, Kirkwood, & Elliott, 2009). The older group performed much worse than the younger children in standardized language and mathematics tests. The effect of poor working memory appears to be cumulative across development, resulting in greater decrements in learning as a student gets older (see Alloway, 2009). This difference in performance can be explained in part by the classroom environment of the two age groups. Younger children are more likely to have additional adult support and memory aids made available for them in the classroom. However, as they get older, they are typically expected to be more autonomous in their learning and thus may be left to develop their own strategies. In older classrooms, teachers are also more likely to use longer and more complex sentences, which require the students to rely on their working memory.

The poor working memory of some students means that they struggle to acquire key learning skills and concepts. Without these building blocks in place, they are unable to keep up with their peers. Research suggests that a child with a low working memory will not "catch up" with their peers. Without intervention, they will continue to struggle in all areas of learning (Alloway, 2009). In a recent study, teenagers who were diagnosed with low working memory two years earlier were still performing very poorly in school compared to their peers.

There are a number of different learning disorders that are accommodated within a mainstream classroom. Each group has a specific area of strength and weakness in working memory and it is important to know what this is in order to provide targeted support. In the next few paragraphs, we briefly outline the working memory profile of students with different learning disorders.

Students with reading and language problems (e.g., dyslexia) exhibit problems in verbal short-term memory tasks (e.g., remembering instructions and words), but these problems are greatly exacerbated when the student has to process additional information simultaneously. It takes considerable working memory space to keep in mind the relevant speech sounds and concepts necessary for identifying words and understanding text, which can exceed the capacity of the dyslexic individual (Swanson, 2003). Thus, the combination of processing and remembering verbal information, rather than just remembering information, is very difficult for the individual with dyslexia. Their visuo-spatial working memory is in the average range (see Archibald & Alloway, 2008, for similar working memory patterns in those with language impairments).

In students with Developmental Coordination Disorder (motor dyspraxia), poor visuo-spatial memory is the trademark memory deficit (Alloway, 2007b). When compared to their peers who don't have motor difficulties, they are more likely than typically developing children to achieve very poor scores in visuo-spatial memory (Alloway & Temple, 2007). In the classroom, a student with dyspraxia will find it more difficult to complete two visuo-spatial tasks at the same time, such as organizing their work station while visualizing their next task.

A student with ADHD typically does not have difficulties in short-term memory. In a standardized test like the Automated Working Memory Assessment (AWMA), they can recall digits, words, instructions, and spatial locations at the same rate as their peers (Roodenrys, 2006). In the classroom, they can usually remember what you have told them and repeat it back. The problem arises when they have to manage or manipulate that information, in both verbal and visual domains. They struggle when they have to hold information in mind and use that to guide their behavior towards tasks or goals (Castellanos, Sonuga-Barke, Milham, & Tannock, 2006; Martinussen, Hayden, Hogg-Johnson, & Tannock, 2005). In fact, visuo-spatial working memory deficits are such a prominent feature of students with ADHD that such difficulties reliably distinguish them from their typically developing peers (Barkley, 1997; Holmes et al., 2010).

The working memory profile of the student with Autistic Spectrum Disorder is varied and depends on whether they are low or high functioning. For instance, low-functioning ASD individuals perform more poorly than chronological age-matched participants, but do not differ from IQ-matched participants on measures of both verbal and visuo-spatial working memory (Russell, Jarrold & Henry, 1996). In contrast, high-functioning ASD persons performed in a similar manner as age- and IQ-matched controls (Belleville, Rouleau & Caza, 1998). In research using the AWMA, high-functioning ASD teenagers displayed verbal short-term memory problems, but average working memory skills (Alloway, Rajendran & Archibald, 2009). One explanation is that these verbal short-term memory deficits are linked to the problems of language and communication in this disorder, as they are required to engage in social reciprocity, which includes remembering conversations in order to participate (Belleville et al., 1998).

A final group of interest is high-ability or gifted students, as some are known as "twice-exceptional" and can have additional needs (Baum & Olenchak, 2002). Gifted or high-ability students often outperform their peers on measures of cognitive skills. However, it was not clear whether they would also demonstrate a marked advantage in working memory tasks. In a recent study, the high-ability group outperformed the average and low-ability students in both verbal and visuo-spatial working memory tasks, even after non-verbal IQ scores were statistically accounted for (Alloway & Elsworth, in press). This finding suggests that assessments of working memory can yield accurate estimations of ability.

FUTURE DIRECTIONS

Testing Working Memory

Given the importance of Working Memory in the classroom, it seems critical to be aware of a students' skills in this area. However, research to date indicates that teachers' awareness of working memory deficits in the classroom can still be quite low. In a recent study, the majority of teachers interviewed only picked up early warning signs of working memory failure in their students 25 percent of the time, despite high teacher ratings of working memory behavioral difficulties in the majority of the troublesome children (Alloway, Doherty-Sneddon & Forbes, 2012). The interviews also revealed that teachers never listed working memory as an explanation for the students' troublesome behavior. This pattern is consistent with anecdotal evidence that teachers tend to misattribute signs of poor working memory as "lacking motivation" or "daydreaming" (Gathercole, Lamont & Alloway, 2006).

Given the difficulty in detecting working memory failures in the classroom, the availability of effective diagnostic tools is crucial. As highlighted above, it is clear that working memory plays an important role in learning; therefore, it is vital to have the means to assess it directly. While many standardized IQ test batteries include working memory subtests, such as the Wechsler Intelligence Scale for Children – IV (Wechsler, 2006), the Stanford-Binet Intelligence Scales (Roid, 2003), and the Woodcock-Johnson Battery (Woodcock, McGrew, & Mather, 2001), the use of such tools requires considerable experience in the administration, scoring, and interpretation of cognitive tests, and are thus restricted to individuals who have training in psychometrics, which effectively excludes teachers.

In the following sections, we will highlight a computerized tool to assess working memory—the Automated Working Memory Assessment (AWMA; Alloway, 2007a). The AWMA is a computer-based assessment of working memory that has automatized test administration and presents results in a form that is easy to interpret by non-experts. Not only does the AWMA eliminate the need for prior training in test administration, it also provides a practical and convenient way for educators to screen students for significant working memory problems. It is standardized for use from early childhood (four years) to adulthood (22 years), with norms to be extended up to 85 years of age in the revised version (AWMA-II, due 2012). The AWMA provides three measures each of verbal and visuo-spatial short-term memory and working memory (Alloway, Gathercole & Pickering, 2006). Currently, it is the only standardized assessment of working memory available for educators to use, and to date has been translated into 15 languages.

A study assessing each memory component in the AWMA in a large sample of children aged 4 to 11 years provided the opportunity to investigate the underlying structure of working memory using confirmatory factor analyses (Alloway et al., 2006). The findings confirmed that the processing aspect of both the verbal and visuo-spatial working memory tasks was controlled by a centralized component, while the short-term storage aspect was supported by a domain-specific component—one for verbal information and another for visuo-spatial information. The underlying cognitive structure for working memory was in place even for those in the youngest age group, who were four years old.

Test–retest reliability refers to the consistency with which a test can accurately measure what it aims to do. If an individual's performance remains consistent over repeated trials, it is considered to be reliable. The test-retest coefficients for the AWMA are high, indicating a consistency in measuring working memory skills. These coefficients range from .69 to .90 (Alloway et al., 2006). Test validity of the AWMA was established by comparing it with performance on the WISC-IV Working Memory Index (Alloway, Gathercole, Kirkwood, & Elliott, 2008). The findings demonstrate that the AWMA has good diagnostic validity, as evidenced by the high classification accuracy (91%) of the digit span subtest of the WISC-IV.

A benefit to using the AWMA to identify students who merit additional learning support is that it is quick to administer: the Screener version is made up of two working memory tests (one verbal and the other visuo-spatial). The AWMA is a standardized test battery, which means that the scores follow the same pattern. As with other standardized test batteries, a standard score that falls between 85 and 115 is considered to be in the average range. Standard scores above 115 are higher than the average level of performance, while standard scores below 85 are representative of a working memory deficit that will lead to learning difficulties. As a result, these students may have access to special education services and accommodations, such as curriculum modification and adaptations. With time at a premium, the automated presentation of tests and automatic generation of a report with standard scores and percentiles make it easy for educators to use.

Training Working Memory

Once the specific strengths and weaknesses of a student's working memory profile are known, specific and targeted accommodations can be made to support learning. The aim in supporting students with learning difficulties is not just to help them survive in the classroom, but to thrive as well. Strategies can provide scaffolding and support that will unlock their working memory potential to boost learning (Alloway, 2010; Gathercole & Alloway, 2008). They can be easily integrated within the classroom setting as a dimension of an inclusive curriculum and used in developing Individualized Education Programs (IEPs) for the student.

Another approach to support working memory difficulties is through cognitive training (see Chapters 14 and 15 this volume). There is a growing body of evidence to suggest considerable cerebral plasticity within the developing brain and that working memory capacity may potentially be improved by training. For instance, studies to date have established that gains are evident in children with ADHD (Klingberg et al., 2005), those with intellectual disability (Van der Molen et al., 2010), and in those with poor working memory (Holmes, Gathercole & Dunning, 2009). Recent research in college students has demonstrated transfer effects to IQ (Jaeggi, Buschkuehl, Jonides, & Perrig, 2008), which may be the result of sharing neural substrates, such as the prefrontal and parietal cortices (Gray, Chabris, & Braver, 2003; Kane & Engle, 2002).

We recently explored the potential benefit of cognitive training in a study of students with learning difficulties. The training compromised of *Jungle Memory*™ (2008), a web-based training program aimed at 7–16-year-old children. The program uses three interactive computer games with up to 30 levels of difficulty in each game to train working memory. The results indicated that the students showed significant improvements in verbal and visual-spatial working memory, verbal and non-verbal IQ scores, as well as literacy scores as measured by the Wechsler Reading Dimension test (Alloway, 2012). In a different set of clinical trials with Dyslexia Scotland and an autistic charity, we compared the efficacy of regular

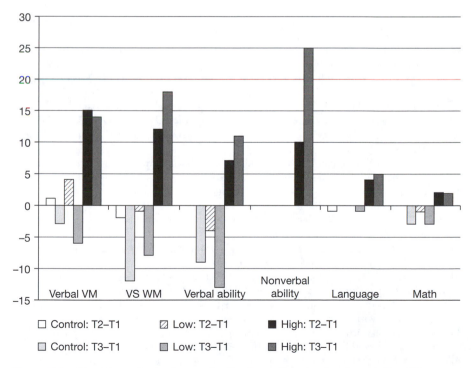

Figure 4.4 Cognitive gains in the standardized tests from testing times 1, 2, and 3, as a function of training group

versus interval training (Alloway, Bibile, & Lau, 2012). The findings indicated that students who used Jungle Memory four times a week showed significant improvements in many areas compared to the control group and those engaged in interval training. An eight-month follow-up also found that improved scores in tests of IQ and working memory were maintained. There were also improvements in scores in language and math, that also remained constant eight months later. Figure 4.4 indicates the difference in standard scores between the three testing times: from pre-training (T1) to post-training (T2); and from pre-training (T1) to an eight-month follow-up (T3).

Summary

Working Memory is a cognitive ability that experiences tremendous growth during childhood. There is substantial evidence that the capacity of Working Memory plays a crucial role in a range of educational activities, from language skills, to comprehension, to mathematical reasoning. Working Memory is also implicated in a range of learning difficulties such as ADHD, dyslexia, motor dyspraxia (DCD), and autistic spectrum disorder. With growing awareness of the importance of Working Memory in development and the increased attention to diagnostic tools and evidence-based training programs, the hope is that such theoretical advances will soon make their way into educational and clinical settings.

REFERENCES

Alloway, T.P. (2007a). *Automated working memory assessment*. London: Pearson Assessment.

Alloway, T.P. (2007b). Working memory, reading and mathematical skills in children with developmental coordination disorder. *Journal of Experimental Child Psychology, 96,* 20–36.

Alloway, T.P. (2009). Working Memory, but not IQ, predicts subsequent learning in children with learning difficulties. *European Journal of Psychological Assessment, 25,* 92–98.

Alloway, T.P. (2010). *Improving working memory: Supporting students' learning.* London: Sage Press.

Alloway, T.P. (2012). Can interactive working memory training improving learning? *Journal of Interactive Learning Research, 23*(3) 197–207.

Alloway, T.P. & Alloway, R.G. (2010). Investigating the predictive roles of working memory and IQ in academic attainment. *Journal of Experimental Child Psychology, 106,* 20–29.

Alloway, T.P. & Alloway, R.G. (2012). Working memory across the lifespan: A cross-sectional approach. *Manuscript under review.*

Alloway, T.P., Alloway, R.G., & Wooten, S. (2012). Home sweet home: The impact of zipcode on cognitive skills. *Manuscript under review.*

Alloway, T.P., Bibile, V., & Lau, G. (2012). The efficacy of working memory training in improving IQ in students with learning difficulties. *Manuscript submitted.*

Alloway, T.P., Doherty-Sneddon, G., & Forbes, L. (2012). Teachers' perceptions of classroom behavior and working memory. *Education Research and Reviews.*

Alloway, T.P. & Elsworth, S. (in press). A comparison of IQ and working memory across high, average, and low ability students. *Learning and Individual Differences.*

Alloway, T.P. & Gathercole, S.E. (2005). The role of sentence recall in reading and language skills of children with learning difficulties. *Learning and Individual Differences, 15,* 271–282.

Alloway, T.P. & Gathercole, S.E. (2006). How does working memory work in the classroom? *Educational Research and Reviews, 1*, 134–139.

Alloway, T.P., Gathercole, S.E., Adams, A.M., Willis, C., Eaglen, R., & Lamont, E. (2005). Working memory and other cognitive skills as predictors of progress towards early learning goals at school entry. *British Journal of Developmental Psychology, 23*, 417–426.

Alloway, T.P., Gathercole, S.E., Holmes, J., Place, M., & Elliott, J. (2009) The diagnostic utility of behavioral checklists in identifying children with ADHD and children with working memory deficits. *Child Psychiatry & Human Development, 40*, 353–366.

Alloway, T.P., Gathercole, S.E., Kirkwood, H.J., & Elliott, J.E. (2008). Evaluating the validity of the Automated Working Memory Assessment. *Educational Psychology, 7*, 725–734.

Alloway, T.P., Gathercole, S.E., Kirkwood, H.J., & Elliott, J.E. (2009). The cognitive and behavioral characteristics of children with low working memory. *Child Development, 80*, 606–621.

Alloway, T.P., Gathercole, S.E., & Pickering, S.J. (2006). Verbal and visuo-spatial short-term and working memory in children: Are they separable? *Child Development, 77*, 1698–1716.

Alloway, T.P., Gathercole, S.E., Willis, C., & Adams, A.M. (2004). A structural analysis of working memory and related cognitive skills in early childhood. *Journal of Experimental Child Psychology, 87*, 85–106.

Alloway, T.P. & Passolunghi, M.C. (2011). The relations between working memory and arithmetical abilities: A comparison between Italian and British children. *Learning and Individual Differences, 21*, 133–137.

Alloway, T.P., Rajendran, G., & Archibald, L.M. (2009). Working memory profiles of children with developmental disorders. *Journal of Learning Difficulties, 42*, 372–382.

Alloway, T.P. & Temple, K.J. (2007). A comparison of working memory profiles and learning in children with developmental coordination disorder and moderate learning difficulties. *Applied Cognitive Psychology, 21*, 473–487.

Archibald, L.M. & Alloway, T.P. (2008). Comparing language profiles: Children with specific language impairment and developmental coordination disorder. *International Journal of Communication and Language Disorders, 43*, 165–180.

Ashcraft, M. & Kirk, E.P. (2001). The relationships among working memory, math anxiety, and performance. *Journal of Experimental Psychology: General, 130*, 224–237.

Astle, D.E., Nobre, A.C., & Scerif, G. (2010). Attentional control constrains visual short-term memory: Insights from developmental and individual differences. *Quarterly Journal of Experimental Psychology, 30*, 1–18.

Baddeley, A.D. & Hitch, G. (1974). Working memory. In G. Bower (Ed.), *The psychology of learning and motivation, 8*, 47–90. New York: Academic Press.

Barkley, R.A. (1997). *ADHD and the nature of self-control.* New York: Guilford.

Barrouillet, P., Bernardin, S., & Camos, V. (2004). Time constraints and resource sharing in adults' working memory spans. *Journal of Experimental Psychology: General, 133*, 83–100.

Baum, S.M. & Olenchak, F.R. (2002). The alphabet children: GT, ADD/ADHD, and more. *Exceptionality, 10*, 77–91.

Belleville, S., Rouleau, N., & Caza, N. (1998). Effect of normal ageing on the manipulation of information in working memory. *Memory and Cognition, 26*, 572–583.

Blakemore, S.J. & Choudhury, S. (2006). Development of the adolescent brain: Implications for executive function and social cognition. *Journal of Child Psychology and Psychiatry, 47*, 296–312.

Boonen, A.J.H., Kolkman, M.E., & Kroesbergen, E.H. (2011). The relation between teachers' math talk and the acquisition of number sense within kindergarten classrooms. *Journal of School Psychology, 49*, 281–299.

Brody, G.H. & Flor, D.L. (1998). Maternal resources, parenting practices, and child competence in rural, single-parent African American families. *Child Development*, 69, 803–816.

Bull, R. & Scerif, G. (2001). Executive functioning as a predictor of children's mathematics ability: Shifting, inhibition and working memory. *Developmental Neuropsychology*, 19, 273–293.

Campbell, T., Dollaghan, C., Needleman, H., & Janosky, J. (1997). Reducing bias in language assessment: A processing-dependent measure. *Journal of Speech, Language and Hearing Research*, 40, 519–525.

Castellanos, F.X., Sonuga-Barke, E.J.S., Milham, M.P., & Tannock, R. (2006). Characterising cognition in ADHD: Beyond executive dysfunction. *Trends in Cognitive Sciences*, 10, 117–123.

Conners, K. (2005). *Conners' Teacher Rating Scale-Revised (S)*. New York: Multi-Health Systems Inc.

Cowan, N. (2001). The magical number 4 in short-term memory: A reconsideration of mental storage capacity. *Behavioral and Brain Sciences*, 24, 87.

Cowan, N. (2005). *Working memory capacity*. Hove, East Sussex, UK: Psychology Press.

Ellis, N.C. & Hennelly, R.A. (1980). A bilingual word-length effect: Implications for intelligence testing and the relative ease of mental calculations in Welsh and English. *British Journal of Psychology*, 71, 43–52.

Engel, P.M.J., Heloisa Dos Santos, F., & Gathercole, S.E. (2008). Are working memory measures free of socio-economic influence? *Journal of Speech, Language, and Hearing Research*, 51, 1580–1587.

Engle, R.W., Carullo, J.J., & Collins, K.W. (1991). Individual differences in working memory for comprehension and following directions. *Journal of Educational Research*, 84, 253–262.

Fuster, J.M. (2005). The cortical substrate of general intelligence. *Cortex*, 41, 228–229.

Fuster, J.M. (2008). *The prefrontal cortex* (Fourth Edition). London: Academic Press.

Fuster, J.M. & Alexander, G.E. (1971). Neuron activity related to short-term memory. *Science*, 173, 652–654.

Gathercole, S.E. (1998). The development of memory. *Journal of Child Psychology and Psychiatry*, 39, 3–27.

Gathercole, S.E. (2006). Complexities and constraints in nonword repetition and word learning. *Applied Psycholinguistics*, 27, 599–613.

Gathercole, S.E. & Alloway, T.P. (2008). *Working memory and learning: A practical guide*. London: Sage Press.

Gathercole, S.E., Durling, J., & Evans, S. (2008). Working memory abilities and children's performance in laboratory analogues of classroom activities. *Applied Cognitive Psychology*, 22, 1019–1037.

Gathercole, S.E., Lamont, E., & Alloway, T.P. (2006). Working memory in the classroom. In S. Pickering (Ed.), *Working memory and education*, pp. 219–240. Oxford: Elsevier Press.

Geary, D.C., Hoard, M.K., & Hamson, C.O. (1999). Numerical and arithmetical cognition: Patterns of functions and deficits in children at risk for a mathematical disability. *Journal of Experimental Child Psychology*, 74, 213–239.

Gersten, R., Jordan, N.C., & Flojo, J.R. (2005). Early identification and interventions for students with mathematics difficulties. *Journal of Learning Disabilities*, 38, 293–304.

Gray, J.R., Chabris, C.F. & Braver, T.S. (2003). Neural mechanisms of general fluid intelligence. *Nature Neuroscience*, 6, 316–322.

Groth, N. (1975). Mothers of gifted. *The Gifted Child Quarterly*, 19, 217–222.

Holmes, J., Gathercole, S.E., Place, M., Alloway, T.P., & Elliott, J. (2010). An assessment of the diagnostic utility of executive function assessments in the identification of ADHD in children. *Child and Adolescent Mental Health*, 15, 37–43.

Holmes, J., Gathercole, S.E., & Dunning, D.L. (2009). Adaptive training leads to sustained enhancement of poor working memory in children. *Developmental Science, 12*, 9–15.

Hulme, C., Maughan, S., & Brown, G.D.A. (1991). Memory for familiar and unfamiliar words: Evidence for a longer term memory contribution to short-term memory span. *Journal of Memory and Language, 30*, 685–701.

Jaeggi, S.M., Buschkuehl, M., Jonides, J., & Perrig, W.J. (2008). Improving fluid intelligence with training on working memory. *Proceedings of the National Academy of Science, 105*, 6829–6833.

Janelle, C.M., Singer, R.N., & Williams, A.M. (1999). External distraction and attentional narrowing: Visual search evidence. *Journal of Sport and Exercise Psychology, 21*, 70–91.

Kane, M.J. & Engle, R.W. (2002). The role of prefrontal cortex in working-memory capacity, executive attention, and general fluid intelligence: An individual-differences perspective. *Psychonomic Bulletin and Review, 9*, 637–671.

Kaufman, A.S. (2001). WAIS-III IQs, Horn's theory, and generational changes from young adulthood to old age. *Intelligence, 29*, 131–167.

Klingberg, T., Fernell, E., Olesen, P.J., Johnson, M., Gustafsson, P., Dahlstrom, K. et al. (2005). Computerised training of working memory in children with ADHD: A randomized, controlled trial. *Journal of the American Academy of Child and Adolescent Psychiatry, 44*, 177–186.

Leseman, P., Scheele, A., Mayo, A., & Messer, M. (2007). Home literacy as a special language environment to prepare children for school. *Zeitschrift für Erziehungswissenschaft, 10*, 334–355.

MacLeod, C. & Donnellan, A.M. (1993). Individual differences in anxiety and the restriction of working memory capacity. *Personality and Individual Differences, 15*, 163–173.

Martinussen, R., Hayden, J., Hogg-Johnson, S., & Tannock, R. (2005). A meta-analysis of working memory impairments in children with attention-deficit/hyperactivity disorder. *Journal of the American Academy of Child and Adolescent Psychiatry, 44*, 377–384.

Messer, M.H., Leseman, P.P.M., Boom, J., & Mayo, A.Y. (2010). Phonotactic probability effect in nonword recall and its relationship with vocabulary in monolingual and bilingual preschoolers. *Journal of Experimental Child Psychology, 105*, 306–323.

Miyake, A. & Shah, P. (Eds.) (1999). *Models of working memory: Mechanisms of active maintenance and executive control.* New York: Cambridge University Press.

Morris, E. (2002). *Insight primary.* Hampshire, UK: NFER Nelson.

Owens, M., Stevenson, J., Norgate, R., & Hadwin, J. (2008). Processing efficiency theory in children: Working memory as a mediator between trait anxiety and academic performance. *Anxiety, Stress, and Coping, 21*, 417–430.

Pimperton, H. & Nation, K. (2010). Suppressing irrelevant information from working memory: Evidence for domain-specific deficits in poor comprehenders. *Journal of Memory and Language, 62*, 380–391.

Reynolds, C.R., Willson, V.L., & Ramsey, M. (1999). Intellectual differences among Mexican Americans, Papagos and Whites, independent of g. *Personality and Individual Differences, 27*, 1181–1187.

Rogalsky, C., Matchin, W., & Hickok, G. (2008). Broca's area, sentence comprehension, and working memory: An fMRI study. *Frontiers in Human Neuroscience, 2*, 14.

Roid, G.H. (2003). *Stanford-Binet Intelligence Scales, Fifth Edition.* Itasca, IL: Riverside Publishing.

Roodenrys, S. (2006). Working memory function in Attention Deficit Hyperactivity Disorder. In T.P. Alloway & S.E. Gathercole (Eds.), *Working memory and neurodevelopmental conditions* (pp. 336–383). Hove, England: Psychology Press.

Russell, J., Jarrold, C., & Henry, L. (1996).Working memory in children with autism and with moderate learning difficulties. *Journal of Child Psychology and Psychiatry, 37*, 673–686.

Siegel, L.S., & Ryan, E.B. (1989). The development of working memory in normally achieving and subtypes of learning disabled children. *Child Development*, *60*, 973–980.

Silk, T.J., Bellgrove, M.A., Wrafter, P., Mattingley, J.B., & Cunnington, R. (2010). Spatial working memory and spatial attention rely on common neural processes in the intraparietal sulcus. *Neuroimage*, *53*, 718–724.

St Clair-Thompson, H. & Sykes, A. (2010). Scoring methods and the predictive ability of working memory tasks. *Behavior Research Methods*, *4*, 969–975.

Swanson, H.L. (2003). Age-related differences in learning disabled and skilled readers' working memory. *Journal of Experimental Child Psychology*, *85*, 1–31.

Turner, M.L. & Engle, R.W. (1989). Is working memory capacity task dependent? *Journal of Memory and Language*, *28*, 127–154.

US Department of Education, National Center for Education Statistics (2010). *Digest of education statistics, 2009* (NCES 2010–013).

Van der Molen, M.J., Van Luit, J.E.H., Van der Molen, M.W., Klugkist, I., & Jongmans, M.J. (2010). Effectiveness of a computerised working memory training in adolescents with mild to borderline intellectual disabilities. *Journal of Intellectual Disability Research*, *54*, 433–447.

Visu-Petra, L., Cheie, L., Benga, O., & Alloway, T.P. (2011). Effects of anxiety on simple retention and memory updating in young children. *International Journal of Behavioral Development*, *35*, 38–47.

Wechsler, D. (2006). *Wechsler Intelligence Scale for Children (UK Version IV)*. Oxford: Psychological Corporation.

Weismer, S.E., Tomblin, J.B., Zhang, X., Buckwalter, P., Chynoweth, J.G., & Jones, M. (2000). Nonword repetition performance in school-age children with and without language impairment. *Journal of Speech, Language, and Hearing Research*, *43*, 865–878.

Woodcock, R., McGrew, R., & Mather, N. (2001). *Woodcock Johnson tests of achievement*. Rolling Meadow, IL: Riverside Publishing.

5

A Hierarchical Model of Working Memory and its Change in Healthy Older Adults

CHANDRAMALLIKA BASAK

The Center for Vital Longevity, University of Texas, Dallas, TX, USA

ELIZABETH M. ZELINSKI

Leonard Davis School of Gerontology, University of Southern California,
Los Angeles, CA, USA

Do not dwell in the past, do not dream of the future, concentrate the mind on the present moment.

Buddha (ca. 563–483 BC)

The true art of memory is the art of attention.

Samuel Johnson (1709–1784)

Any man who can drive safely while kissing a pretty girl is simply not giving the kiss the attention it deserves.

Albert Einstein (1879–1955)

The quotes above reflect views of attentional focus and capacity, constructs closely associated with working memory (WM). Although the quotes come from authors of different historical periods and cultures, they capture contemporary views of WM function. The first suggests the importance of focus. The second suggests that attention, therefore WM, is critical to memory. The third quote suggests that the proper focus is unitary even when multiple goal sets are maintained.

In this chapter, we extend the discussion of WM to detail what is known about changes and differences as people grow older. We begin with a historical perspective of observations of age-related decline in WM, including how individual differences in older adults' WM affects performance on other cognitive abilities. We subsequently present findings from a modern hierarchical account of WM that identifies the specific processes that change with aging. This view was first proposed by Cowan (1988), initially adapted to explain contradictory findings, by Oberauer (2002), and recently reconciled with identification of the boundary conditions that accommodate features of both models by Basak & Verhaeghen (2011a; 2011b). We examine how other high-level processes like the maintenance of goal set may reflect capacity in WM. We discuss interventions suggesting approaches that have promise to reduce WM declines and thereby offset changes in cognitive abilities. We conclude with a discussion of the impact of WM changes on everyday functional abilities in older adults.

BACKGROUND INFORMATION

An Historical Perspective on the Aging of WM

Working memory can be defined as the ability to simultaneously store and actively transform information (e.g., Baddeley & Hitch, 1974). Most of the initial research on the effects of aging on WM have been based on the Baddeley and Hitch model of a central executive that operates on two systems of WM, namely, verbal, and visuo-spatial stores. Studies initially seeking to describe age effects approached the measurement of age differences with WM span tasks as well as experiments to examine the interaction of age with increases in storage or processing requirements.

Adult age comparisons on span tasks consistently show age deficits. A meta-analysis of 123 studies of age-related differences in forward digit span showed that older adults have a smaller simple storage span (~7.1 items) compared to younger adults (~7.6 items), a mean age difference of 0.53, and that backwards digit span, that is, recitation of strings of digits in the reverse order of presentation, shows equivalent age differences (old M = 5.34 and young M = 5.88, with a mean difference of 0.54; Bopp & Verhaeghen, 2005). In contrast, the differences between mean spans are about twice as large for complex span tasks that require, in addition to storage, processing and coordination of multiple items before providing the final response. These include sentence span, listening span, and computation span (M age difference = 1.01, 1.27, and 1.54, respectively). Mathematical modeling of data from the meta-analysis additionally suggests that younger adults can hold about four items in WM whereas older adults can hold only three. These results are in line with findings by Basak & Verhaeghen (2003). They evaluated the subitizing span in older adults. Subitizing is a rapid process whereby people "see" or know how many elements are in a display just at a glance, without counting. It is considered to be a measure of focus of attention in WM. Basak and Verhaeghen found that older adults have a subitizing span of 2.07 items compared to 2.83 in younger adults. Thus, older adults appear to have smaller WM spans and therefore capacity than younger ones in a number of tasks.

The Role of Cohort in Estimates of Age Differences in WM

However, it is possible that the size of age-related declines in WM, as measured in cross-sectional studies with young and old individuals, as in the studies reported by Bopp and Verhaeghen (2005), are confounded by cohort effects. These are generational differences that enhance performance in the more recently born and younger participants because of historical changes that have produced a more cognitively complex environment. Effects of cohort must therefore be ruled out in order to make appropriate inferences about age changes in WM from cross-sectional studies comparing young and older adults.

This issue is partially resolved by longitudinal comparisons over time in the same individuals. The Victoria Longitudinal Study used several span measures and reported three-year declines in individuals in their sixties and seventies (Hultsch, Hertzog, Small, McDonald-Miszczak, & Dixon, 1992). The Rush Religious Orders Study, a sample of Catholic religious people aged 65 and up, used a composite of four span measures administered annually over eight years. After accounting for practice effects in the working memory composite, which were substantial, Wilson, Li, Bienias, and Bennett (2006) found declines. These studies confirm relatively short-term declines in WM in older adults but do not address possible generational differences.

Although there are virtually no studies examining longer-term declines in WM in an adult life span sample, we make inferences about WM changes from studies of reasoning change because reasoning is highly correlated with WM, at about $r = .90$ (Kyllonen & Christal, 1990). Age-related declines in reasoning have been reported over 16 years in adults aged 30–36 and 55–81 at baseline in the Long Beach Longitudinal Study (Zelinski & Burnight, 1997). These differences were about the same for the longitudinal comparisons as for an annualized estimate of age decline based on a cross-sectional baseline comparison. This would suggest persistent and cumulative declines in WM from early adulthood on. However, the 16-year span does not match the 40–50-year age range evaluated in cross-sectional comparisons of people in their twenties and people in their sixties and seventies. Additionally, no direct comparison of people matched on age from different birth cohorts of participants could be made in those data.

The issue of cohort is important in studies of reasoning, and implicitly, WM, because reasoning, as an indicator of fluid intelligence (Horn & Cattell, 1967), has been shown to be related to birth cohort in young adults (Flynn, 1987), whereby scores have increased by up to 1.5 standard deviations in same-age comparisons over a generation. In order to determine whether cohort differences reduce the longitudinal effects of age, Zelinski and Kennison (2007) compared two groups of adults over the ages of 55–87 that were born 16 years apart, on longitudinal changes in reasoning in the Long Beach Longitudinal Study. They found that at age 74, the cohort born before World War II had substantially higher scores than the cohort born 16 years earlier. The average performance estimates at age 74 of the people born more recently were approximately the same as those of people from the earlier-born cohort at the age of 59. Yet both cohorts showed robust age declines, and the slopes of age declines did not differ for the two cohorts despite their being born nearly a generation apart. Thus, age declines in reasoning, and by extension,

WM, were not accounted for by cohort. Nevertheless, the findings also suggested that cohort can play a major role in the size of observed age differences in cross-sectional studies. This indicates that WM deficits with age may not be quite as substantial as implied in such studies. We make this point because the remainder of the research studies described in this chapter use cross-sectional designs and this should be kept in mind when interpreting findings.

CURRENT EVIDENCE

WM and its Associations with Other Cognitive Abilities

Besides affecting memory, age differences in WM are likely to have consequences for the rest of the cognitive system, particularly abilities associated with fluid intelligence. There is clear evidence from studies of young adults that WM correlates well with general intelligence (Conway, Kane, & Engle, 2003), reading comprehension (Just & Carpenter, 1992), mathematics (Gathercole, Pickering, Knight, & Stegmann, 2003), and general language abilities (Kemper, Herman, & Liu, 2004).

Working memory has also been studied in aging as a source of individual differences in predicting other abilities, and WM span is associated with many abilities in older adults. In fact, very strong relationships of WM and reasoning have been found, not only in young adults (e.g., Kyllonen & Christal, 1990), but also in an adult life span sample with an age range at baseline of 28–97 (Zelinski & Lewis, 2003). Other abilities associated with WM include memory for lists of words and for discourse (Lewis & Zelinski, 2010), complexity of both spoken and written language production (see Kemper & Mitzner, 2001), word-by-word processing of complex sentences (Stine-Morrow, Miller, Gagne, & Hertzog, 2008), prospective memory (see Braver & West, 2008 for a review), and the ability to identify the meaning of unfamiliar words from context (McGinnis & Zelinski, 2000).

How WM might affect task performance is illustrated in a study by Light, Zelinski, and Moore (1982; Exp. 3), who used an experimental approach to evaluate older adults' ability to draw inferences from linear ordering tasks that varied in the amount of rearrangement of terms needed to construct the ordering. The terms were either adjacent, as in: *David was taller than Bob. Bob was taller than James. James was taller than Ron*; or required reordering, e.g., *James was taller than Ron. Bob was taller than James. David was taller than Bob.* Participants were asked either fact (*Was James taller than Ron?*) or inference questions requiring integration of the terms across sentences (*Was David taller than Ron?*). Findings indicated that older adults had more difficulty than younger ones in making inferences as well as remembering the facts but only for the sequences requiring rearrangement. This suggested that the requirements to rearrange terms mentally burdened WM capacity to a greater extent in the older adults. Alternative explanations, such as a reduction in ability to reason, less confidence in responses, and poorer overall memory, were ruled out. Because the older adults also had difficulty remembering facts in the rearrangement condition, the findings also suggested that tasks producing an excessive burden on WM capacity affect memory in older adults.

Much more recently, but in a similar vein, computational modeling confirmed that older adults have greater difficulty in forming new unfamiliar associations than younger adults due to impairments that appear under the greater WM demand of associating unfamiliar rather than familiar material (Buchler, Faunce, Light, Gottfredson, & Reder, 2011).

Correlated Change in WM and Other Abilities

There are only a few studies specifically evaluating the relationship between longitudinal changes in WM and cognitive outcomes. One of the earliest studies of correlates of cognitive changes (Zelinski, Gilewski, & Schaie, 1993) found that three-year changes in reasoning predicted changes in memory in people aged 55 and older in the Long Beach Longitudinal Study. It was subsequently found that reasoning and WM were highly correlated in this sample (Zelinski & Lewis, 2003), suggesting that memory changes could be predicted by declines in WM. In the Victoria Longitudinal Study, six-year changes in WM span were associated with changes in episodic memory (Hertzog, Dixon, Hultsch, & MacDonald, 2003; Hultsch, Hertzog, Dixon, & Small, 1998). In the Rush Religious Orders Study, six-year changes in verbal WM were correlated with changes in a range of other abilities, including story and word memory, perceptual speed, and visuospatial abilities (Wilson et al., 2002).

WM: A Cognitive Primitive Underlying Aging?

It has been suggested that cognitive primitives, or basic processes, underlie more complex ones, and that decline in a small number of primitives therefore accounts for most age changes in more complex abilities (e.g., Salthouse, 2004). The consistency of both cross-sectional and longitudinal findings in indicating that age differences and age changes in WM or related measures are related to age differences and declines in other cognitive abilities raises the question of the extent to which decline in WM is a mechanism of cognitive aging effects and therefore a cognitive primitive.

Previous work by Salthouse (1996) suggested that age-related slowing in processing speed was the cognitive primitive underlying most aging phenomena because measures of speed tend to be more strongly predictive of other cognitive measures than vice versa. However, recent findings suggest that although processing speed is an important correlate of the aging of memory as measured by list recall (e.g., Verhaeghen & Salthouse, 1997), it does not account for all variance in memory after accounting for age (e.g., Salthouse, 2004). Lewis and Zelinski (2010), for example, found in structural equation models that in addition to speed, WM directly predicted list recall. Text recall was not predicted by speed but by WM. Further, the effects of WM on text recall were independent of age as found by others (e.g., Kemper & Liu, 2007). Basak and Verhaeghen (2003) proposed that WM capacity deficits could account for increased slowing in the elderly because a smaller capacity could increase processing latency due to the time needed to move items in and out of attentional focus.

The studies described here not only cast doubt on the status of processing speed as the only cognitive primitive, but also provide indirect evidence that WM may be one of the handful of cognitive primitives. In addition, differences in WM capacity can explain age-related deficits in the maintenance of multiple goal sets; recent meta-analytic evidence reveals the existence, over and above general slowing, of age differences in tasks involving *global switching* from maintenance of one goal set to multiple goal sets, measured as the difference between carrying out one type of operation repeatedly over trial blocks versus carrying out one of two possible types of operation within the same block. However, after accounting for general slowing, there were no age differences in *local switching*, that is, measured as the difference in performance of trials, within the same block, where the preceding trial had the same operation type vs. trials where the preceding trial had a different operation (e.g., Wasylyshyn, Verhaeghen, & Sliwinski, 2011). It is possible that the set of processes related to supervisory processes of managing multiple goals, which are not easily differentiated from WM, is the underlying primitive (see e.g., Braver & West, 2008 for that interpretation). We next turn to the literature on a hierarchical model of WM to home in on the specific processes that may clarify how WM changes with aging.

A Hierarchical Model Of WM: Age Differences in Availability versus Accessibility

A crucial aspect of the WM system is its limited capacity of only a few items or ideas in consciousness (e.g., Baddeley & Hitch, 1974). The original conceptualization of storage in WM was that its capacity was unitary but separate for auditory and visual inputs. Hierarchical theories, most notably Cowan's (e.g., 1988; 1995), propose a hierarchy within capacity limits whereby some items in WM are more accessible than others. Cowan's model proposes a two-store structure for WM. It distinguishes between a zone of immediate access of about 4±1 items, labeled the *focus of attention* from a larger, activated zone of long-term memory (LTM) in which items are stored in a readily available but not as immediately accessible state. Oberauer (2002) adapted Cowan's model, suggesting a tripartite, no bipartite, architecture of the WM system. Like Cowan's model, there is an inner, limited focus of attention, but it holds only one information unit. It is surrounded by the outer store where to-be-updated information units are maintained, surrounded by an activated LTM called passive LTM store. Unlike Cowan's model, recent findings suggest that these two zones are firewalled from the passive LTM store where not-to-be-updated information is stored and maintained for later recall (Basak & Verhaeghen, 2011b). A simplified version of the model resulting from Basak and Verhaeghen's result is shown on the left side of Figure 5.1. This model has been supported by other work that suggests that the focus capacity of one item is observed when continuous memory updating is required and there are no practice effects (see below); under other conditions, however, the capacity may be larger.

According to the hierarchical models, when the number of informational units to be retained in WM is less than or equal to the capacity of the focus of attention, they will be contained within the focus. There they will be immediately

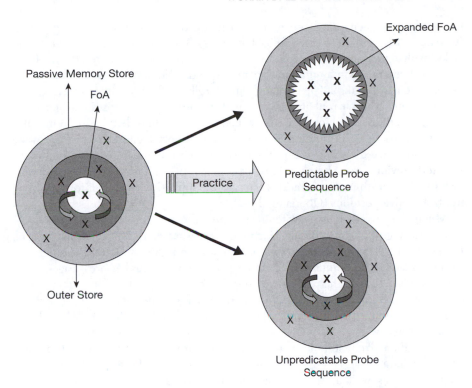

Figure 5.1   A simple representation of the tripartite architecture of working memory. Our model proposes that focus first directs attention to the relevant information, then accesses and subsequently updates it in a continuous memory updating task; (un)predictability of probe cue affects the first role. With extensive practice, the focus expands from one to about four items in a predictable probe order, following Cowan's (1995) model, but focus does not expand for unpredictable probe order

retrievable—the latency to access those items will be fast and indicate near-automatic processing with a slope of about 40 ms/number of informational units. When the number of informational units to be retained in WM exceeds the capacity of the focus, however, the additional units will be stored outside the focus (outer store). In that case, processing of informational units in the outer store will require a retrieval operation that brings them from the outer store into the focus of attention, that is, a *focus switch*, and this will increase the latency to access those items (Verhaeghen & Basak, 2005). Measurement of the capacity of the focus of attention involves assessment of *focus switch costs*, measured by the difference in response latency observed as a function of the number of items in WM; such costs are quite substantial (between 200 and 600 ms/number of informational units), indicating controlled processing, and different from the shallow latency rate inside the focus. Studies of focus switch costs show that the capacity of the focus of attention varies with task requirements.

For tasks involving parallel processes in deployment of attention, such as subitizing span, the number of items that can be accurately estimated with a glance, the capacity of focus has been identified as up to four items for young adults (Cowan, 2001), and up to three for older adults (Basak & Verhaeghen, 2003). For tasks involving serial attention processes, the size of the focus is limited to one item. This has been noted in a number of paradigms: the N-back task (McElree, 2001; Verhaeghen & Basak, 2005; Verhaeghen, Cerella, & Basak, 2004) where participants match the current item with an item presented N positions before; a running count task in which participants keep track of multiple types of items, like circles and triangles in a visual display (Basak & Verhaeghen, 2011b; Garavan, 1998); randomized N-back, where the current item is compared with a randomly selected previous item (Basak & Verhaeghen, 2011a); and an arithmetic updating task in which arithmetic operations have to be applied to update information in multiple active positions (Oberauer, 2002).

Much of the work on focus switching in aging has used a modified, self-paced, N-back task (e.g., Vaughan, Basak, Hartman, & Verhaeghen, 2008; Verhaeghen & Basak, 2005). Participants press one of two keys to indicate whether the current stimulus matches the stimulus presented N positions back; this key press triggers the next stimulus. To help the participant keep track of item positions, stimuli are presented on the computer screen in N-colored virtual columns, one at a time, the first stimulus in column 1, the second in column 2, and so on; after N stimuli have been presented, a new "row" of stimulus sequence starts at column 1. Thus the participant compares the current stimulus with the stimulus presented previously in the same colored column. The paradigm thus allows measurement of the speed of an item's *accessibility*, as well as the accuracy of its retrieval or its *availability*, while minimizing the participant's effort in keeping track of item positions.

Models of serial processing indicate that response times increase stricly monotonically as a function of the number of information units when searching for a particular unit in a set of multiple units in memory, indicating that we check the units individually until the target unit is found. According to Oberauer (2002), the retrieval rate of informational units in the outer store increases as a function of number of units, which would suggest a serial search process. But, this has not been replicated in other studies of processing from the outer store (e.g., Verhaeghen & Basak, 2005; Verhaeghen et al., 2004), where serial search was not evident, allowing us to propose that the manifestation of the serial search process may be related to predictability of the probe cue.

Basak & Verhaeghen (2011b), using the running count paradigm, proposed that the focus of attention has to point to the relevant information unit in the outer store before it can be accessed and retrieved into the focus for subsequent updating. If the probe cue to select the information is *predictable*, the focus switch cost is unchanged across the number of information units in the outer store; if *unpredictable*, a controlled serial search is required to point attention to the appropriate target in the outer store, increasing the focus switch cost as the number of information units increase. In the N-back paradigm, the probe cue is predictable, therefore the focus switch cost is constant from $N = 1$ to $N = 5$ (Verhaeghen & Basak, 2005); in a *randomized* N-back or the running count task where the probe cue is unpredictable, the focus switch cost increases with N for $N > 1$ (Basak & Verhaeghen, 2011a, 2011b; see Figure 5.2 for a proposed model).

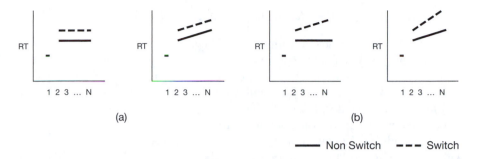

Figure 5.2 Focus switch cost is computed as the difference between switch and non-switch response times for N > 1. (a) When the probe order is predictable, the focus switch cost is constant as the switch and non-switch response time slopes are expected to be parallel. (b) When the probe order is unpredictable, the focus switch cost increases as a function of memory set-size

Analysis of the switch trials of the randomized N-back task, where the to-be-presented column is unpredictable, was conducted to further test the prediction of the Basak and Verhaeghen (2011a) explanation. Within each row, the number of the information units to be searched decreased with probe order (e.g., in the 4-back version, in the first switch trial, three items needed to be searched; in the second switch trial, only two items needed to be searched; in the final switch trial, only one item was left to be checked). The expectation was that reaction times decrease over probe cue order within a row only when a serial search process is taking place; this was supported. In another study, using the running count paradigm, alternative explanations, such as number of intervening columns and lag effects for the switch trials were ruled out (Basak & Verhaeghen, 2011b). In a recent study, Basak and her colleagues used a novel memory-updating paradigm to explore the neural correlates of the predictability of probe cue. The results support the behavioral evidence of our model; that is, predictability matters in accessing and updating of information in working memory (Basak & Hamilton, 2012).

Basak and colleagues have also observed that the size of the attentional focus of one item can expand with extensive practice in a modified N-back task (Verhaeghen, Cerella & Basak, 2004), but not in the random N-back or N-count tasks (Basak, 2006; Oberauer, 2006). We argue that when the probe cue is predictable, extensive practice can expand the focus from one to four items, but when it is unpredictable, extensive practice cannot expand the focus beyond one item because unpredictability invokes a controlled serial search. Thus, both extensive practice with a predictable probe cue order or tasks involving parallel processes like subitizing span are associated with an expanded focus of attention. This is further illustrated on the right side of Figure 5.1, where it is shown that under certain circumstances the focus of one in memory updating tasks can be expanded with practice, thus integrating the single focus models (Basak and Verhaeghen, 2011b; Oberauer, 2002; Verhaeghen & Basak, 2005) with Cowan's (1988; 1995) model.

Aging Findings from the Hierarchical WM Model

With respect to aging, research with the virtual column paradigm has yielded four main findings. The first finding concerns the age-equivalence in the capacity limits of the focus of attention. That is, in serial attention tasks both *older and younger adults can hold a maximum of one information unit in their focal attention of working memory*; needless to say, the focus cannot be empty provided individuals are involved in active processing of information in their working memory.

The second finding concerns age effects in item accessibility during a focus switch process in working memory. No age differences in focus switch costs in response latency for correct responses are observed once baseline age-related slowing in the comparison process itself is taken into account. This is contrary to the findings in cognitive aging that older adults' response latencies (Cerella, Poon, & Williams, 1980), compared to those of younger adults, increases as task difficulty increases. This finding holds true even for more difficult versions of the task, for example, when items are randomly presented in sequence (Basak & Verhaeghen, 2011a), when all items are displayed at the same location on the screen (Vaughan et al., 2008, Exp, 1), or when all stimuli are three-digit numbers rather than single digits (Vaughan et al., 2008, Exp. 2). This positive finding is not merely unexpected; it leads to the conclusion that *older adults can access information units in and out of the focus of attention in working memory as effectively as younger adults provided the units are available*.

The third finding with respect to aging concerns item availability, that is, the probability of successful retrieval after a focus switch. Items in the focus are highly available, as evidenced by near-perfect accuracy. Items in the outer store become less available, as evidenced by monotonic decline in accuracy. In the N-back task, although there were no age-related differences in the retrieval dynamics of the focus-switch process, age interacted with focus switch accuracy, such that older adults were much less accurate when they had to switch focus, compared to when they did not (Vaughan et al., 2008, Exp. 1; Verhaeghen & Basak, 2005, Exp. 1). This suggests that the focus switch process requiring retrieval of information from the outer store into the focus was less available to the older adults compared to the younger adults. Similarly, in the randomized N-back task, the focus switch trials yielded lower accuracy than the non-switch trials, and age differences in accuracy were larger on the focus switch than the non-switch trials (Basak & Verhaeghen, 2011a; see Figure 5.3a). These findings indicate that *age differences exist in the item availability in the outer store*.

The fourth age-related finding concerns the dynamics of search within the outer store. As described previously, the slope of retrieval speed of an information unit from the outer store over the memory set-size varies with the predictability of probe cue. When the probe cue is predictable, the slope is zero or near zero; if unpredictable, the slope increases with N in the N-back experiments, indicating a controlled search (Basak & Verhaeghen, 2011a; see Figure 5.3b). Importantly, there is little or no age difference in that slope, once general slowing is accounted for, regardless of the predictability of the task. That is, *both young and older adults can search the outer store with similar efficiency*.

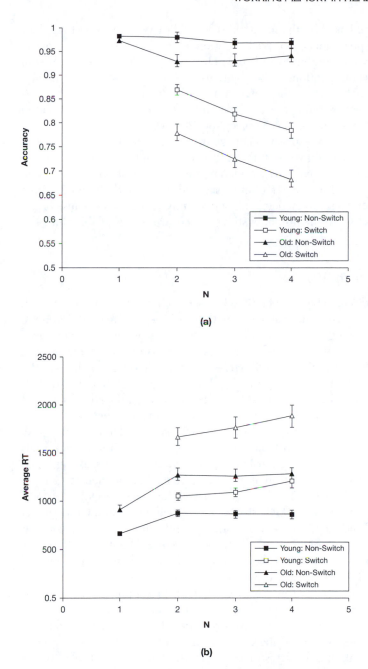

Figure 5.3   Availability and accessibility in younger and older adults in the unpredictable version of the *N*-back task (adapted from Basak & Verhaeghen, 2011a). (a) Age-related differences in accuracy exist between switch and non-switch trials at N=2, but the difference does not increase for N>2. (b) The focus switch cost increases as a function of set-size, indicating a controlled search process, but no age-related differences exist in the search efficiency

In sum, the work based on the hierarchical model of WM suggests that older adults' poorer WM performance in serial attention tasks is based on only one of the four processes identified in that line of research. There are no age differences in the size of the focus of attention, in the ability to switch focus, or in the dynamics of retrieving information from the outer store in both predictable and unpredictable trials. However, there are age-related differences in the information available in the outer store (Basak & Verhaeghen, 2011a).

It is less clear what the interpretation of age differences in the size of the focus in parallel processing might involve. Basak and Verhaeghen (2003) suggested that in subitizing, older adults have a narrower range of focus of attention, with one fewer item in focus than for younger adults. As already suggested, this could affect not only the speed but also efficiency of higher cognitive processes because of the need to retrieve items from the outer store, which are less available, into the attentional focus.

Goal Maintenance in WM

All of the research discussed to this point has focused on the evaluation of WM with respect to age differences and changes in within-task performance differences. Some views of the aging of WM are broader, including phenomena not easily differentiated from those associated with supervisory processes, such as goal maintenance (see Braver & West, 2008). Here, too, the role of age declines in the availability of information is a key aspect of performance, though that information may be at the level of task set or goals. Recent accounts of age differences in WM have suggested that aging is associated with difficulties in maintaining two task sets.

Global task switch costs, an overall increase in response latency when task switching is required in a switch-block of trials, compared to pure-block trials where no switching occurs, are greater in older than younger adults, as suggested earlier, even after accounting for general slowing (e.g., Verhaeghen & Cerella, 2002; Wasylyshyn et al., 2011). The behavioral age differences for global vs. local task switching are paralleled in fMRI studies of cortical activation. Older adults show less sustained and more transient activation in prefrontal cortex than younger ones in task switching paradigms (Jimura & Braver, 2010). These age differences in the dynamics of cortical activation thus support the idea that maintaining the general set for multiple tasks is impaired in older adults.

Braver and colleagues (e.g., Braver & West, 2008) have proposed context-based models of set maintenance whereby older adults are more reliant on stimulus-driven bottom-up cues than goal-based top-down cues. This has been tested in the AX-CPT, a continuous performance task. When participants see the probe letter X, they are to press a button only if it is preceded by the letter A (AX trials). If X is preceded by a B, they are to withhold the response (BX trials). If the letter Y is presented, they are also to withhold the response, even if it is preceded by an A (AY trials). The majority of trials are of the AX pairing in order to bias responses to the A context. The model predicts that the context (the letter A or B) would have a greater effect on the older adults' accuracy scores than on younger adults' scores. This was supported: Older adults made more errors on BX trials than younger ones and fewer errors on AY trials. This suggested greater reliance on the A context than on the maintenance of the A and B task sets.

These findings gave rise to the Dual Mechanisms of Control model that suggests that there is flexible allocation of two modes of cognitive control: proactive and reactive. Proactive control involves the sustained maintenance of goal representations and anticipatory biasing of attention and action systems, whereas reactive control involves transient stimulus-driven reactivation of goal information when necessary to avoid errors (Braver, Gray, & Burgess, 2007). The fMRI correlates of these activation dynamics are seen in lateral prefrontal cortex (PFC) whereby sustained activation in lateral PFC is associated with proactive control whereas transient activation in lateral PFC and other areas including anterior cingulate and posterior associational cortices is associated with reactive control. The prediction that older adults have difficulties with proactive but not with reactive control, compared to younger ones, was confirmed in cortical activation patterns during an AX-CPT experiment (Paxton, Barch, Racine, & Braver, 2008). Younger adults were more likely to engage in proactive control and its associated activation patterns. These findings suggest that older adults do engage less in goal maintenance activities, as they do not spontaneously sustain the activation needed to maintain top-down goals.

Expanding WM Through Training: Training and Transfer Effects

It is clear from the discussion thus far that aging is associated with greater limitations in the functioning of the WM system than in younger adults. However, research in neuroplasticity suggests that some of the declines may be remediated by cognitive training and, critically, that performance on tasks associated with WM, even if not directly trained, may improve as well (see Zelinski, 2009).

Cognitive Training

Early work on memory training in older adults emphasized strategy use to improve episodic memory, such as the method of loci. A meta-analysis of the effects of episodic memory training on within-subject change in targeted memory performance showed that older adults benefited from memory training, with a mean effect size of .73, which was about twice the effect size shown by no-treatment control and placebo treatment groups. The specific type of mnemonic trained, however, did not matter (Verhaeghen, Marcoen, & Goossens, 1992). However, strategy training studies have generally shown very narrow transfer to untrained materials or tasks. For example, imagery-based training creates improvement in memory for concrete words, which can easily be visualized, but not abstract words, which are not (Stigsdotter Neely & Bäckman, 1995). Interestingly, from the standpoint of WM deficits, older adults may find it difficult to implement trained strategies in everyday contexts (Brooks, Friedman, & Yesavage, 1993; see Rebok, Carlson, & Langbaum, 2007). Memory strategy training is effortful, that is, it requires that the trained techniques be retrieved and maintained in WM (see Zelinski, 2009), and it may require avoiding highly overlearned but ineffective encoding habits, which would imply actively maintaining a goal set. This suggests that direct training of WM may be important for transfer.

Training on working memory paradigms have mixed results, with some of them indicating transfer to broader skills. Paradigms including dual task, task switching, N-back training, task switching, and WM span have been evaluated.

Kramer, Larish, and Strayer (1995) trained young and old adults in the dual tasks of monitoring a changing display while responding to alphabet arithmetic items. The transfer tasks, also completed in a dual task format, were scheduling and paired associates running memory and were thus functionally different from those trained. After training, the older adults did not differ from young adults in the difference between doing tasks individually and simultaneously, that is, the dual task costs, after training, and showed similar cost reductions with the transfer tasks as did the younger people. Bherer et al. (2005) found that for both auditory and cross-modality transfer tasks, the trained older adults showed a dual task cost reduction not seen in the control group. Kramer, Larish, Weber, and Bardell (1999) additionally found that dual task training effects were still observed in older adults approximately two months later.

Several studies have directly trained performance on the N-back task. Buschkuehl et al. (2008) trained participants over the age of 80 on N-back recall of visual materials and in choice response time. There were improvements in speed and accuracy on the trained tasks and transfer to recall of visual materials and digit span. A one-year follow-up showed that both training and transfer findings persisted, though these effects were weaker. Li et al. (2008) trained spatial working memory with a 2-back task. Besides improvement on the trained 2-back task, there was transfer to a 3-back spatial task and to N-back recall of digits.

Older adults show large training improvements in task switching, with reductions in switch cost that bring them to the level of younger adults (Kramer, Hahn, & Gopher, 1999). Training on task-switching resulted in transfer to reduced switch costs in a different task switching paradigm (Karbach, Mang, & Kray, 2010), and to reductions in Stroop interference, and verbal and spatial WM span tasks (Karbach & Kray, 2009). Finally, training of WM span in a sample of older adults resulted in improvements compared to controls on backwards digit span, fluid intelligence, Stroop interference, and processing speed (Borella, Carretti, Riboldi, and De Beni, 2010).

However, not all studies have reported transfer. In one study, older adults, like younger adults, benefited from extended practice in a letter span task (Dahlin, et al., 2008). Unlike the younger adults, the older ones showed no transfer to a 3-back task. Patterns of fMRI brain activation at pretest showed that among younger adults, the updating task and N-back task produced similar patterns of activation in the left striatum, which is thought to serve a gate-keeping function for WM and frontal-parietal regions, but older adults did not display such overlap in striatal activations between the two tasks.

The authors argued that transfer of training depends on common neural systems required for target and transfer tasks, and that in this case, the lack of transfer among older adults may be due to deficiencies in striatal functioning. But, ideally, activations should be measured for both the training and transfer tasks not just at pretest, as done in this study, but also at post-test. This would allow a direct test of the hypothesis that although older adults may be learning the training task, they may not be engaging the same brain regions post-training, unlike the younger adults, that subserve the training and transfer tasks.

Age differences in characteristic activation patterns during task performance can be changed along with behavioral outcomes, however. Braver, Paxton, Locke, and Barch (2009) provided task strategy training to older adults and monetary incentives to younger ones to change their habitual control patterns in the AX-CPT paradigm. Older adults shifted to a proactive control pattern and younger ones to a reactive one as a result of the biasing interventions. The temporal dynamics of their fMRI activations reflected the behavioral changes, suggesting that activation patterns, along with performance, are manipulable in older adults with training.

It is also important to consider that although experimental evaluations of age differences in WM with paradigms such as N-back or dual task training can be used to pinpoint age deficits in processes theorized to represent WM, the extent to which the specific processes are trained in the tasks and instantiated in the transfer tasks has not been empirically determined. That is, few studies have examined whether the cognitive processes measured in WM training are equally trainable and are represented equivalently in different transfer tasks. Miyake et al. (2000) used latent variable modeling of a wide range of tasks to test hypotheses about independence of constructs in "frontal lobe" tasks, which can be construed as having considerable overlap with WM. They found three separate but correlated factors, including updating and monitoring of information in WM, shifting between task sets, and the withholding of prepotent responses. Until the representativeness of WM processes across tasks has been identified, it seems prudent to engage training with multiple WM-related processes to produce transfer.

A commercially available computerized training program that targets sensory discrimination—in which participants perform computer exercises requiring increasingly finer discrimination in auditory signal processing, requiring both speed and accuracy, at the level of sound sweeps, phonemes, and syllables—was evaluated for transfer potential (Mahncke, Bronstone, & Merzenich, 2006; Mahncke et al., 2006). The training tasks also engaged working memory, as they required participants to store responses until the stimuli in each trial had been presented. Several of the training tasks involved increasing WM loads. One of the training tasks involved monitoring the spatial location of matching pairs of syllables in a matrix that became increasingly larger over trials, another trained increases in syllable span, and another trained participants to enact auditory instructions that increasingly required more actions to complete and were more linguistically complex over trials. The intervention improved both directly trained and transfer performance, including a global auditory memory score compared to active controls or retest controls (Mahncke, Bronstone, & Merzenich, 2006; Mahncke et al., 2006). In a multi-site double-blind randomized controlled clinical trial of the training with nearly 500 participants over the age of 65, Smith et al. (2009) showed that the experimental group improved more than an active control group in multiple memory recall tasks, including backwards digit span, letter-number sequencing, word list delayed recall, and word list total score. A three-month follow-up with no additional training indicated that the gains generally persisted in the experimental group, but the effects did fade (Zelinski et al., 2011).

The studies cited here suggest that training with WM paradigms is generally associated with transfer. More complex multimodal approaches may also be important in improvements in WM as an outcome. Gopher (2007) suggested that training in a speeded task with multiple attentional demands, such as driving, produces better learning if the training involves variable emphasis on different components of the task rather than training on individual components sequentially. This approach requires that participants train holistically on all of the components of the task to encourage generalization of skills across multiple subprocesses. Kramer et al. (1995) found that a variable priority approach to dual task performance, whereby participants were instructed on which task to prioritize for each trial, produced better performance than fixed priority instructions, which encouraged prioritizing one task within a block of trials. Bherer et al. (2005) showed that variable priority training did not enhance performance on easy tasks, suggesting that variable emphasis is more beneficial for difficult tasks. A recent study by Boot et al. (2010) trained younger adults for 20 hours in a complex digital game, called *Space Fortress*. The training group received variable priority training, while the control group was asked to focus on improvements in the total score. The training group not only improved in the game, as evidenced from a faster learning rate, they also displayed significantly greater transfer effects to short-term memory, measured by Sternberg's memory scanning paradigm, as well as to dual task cost reductions in a flight simulator performance.

Digital video games have been used to improve WM in older adults. Video games inherently use variable priority methods to allow integrated training in core WM skills that are adversely affected by age, such as goal maintenance and sensory discrimination. The key rationale is that the remediation of these core skills in an integrated manner will have broad-based effects on the cognitive system (Basak, Boot, Voss & Kramer, 2008; Buschkuehl et al., 2008; Kramer, Larish, Weber, & Bardell, 1999).

A few studies have explored the effect of training in integrative, multimodal digital games on untrained cognitive skills. Training older adults on first-generation arcade-type games, such as Pac-Man, Donkey Kong, or Super Tetris, improves merely their response latencies, not cognitive control (Clark, Lanphear, & Riddick, 1987; Dustman et al., 1992; Goldstein et al., 1997). For example, older adults who trained on Super Tetris for 25 hours improved in a reaction time task, but not in the Stroop Color Word Test, a measure of the ability to inhibit a prepotent response tendency, than controls (Goldstein et al., 1997).

Recent-generation digital games use mechanics that are more likely to support improvements in working memory and its correlates than arcade games (see, e.g., Zelinski & Reyes, 2009). Real-time strategy games require remembering the game rules and applying them while adapting to increasingly difficult challenges; they marry the complexity of turn-based strategy games or strategy board games with the speed of action games. For example, the order of actions used to build a structure like a library in a strategy game must be followed as required for its successful construction and use; when, where and why to build it must be evaluated by the player. Digital games motivate players to improve their performance through failures to progress in the game. This forces players to develop alternative strategies and to learn from mistakes, thereby changing goal sets. Another element of game design relevant to working memory is backtracking, a requirement to return to previously visited areas to complete a task that was not previously attainable until a subsequent goal was met.

More than 23 hours of training on a complex real-time strategy game, *Rise of Nations*, that uses some of the mechanics just described, was shown to improve visuo-spatial WM and focus switch cost in an *N*-back task in older adults relative to retest controls (Basak, Voss, Boot, & Kramer, 2008). Moreover, improvements in measures of game performance predicted improvements in switching between tasks and objects in working memory, assessed by the local switch cost in a task switching paradigm and the focus switch cost in an *N*-back task, respectively. Individual differences in volumes of frontoparietal brain regions and cerebellum also predicted improvements in game performance in older adults (Basak et al., 2011), suggesting that larger brain volumes of regions that subserve cognitive control and motor control are related to faster learning rates of complex cognitive skills.

Page limitations preclude a more thorough review of the training literature (though see Chapters 14 and 15 in this volume). A growing body of evidence suggests that a variety of approaches can improve WM in older adults, including aerobic fitness (e.g., Hindin & Zelinski, 2012), self-efficacy (West, Bagwell, & Dark-Freudeman, 2008), and cognitive engagement (e.g., Carlson et al., 2008; Stine-Morrow, Parisi, Morrow, & Park, 2008). More extensive reviews discuss these findings (Stine-Morrow & Basak, 2011; Zelinski, Dalton, & Smith, 2011).

FUTURE DIRECTIONS

It is important to understand that the research described here pushes older adults to the limits of their performance so as to clearly identify possible deficits in WM and other abilities. We also acknowledge the relevance of cohort effects to some of the apparent age effects that may exacerbate the size of age differences, but it is clear that there are measurable age declines in WM. Most important, though, is the scarcity of literature on the possible effect of WM decline on everyday activities. There is very little research dedicated to the development of outcome measures that would validly approximate the cognitive demands of everyday functional abilities so that their relationship with WM can be assessed. One area, however, that hints at the relevance of WM to everyday life is that of subjective memory appraisal.

Subjective Memory

Memory self-efficacy declines with age (e.g., Cutler & Grams, 1988), and though it is thought of as indicative of subjective rather than objective memory perform-ance, it is defined by questions about failures of WM as well as of retrieval from long-term memory. Items from the 33-item Frequency of Forgetting scale from the Memory Functioning Questionnaire (Gilewski, Zelinski, & Schaie, 1990) that discriminate among respondents and that add unique variance were empirically selected to create a short but equally reliable and valid version of the scale using

Rasch modeling. Of ten items that were included in the short version of the scale, renamed the Frequency of Forgetting-10 (FOF-10), four items suggested WM or attentional failures. These included how often people reported forgetting "where you put things," "beginning to do something and forgetting what it was," and two questions about forgetting previously read material while continuing to read (Zelinski & Gilewski, 2004). Although responses to the FOF-10 are associated negatively with depression scores and positively with the personality trait of conscientiousness, they are associated also with list recall and with WM span (Zelinski, in preparation). In a similar vein, the complex auditory discrimination and working memory training that was assessed in the randomized clinical trial described earlier was associated with improvements in subjective memory appraisals in healthy older adults compared to those of active controls in the study reported by Smith et al. (2009).

We note that subjective memory is of clinical importance because subjective complaints in the absence of neuropsychologically observable deficits are traditionally interpreted as suggesting subclinical deficits and possible risk of development of cognitive impairment. In addition, deficits in processes related to goal management and planning, independent of memory impairment, have been identified as suggesting risk for development of dementia (Storandt, 2008). Persistent deficits in WM that may not be amenable to training may therefore be implicated, not only as indicative of decline in healthy aging, but as an early indicator of dementia.

Compensation

For healthy older adults, who are the majority of the elderly, little is known about how they might compensate for WM deficits in everyday life. However, there are implications that compensation is possible. For example, where the stakes are high, such as remembering to go to a medical appointment, little evidence of failure is seen in healthy older adults (see also Salthouse, 2004). In contrast to the deficits observed in laboratory-based prospective memory, real-life prospective memory is *better* in older than younger people because the older ones engage in compensatory behavior: they acknowledge the risk of cognitive fallibility, and they plan to remember the task, using cues, such as calendar reminders, for example (Henry, MacLeod, Phillips, & Crawford, 2004).

Driving is another example of an everyday activity with strong WM components. Driving failures, such as crashes, are rare, but can be very serious. Between 1995 and 2008, the number of drivers at or over the age of 70 increased, but the proportion of crashes, both fatal and nonfatal, declined more in that group, as well as for drivers age 80 and up than for drivers aged 35–54 (Cheung & McCartt, 2010). This is not apparently due only to safer cars and more stringent licensing laws for older drivers; it has been suggested that better health, including better vision as well as cognition in the older population (e.g., Zelinski & Kennison, 2007), is a critical factor (Cheung & McCartt, 2010). In addition, drivers over the age of 65 are much more likely to use seat belts, to drive only under the safest conditions, and are less likely to drive impaired or distracted. For example, older adults are much less likely to drink and drive, to use cellular phones, or to text message while driving than other age groups (Centers for Disease Control Data and Statistics, 2011). A large percent of older adults self-regulate driving because of concerns about visual and cognitive impairments (Braitman & McCartt, 2008). Relevant to these concerns, new evidence suggests that errors in driving may be reduced with WM training. A study that combined N-back and dual task training was associated with improvements in older adults' performance on a driving simulator (Cassavaugh & Kramer, 2009). This is one of the first demonstrations that WM training may improve functional performance, and presents exciting possibilities for supporting older adults' independence.

WM, Functional Abilities, and Health

In aging, preservation of functional ability so that older adults maintain their independence is important because of the sheer number of older adults projected to be in the worldwide population by 2050. The median age of the world's population is projected to increase by 20 years (United Nations, 2002). The population of adults aged 65 years and older is projected to increase from 6.9 percent to 12 percent worldwide, from 12.6 percent to 20.3 percent in North America, from 15.5 percent to 24.3 percent in Europe, from 6.0 percent to 12.0 percent in Asia, and from 5.5 percent to 11.6 percent in Latin America and the Caribbean (Kinsella & Velkoff, 2001). This worldwide increase in the proportion of older adults brings with it the increased incidence and prevalence of age-related cognitive declines, such as mild cognitive impairment, and dementia, and makes solutions to reducing and delaying dependence critical. The delay of as little as one year of dependency for a number of health conditions that increase with old age has far reaching implications (e.g., Brookmeyer, Johnson, Ziegler-Graham & Arrighi, 2007). Murphy and Topel (2006) suggested that the one-year gain in life expectancy from 1970 to 2000 because of reductions in cardiovascular disease mortality increased US social wealth by $95 trillion dollars. It is estimated that a one-year gain in quality of health might double the economic effect. Cognitive performance, broadly defined, is considered by epidemiologists to be a health indicator; there is likely to be a bidirectional association between cognition and functional abilities; that is, neurological function may underlie both cognition and ability to perform tasks (e.g., Li, Lindenberger, Freund, & Baltes, 2001). If this is the case, reducing or reversing cognitive performance declines might be associated with improved physical functioning outcomes (see also Jobe et al., 2001). Working memory pervades many higher level cognitive processes that we assume are relevant to everyday activities. A better understanding of age change in WM and its relation to functional outcomes and studies of the efficacy of WM training on a range of cognitive and behavioral outcomes is critical to determining how to increase the quality of life for older adults.

REFERENCES

Baddeley, A. D., & Hitch, G. J. (1974). Working memory. In G. H. Bower (Ed.), *The psychology of learning and motivation*, (Vol. 8, pp. 47–89). New York, NY: Academic Press.

Basak, C. (2006). Capacity limits of the focus of attention and dynamics of the focus switch cost in the working memory [Dissertation Abstract]. *Dissertation Abstracts International: Section B: The Sciences and Engineering*. Vol 66(10-B), pp. 5715.

Basak, C., Boot, W. R., Voss, M. W., & Kramer, A. F. (2008). Can training in a real-time strategy videogame attenuate cognitive decline in older adults? *Psychology and Aging, 23,* 765–777.

Basak, C., & Hamilton, A. C. (2012). Aging and neural correlates of predictability of focus switching in working memory. Poster presented at the 2012 Cognitive Aging Conference, Atlanta.

Basak, C., & Verhaeghen, P. (2003). Subitizing speed, subitizing range, counting speed, the Stroop effect, and aging: Capacity differences, speed equivalence. *Psychology and Aging, 18,* 240–249.

Basak, C., & Verhaeghen, P. (2011a). Aging and switching the focus of attention in working memory: Age differences in item availability but not in item accessibility. *Journals of Gerontology: Psychological Sciences, 66(5),* 519–526.

Basak, C., & Verhaeghen, P. (2011b). Three layers of working memory: Focus-switch costs and retrieval dynamics as revealed by the *N*-count task. *Journal of Cognitive Psychology, 23(2),* 204–219.

Basak, C., Voss, M. W., Erickson, K. I., Boot, W. R., & Kramer, A. F. (2011). Regional differences in brain volume predict the acquisition of skill in a complex real-time strategy video game. *Brain and Cognition, 76(3),* 407–414.

Bherer, L., Kramer, A. F., Peterson, M. S., Colcombe, S., Erickson, K., & Becic, E. (2005). Training effects on dual-task performance: Are there age-related differences in plasticity of attentional control? *Psychology and Aging, 20,* 695–709.

Boot, W. R., Basak, C., Erickson, K. I., Neider, M., Simons, D. J., Fabiani, M., Gratton, G., Voss, M. W., Prakash, R., Lee, H., & Kramer, A. F. (2010). Strategy, individual differences, and transfer of training in the acquisition of skilled Space Fortress performance. *Acta Psychologica, 135,* 349–357.

Bopp, K. L., & Verhaeghen, P. (2005). Aging and verbal memory span: A meta-analysis. *Journals of Gerontology: Psychological Sciences*, 60B, 223–233.

Borella, E., Carretti, B., Riboldi, F., & De Beni, R. (2010, October 25). Working memory training in older adults: Evidence of transfer and maintenance effects. *Psychology and Aging, 25,* 767–778.

Braitman, K. A., & McCartt, A. T. (2008). Characteristics of older drivers who self-limit their driving. *Annals of Advances in Automotive Medicine, 52,* 245–254.

Braver, T. S., Gray, J. R., & Burgess, G. C. (2007). Explaining the many varieties of working memory variation: Dual mechanisms of cognitive control. In A. R. A. Conway, C. Jarrold, M. J. Kane, A. Miyake, & J. N. Towse (Eds.), *Variation in working memory* (pp. 76–106). New York: Oxford University Press.

Braver, T. S., Paxton, J. L., Locke, H. S., & Barch, D. M. (2009). Flexible neural mechanisms of cognitive control within human prefrontal cortex. *Proceedings of the National Academy of Sciences, 106,* 7351–7356.

Braver, T. S., & West, R. (2008). Working memory, executive control, and aging. In F. I. M. Craik & T. A. Salthouse (Eds.), *The handbook of aging and cognition* (pp. 311–372). New York: Psychology Press.

Brookmeyer, R., Johnson, E., Ziegler-Graham, K., & Arrighi, H. M. (2007). Forecasting the global burden of Alzheimer's disease. *Alzheimer's and Dementia, 3,* 186–191.

Brooks, J. O., Friedman, L., & Yesavage, J. A. (1993). A study of the problems older adults encounter when using a mnemonic technique. *International Psychogeriatrics, 5,* 57–65.

Buchler, N. G., Faunce, P., Light, L. L., Gotfreddson, N., & Reder, L. M. (2011). Effects of repetition on associative recognition in young and older adults: Item and associative strengthening. *Psychology and Aging, 26,* 111–126.

Buschkuehl, M., Jaeggi, S. M., Hutchison, S., Perrig-Chiello, P., Däpp, C., Müller, M., ... Perrig, W. J. (2008). Impact of working memory training on memory performance in old-old adults. *Psychology and Aging, 23,* 743–753.

Carlson, M. C., Saczynski, J. S., Rebok, G. W., Seeman, T., Glass, T. A., McGill, S., et al. (2008). Exploring the effects of "everyday" activity programs on executive functions and memory in older adults: Experience Corps®. *The Gerontologist, 48,* 793–801.

Cassavaugh, N. D., & Kramer, A. F. (2009). Transfer of computer-based training to simulated driving in older adults. *Applied Ergonomics, 40,* 943–952.

Centers for Disease Control Data and Statistics (2011). New data on older drivers. Retrieved April 19, 2011 from: http://www.cdc.gov/Features/dsOlderDrivers/

Cerella, J., Poon, L. W., & Williams, D. M. (1980). Age and the complexity hypothesis. In L. W. Poon (Ed.), *Aging in the 1980s* (pp. 332–340), Washington, DC: American Psychological Association.

Cheung, I., & McCartt, A. T. (2010). *Declines in fatal crashes of older drivers: Changes in crash risk and survivability.* Arlington, VA: Insurance Institute for Highway Safety.

Clark, J. E., Lanphear, A. K., & Riddick, C. C. (1987). The effects of videogame playing on the response selection processing of elderly adults. *Journals of Gerontology, 42,* 82–85.

Conway, A. R. A., Kane, M. J., & Engle, R. W. (2003). Working memory capacity and its relation to general intelligence. *Trends in Cognitive Sciences, 7,* 547–552.

Cowan, N. (1988). Evolving conceptions of memory storage, selective attention, and their mutual constraints within the human information-processing system. *Psychonomic Bulletin, 104,* 163–191.

Cowan, N. (1995). *Attention and memory: An integrated framework.* New York: Oxford University Press.

Cowan, N. (2001). The magical number 4 in short-term memory: A reconsideration of mental storage capacity. *Behavioral and Brain Sciences, 24,* 87–185.

Cutler, S. J., & Grams, A. E. (1988). Correlates of self-reported everyday memory problems. *Journals of Gerontology: Social Sciences, 43,* S82–S90.

Dahlin, E., Stigsdotter Neely, A., Larsson, A., Bäckman, L., & Nyberg, L. (2008). Transfer of learning after updating training mediated by the striatum. *Science, 320,* 1510–1512.

Dustman, R. E., Emmerson, R. Y., Steinhaus, L. A., Shearer, D. E., & Dustman, T. J. (1992). The effects of videogame playing on neuropsychological performance of elderly individuals. *Journals of Gerontology, 47,* 168–171.

Flynn, J. R. (1987). Massive IQ gains in 14 nations: What IQ tests really measure. *Psychological Bulletin, 101,* 171–191.

Garavan, H. (1998). Serial attention within working memory. *Memory and Cognition, 26,* 263–276.

Gathercole, S. E., Pickering, S. J., Knight, C., & Stegmann, Z. (2003). Working memory skills and educational achievement: Evidence from National Curriculum Assessments at 7 and 14 years of age. *Applied Cognitive Psychology, 18,* 1–16.

Gilewski, M. J., Zelinski, E. M, and Schaie, K. W. (1990). The Memory Functioning Questionnaire. *Psychology and Aging, 5,* 482–490.

Goldstein, J., Cajko, L., Oosterbroek, M., Michielsen, M., Van Houten, O., & Salvedera, F. (1997). Videogames and the elderly. *Social Behavior and Personality, 25*(4), 345–352.

Gopher, D. (2007). Emphasis change as training protocol for high-demand tasks. In A. F. Kramer, D. A. Wiegmann, & A. Kirlik (Eds.), *Attention: From theory to practice* (pp. 209–224). New York: Oxford University Press.

Henry, J. D., MacLeod, M. S., Phillips, L. H., & Crawford, J. R. (2004). A meta-analytic review of prospective memory and aging. *Psychology and Aging, 19,* 27–39.

Hertzog, C., Dixon, R. A., Hultsch, D. R., & MacDonald, S. W. S. (2003). Latent change models of adult cognition: Are changes in processing speed and working memory associated with changes in episodic memory? *Psychology and Aging, 18,* 755–769.

Hindin, S., & Zelinski, E. M. (2012). Extended practice and aerobic exercise interventions benefit untrained cognitive outcomes in older adults: A meta-analysis. *Journal of the American Geriatrics Society, 60*, 136–141.

Horn, J. L., & Cattell, R. B. (1967). Age differences in fluid and crystallized intelligence. *Acta Psychologica, 26*, 107–129.

Hultsch, D. F., Hertzog, C., Dixon, R. A., & Small, B. J. (1998). *Memory change in the aged.* Cambridge, England: Cambridge University Press.

Hultsch, D. F., Hertzog, C., Small, B. J., McDonald-Miszczak, L., & Dixon, R. A. (1992). Short-term longitudinal change in cognitive performance in later life. *Psychology & Aging, 7*, 571–584.

Jimura, K., & Braver, T. S. (2010). Age-related shifts in brain activity dynamics during task switching. *Cerebral Cortex, 20*, 1420–1431.

Jobe, J. B., Smith, D. M., Ball, K., Tennstedt, S. L., Marsiske, M., Willis, S. L., et al. (2001). ACTIVE: A cognitive intervention trial to promote independence in older adults. *Controlled Clinical Trials, 22*, 453–479.

Just, M. A., & Carpenter, P. A. (1992). A capacity theory of comprehension: Individual differences in working memory. *Psychological Review, 99*, 122–149.

Karbach, J., & Kray, J. (2009). How useful is executive control training? Age differences in near and far transfer of task-switching training. *Developmental Science, 12*, 978–990.

Karbach, J., Mang, S., & Kray, J. (2010). Transfer of task-switching training in older age: The role of verbal processes. *Psychology and Aging, 25*, 677–683.

Kemper, S., Herman, R. E., & Liu, C.-J. (2004). Sentence production by young and older adults in controlled contexts. *Journals of Gerontology: Psychological Sciences, 59B*, 220–224.

Kemper, S., & Liu, C.-J. (2007). Eye movements of young and older adults during reading. *Psychology and Aging, 22*, 84–93.

Kemper, S., & Mitzner, T. L. (2001). Language production and comprehension. In J. E. Birren & K. W. Schaie (Eds.), *Handbook of the psychology of aging* (pp. 378–398). San Diego, CA: Academic Press.

Kinsella, K., & Velkoff, V. (2001). *An aging world: 2001.* Washington, DC: U.S. Government Printing Office, series P95/01-1.

Kramer, A. F., Hahn, S., & Gopher, D. (1999). Task coordination and aging: Explorations of executive control processes in the task switching paradigm. *Acta Psychologica, 101*, 339–378.

Kramer, A. F., Larish, J. F., & Strayer, D. L. (1995). Training for attentional control in dual task settings: A comparison of young and old adults. *Journal of Experimental Psychology: Applied, 1*, 50–76.

Kramer, A. F., Larish, J. F., Weber, T. A., & Bardell, L. (1999). Training for executive control: Task coordination strategies and aging. In D. Gopher & A. Koriat (Eds.), *Attention and performance XVII: Cognitive regulation of performance: Interaction of theory and application* (pp. 617–652). Cambridge, MA: MIT Press.

Kyllonen, P. C., & Christal, R. E. (1990). Reasoning ability is (little more than) working-memory capacity?! *Intelligence, 14*, 389–433.

Lewis, K. L., & Zelinski, E. M. (2010). List and text recall differ in their predictors: Replication over samples and time. *Journals of Gerontology: Psychological Sciences, 65B*, 449–458.

Li, K. Z. H., Lindenberger, U., Freund, A. M., & Baltes, P. B. (2001). Walking while memorizing: Age-related differences in compensatory behavior. *Psychological Science, 12*, 230–237.

Li, S., Schmiedek, F., Huxhold, O., Rocke, C., Smith, J., & Lindenberger, U. (2008). Working memory plasticity in old age: Practice gain, transfer, and maintenance. *Psychology and Aging, 23*, 731–742.

Light, L. L., Zelinski, E. M., & Moore, M. G. (1982). Adult age differences in inferential reasoning from new information. *Journal of Experimental Psychology: Learning, Memory, and Cognition, 8*, 435–447.

Mahncke, H. W., Bronstone, A., & Merzenich, M. M. (2006a). Brain plasticity and functional losses in the aged: Scientific bases for a novel intervention. *Progress in Brain Research, 157*, 81–109.

Mahncke, H. W., Connor, B. B., Appelman, J., Ahsanuddin, O. N., Hardy, J. L., Wood, R. A., et al. (2006b). Memory enhancement in healthy older adults using a brain plasticity-based training program: A randomized, controlled study. *Proceedings of the National Academy of Science, 103*, 12523–12528.

McElree, B. (2001). Working memory and focal attention. *Journal of Experimental Psychology: Learning, Memory, and Cognition, 27*, 817–835.

McGinnis, D., & Zelinski, E. M. (2000). Understanding unfamiliar words: The influence of processing resources, vocabulary knowledge, and age. *Psychology and Aging, 15*, 335–350.

Miyake, A., Friedman, N. P., Emerson, M. J., Witzki, A. H., Howerter, A., & Wager, T. D. (2000). The unity and diversity of executive functions and their contributions to complex "frontal lobe" tasks: A latent variable analysis. *Cognitive Psychology, 41*, 49–100.

Murphy, K. M., & Topel, R. H. (2006). The value of health and longevity. *Journal of Political Economics, 114*, 871–904.

Oberauer, K. (2002). Access to information in working memory. Exploring the focus of attention. *Journal of Experimental Psychology: Learning, Memory, and Cognition, 28*, 411–421.

Oberauer, K. (2006). Is the focus of attention in working memory expanded through practice? *Journal of Experimental Psychology: Learning, Memory, and Cognition, 32(2)*, 197–214.

Paxton, J. L., Barch, D. M., Racine, C. A., & Braver, T. S. (2008) Cognitive control, goal maintenance, and prefrontal function in healthy aging. *Cerebral Cortex, 18*, 1010–1028.

Rebok, G. W., Carlson , M. C., & Langbaum, B. S. (2007). Training and maintaining memory abilities in healthy older adults: Traditional and novel approaches. *Journals of Gerontology: Psychological Sciences, 62B*, 53–61.

Salthouse, T. A. (1996). The processing-speed theory of adult age differences in cognition. *Psychological Review, 103*, 403–428.

Salthouse, T. A. (2004). What and when of cognitive aging. *Current Directions in Psychological Science, 13*, 140–144.

Smith, G. E., Housen, P., Yaffe, K., Ruff, R., Kennison, R. F., Mahncke, H. W., & Zelinski, E. M. (2009). A cognitive training program based on principles of brain plasticity: Results from the improvement in memory with plasticity-based adaptive cognitive training (IMPACT) study. *Journal of the American Geriatrics Society, 57*, 594–603.

Stigdotter Neely, A. S., & Bäckman, L. (1995). Effects of multifactorial memory training in old age: Generalizability across tasks and individuals. *Journals of Gerontology: Psychological Sciences, 50B*, 134–140.

Stine-Morrow, E. A. L., & Basak, C. (2011). Cognitive interventions. In K. W. Schaie & S. L. Willis (Eds.), *Handbook of the psychology of aging*, seventh edition (pp. 153–171). New York: Elsevier.

Stine-Morrow, E. A. L., Miller, L. M. S., Gagne, D. D., & Hertzog, C. (2008). Self-regulated reading in adulthood. *Psychology and Aging, 23*, 131–153.

Stine-Morrow, E. A. L., Parisi, J. M., Morrow, D. G., & Park, D. C. (2008). The effects of an engaged lifestyle on cognitive vitality: A field experiment. *Psychology and Aging, 23*, 778–786.

Storandt, M. (2008). Cognitive deficits in the early stages of Alzheimer's disease. *Current Directions in Psychological Science, 17*, 198–202.

United Nations (2002). *Report of the Second World Assembly on Aging.* Madrid, Spain: United Nations.

Vaughan, L., Basak, C., Hartman, M., & Verhaeghen, P. (2008). Aging and working memory inside and outside the focus of attention: Dissociations of availability and accessibility. *Aging, Neuropsychology and Cognition, 15,* 1–22.

Verhaeghen, P., & Basak, C. (2005). Ageing and switching of the focus of attention in working memory: Results from a modified N-back task. *The Quarterly Journal of Experimental Psychology, 58A,* 134–154.

Verhaeghen, P., Cerella, J., & Basak, C. (2004). A working-memory workout: How to expand the focus of serial attention from one to four items, in ten hours or less, *Journal of Experimental Psychology: Learning, Memory and Cognition, 30,* 1322–1337.

Verhaeghen, P., & Cerella, J. (2002). Aging, executive control, and attention: A review of meta-analyses. *Neuroscience and Biobehavioral Reviews, 26,* 849–857.

Verhaeghen, P., Marcoen, A., & Goossens, L. (1992). Improving memory performance in the aged through mnemonic training: A meta-analytic study. *Psychology and Aging, 7,* 242–251.

Verhaeghen, P., & Salthouse, T. A. (1997). Meta-analyses of age-cognition relations in adulthood: Estimates of linear and nonlinear age effects and structural models. *Psychological Bulletin, 122,* 231–249.

Wasylyshyn, C., Verhaeghen, P., & Sliwinski, M. J. (2011). Aging and task switching: A meta-analysis. *Psychology and Aging, 26,* 15–20.

West, R. L., Bagwell, D. K., & Dark-Freudeman, A. (2008). Self-efficacy and memory aging: The impact of a memory intervention based on self-efficacy. *Aging, Neuropsychology, and Cognition, 15,* 302–329.

Wilson, R. S., Beckett, L. A., Barnes, L. L., Schneider, J. A., Bach, J., Evans, D. A., & Bennett, D. A. (2002). Individual differences in rates of change in cognitive abilities of older persons. *Psychology and Aging, 17,* 179–193.

Wilson, R. S., Li, Y., Bienias, J. L., & Bennett, D. A. (2006). Cognitive decline in old age: Separating retest effects from the effects of growing older. *Psychology and Aging, 21,* 774–789.

Zelinski, E. M. (2009). Far transfer in cognitive training of older adults. *Restorative Neurology and Neuroscience, 27,* 455–471.

Zelinski, E. M., & Burnight, K. P. (1997). Sixteen-year longitudinal and time lag changes in memory and cognition in older adults. *Psychology and Aging, 12,* 503–513.

Zelinski, E. M., Dalton, S. E., & Smith, G. E. (2011). Consumer-based brain fitness programs. In A. Larue & P. Hartman-Stein (Eds.), *Enhancing cognitive fitness in adults: A guide to the use and development of community programs* (pp. 45–66). New York: Springer.

Zelinski, E. M., & Gilewski, M. J. (2004). A 10-item Rasch modeled memory self efficacy scale. *Aging and Mental Health, 8,* 293–306.

Zelinski, E. M., Gilewski, M. J., & Schaie, K. W. (1993) Individual differences in cross-sectional and three-year longitudinal memory performance across the adult lifespan. *Psychology and Aging, 8,* 176–186.

Zelinski, E. M., & Kennison, R. F. (2007). Not your father's test scores: Cohort reduces psychometric aging effects. *Psychology and Aging, 22,* 546–557.

Zelinski, E. M., & Lewis, K. L. (2003). Adult age differences in multiple cognitive functions: Differentiation, dedifferentiation or process-specific change? *Psychology and Aging, 18,* 727–745.

Zelinski, E. M., & Reyes, R. (2009). Cognitive benefits of computer games for older adults. *Gerontechnology, 8,* 220–235.

Zelinski, E. M., Spina, L. M., Yaffe, K., Ruff, R., Kennison, R. F., Mahncke, H. W., & Smith, G. E. (2011). Improvement in memory with plasticity-based adaptive cognitive training (IMPACT): Results of the 3-month follow-up. *Journal of the American Geriatrics Society, 59,* 258–265.

Part III

Working Memory and Expertise

6

Working Memory that Mediates Experts' Performance

Why it is Qualitatively Different from Traditional Working Memory

K. ANDERS ERICSSON

Department of Psychology, Florida State University, Tallahassee, FL, USA

JERAD H. MOXLEY

Department of Psychology, Florida State University, Tallahassee, FL, USA

*I*n the late nineteenth century the science of psychology (general psychology) was established as a laboratory science, and the research focused on identifying basic processes and associated general laws of learning and memory (Ebbinghaus, 1885/1913) that would mediate all types of cognitive activity. During this pioneering time scientists made a fundamental distinction between attention/awareness (primary memory) and long-term memory (secondary memory) based on their introspective salience (James, 1890). Because the introspective method was eventually unable to resolve scientific issues in the early twentieth century (Ericsson & Simon, 1993), researchers turned away from complex mental mechanisms toward behavior and observable associations between stimuli and responses (Watson, 1913). In the pioneering research on telegraphers, Bryan and Harter (1899) had shown that many skills, such as sending and receiving Morse code, were gradually acquired during extended periods of training and thus were very complex and mediated by a massive number of acquired domain-specific associations. Because the same processes were thought to mediate the full range of behavior, it was, therefore, reasonable to turn away from the study of complex skills and study simple paired-associate learning in the laboratory, where the complete process of learning associations between unfamiliar items, such as nonsense syllables, could be studied within an hour-long session. Although there were a small number of researchers who continued to study complex skills it was not until the 1950s that a large number of American psychologists became interested in research on more complex cognitive processes.

In his influential paper on the magical number seven plus/minus two, George Miller (1956) demonstrated a highly reproducible performance limit for immediate recall of rapidly presented items. He showed that immediate recall was limited to around seven unrelated chunks (familiar patterns) and this type of recall was assumed to measure individuals' limited short-term memory (STM). The capacity-limited STM became the central mechanism constraining cognitive processes in the new information-processing model of human cognition (Newell & Simon, 1972). It is important to note that the new concept of STM did not rely on introspective reports; instead it was a theoretical construct meant to explain the capacity limits on performance on a wide range of tasks involving thinking, such as concept formation (Bourne, Goldstein, & Link, 1964), problem solving (Atwood, Masson, & Polson, 1980; Newell & Simon, 1972), and decision making (Payne, 1976; Svenson, 1979). Once the human range of capacity limits had been established, researchers started to examine the effects of individual differences in STM capacity and to what extent these differences could be explained by differences in performance. The traditional method to measure the capacity of a given individual's STM used direct tests of immediate memory, such as memory spans for digits and consonants, reviewed by Miller (1956). In seminal work Baddeley and Hitch (1974; Baddeley, 1986) argued that the critical limit did not concern only storage but concerned working memory, which required measurement of capacity both for processes and for storage of intermediate results. In support of that proposal researchers found that higher correlations to target performance were obtained by memory tests that measure both storage and processing (Daneman & Carpenter, 1980, and later Turner & Engle, 1989). This is the theoretical background for the laboratory study of the domain-general capacity limits of working memory at the time of the first modern studies of the memory and working memory of experts.

This chapter will start with a review of the history of the study of working memory of experts. We will start with the classic theory of expertise by Simon and Chase (1973) and progress to more complex theories of working memory (Baddeley, 1986) to theories that view working memory as an acquired and integrated aspect of the experts' skill (Ericsson & Kintsch, 1995) and other extensions of the classic theory of expert memory (Gobet & Simon, 1996; Vicente & Wang, 1998). Our review chapter will focus on some central theoretical issues related to working memory mediating expert performance. Is the working memory of experts mediated by the general working memory system, as assessed by traditional psychometric tests? If it is not, what kind of acquired mechanisms can explain the experts' working memory and its large capacity? If this enhanced working memory is associated with higher skilled performance, how can one explain its acquisition and its relation to increased task performance?

BACKGROUND INFORMATION

The start of modern laboratory research on expertise is typically credited to the work of Herbert Simon and Bill Chase (Simon & Chase, 1973). They proposed an information-processing model for expertise in chess, where skilled chess players were hypothesized to retrieve a chess move from long-term memory (LTM) based on recognized patterns (chunks) of chess pieces in the current chess position. One of the most important characteristics of this model was that it explained expertise as a gradual acquisition of increasingly complex familiar patterns (particular configurations of chess pieces) and thus did not need to assume any superior capacity of chess masters to maintain patterns (chunks) to explain their superior chess-playing performance. The most compelling feature of the model was that it could also explain very large differences in the recall performance for briefly presented chess positions as a function of the players' chess skill.

Many decades earlier Djakow, Petrowski, and Rudik (1927) had documented skilled chess players' superior memory for chess positions, but that their superior memory was limited to chess stimuli and was not observed for other types of materials and information. About two decades later Adrian de Groot (1978/1946) completed his pioneering research on highly skilled chess players and how they identify the best move for a position. He instructed the chess players to think aloud while they searched for the best move and found that the world-class players were able to find good moves very rapidly so he would present the chess position only for some three to 15 seconds before requesting a chess move, and then de Groot would ask the chess players to give retrospective reports on their thought processes. He found that with even very short presentations of an unfamiliar chess position, highly skilled players were able to virtually perfectly reproduce all the pieces in the position, whereas less skilled club players were only able to remember the locations of a fraction of the pieces.

In a classic series of studies Chase and Simon (1973) converted the move selection task into an explicit test of memory for chess pieces in positions taken from regular games of chess masters, and presented the positions to players differing in level of chess expertise. The chess positions were presented for five seconds followed by the participant's immediate recall of the position by placing pieces on a chess board. Most notably, Chase and Simon (1973) also presented stimuli with randomly arranged chess pieces under the same conditions and with immediate recall. For stimuli reflecting game positions, the performance of the three studied chess players was strikingly different as a function of their level of expertise. The chess master was much better than the skilled chess player, who in turn was better than the beginner in recalling positions from chess games. In contrast, for the randomly scrambled chess positions there was no reliable difference and all three chess players performed equally poorly only recalling a handful of chess pieces—essentially the same level of recall by the beginner for positions from chess games. Furthermore, Chase and Simon (1973) monitored the process of recall and found that the more skilled players would place several pieces in quick succession, which is consistent with their hypothesis of patterns and chunks stored in LTM. In sum, they found clear evidence that the difference between chess players was not in terms of the number of patterns recalled but in terms of the number of pieces contained in each pattern. Hence, the experts' larger storehouse of game-related patterns in LTM permitted them to find meaningful patterns in the game positions but not in the randomly re-arranged stimuli. This finding supports the hypothesis that all chess players are able to hold about the same number of chunks in short-term memory as Miller (1956) had found in laboratory experiments using more traditional stimuli, such as digits, consonants, and unrelated words.

The Chase-Simon paradigm provided a new laboratory method for studying differences related to expertise by studying differences in immediate memory between experts and less skilled individuals for representative stimuli from game situations and for random/unstructured stimuli. Their original finding of an expert advantage in memory recall for representative situations but not for unstructured domains was replicated in many other domains, such as bridge (Charness, 1979; Engle & Bukstel, 1978), Go (Reitman, 1976), Othello (Wolff, Mitchell, & Frey, 1984), medicine (Norman, Brooks, & Allen, 1989), electronic circuit diagrams (Egan & Schwartz, 1979), computer programming (McKeithen, Reitman, Rueter, & Hirtle. 1981), dance (Starkes, Deakin, Lindley, & Crisp, 1987), basketball (Allard, Graham, & Paarsalu, 1980), field hockey (Starkes & Deakin, 1984), and volleyball (Bourgeaud & Abernethy, 1987) (see Ericsson and Lehmann, 1996, for a more complete review).

CURRENT EVIDENCE

Challenges against the Pattern-Action Mechanism in the Simon-Chase Theory of Expertise

The Simon-Chase theory of expertise (Simon & Chase, 1973) focused virtually completely on slow acquisition of patterns (chunks) and pattern-action associations in LTM. In contrast, the empirical paper on experts' memory by Chase and Simon (1973) examined many aspects of chess players' memory beyond their immediate memory for briefly presented information, such as their use of the mind's eye for planning and storage in LTM of sequences of chess moves. Nonetheless, it was their theory of expertise based on the mediation of chunks kept in the capacity-limited STM that stimulated other research on experts and their superior memory.

One of the first criticisms was given by Neil Charness in his dissertation supervised by Bill Chase. Charness (1976) found that if one interfered with STM by executing STM-demanding tasks immediately after the five-second presentation of the chess position, but before recall, the recall of skilled chess players was virtually unaffected. This finding clearly raised doubt that during the normal memory tests with five-second presentation of chess positions that the expert stored pointers to the patterns (chunks) only in STM. If the information was stored in both LTM and STM then it was not clear how the capacity of STM constrained the level of recall.

Another criticism centered on the trainability of performance on tasks assumed to measure the fixed capacity of STM. In an extended training study Bill Chase and

Anders Ericsson (Chase & Ericsson, 1981, 1982; Ericsson, Chase, & Faloon, 1980) showed that memory performance on the digit span task could increase from a normal level of 7 digits to over 80 digits. In some research, more directly related to memory for chess positions, Ericsson and Harris (1990) found that a participant without any chess skill was able to increase her recall level from that of a beginner to that of a chess master within 50 hours of training. The trainability of memory for briefly presented chess positions was later replicated by Gobet and Jackson (2002). Even skilled chess players do not have any experience of memorizing briefly presented chess positions and thus they seem to change their cognitive processes and improve their performance with practice memorizing chess positions (see Ericsson, Patel, & Kintsch, 2000, for a review).

A more general criticism was directed toward the Simon-Chase hypothesis that the immediate memory task and performance on representative tasks, such as selecting the best move for a chess position, were mediated by the same processes and memory capacity. For example, tournament performance in chess is more closely associated with performance on a selecting-the-best-move task than by the memory performance for briefly presented chess positions (see Ericsson et al., 2000, for a review). More generally, Daneman and Carpenter (1980) found that individual differences in comprehension of texts was not correlated with memory performance on the digit span task (a traditional test of STM), but was correlated with a task that attempted to measure both processing and storage of information. This finding has led to a very large body of research examining the correlation between memory tasks measuring both processing and storage, such as the sentence span (Daneman & Carpenter, 1980) and the OSPAN (Turner & Engle, 1989), and the target performance on a wide range of laboratory tasks. In the next major section of our chapter we will examine whether expert performance is correlated with individual differences for these types of memory tasks that measure capacity of the general working memory. We will first explicate the working memory demands while performing representative tasks from the experts' domain of expertise.

From Experts' Working Memory to Memory Demands During Expert Performance

The Chase-Simon paradigm altered the focus on de Groot's (1978/1946) early studies of selecting moves for chess positions to maximizing immediate memory performance for game positions. Ericsson and Smith (1991) argued that researchers needed to refocus on the core performance in the domain of expertise, such as selecting the best moves for chess positions, and continue the research approach initiated by de Groot (1978/1946). In order to measure performance it is necessary to give participants similar tasks many times, notwithstanding the threat of changes in performance due to practice effects. However, if one were to test the defining performance in a domain of expertise it would be very surprising if a few more hours of testing would change the performance of skilled participants with hundreds or thousands of hours of related performance. In contrast, when one is giving participants a task that they have never encountered before, then a few hours of practice can have a substantial effect, as demonstrated by the training studies reported earlier.

Ericsson and Smith (1991) proposed the expert performance approach, where the first step involves the demonstration of reproducibly superior performance and how this performance can be captured by representative tasks. De Groot (1978/1946) had already demonstrated how superior chess performance can be captured by presenting chess positions and asking participants to select the best move. Subsequent research has shown that this general method of presenting representative situations from real chess games and requiring participants to generate the best available actions provides the best available measure of chess skill that predicts performance in chess tournaments (Ericsson et al., 2000; van der Maas & Wagenmakers, 2005). The second step is to identify the mechanisms that mediate the reproducibly superior performance. This is typically accomplished by a combination of tracing the processes on the representative task and experimental manipulations (Ericsson, 2006a). In his pioneering research de Groot (1978/1946) instructed his participants to think aloud while they selected the best move for the presented chess positions. From the protocols de Groot (1978/1946) found that the chess players selected a series of moves one move at a time to examine the consequences of playing one of the possible moves for the chess position. After considering one move they may turn to evaluate another and so on. This data implies that skilled chess players must be able to generate a large amount of information in working memory to be able to evaluate the consequences of mentally moving some five to 15 chess pieces. To his surprise, de Groot (1978/1946) found that both world-class chess players and skilled club players explored move sequences to a similar depth. This null finding, however, has not held up to further research, and higher chess skill is associated with deeper search (Charness, 1981b).

Working Memory Theories for Experts Based on Encoding and Retrieval from LTM

The most influential theories of working memory defined working memory as transiently activated information in memory, which precluded reliance on storage in LTM (Baddeley, 1986). This model of working memory consisted of two slave systems that could hold phonemic information (the rehearsal loop) and visuo-spatial information (the visuo-spatial scratch pad) that supplemented the central system of attention. Some of the most compelling evidence for supplementary memory systems comes from research where participants were asked to engage in primary tasks along with a task that was designed to interfere with storage in the rehearsal loop (for example, by saying "hiya, hiya," and so on during the trial) or in the visuo-spatial scratch pad (by engaging in a concurrent task involving visual scanning). In a wide range of laboratory tasks Baddeley (1986) found evidence for an interaction where one of these dual tasks interfered with performance more, thus implying that single-task performance would have relied more on storage in the slave system with the most degraded performance.

This dual-task methodology has been applied to some types of skilled performance. One of the earliest studies was conducted by Chase and Ericsson (1981), who had one of their trained experts (SF) on digit-span perform the digit span task under several conditions. Based on their earlier experiments they hypothesized that

SF segmented the orally presented digits into groups of three or four digits using the phonemic buffer and then encoded the groups with associations to running times and other meaningful categories, ideas, and patterns in LTM. In order to reconstruct the linear order of the digit groups at the time of recall, SF constructed a retrieval structure (Chase & Ericsson, 1981, 1982). SF's retrieval, structure was found to be hierarchically organized so that at the lowest level was a meaningfully encoded group of digits. These digit groups were then grouped into super groups with initially three groups where each digit group had associations to the spatial position within the super-group (left, middle, and right) in hierarchical manner. Thus at each point during the presentation the expert digit-span participant would have stored essentially all of the digit groups in LTM, except for the current group of digits held in the rehearsal buffer. When Chase and Ericsson (1981) asked SF to say "hiya, hiya, hiya, . . ." while performing the digit span task his performance was only reduced from around 26 (standard presentation) to around 24 (chanting hiya). This finding is consistent with his ability to memorize digits in LTM and may have primarily interfered with his ability to generate a phonemic code to maximize the storage capacity of the phonemic buffer (four to six digits) to around three to four digits. SF was also asked to copy and rotate geometrical figures while he performed the digit-span task, but his performance was not reliably different from his regular digit span of 26 with standard presentation. These findings demonstrate that SF's digit-span was not affected by the visual suppression of the visuo-spatial scratchpad and only slightly affected by the concurrent chanting. SF's resilience, despite the effects of concurrent task interference with transient working memory, supports the argument that with training it is possible to acquire memory skills that permit vastly superior memory performance on tasks that measure untrained participants' highly constrained working memory.

Chase and Ericsson (1982) demonstrated that memory skills similar to the trained digit-span experts were acquired by a mental calculator who squared five-digit numbers and a waiter, who memorized dinner orders from up to 16 customers without writing anything down (Ericsson & Polson, 1988). Over a decade later Ericsson and Kintsch (1995) generalized Chase and Ericsson's Skilled Memory theory to account for a wide range of demonstrations of increased working memory capacity in skilled and expert performers. The primary challenge for Long-Term Working Memory (LTWM), using LTM as the means to support working memory, is attaining rapid encoding of intermediate products and new information in LTM in such a manner that it can be efficiently retrieved when needed during sub-sequent processing. This means that the memory skill is acquired and developed in parallel with the increases in task-related performance. Consequently, increased working memory capacity is limited to the types of memory that are essential to improved levels of task performance rather than some level of memory per-formance that increases for any type of domain-related materials (Ericsson et al., 2000; Ericsson & Roring, 2007). Inconsistent with Vicente and Wang's (1998) constraint attunement hypothesis, increased experience in the domain is not always associated with superior memory performance for representative stimuli in the domain. Ericsson and colleagues (Ericsson & Lehmann, 1996; Ericsson et al., 2000) enumerated many examples of highly experienced experts who failed to demonstrate superior memory. For example, expert musicians did not show superior memory for melodies that were auditorily presented compared to less skilled individuals (Sloboda & Parker, 1985), expert actors were not superior to less skilled individuals for memorizing text (Intons-Peterson & Smyth, 1987; Noice 1993), and map experts did not show better memory for the traditional types of maps (Gilhooly, Wood, Kinnear, & Green, 1988).

Domain-Specific and Generalizable Characteristics of Experts' Working Memory

In the main part of this chapter we will review evidence from experts' working memory performance and whether generalized innate capacities for transient working memory continue to mediate highly skilled and expert performance. The most common procedure for establishing the involvement of general working memory is to measure its capacity with some standardized test, such as the operation span test (Turner & Engle, 1989), and then show that these individual differences correlate with the experts' memory performance. A slightly less direct method is to measure individuals' basic general abilities such as fluid intelligence and basic memory abilities, and assess their correlations with current performance of expert performers or correlation with future performance of beginners in a domain. A highly significant correlation of the latter type would imply that basic abilities are predictive of children's and adolescents' potential for high performance in a given domain.

To assess the evidence that would more directly support the hypothesis of acquired memory skill based on LTWM, one could also review evidence for the distinctive characteristics of LTWM. The acquired memory skill hypothesis predicts that participants relying on LTWM would reveal memory at the end of the trial, when unexpectedly asked to recall their thoughts and other relevant information. In contrast, the hypothesis of performance mediated by transient working memory would predict the absence of recallable memory from the processing on a trial. Furthermore, the acquired skill hypothesis would predict that the mechanisms of LTWM have to be acquired through training in a manner coordinated with the development of other aspects mediating superior performance. In the beginning there would be no acquired LTWM skills to support the memory performance in the domain-specific task, and thus one would predict that beginners would rely on more general memory strategies and skills—similar to those used in unfamiliar memory tasks in the laboratory.

The most influential contemporary model for acquisition of everyday skills, such as typing, driving, and other skills, was proposed by Fitts and Posner (1967) over 40 years ago. This model consists of three different stages and is illustrated in the lower arm of Figure 6.1. When individuals are introduced to an unfamiliar type of activity, they first need to understand the rules and acquire the necessary knowledge, For example, when someone tries to learn to type by touch they need to memorize the locations of all the keys so they can strike them without looking. During the first "cognitive" stage (see lower arm of Figure 6.1) behavior is intentionally generated and thus is typically slow and error prone. These errors lead to clear observable consequences such as a missed ball in tennis or incorrectly typed words and thus can be corrected and gradually improved by repeated practice opportunities. When individuals are able to learn and execute sequences of associated actions they enter the second "associative" stage. For most recreational activities such as skiing, tennis, and driving a car, as well as professional activities such as telegraphy and typing (see Ericsson, 2006b for a review), 50 hours of experience is generally sufficient for individuals to reach an acceptable level of performance in the domain of activity. With more experience the execution becomes increasingly automated and the performers cease monitoring many aspects of their behavior and reach the third "autonomous" phase (Fitts & Posner, 1967). Based on this model Ackerman (1988, 2000) proposed that different types of individual differences would be associated with different stages. For the first stage, Ackerman (1988) predicted and found that performance on tests of general working memory and general cognitive abilities would be predictive of performance in the beginning of training, but when performance became increasingly fluid and smooth this new performance would reflect different characteristics, such as visuo-spatial abilities, and eventually, after extended acquisition, the resulting automated performance would correlate with basic perceptual-motor abilities. Given that we are focusing on experts' memory performance our predictions will differ from Ackerman's (1988, 2000) because he studied primarily comparatively simple tasks, where automated performance was attained within five to ten hours. Our hypothesis about acquired memory skills predicts that the domain-specific memory representation is refined and improved in parallel with the increased skill and will continue to be changed with further training, thus corresponding to the upper arm of Figure 6.1. The acquired memory skills will become increasingly able to manage the working memory demands and eventually will solely determine the experts' performance on the domain-related memory tasks. With very high levels of performance in the domain, we would not predict performance on representative tasks to be determined by general working memory processes.

Finally, Ericsson and Kintsch (1995; see also Ericsson et al., 2000, and Ericsson & Roring, 2007) argue that the superior performance on a memory task that has not been explicitly practiced can be explained by the expert's ability to use mechanisms acquired to support representative task performance, which can allow a high level of performance on the memory task. For example, expert chess players do not spend much time, if any, memorizing briefly presented chess positions, yet they show highly superior memory when tested on this task. It is thus necessary to develop an account of how the structure of the mechanisms for the representative performance in the domain is acquired through effective practice and how these mechanisms can sometimes be relied on to generate superior performance on an unfamiliar memory task. In some cases the match between the demands of the memory tasks and the acquired mechanisms is very good. For example, in chess, skilled players must rapidly encode chess position in LTWM to support their analysis during move selection. The same mechanisms mediate superior memory for briefly presented chess positions in the memory task, leading to a high correlation between level of skill and memory. In other domains the match is poor, as in the case of expert actors and concert pianists, and no reliable memory

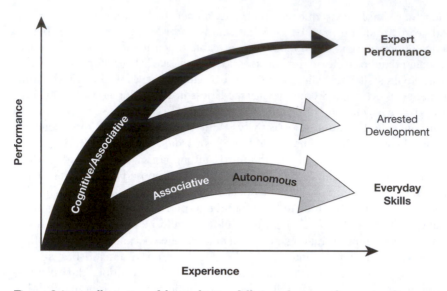

Figure 6.1   An illustration of the qualitative difference between the course of improvement of expert performance and of everyday activities. The goal for everyday activities is to reach a satisfactory level that is stable and "autonomous" as rapidly as possible. After individuals pass through the "cognitive" and "associative" phases, they can generate their performance virtually automatically with a minimal amount of effort (see the gray/white plateau at the bottom of the graph). In contrast, expert performers counteract automaticity by developing increasingly complex mental representations to attain higher levels of control of their performance and will therefore remain within the "cognitive" and "associative" phases. Some experts will at some point in their career give up their commitment to seeking excellence and thus terminate regular engagement in deliberate practice to further improve performance, which results in premature automation of their performance. (Adapted from "The scientific study of expert levels of performance: General implications for optimal learning and creativity" by K. A. Ericsson in *High Ability Studies*, 9, p. 90. Copyright 1998 by European Council for High Ability).

superiority is found for experts, as reviewed in an earlier section. Let us now review evidence relevant to these hypotheses; we will start with the hypothesis that predicts that general working memory and general cognitive abilities mediate experts' performance, and in particular, their memory performance.

Individual Differences in General Working Memory and General Cognitive Abilities

It is assumed that general capacities and basic abilities are very stable across adulthood, but they can develop until adulthood and are subject to decreases due to aging. Within the research on expert performance, recent reviews (Ericsson, 2007a, 2007b; Ericsson, Roring, & Nandagopal, 2007a, 2007b) have not uncovered reproducible evidence for basic and unmodifiable characteristics that are predictive of future level of expert performance, with the exception of height and body size.

These reviews do not, however, preclude the possibility that future research will uncover such relations between expert performance and individual genes or combinations of genes.

One of the challenges for this type of research is that we need objective measures of reproducibly superior performance in the studied domain of expertise. Unfortunately, some researchers have studied groups of professionals based on self-nomination or social judgments of expertise by peers or subordinates. In many domains experienced professionals do not always exhibit superior perform-ance to less skilled individuals (Ericsson, 2006b), as exemplified by translators (Jääskeläinen, 2010), computer programmers (Doane, Pellegrino, & Klatzky, 1990), nurses (Ericsson, Whyte, & Ward, 2007), and doctors (Ericsson, 2004).

When we limit our review to only objective measures of performance in domains of skill, we find support for our hypothesis that general cognitive ability and intelligence may be correlated with initial performance on a new task. However, after extended periods of skill acquisition the relation between performance and general ability is no longer statistically reliable.

In the domain of chess, the level of attained chess performance has often been assumed to be highly correlated with individual differences in intelligence and visuo-spatial memory. Consistent with these assumptions, Robbins et al. (1996) found that chess performance was interfered with by a concurrent visuo-spatial task, namely, performing a pre-determined sequence of key presses on a hidden keypad. This concurrent task interfered with memory for briefly presented chess positions—a decrease of around 85% from the score obtained in the control condition. Performing this concurrent visuo-spatial task also interfered with the selection of a move for presented chess positions—a decrement in the score of around 30 percent. In contrast, neither of these two tasks was significantly influenced by concurrent articulatory suppression, which involved saying "the" once a second at the beat of a metronome. These findings support the view that visuo-spatial memory is critical to chess performance.

In an early study of high-skilled chess players Doll and Mayr (1987) failed to find a significant correlation between chess ratings and scores from an intelligence test. There have been a few studies of children, where one reported a significant association with one aspect of general intelligence (Frydman & Lynn, 1992). In an exemplary longitudinal study of children's acquisition of chess skill, Bilalić, McLeod, and Gobet (2007) found that the predictive power of IQ diminishes dramatically as skill increases and did not predict rate of improvement after accounting for practice activity. In fact when Bilalić et al. (2007) restricted their analysis to rated chess players in their sample they found a negative correlation with intelligence, probably due to a negative correlation between practice and intelligence. Similarly, Waters, Gobet, and Leyden (2002) did not find a significant correlation between tests of visuo-spatial ability and chess skill. In another domain, namely the Japanese game Go, Masunaga and Horn (2001) studied over 250 players at different levels of expertise and found only significant negative relations between general abilities, such as fluid intelligence and general working memory, and memory and performance within the domain of Go. Studies of performance in games, such as chess and Go, do not find evidence for a mediation of general cognitive abilities for individuals who have acquired domain-specific mechanisms that mediate their superior skilled performance.

Similar findings have been observed in music performance. Ruthsatz, Detterman, Griscom, and Cirullo (2007) found that intelligence was correlated with music performance at the introductory level of musicians in the school band, but not for advanced musicians at a music academy. They did, however, find that the average IQ of the academy musicians was significantly higher than average. Similarly, Doll and Mayr (1987) found that the sample of chess masters had an average IQ similar to that of college students. Some researchers have argued that these findings demonstrate that there is a threshold of intelligence that is necessary for reaching an expert level of performance. Unfortunately, there is currently no conclusive evidence explaining the group differences of experts. There is compelling evidence that individuals with an IQ below the average 100 can become chess masters (Grabner, Neubauer, & Stern, 2006) or even an international master in chess (Doll & Mayr, 1987). At the same time Grabner et al. (2006) found significant moderate correlations between chess rating and measures of intelligence, particularly verbal intelligence. The exploratory nature of Grabner et al.'s study requires that it should be replicated in the future with standardized methods to recruit participants and to collect data on estimated hours of engagement in chess playing and solitary practice.

Furthermore, some top players in Scrabble have below average verbal ability (Tuffiash, Roring, & Ericsson, 2007). Another issue is that many educational environments, such as music academies and universities, require their students to achieve high grades and high scores on admissions tests that are likely to preclude students with low IQ scores to be admitted. When Unterrainer, Kaller, Halsband, and Rahm (2006) compared a group of chess players with a group matched on age and education, they found no differences in fluid intelligence nor visuo-spatial memory, although they did find a difference in ability to solve the Tower of London task, possibly due to the fact that chess players persisted longer before giving their responses. Similarly, Helmbold, Rammsayer, and Altenmuller (2005) compared a group of music majors to other university students and did not find any differences in intelligence. There is now a rather compelling body of evidence that documents a large number of differences in the brain activity and brain structure of musicians compared to non-musicians. The largest difference in memory performance concerns memory for auditory stimuli (Cohen, Evans, Horowitz, & Wolfe, 2011). Hence, the current evidence clearly supports that observed differences are the result of music training rather than the indicators of underlying innate abilities (Trainor & Corrigall, 2010).

One of the domains with the obvious demand for working memory is simultaneous translation. While engaging in simultaneous interpreting, the interpreter must be both listening and speaking at the same time. The spoken translation lags the listening (current speech generated by the speaker) by two to six words (Christoffels & de Groot, 2005). Numerous investigators have therefore conducted research comparing the working memory capacity of professional interpreters, bilinguals, and monolinguals. Although some studies have found significant differences between groups, recent reviews argue that tests of general memory and traditional working memory cannot explain the abilities of professional interpreters to simultaneously listen and verbalize the translation of earlier speech (Liu, 2008). In a comprehensive review, Signorelli (2008) shows how confounding influences of age, level of interpreting experience, and differences in method might explain the pattern of differences and lack of differences for tests, with two exceptions. Professional interpreters show consistently higher performance on tests of non-word repetition and the reading span test. Signorelli (2008) argues that the professional demands of interpreters are consistent with the differences in performance. Interpreters need the skill to retain non-words to maintain names of people. The reading span test where people need to hold on to the meaning of presented items while comprehending the next sentence seem to mimic some aspects of the situation in simultaneous translation. In a review paper Ericsson (2010/2001) explicitly looked for research that objectively measured the ability to interpret by having several interpreters perform the same set of interpreting tasks. Only a small number of studies have developed tasks for objective measurement. Dillinger (1994) found that professional interpreters were able to translate more units of meaning than a group of untrained bilinguals. In a longitudinal study Gerver, Longley, Long, and Lambert (1984) examined changes in performance during an intensive course for interpreters and found that logical memory and depth of understanding in one's first language predicted the quality of their translations at the end of the course. The most predictive factor for the quality of simultaneous translation at the end of the course was their ability to generate synonyms and missing words in texts. These findings are consistent with many translation researchers' arguments (Ericsson, 2010/2001) that professional interpreters do not reach an automatic phase but retain their monitoring and control over the translation process by developing increasingly complex representations. Similarly, Moser-Mercer (2000) documents how interpreters improve their performance by gradually eliminating certain types of mistakes. The research studying professional interpreters is consistent with the hypothesis that their performance reflects complex representations and skills that are acquired over time rather than individual differences in their basic abilities. It appears plausible that it is these acquired skills that mediate differences in performance on some types of memory tasks.

Other domains where working memory is required are transcription typing and sight-reading of music. In these domains superior performance is associated with longer spans between the executed actions and the information fixated with the eyes. A skilled sight-reading musician is looking further ahead in the music score than less skilled sight readers (Sloboda, 1974; Thompson, 1987) and skilled transcription typists look further ahead in the text than less skilled typists (Salthouse, 1984). The most skilled sight readers are accompanists who perform with limited or no preparation; they can often easily outperform concert pianists at playing an unfamiliar music piece directly from the music score. The concert pianists are of course able to master each piece after sufficient memorization and preparation (Lehmann & Ericsson, 1993). We know of three studies that have measured working memory capacity and sight-reading performance. In the first study, Thompson (1987) measured memory span in flute players at different levels of music skill. This study found significant relations between music memory, eye-hand span, and skill. It did not, however, find any significant relation between memory span and skill. In the first study to examine the relations with measures of complex working memory, Kopiez and Lee (2006, 2008) administered a psychometric battery and interviewed participants about their current and past practice to predict individual differences in sight-reading skill in a sample of student musicians and accompanists. In their general model Kopiez and Lee (2008) found one component skill of piano performance, namely speed of alternating finger movements, and sight-reading experience were the significant predictors of sight-reading performance, but not working memory. Of particular relevance to the relation between level of sight-reading skill and working memory, Kopiez and Lee (2006) analyzed performance as a function of the difficulty level of the sight-reading task. For the three lowest difficulty levels (Levels 1–3) Kopiez and Lee (2006) found a significant correlation between sight-reading performance and working memory. For the second highest difficulty level (Level 4) the correlation was no longer significant, and for the highest difficulty level (Level 5) the correlation was not significant ($r=0.08$). In a very recent study Meinz and Hambrick (2010) collected both psychometric measures of working memory and the level of past and current music practice to predict sight-reading performance. They found that even after controlling for the level of piano practice, individual differences in working memory significantly predicted skill. Meinz and Hambrick interpret their results as showing the influence on stable basic working memory differences on acquired level of skill. An alternative account is that Meinz and Hambrick (2010) included a sample of individuals with a vast range of sight reading ability. By including data on lower levels of sight reading their analysis would be predicted to show correlation between sight-reading performance and working memory—as found by Kopiez and Lee (2006). Hence, Meinz and Hambrick (2010) did not satisfy Ericsson and Charness' (1994) assumption that all the individuals had acquired a high level of sight-reading performance and the associated LTWM mechanisms. Most recently, Drai-Zerbib, Baccino, and Bigand (2012) showed how sight-reading experts were able to improve their performance by hearing a music piece prior to sight reading it. During the presentation they engaged in "fingering" that involves deciding and remembering which finger would hit which piano key in difficult passages during the subsequent sight-reading performance. They propose that Ericsson and Kintsch's (1995) LTWM can explain this efficient cross-modal integration among expert musicians.

Research on skilled typing has not focused on the relation between individual differences in working memory and typing performance, although it is generally accepted that eye-hand span is the best predictor of typing speed. In his classic study, Salthouse (1984) found no significant relation between typing speed and traditional measures of STM, namely the memory span. A more recent study has, however, found other types of evidence for the involvement of working memory in typing. Hayes and Chenoweth (2006) showed that articulatory suppression—saying "tap" for every beat of a metronome—performed concurrently with typing interfered with typing performance. Typing speed was slowed down by around 10 percent, errors were increased by 10–20 percent, and the memory for the typed texts decreased.

In sum, most of the evidence suggests that the expanded working memory performance necessary for expert performance is not related to differences in basic cognitive abilities. If these differences are not related to pre-existing differences in general abilities and capacities then this would support the hypothesis that expert performance is acquired and that the expanded working memory is one aspect of the acquired superior performance. In the next section we will examine and review evidence for the use of LTM and in particular the plausibility of acquired LTWM.

Memory from Representative Performance in the Domain of Expertise

In the historical background section we described the classic studies of Chase and Simon (1973), where they showed that briefly presented positions from chess games were recalled better as the skill level of the players increased. When the presented stimuli lacked a meaningful structure, such as randomly rearranged chess pieces on a board, the memory advantage for chess experts was dramatically reduced and often not significant. Given that chess players in these studies were instructed to memorize the presented stimuli, these studies do not present the best evidence for how much LTM and LTWM is in involved in the execution of superior performance. There are a few studies that have studied incidental memory of chess positions, when the representative task involved selecting the best move. The first study was conducted by Neil Charness (1981a), who unexpectedly asked participants to recall the chess positions for which they had selected the best move during an earlier part of the experiment. He found that the amount of accurate recall was related to chess skill. In a study designed to study incidental memory for a chess position while selecting the best move, Lane and Robertson (1979) found that when more skilled chess players were unexpectedly asked to recall the position after having completed a move-selection task, they reproduced significantly more pieces than less skilled players. Most interestingly, when two groups of players differing in skill were presented with the same chess position and asked to count the number of pieces, where the color of the piece matched the color of its square on the chess board, there were no reliable differences as a function of chess skill. As noted earlier, de Groot's (1946/1978) original research focused on the task of selecting moves, and he discovered that the retrospective reports on the thoughts from the move selection revealed that highly skilled chess players were better able to reproduce the associated chess position than less skilled players.

There are similar findings in other domains of expertise. For example, Gerver (1975) found that a text was better recalled when it was translated than when it was merely shadowed (repeated in the same language).

The essence of expert performance in many sports involves knowing the best action in a given situation and being able to execute that action. For example, when soccer players are shown videos of real match situations, and at some indicated point in time are cued to select the best future action, the quality of the selected action, and in some cases even in the speed of the execution of the action, increases as a function of the expertise of the soccer players at the local, national, and international levels (Helsen & Starkes, 1999; Ward & Williams, 2003). In sports, expertise is associated with more accurate anticipation of an opponent's actions based on the processing of perceptual cues (such as locations of players on the field and body movement information from the players possessing the soccer ball). This permits the experts to prepare superior actions as well as better countermeasures to opponents' actions.

In soccer, evidence suggests that better players have greater selective access to possible alternative plays at points in a game (Ward & Williams, 2003). Studies have presented videos of games with dynamically changing situations in team sports, where the tape is stopped and the screen blanked. At this point the players' memory for the last seen situation is tested and in some studies the player is asked to report the best available action of the player in control of the ball. Players at the higher level of competition show superior memory, not just in soccer (Ward & Williams, 2003), but also in volleyball (Borgeaud & Abernethy, 1987). Similarly, players at higher levels of competition also demonstrate better memory for snapshots of game situations in basketball (Allard et al., 1980). These results are similar to those observed in chess; however, the game situations in team sports change very rapidly, which leaves little room for planning, and future situations are also less predictable, which makes deeper planning less successful, even if sufficient time were available.

Amount of Time Required to Acquire the LTWM Mechanisms

If the superior memory of expert performers reflects acquired memory skills then it should be possible to trace its development as a function of engagement in relevant training. In the same manner that we have documented the need for extensive practice to attain exceptional memory performance for lists of digits, letters, and words (see Ericsson, 2003, 2006b; Ericsson & Kintsch, 1995) we predict that focused training is necessary to attain high levels of performance, which in turn is highly correlated with superior performance on memory tasks that are relevant to representative task performance (Ericsson, 2006a; Ericsson & Kintsch, 1995; Ericsson, Krampe, & Tesch-Römer, 1993; Ericsson et al., 2000; Ericsson & Lehmann, 1996).

In their paper on the role of deliberate practice in expert performance (Ericsson et al., 1993) showed that the amount of solitary practice by expert musicians was closely related to their attained level of performance, but that other music-related activities were not. In a very similar manner, higher skill in chess has been found to correlate significantly with the amount of solitary study in chess (Charness, Krampe, & Mayr, 1996; Charness, Tuffiash, Krampe, Reingold, & Vasyukova, 2005), explaining almost half the variance among chess players that compete in chess tournaments. The amount of time that elite chess players invest in solitary chess study is impressive. For example, Charness et al. (1996) estimated that international-level chess players had engaged in around 6,000 hours in solitary study of chess during their first ten years of chess playing, whereas national-level and club-level chess players only averaged round 3,000 and 1,500 hours respectively during the same time period. A similar pattern of results has been found by Duffy, Baluch, and Ericsson (2004) for dart throwing, where the accumulated amount of solitary practice is predictive of dart performance but the amount of time spent in dart games is unrelated to dart performance.

In sports, athletes who compete in higher levels of events (amateur, local, district, national, and international) have been found to have engaged in more different types of practice activities (Helsen, Starkes, & Hodges, 1998; Starkes, Deakin, Allard, Hodges, & Hayes, 1996; Ward, Hodges, Williams, & Starkes, 2004). In team sports there are some current controversies about which types of practice activities constitute deliberate practice as opposed to more playful activities (Côté, Ericsson, & Law, 2005). Amounts of practice activities that combine deliberate practice and play (deliberate play, Côté, 1999) have been found to be significantly correlated with attained skilled performance (Côté, Baker, & Abernethy, 2003).

The detailed practice activities will certainly differ from one domain of expertise to another, but the general principle is the same, namely that aspiring expert performers need to engage in training activities that are designed to improve particular aspects of performance. Once these aspects are mastered, then they direct their attention to other improvable aspects (see Figure 6.2). The aspiring expert performers image the goal states, monitor the outcome of their attempts, and make corrections. When this type of practice is executed with full concentration, immediate feedback, and opportunities to make repetitions, it meets the requirements for deliberate practice (Ericsson et al., 1993) (see Figure 6.2).

Not all goals for performance improvements will be associated with differences in the acquired mechanisms that are associated with increases in memory

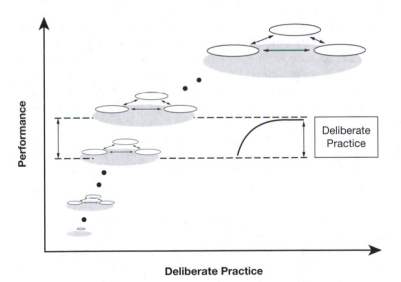

Figure 6.2   A schematic illustration of the acquisition of expert performance as a series of states with mechanisms of increasing complexity for monitoring and guiding future improvements of specific aspects of performance. (Adapted from "The scientific study of expert levels of performance can guide training for producing superior achievement in creative domains" by K. A. Ericsson in Proceedings from International conference on the cultivation and education of creativity and innovation (p. 14). Beijing, China: Chinese Academy of Sciences. Copyright 2009 by International Research Association for Talent Development and Excellence.)

performance. In the domains where we have observed increases in domain-specific memory performance we have also observed the relation between attained level of skill and amount of deliberate practice. Although we know of few studies that have studied the relation between memory performance and deliberate practice directly, the high correlations between skill level and memory performance and between skill level and amount of practice strongly supports our argument that the superior memory performance of experts reflects a skill, that has been acquired over months and years of deliberate practice.

Process Descriptions of the Development of LTWM

Based on the findings already reviewed, a full account of superior memory of experts would require detailed models of its development in individuals. This will be particularly challenging to achieve for expert performers in domains where the superior memory is not a goal in itself but rather an aspect supporting the execution of the expert performance, as well as the means to keep improving one's performance by sustained deliberate practice.

In some domains, such as chess, the superior memory of highly skilled chess players is so much larger than for less skilled players that it becomes easier to relate the training activities to the expanded working memory. The task that captures expert performance in chess is the selection of the best next move for a game position, as identified by de Groot (1946/1978). When chess players think aloud while selecting the best move for a presented position, they first familiarize themselves with it to assess its general characteristics and especially weaknesses. They then engage in examining the consequences of a certain moves, likely countermoves, and moves responding to these, and so on. This type of planning requires extensive working memory use to be able to mentally represent the new chess position after several move exchanges. When players engage in deliberate practice in chess they will thus spend considerable time generating and planning to find their best move. By getting immediate feedback on whether they found the best move (by checking what the grandmaster selected for the studied position), they can then determine when they overlooked a better move. It is likely that a major proportion of the reasons for failure to find the best move can be linked to failure to represent the consequences of a series of moves fully and accurately. These failures can then be addressed by extended analysis of the mental representations of the critical chess positions.

There is now a considerable body of evidence that confirms that highly skilled players are more able to mentally plan out accurate consequences of sequences of chess moves than less skilled players. In fact, Ericsson and Oliver (for a description see Ericsson & Staszewski, 1989) found that a candidate chess master without prior "blindfold" training could play at a very high level of chess without seeing the chess board. More generally chess masters, unlike less skilled players, are all able to play blindfold, without a visible board showing the current position, at a level near their normal level (Chabris & Hearst, 2003; Karpov, 1995; Koltanowski, 1985). Experiments show that chess masters, but not less skilled players, are able to mentally update multiple chess games without any external memory support when an experimenter reads sequences of moves from multiple chess games (Saariluoma, 1991, 1995). Cowley and Byrne (2004) demonstrated that higher-level players were more accurate in evaluating chess positions after a series of moves had been mentally applied, which is equivalent to evaluating the end state of a planning sequence. One of the most intriguing studies was conducted by Saariluoma and Kalakoski (1998). They did not allow the chess masters to see the whole chess position at once, but presented it auditorily by having the experimenter speak the location of each of the individual pieces. Not only were the chess masters able to integrate this piecemeal information, but they were able to examine the position mentally and then select the best move. These impressive memory performances cannot be explained in terms of general memory superiority because they are limited to chess; nor in terms of transient working memory capacity because they are mediated by storage in LTM.

There are a few studies that have come as close as possible to studying the detailed processes mediating the acquisition of a memory skill (LTWM) in an individual participant. In fact, the pioneering training study by Chase and Ericsson (1981, 1982; Ericsson et al., 1980) collected detailed data on the 200 hours of training of a college student (SF), whose initial immediate memory for rapidly presented digits was around seven, in correspondence with the typical average (Miller, 1956). During the 200+ hour-long training periods, we monitored any changes in SF's cognitive processes by having him give retrospective reports on his thought processes after most memory trials (cf. Ericsson and Simon, 1993). As his memory performance for digits started to increase, he reported breaking the presented lists into three-digit groups and whenever possible encoded them with associations to running times for various races, because SF was an avid cross-country runner. For example, SF would encode 358 as a very fast mile time, three minutes and 58 seconds, just below the four-minute mile.

The central issue that concerns any type of verbal reports is whether these reports reflect a valid process where the ability to generate mnemonic running-time encodings improves his memory performance. To address that issue, we designed an experiment to test the effects of mnemonic encodings and presented SF with special types of designed lists of digits, in addition to the lists of random digits. One of the lists was designed to contain only three-digit groups that could not be encoded as running times, such as 364 as three minutes and 64 seconds, in a list (364 895 481 [...]). As predicted, his memory performance was reliably worse than for random lists of digits. In another experiment, we constructed lists of digits where all three-digit groups could be encoded as running times (412 637 524 . . .), with a reliable increase in his associated performance. In over a dozen specially designed experiments, it was possible to validate several aspects of SF's acquired memory skill (Chase & Ericsson, 1981, 1982; Ericsson, 1985), such as his retrieval structure and his speed-up of memorizing digit sequences well below his current digit span. The training given to SF matched all the characteristics of what was later called deliberate practice (Ericsson et al., 1993). Most importantly, SF was focused on mastering the memory for the digits sequences and improving his performance. The lengths of the presented digit sequences were at the limits of SF's ability (on average he would get them correct 50% of the time) and were continuously adjusted to be at that difficulty level even when his memory performance increased. SF would get immediate feedback about errors after his recall and retrospective verbal report. SF had repeated opportunities to master digit sequences of a given length. Using this methodology of collecting verbal reports followed up by designed experiments to assess the mechanisms mediating the developing memory skill, two other college students both attained exceptional memory after 50–200 hours of training (Chase & Ericsson, 1981, 1982). In fact, one of the participants was later trained by Jim Staszewski and reached a digit span of over 100 digits (Richman, Staszcwski, & Simon, 1995). Other investigators, such as Wenger and Payne (1995), have also relied on protocol analysis and other process tracing data to assess the mechanisms of individuals who, with practice, dramatically increased their memory performance on a list learning task.

A similar methodology has also been applied to the study of superior memory of mental calculators (Staszewski, 1988), waiters (Ericsson & Polson, 1988), and other individuals with exceptional memory in domains where memory is the focus of the exceptional performance. The latter type of study has examined the superior memory abilities of individuals who have memorized over 30,000 digits (Thompson, Cowan, & Frieman, 1993) and over 60,000 digits (Hu, Ericsson, Yang, & Lu, 2009) of the mathematical constant pi. There is currently no firm evidence that these or other memorists have been endowed with an innate advantage in general memory abilities (Ericsson, Delaney, Weaver, & Mahadevan, 2004; Hu et al., 2009), but mechanisms of acquired LTWM have successfully explained their superior performance.

In other types of domains of expertise, the focus is not on rapidly encoding and memorizing information, still, through the processes of preparing for a public performance, memory is extended. For instance, stage actors must accurately remember all their lines while giving a moving interpretation of the character that they portray. Similarly, a concert pianist faces a very demanding memory task of playing complex pieces from memory while giving their own, often unique, emotional interpretation. There is considerable evidence for the use of LTWM skill and particularly retrieval structures mediating memory and recall of music pieces. In an intensive study of a concert pianist learning a piece, Chaffin and Imreh (2002) showed that the pianist organized the piece into sections using both technical and interpretative cues. During later recall of the piece she showed predicted hesitations at cue boundaries consistent with a switch from cue to cue in a retrieval structure (Chase & Ericsson, 1982). The development of these memory structures during practice prepares the musician to play from memory without the constraints and distractions of maintaining access to the sheets of notes (Chaffin, 2007). Intensive studies of cellists preparing a piece (Chaffin, Lisboa, Logan, & Begosh, 2010) as well as a jazz pianist (Noice, Jeffery, Noice, & Chaffin, 2008) have shown similar patterns of the use of a retrieval structure to support preparation and performance of a piece. With a large number of musicians at multiple skill levels, Williamon and Valentine (2002) found that segmenting music pieces was done by all pianists in a meaningful way and they organized these segments into super segments reflecting the hierarchical structure of the piece. The use of expert memory by concert pianists and accomplished actors is guided by the ultimate goal

Memory skills are particularly attractive and easy to study as exceptional performance can be attained within a few hundred hours of practice. An important part of the reason for the relatively easy acquisition is that the representative task performance is essentially identical to the performance on the memory tasks. We also discussed some domains of expertise, such as public performance as solo musicians and actors. In these types of domains the focus is on slowly preparing a unique experience for the audience, where speed of memorization and thus working memory capacity frequently does not clearly differentiate expert performers from less skilled performers or even novices and people in the general population.

If we are to make progress on understanding the structure and acquisition of expert performance it is important to recognize that the reviewed findings on experts' memory performance do not support the mediation of a generalizable component or mechanism. The evidence points to the slow acquisition of complex mental mechanisms and representations in response to deliberate practice. In some domains of expertise these mechanisms will permit experts to display superior memory performance on a memory task compared to less skilled individuals. When the cognitive processes mediating this superior memory performance are analyzed, we have found that they can be best understood by describing the development of the mechanisms mediating the expert performance rather than attempting to explain them with general characteristics such as working memory capacity. It is likely that if and when we can describe the cognitive processes and mechanisms mediating the expert performance of a few individual participants we will discover what Chase and Ericsson (1982; Ericsson, 1985, 1988, 2003) found: namely, that detailed associations and knowledge (e.g., SF's and DD's running times) mediating the memorization of lists of digits will differ, but the principles restricting the types of structures of the memory encodings and their associated retrieval structures may be very general for a given domain of expertise. We believe that similar studies of a few expert performers are likely to uncover similar principles and new types of structures that are associated with the acquisition of different levels of performance. A better understanding of these structures is likely to be able to guide the development of deliberate practice activities and help future performers to achieve higher levels of performance in better and more efficient ways. Further insights in the detailed mechanisms mediating performance on laboratory tasks as well as mechanisms mediating the superior representative performance of experts will help us understand the prospects and limits of general mechanisms, such as general working memory and intelligence, to explain human performance.

REFERENCES

Ackerman, P. L. (1988). Determinants of individual differences during skill acquisition: Cognitive abilities and information processing. *Journal of Experimental Psychology: General, 117*, 288–318.

Ackerman, P. L. (2000). A reappraisal of ability determinants of individual differences in skilled performance. *Psychologische Beiträge, 42*, 4–17.

Allard, F., Graham, S., & Paarsalu, M. E. (1980). Perception in sport: Basketball. *Journal of Sport Psychology, 2*, 14–21.

of providing freedom to present an emotional experience to the people in the audience. Their acquired memory skills are not designed to acquire information rapidly and superficially, but instead to permit the musicians and the actors to find a deep interpretation that they can communicate to the audience. Depending on the domain of expertise and the representative demands and constraints on expert performers, the types of memory skills acquired will differ markedly from each other and can only be understood through a careful analysis of task demands for each type of expert performer.

FUTURE DIRECTIONS

In this chapter we have shown how the ideas of a transient STM or general working memory with invariant capacity was the original mechanism for explaining how the superior memory of experts could be attained by the accumulation of patterns and chunks stored in LTM. We described the emerging evidence that raised doubts about sufficiency of such an explanation to explain the working memory of experts. We proceeded to describe alternative proposals for accounting for storage in LTM and how acquired memory skills could be made functionally equivalent to storage in capacity-limited transient working memory with an emphasis on LTWM (Ericsson & Kintsch, 1995; Ericsson et al., 2000), but we acknowledge other theoretical proposals for accounting for superior memory performance based on templates (Gobet & Simon, 1996).

We reviewed the evidence for general transient working memory mediating superior memory associated with highly skilled and expert performance. Although we found some evidence that performance of beginners was correlated with individual differences in general abilities and general working memory capacity, we found no evidence that individual differences in these capacities mediated expert performance. Our review also found evidence that was directly inconsistent with accounts of performance based on individual differences in general transient working memory. For example, experts' memory is mediated by encoding in LTM, which is consistent with LTWM (Ericsson & Kintsch, 1995; Ericsson et al., 2000) and templates (Gobet & Simon, 1996). There was also considerable evidence showing that experts' memory performance was domain-specific and even task-specific, where working memory performance was closely connected to the particular working memory demands of the tasks that capture expert performance in the corresponding domain. Similarly, we found that mere experience of activities in the domain was not sufficient to improve performance but that engagement in particular training activities (deliberate practice) was necessary for increasing performance and, by inference, the memory skills corresponding to the experts' superior performance. In the final section we went even further and tried to determine more specifically how the deliberate practice activities changed the cognitive structures that mediate both the representative task performance and performance on memory tasks. By specifying the detailed mechanisms and validating the mechanisms by a systematic sequence of experiments, this analysis has shown how the acquisition of memory skill by individual participants can be explained by deliberate practice and the development of expert performance skills.

Atwood, M. E., Masson, M. E., & Polson, P. G. (1980). Further explorations with a process model for water jug problems. *Memory and Cognition, 8,* 182–192.

Baddeley, A. D. (1986). *Working memory.* New York: Oxford University Press.

Baddeley, A. D., & Hitch, G. J. (1974). Working memory. In G. H. Bower (Ed.), *The psychology of learning and motivation Vol. 8,* (pp. 47–90). New York: Academic Press.

Bilalić, M., McLeod, P., & Gobet, F. (2007). Does chess need intelligence? – A study with young chess players. *Intelligence, 35,* 457–470.

Bourgeaud, P., & Abernethy, B. (1987). Skilled perception in volleyball defense. *Journal of Sport Psychology, 9,* 400–406.

Bourne, L. E., Jr., Goldstein, S., & Link, W. E. (1964). Concept learning as a function of availability of previously presented information. *Journal of Experimental Psychology, 67,* 439–448.

Bryan, W. L., & Harter, N. (1899). Studies of telegraphic language: The acquisition of a hierarchy of habits. *Psychological Review, 6,* 345–375.

Chabris, C. F., & Hearst, E. S. (2003). Visualization, pattern recognition, and forward search: Effects of playing speed and sight of the position on grandmaster chess errors. *Cognitive Science, 27,* 637–648.

Chaffin, R. (2007). Learning *Clair de Lune*: Retrieval practice and expert memorization. *Music Perception, 24,* 377–393.

Chaffin, R., & Imreh, G. (2002). Practicing perfection: Piano performance as expert memory. *Psychological Science, 13,* 342–349.

Chaffin, R., Lisboa, T., Logan, T., & Begosh, K. T. (2010). Preparing for memorized cello performance: The role of performance cues. *Psychology of Music, 38,* 3–30.

Charness, N. (1976). Memory for chess positions: Resistance to interference. *Journal of Experimental Psychology: Human Learning and Memory, 2,* 641–653.

Charness, N. (1979). Components of skill in bridge. *Canadian Journal of Psychology, 33,* 1–16.

Charness, N. (1981a). Aging and skilled problem solving. *Journal of Experimental Psychology: General, 110,* 21–38.

Charness, N. (1981b). Search in chess: Age and skill differences. *Journal of Experimental Psychology: Human Perception and Performance, 7,* 467–476.

Charness, N., Krampe, R., & Mayr, U. (1996). The role of practice and coaching in entrepreneurial skill domains: An international comparison of life-span chess skill acquisition. In K. A. Ericsson (Ed.), *The road to excellence: The acquisition of expert performance in the arts and sciences, sports and games* (pp. 51–80). Mahwah, NJ: Erlbaum.

Charness, N., Tuffiash, M., Krampe, R., Reingold, E., & Vasyukova, E. (2005). The role of deliberate practice in chess expertise. *Applied Cognitive Psychology, 19,* 151–165.

Chase, W. G., & Ericsson, K. A. (1981). Skilled memory. In J. R. Anderson (Ed.), *Cognitive skills and their acquisition* (pp. 141–189). Hillsdale, NJ: Lawrence Erlbaum Associates.

Chase, W. G., & Ericsson, K. A. (1982). Skill and working memory. In G. Bower (Ed.), *The psychology of learning and motivation* (Vol. 16, pp. 1–58). New York: Academic Press.

Chase, W. G., & Simon, H. A. (1973). The mind's eye in chess. In W. G. Chase (Ed.), *Visual information processing* (pp. 215–281). New York: Academic Press.

Christoffels, I. K., & de Groot, A. M. B. (2005). Simultaneous interpreting: A cognitive perspective. In J. F. Kroll & A. M. B. de Groot (Eds.), *Handbook of bilingualism: Psycholinguistic approaches* (pp. 454–479). Oxford, UK: Oxford University Press.

Cohen, M. A., Evans, K. K., Horowitz, T. S., & Wolfe, J. M. (2011) Auditory and visual memory in musicians and non-musicians. *Psychonomic Bulletin and Review, 18,* 586–591.

Côté, J. (1999) The influence of the family in the development of talent in sports. *The Sport Psychologist, 13,* 395–417.

Côté, J., Baker, J., & Abernethy, B. (2003). From play to practice: A developmental framework for the acquisition of expertise in team sports. In K. A. Ericsson & J. L. Starkes (Eds.), *Expert performance in sports: Advances in research on sport expertise*. Champaign, IL: Human Kinetics.

Côté, J., Ericsson, K. A., & Law, M. (2005). Tracing the development of athletes using retrospective interview methods: A proposed interview and validation procedure for reported information. *Journal of Applied Sport Psychology, 17*, 1–19.

Cowley, M., & Byrne, R. M. J. (2004). Chess masters' hypothesis testing. *Proceedings of the Twenty-sixth Annual Conference of the Cognitive Science Society* (pp. 250–255). Mahwah, NJ: Erlbaum.

Daneman, M., & Carpenter, P. A. (1980). Individual differences in working memory and reading. *Journal of Verbal Learning and Verbal Behavior, 19*, 450–466.

de Groot, A. D. (1978). *Thought and choice in chess* (2nd English ed.: first Dutch edition published in 1946). The Hague: Mouton Publishers.

Dillinger, M. (1994). Comprehension during interpreting: What do interpreters know that bilinguals don't? In S. Lambert and B. Moser-Mercer (Eds.), *Bridging the gap: Empirical research in simultaneous interpretation* (pp. 155–189). Amsterdam, The Netherlands: John Benjamins Publishing Co.

Djakow, J. N., Petrowski, N. W., & Rudik, P. A. (1927). *Psychologie des Schachspiels [The psychology of chess]*. Berlin: Walter de Gruyter.

Doane, S. M., Pellegrino, J. W., & Klatzky, R. L. (1990). Expertise in a computer operating system: Conceptualization and performance. *Human–Computer Interaction, 5*, 267–304.

Doll, J., & Mayr, U. (1987). Intelligenz und Schachleistung: Eine Untersuchung an Schachexperten. [Intelligence and achievement in chess: A study of chess masters]. *Psychologische Beiträge, 29*, 270–289.

Drai-Zerbib, V., Baccino, T., & Bigand, E. (2012). Sight-reading expertise: Cross-modality integration investigated using eye tracking. *Psychology of Music, 40*, 201–215.

Duffy, L. J., Baluch, B., & Ericsson, K. A. (2004). Dart performance as a function of facets of practice amongst professional and amateur men and women players. *International Journal of Sport Psychology, 35*, 232–245.

Ebbinghaus, H. (1913). *Memory: A contribution to experimental psychology*. (originally published in German in 1885). New York: Teachers College, Columbia University.

Egan, D. E., & Schwartz, B. J. (1979). Chunking in recall of symbolic drawings. *Memory and Cognition, 7*, 149–158.

Engle, R. W., & Bukstel, L. H. (1978). Memory processes among bridge players of differing expertise. *American Journal of Psychology, 91*, 673–689.

Ericsson, K. A. (1985). Memory skill. *Canadian Journal of Psychology, 39*, 188–231.

Ericsson, K. A. (1988). Analysis of memory performance in terms of memory skill. In R. J. Sternberg (Ed.), *Advances in the psychology of human intelligence, Vol. 4* (pp. 137–179). Hillsdale, NJ: Erlbaum.

Ericsson, K. A. (2003). Exceptional memorizers: Made, not born. *Trends in Cognitive Sciences, 7*, 233–235.

Ericsson, K. A. (2004). Deliberate practice and the acquisition and maintenance of expert performance in medicine and related domains. *Academic Medicine, 79*, S70–S81.

Ericsson, K. A. (2006a). The influence of experience and deliberate practice on the development of superior expert performance. In K. A. Ericsson, N. Charness, P. Feltovich, & R. R. Hoffman (Eds.), *Cambridge handbook of expertise and expert performance* (pp. 685–706). Cambridge, UK: Cambridge University Press.

Ericsson, K. A. (2006b). Protocol analysis and expert thought: Concurrent verbalizations of thinking during experts' performance on representative tasks. In K. A. Ericsson, N. Charness, P. Feltovich, & R. R. Hoffman (Eds.), *Cambridge handbook of expertise and expert performance* (pp. 223–242). Cambridge, UK: Cambridge University Press.

Ericsson, K. A. (2007a). Deliberate practice and the modifiability of body and mind: Toward a science of the structure and acquisition of expert and elite performance. *International Journal of Sport Psychology, 38*, 4–34.

Ericsson, K. A. (2007b). Deliberate practice and the modifiability of body and mind: A reply to the commentaries. *International Journal of Sport Psychology, 38*, 109–123.

Ericsson, K. A. (2010/2001). Expertise in interpreting: An expert-performance perspective. Republished in G. M. Shreve & E. Angleone (Eds.), *Translation and cognition* (pp. 231–262). Amsterdam, the Netherlands: John Benjamin Publishing Company.

Ericsson, K. A., & Charness, N. (1994). Expert performance: Its structure and acquisition. *American Psychologist, 49(8)*, 725–747.

Ericsson, K. A., Chase, W. G., & Faloon, S. (1980). Acquisition of memory skill. *Science, 208*, 1181–1182.

Ericsson, K. A., Delaney, P. F., Weaver, G., & Mahadevan, R. (2004). Uncovering the structure of a memorist's superior memory capacity. *Cognitive Psychology, 49*, 191–237.

Ericsson, K. A., & Harris, M. S. (1990). *Expert chess memory without chess knowledge: A training study.* Poster presented at the 31st Annual Meeting of the Psychonomic Society, New Orleans, Louisiana.

Ericsson, K. A., & Kintsch, W. (1995). Long-term working memory. *Psychological Review, 102*, 211–245.

Ericsson, K. A., Krampe, R. T., & Tesch-Römer, C. (1993). The role of deliberate practice in the acquisition of expert performance. *Psychological Review, 100*, 363–406.

Ericsson, K. A., & Lehmann, A. C. (1996). Expert and exceptional performance: Evidence on maximal adaptations on task constraints. *Annual Review of Psychology, 47*, 273–305.

Ericsson, K. A., Patel, V. L., & Kintsch, W. (2000). How experts' adaptations to representative task demands account for the expertise effect in memory recall: Comment on Vicente and Wang (1998). *Psychological Review, 107*, 578–592.

Ericsson, K. A., & Polson, P. G. (1988). An experimental analysis of the mechanisms of a memory skill. *Journal of Experimental Psychology: Learning, Memory and Cognition, 14*, 305–316.

Ericsson, K. A., & Roring, R. W. (2007). Memory as a fully integrated aspect of skilled and expert performance. *The Psychology of Learning and Motivation, 48*, 351–380.

Ericsson, K. A., Roring, R. W., & Nandagopal, K. (2007a). Giftedness and evidence for reproducibly superior performance: An account based on the expert-performance framework. *High Ability Studies, 18*, 3–56.

Ericsson, K. A., Roring, R. W., & Nandagopal, K. (2007b). Misunderstandings, agreements, and disagreements: Toward a cumulative science of reproducibly superior aspects of giftedness. *High Ability Studies, 18*, 97–115.

Ericsson, K. A., & Simon, H. A. (1993). *Protocol analysis: Verbal reports as data* (Rev. Ed.). Cambridge, MA: MIT Press.

Ericsson, K. A., & Smith, J. (1991). Prospects and limits in the empirical study of expertise: An introduction. In K. A. Ericsson & J. Smith (Eds.), *Toward a general theory of expertise: Prospects and limits* (pp. 1–38). Cambridge, UK: Cambridge University Press.

Ericsson, K. A., & Staszewski, J. J. (1989). Skilled memory and expertise: Mechanisms of exceptional performance. In D. Klahr & K. Kotovsky (Eds.), *Complex information processing: The impact of Herbert A. Simon* (pp. 235–267). Hillsdale, NJ: Lawrence Erlbaum.

Ericsson, K. A., Whyte, J., & Ward, P. (2007). Expert performance in nursing: Reviewing research on expertise in nursing within the framework of the expert-performance approach. *Advances in Nursing Science, 30*, E58–E71.

Fitts, P., & Posner, M. I. (1967). *Human performance.* Belmont, CA: Brooks/Cole.

Frydman, M., & Lynn, R. (1992). The general intelligence and spatial abilities of young Belgian chess players. *British Journal of Psychology, 83*, 233–235.

Gerver, D. (1975). A psychological approach to simultaneous interpretation. *Meta: Translators' Journal, 20*, 119–128.

Gerver, D., Longley, P., Long, J., & Lambert, S. (1984). Selecting trainee conference interpreters: A preliminary study. *Journal of Occupational Psychology, 57*, 17–31.

Gilhooly, K. J., Wood, M., Kinnear, P. R., & Green, C. (1988). Skill in map reading and memory for maps. *Quarterly Journal of Experimental Psychology, 40A*, 87–107.

Gobet, F., & Jackson, S. (2002). In search of templates. *Cognitive Systems Research, 3*, 35–44.

Gobet, F., & Simon, H. A. (1996). Templates in chess memory: A mechanism for recalling several boards. *Cognitive Psychology, 31*, 1–40.

Grabner, R. H., Neubauer, A. C., & Stern, E. (2006). Superior performance and neural efficiency: The impact of intelligence and expertise. *Brain Research Bulletin, 69*, 422–439.

Hayes, J. R., & Chenoweth, N. A. (2006). Is working memory involved in the transcribing and editing of texts? *Written Communication, 23*, 135–149.

Helmbold, N., Rammsayer, T., & Altenmuller, E. (2005). Differences in primary mental abilities between musicians and nonmusicians. *Journal of Individual Differences, 26*, 74–85.

Helsen, W., & Starkes, J. (1999). A multidimensional approach to skilled perception and performance in sport. *Applied Cognitive Psychology, 13*, 1–27.

Helsen, W. F., Starkes, J. L., & Hodges, N. J. (1998). Team sports and the theory of deliberate practice. *Journal of Sport and Exercise Psychology, 20*, 12–34.

Hu, Y., Ericsson, K. A., Yang, D., & Lu, C. (2009). Superior self-paced memorization of digits in spite of a normal digit span: The structure of a memorist's skill. *Journal of Experimental Psychology: Learning, Memory, and Cognition, 35*, 1426–1442.

Intons-Peterson, M. J., & Smyth, M. M. (1987). The anatomy of repertory memory. *Journal of Experimental Psychology: Learning, Memory, and Cognition, 13*, 490–500.

Jääskeläinen, R. (2010). Are all professionals experts? Definitions of expertise and reinterpretation of research evidence in process studies. In G. M. Shreve & E. Angelone (Eds.), *Translation and cognition* (pp. 213–227). Amsterdam, the Netherlands: John Benjamins Publishing Company.

James, W. (1890). *The principles of psychology* (Vols. 1 & 2). New York, NY: Henry Holt.

Karpov, A. (1995). Grandmaster musings. *Chess Life*, November, pp. 32–33.

Koltanowski, G. (1985). *In the dark*. Coraopolis, PA: Chess Enterprises.

Kopiez, R., & Lee, J. L. (2006). Towards a dynamic model of skills involved in sight reading music. *Music Education Research, 8*, 97–120.

Kopiez, R., & Lee, J. L. (2008). Towards a general model of skills involved in sight reading music. *Music Education Research, 10*, 41–62.

Lane, D. M., & Robertson, L. (1979). The generality of levels of processing hypothesis: An application to memory for chess positions. *Memory and Cognition, 7*, 253–256.

Lehmann, A. C., & Ericsson, K. A. (1993). Sight-reading ability of expert pianists in the context of piano accompanying. *Psychomusicology, 12*, 182–195.

Liu, M. (2008). How do experts interpret? Implications from research in Interpreting Studies and cognitive science. In G. Hansen, A. Chesterman, & H. Gerzymisch-Arbogast (Eds.), *Efforts and models interpreting and translation research* (pp. 159–177). Amsterdam, the Netherlands: John Benjamins Publishing Company.

Masunaga, H., & Horn, J. (2001). Expertise and age-related changes in components of intelligence. *Psychology and Aging, 16*, 293–311.

McKeithen, K. B., Reitman, J. S., Rueter, H. H., & Hirtle, S. C. (1981). Knowledge organization and skill differences in computer programmers. *Cognitive Psychology, 13*, 307–325.

Meinz, E. J., & Hambrick, D. Z. (2010). Deliberate practice is necessary but not sufficient to explain individual differences in piano sight-reading skill: The role of working memory capacity. *Psychological Science, 21,* 914–919.

Miller, G. A. (1956). The magical number seven, plus or minus two: Some limits on our capacity for processing information. *Psychological Review, 63,* 343–355.

Moser-Mercer, B. (2000). Simultaneous interpreting: Cognitive potential and limitations. *Interpreting, 5,* 83–94.

Newell, A., & Simon, H. A. (1972). *Human problem solving.* Englewood Cliffs, NJ: Prentice-Hall.

Noice, H. (1993). Effects of rote versus gist strategy on the verbatim retention of theatrical scripts. *Applied Cognitive Psychology, 7,* 75–84.

Noice, H., Jeffery, J., Noice, T., & Chaffin, R. (2008). Memorization by a jazz musician: A case study. *Psychology of Music, 36,* 63–79.

Norman, G. R., Brooks, L. R., & Allen, S. W. (1989). Recall by expert medical practitioners and novices as a record of processing attention. *Journal of Experimental Psychology: Learning, Memory and Cognition, 15,* 1166–1174.

Payne, J. W. (1976). Task complexity and contingent processing in decision making: An informational search and protocol analysis. *Organizational Behavior and Human Performance, 16,* 366–387.

Reitman, J. (1976). Skilled perception in Go: Deducing memory structures from inter-response times. *Cognitive Psychology, 8,* 336–356.

Richman, H. B., Staszewski, J. J., & Simon, H. A. (1995). Simulation of expert memory using EPAM IV. *Psychological Review, 102,* 305–330.

Robbins, T. W., Anderson, E. J., Barker, D. R., Bradley, A. C., Fearnyhough, C., Henson, R., Hudson, S. R., & Baddeley, A. D. (1996). Working memory in chess. *Memory and Cognition, 24,* 83–93.

Ruthsatz, J., Detterman, D., Griscom, W. S., & Cirullo, B. A. (2007). Becoming an expert in the musical domain: It takes more than just practice. *Intelligence, 36,* 330–338.

Saariluoma, P. (1991). Aspects of skilled imagery in blindfold chess. *Acta Psychologica, 77,* 65–89.

Saariluoma, P. (1995). *Chess players' thinking: A cognitive psychological approach.* London: Routledge.

Saariluoma, P., & Kalakoski, V. (1998). Apperception and imagery in blindfold chess. *Memory, 6,* 67–90.

Salthouse, T. A. (1984). Effects of age and skill in typing. *Journal of Experimental Psychology: General, 113,* 345–371.

Signorelli, T. M. (2008). Working memory in simultaneous interpretation. *Dissertation Abstracts International,* B 69/05.

Simon, H. A., & Chase, W. G. (1973). Skill in chess. *American Scientist, 61,* 394–403.

Sloboda, J. (1974). The eye–hand span: An approach to the study of sight reading. *Psychology of Music, 2,* 4–10.

Sloboda, J. A., & Parker, H. H. (1985). Immediate recall of melodies. In I. Cross, P. Howell, & R. West (Eds.), *Musical structure and cognition* (pp. 143–167). New York: Academic Press.

Starkes, J. L., & Deakin, J. (1984). Perception in sport: A cognitive approach to skilled performance. In W. F. Straub & J. M. Williams (Eds.), *Cognitive sport psychology* (pp. 115–128). Lansing, NY: Sport Science Associates.

Starkes, J. L., Deakin, J. M., Allard, F., Hodges, N. J., & Hayes, A. (1996). Deliberate practice in sports: What is it anyway? In K. A. Ericsson (Ed.), *The road to excellence: The acquisition of expert performance in the arts and sciences, sports and games* (pp. 81–106). Hillsdale, NJ: Lawrence Erlbaum Associates.

Starkes, J. L., Deakin, J. M., Lindley, S., & Crisp, F. (1987). Motor versus verbal recall of ballet sequences by young expert dancers. *Journal of Sport Psychology, 9,* 222–230.

Staszewski, J. J. (1988). Skilled memory and experimental calculation. In M. T. H. Chi, R. Glaser, & M. J. Farr (Eds.), *The nature of expertise* (pp. 71–128). Hillsdale, NJ: Erlbaum.

Svenson, O. (1979). Process descriptions of decision making. *Organizational Behavior and Human Performance, 23,* 86–112.

Thompson, C. P., Cowan, T. M., & Frieman, J. (1993). *Memory search by a memorist.* Hillsdale: NJ: Erlbaum.

Thompson, W. B. (1987). Music sight-reading skill in flute players. *Journal of General Psychology, 114,* 345–352.

Trainor, L. J., & Corrigall, K. A. (2010) Music acquisition and effects of musical experience. In M. R. Jones, R. R. Fay, & A. N. Popper (Eds.), *Music perception.* Berlin: Springer Science+Business Media.

Tuffiash, M., Roring, R. W., & Ericsson, K. A. (2007). Expert word play: Capturing and explaining reproducibly superior verbal task performance. *Journal of Experimental Psychology: Applied, 13,* 124–134.

Turner, M. L., & Engle, R. W. (1989). Is working memory capacity task dependent? *Journal of Memory and Language, 28,* 127–154.

Unterrainer, J. M., Kaller, C. P., Halsband, U., & Rahm, B. (2006). Planning abilities and chess: A comparison of chess and non-chess players on the Tower of London task. *British Journal of Psychology, 97,* 299–311.

van der Maas, H. L. J., & Wagenmakers, E. J. (2005). A psychometric analysis of chess expertise. *American Journal of Psychology, 118,* 29–60.

Vicente, K. J., & Wang, J. H. (1998). An ecological theory of expertise effects in memory recall. *Psychological Review, 105,* 33–57.

Ward, P., Hodges, N. J., Williams, A. M., & Starkes, J. L. (2004). Deliberate practice and expert performance: Defining the path to excellence. In A. M. Williams and N. J. Hodges (Eds.), *Skill acquisition in sport: Research, theory and practice* (pp. 231–258). London: Routledge.

Ward, P., & Williams, A. M. (2003). Perceptual and cognitive skill development in soccer: The multidimensional nature of expert performance. *Journal of Sport and Exercise Psychology, 25(1),* 93–111.

Waters, A. J., Gobet, F., & Leyden, G. (2002). Visuo-spatial abilities in chess players. *British Journal of Psychology, 93,* 557–565.

Watson, J. B. (1913). Psychology as the behaviorist views it. *Psychological Review, 20,* 158–177.

Wenger, M. J., & Payne, D. G. (1995). On the acquisition of mnemonic skill: Application of skilled memory theory. *Journal of Experimental Psychology: Applied, 3,* 194–215.

Williamon, A., & Valentine, E. (2002). The role of retrieval structures in memorizing music. *Cognitive Psychology, 44,* 1–32.

Wolff, A. S., Mitchell, D. H., & Frey, P. W. (1984). Perceptual skill in the game of Othello. *Journal of Psychology, 118,* 7–16.

Working Memory Capacity and Musical Skill

DAVID Z. HAMBRICK

Department of Psychology, Michigan State University, East Lansing, MI, USA

ELIZABETH J. MEINZ

Department of Psychology, Southern Illinois University, Edwardsville, IL, USA

BACKGROUND INFORMATION

Working Memory Capacity and Musical Skill

How people acquire and maintain elite levels of performance in complex domains has long been a topic of debate in psychology. Sir Francis Galton, the Victorian polymath, conducted the first scientific research on the topic in the mid-1800s. Inspired by the work of his illustrious cousin, Charles Darwin, Galton believed that intellectual ability is heritable in the same way that physical characteristics such as body size are heritable. To test this idea, Galton studied genealogical records for hundreds of Englishmen of "high reputation"— judges, scientists, poets, musicians, artists, and so on—and asked a straightforward question: Do they tend to be related to one another? As he summarized in his book *Hereditary Genius* (1869), the answer was yes. For example, the 26 musicians in Galton's sample represented just 14 families. Here was his entry for the Bach family:

> The Bachs were a musical family, comprising a vast number of individuals, and extending through eight generations. It began in 1550, it culminated in Sebastian . . . and its last known member was Regina Susanna, who was alive in 1800, but in indigent circumstances. There are far more than twenty *eminent* musicians among the Bachs; the biographical collections of musicians give the lives of no less than fifty-seven of them.

(p. 240)

137

Galton concluded that intellectual ability *must* be hereditary. And although he later popularized the phrase *nature vs. nurture*, he made it clear where he stood: "I HAVE no patience with the hypothesis occasionally expressed . . . that babies are born pretty much alike, and that the sole agencies in creating differences between boy and boy, and man and man, are steady application and moral effort" (p. 14). To be sure, Galton did not deny that a person must work exceptionally hard to become a great writer or scientist or musician. But he *did* deny that *anyone* can become a great writer or scientist or musician. This view is illustrated in Figure 7.1 in terms of learning curves for individuals representing low, medium, and high levels of innate ability. The curves differ in their *asymptotes*—the points at which increases in practice produce no further improvements in performance. (They also differ in the initial performance level, and in the rate of learning.) The talent view can be boiled down to the idea that asymptotic levels of performance differ across individuals, and that these differences reflect innate factors.

Galton's views created a stir. Then, as now, liberally minded thinkers held fast to the idea, championed by British empiricists such as John Locke and Thomas Hobbes, that a person comes into the world a *tabula rasa*—a "blank slate"—and can rise to eminence through sheer determination. The popular novelist Horatio Alger captured this ideology—the cornerstone of what historian James Truslow Adams would later call the American Dream—in his popular stories for young boys. The story was always essentially the same: Hapless young boy impresses a wealthy older gentleman through some valiant act. Wealthy older gentleman becomes the boy's benefactor. Boy rises above poverty through hard work—"pluck"—and clean living and goes on to a life of middle-class respectability.

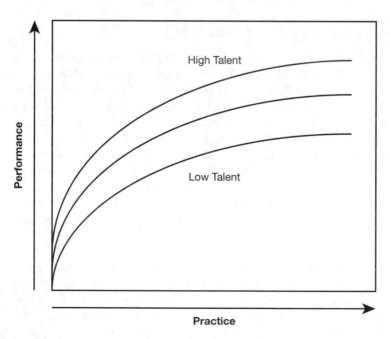

Figure 7.1   Illustration of talent view

Several decades later, John Watson, the founder of behaviorism, put a scientific spin on the rags-to-riches story. Dissatisfied with the vagueness of psychology's central topic of study at the time—consciousness—and by the unreliability of the principal tool used to study it—introspection—Watson believed that a science of psychology should focus exclusively on what *can* be objectively observed: behavior and the circumstances under which it occurs. Watson also believed that behavior reflects *habits*, born of experience, rather than instinct. Indeed, in *Behaviorism* (1970/1930), he famously proclaimed,

> Give me a dozen healthy infants, well-formed, and my own specified world to bring them up in and I'll guarantee to take any one at random and train him to become any type of specialist I might select—doctor, lawyer, artist, merchant-chief and, yes, even beggar-man and thief, regardless of his talents, penchants, tendencies, abilities, vocations, and race of his ancestors.
>
> (p. 104)

In the very next sentence, Watson admitted that he was stretching: "I am going beyond my facts and I admit it, but so have the advocates of the contrary and they have been doing it for many thousands of years" (p. 104). Watson was, however, as emphatic in his rejection of the nature view of exceptional performance as Galton had been in his rejection of the nurture view. One even wonders whether Galton was one of the "advocates to the contrary" to which Watson was referring. Here, later in *Behaviorism*, Watson offers his own view of genius:

> The formation of early work habits in youth, of working longer hours than others, or practicing more intensively than others, is probably the most reasonable explanation we have today not only for success in any line, *but even for genius* (italics added).
>
> (p. 212)

Historical curiosity aside, there are two longstanding positions on expertise in psychology. One is that experts are "born," and the other is that they are "made." We have referred to these views as the *talent view* and the *acquired characteristics view*, respectively (Hambrick & Meinz, 2011a).

CURRENT EVIDENCE

Goal and Organization of Chapter

The goal of this chapter is to review evidence for these views in music. Many people have tried to learn how to play instruments such as the violin, cello, or piano. But very few become skilled enough to pass an audition for the Juilliard School, or even for a community symphony. Many fewer still—a few out of a million—reach a level of skill that could legitimately be called exceptional. Our specific goal is to speculate about the role of *working memory capacity* (WMC) in musical skill. WMC is widely regarded as a major contributor to individual differences in a wide variety of complex tasks, including language comprehension, problem solving, decision making, complex learning, and reasoning, to name a few (see Hambrick, Kane, &

Engle, 2005, for a review). It has even been recently suggested that—beginning some 650,000 years ago—an increase in WMC sparked creative culture in humans, and is the development that allowed modern humans to replace Neanderthals (Coolidge & Wynn, 2009; see also Chapter 3 in this volume). Here, we review the available evidence, what little exists, for the role of WMC in musical skill. We consider evidence from unskilled and skilled musicians, children and adults. The chapter is organized into two major sections. In the first section, we discuss possible reasons for the popularity of music as a domain for expertise research, as well as an approach to the scientific investigation of music skill. In the second section, we review evidence for the role of acquired characteristics and basic capacities—especially WMC—in music skill. We conclude by identifying some unresolved issues and directions for future research.

Music as Venue for Research on Expertise

Music is a frequent venue for research on expertise. In fact, although chess has been described as the "fruit fly" (*Drosophila*) of expertise research, at least as many articles have been published on music expertise as on chess expertise. A likely reason for this interest is that music is simply that it is practical to study. Compared to, say, computer programmers or radiologists, or even chess players, musicians are abundant in the general population. Nearly all colleges and universities have a music department, and thus music majors, and there are always at least a few musicians in any undergraduate subject pool. And most cities have some sort of community symphony.

It is also easy to import music tasks into the lab. What Ericsson and Smith (1991) termed the *expertise approach* is a strategy for scientifically investigating expertise. The major idea of this approach is that expertise should be judged not by reputation, status, or credentials—criteria that are largely subjective—but rather by objectively verifiable performance in the domain. That is, this approach defines expertise as a consistently superior level of performance on tasks that are designed to capture the critical requirements of a domain. This idea is illustrated in Figure 7.2 in terms of a normal distribution of performance on domain-representative tasks for any given instrument. Expert performance is defined as performance that is three or more standard deviations above the mean.

We suspect that the second reason that music has so frequently been used for research on expertise is personal. Nearly everyone likes, even loves, music of some sort, and many people have at least attempted to acquire a high level of skill in music. To put it another way, we suspect that much research on music is "me-search"—research inspired by the researchers' interest in understanding something about themselves. Next, we consider what this research has revealed about the origins of musical expertise.

The Importance of Acquired Characteristics

Research in cognitive psychology has established that one of the most powerful predictors of success in complex domains is simply what people know—the

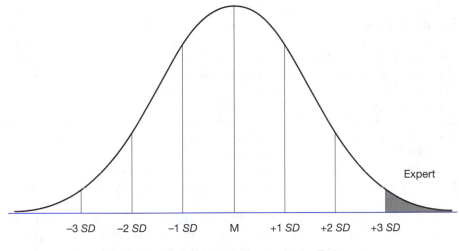

Performance on Domain Representative Tasks

Figure 7.2   Statistical definition of expertise

representations, procedures, processes, and strategies that people acquire through years of experience in a domain, and which reflect adaptations to the unique demands of a given task. Beginning with de Groot's (1946/1978) work, the importance of domain knowledge as a major determinant of higher-level cognition was first demonstrated in studies of chess. Therefore, he proposed that what differentiates skilled and less-skilled chess players is the perception of familiar patterns of pieces. DeGroot (1946/1978) found that chess masters had superior memory for briefly presented chess pieces in game positions, as compared to weaker players. He reasoned "it is evident that 'experience' is the foundation of the superior achievements of the masters" (p. 329). The outcome of this experience, de Groot proposed, is the perception of familiar patterns of pieces. Using more controlled experimental procedures, Chase and Simon (1973) replicated de Groot's finding in a study with players representing three skill levels (expert, intermediate, beginner). In addition to recalling pieces in game positions, the participants recalled random configurations of pieces. Chase and Simon found that expertise enhanced memory for actual (structured) positions but not memory for random (unstructured) positions. Chase and Simon also estimated the average chunk-size for each player, on the assumption that a pause in recall of two seconds or greater indicated a boundary between chunks. Based on the finding of larger chunk sizes for the experts in their study than for the weaker players, Chase and Simon proposed that experts hold in short-term memory a relatively small number of labels for familiar patterns of chess pieces stored in long-term memory. Thereby, experts maintain access to a large amount of information without exceeding the capacity limits of short-term memory. By contrast, weaker players overload short-term memory because they must maintain a large number of individual pieces.

This sort of Skill×Structure interaction was subsequently replicated in a wide variety of domains, including music. For example, Halpern and Bower (1982) presented musicians and non-musicians with *good*, *bad*, and *random* melodies, and found that although there was an overall expertise advantage (i.e., main effect), this advantage was largest for the good melodies, and smallest for the random melodies (see also Meinz & Salthouse, 1998). (Although seldom mentioned in discussions of expertise research, in replications of Chase and Simon (1973), a small, and sometimes significant, expertise advantage is nearly always found for recall of random chess positions (see Gobet & Simon, 1996). Halpern and Bower also created a consistency score for each of several melodies used in a previous study, reflecting the musicians' agreement on groupings of notes in the melody (i.e., chunk), and found that the melodies with high consistency ratings were the ones that showed the largest expertise advantage. The recognition of large, meaningful patterns of domain-relevant information therefore seems to be an important component of musical skill.

Eye-movement studies provide additional support for the role of chunking in chess skill. For example, expert players make more fixations on salient pieces and have a larger *visual span* for chess information than do novices; that is, experts are capable of encoding a greater amount of information from a chess board in a single fixation than are novices (Charness, Reingold, Pomplun, & Stampe, 2001; Reingold, Charness, Pomplun, & Stampe, 2001; Reingold, Charness, Schultetus, & Stampe, 2001). Similarly, evidence from music suggests that skilled sight-readers take in more notes in a single fixation than unskilled sight-readers (Furneaux & Land, 1999; Goolsby, 1994), and that the eye-hand span— the distance the eyes are ahead of the hands—is larger in skilled than unskilled musicians (Gilman & Underwood, 2003; Truitt, Clifton, Pollatsek, & Raynor, 1997).

Deliberate Practice and Music Skill   More recently, research has established that expertise in music reflects a long period of *deliberate practice*. As Ericsson, Krampe, and Tesch-Römer (1993) defined it, deliberate practice refers to engagement in activities that meet three criteria: they are highly relevant to improving performance in the domain, require a high level of concentration, and are not particularly enjoyable. In a pioneering study, Ericsson et al. asked students from a German music academy to rate a variety of music-related activities on these three dimensions (i.e., *relevance*, *effort*, and *pleasure*), and then to provide estimates of the amount of time in a typical week spent engaging in the activities for each year since taking up the instrument. The major finding was that there were large differences in the cumulative amount of engagement in the activity that qualified as deliberate practice—*practice alone*—but not in other activities. By age 20, the "best" violinists, who had been nominated by the faculty as having the potential for a career as an international soloist, had accumulated an average of 10,000 hours of practice alone—thousands of hours more than less accomplished players. In a follow-up study, the difference between expert and amateur pianists was even more dramatic —10,000 hours of practice alone for the experts, compared to only 2,000 hours for the amateurs. Other researchers have observed similarly strong relationships between estimates of deliberate practice and various measures of music skill. For example, Ruthsatz, Detterman, Griscom, and Cirullo (2008) found moderate to strong correlations between deliberate practice and measures of musical achievement in music majors ($r=.54$) and conservatory students ($r=.31$) (for another example, see Sloboda, Davidson, Howe, & Moore, 1996).

Challenges to the Deliberate Practice View   The evidence just discussed is consistent with the possibility that deliberate practice is necessary for the acquisition of expertise, but it has been pointed out that this evidence is purely correlational (e.g., Sternberg, 1996). It is therefore possible that positive correlations between deliberate practice and music skill are spurious and reflect a certain "third-variable"—musical talent. The idea of this account would be that musical talent positively predicts musical skill, as well as engagement in deliberate practice. However, if the question is whether the true correlation between deliberate practice and music skill is *zero*, then the answer is simply no. Exceptional levels of performance in music and other domains are almost never reached without years of full-time engagement in the domain (e.g., Sosniak, 1985), and there is no scientific evidence for exceptional musical performance arising out of "thin air." Even in cases of autistic savants—individuals who excel in one specific area despite overall intellectual deficits—musical performance appears to reflect acquired skills (Ericsson & Faivre, 1988; Howe, 1990).

Nevertheless, Ericsson and colleagues' interpretation of the correlation between deliberate practice and skill—which is that the former causes the latter—is not the only interpretation that makes sense. Although it seems clear that deliberate practice contributes to success, it is possible that success is what keeps a music student motivated to continue engaging in deliberate practice, which leads to acquisition of even higher levels of skill. This account accords with everyday experience—we tend to persist in things that we are good at, which makes us even better at these things, but to quit things we are bad at, or to engage in them on a purely recreational basis. Furthermore, Ericsson and colleagues have never made a convincing case based on evidence that deliberate practice is *sufficient* for the acquisition of expertise—that if two people practice the same amount, with equal intensity, they will reach the same level of performance.

It does seem that some people acquire musical skill with little effort, or at least with much less effort than others, implying that some people have more *talent* for music than others. Take the case of Joshua Bell, one of the greatest living violinists. Legend has it that Bell frequently skipped violin practice to play video games. Sometimes anecdotes are exaggerated, while other times, if not made up altogether, important details are omitted. In an interview for *Mother Jones* magazine (Mechanic, 2011), Bell did confess to ditching practice:

> I was more than *into* video games. I was addicted. Really, looking back, I think I had a severe addiction, with all the classic symptoms of anxiety and release and things that go along with it. I remember going out the back door of the music school where I should have been practicing. My mother would drop me off and I'd go out the back and literally break into a sprint to get to the arcade, feeling that rush of like—I've never done drugs but apparently it's like that—I'd walk into the arcade and I'd just feel this euphoria.

But we don't know how often he ditched and whether he somehow made up for the lost practice time. We also cannot rule out the possibility, as far-fetched as it seems, that Bell's video game playing was somehow beneficial to his violin playing. Perhaps, for example, he mentally practiced some aspect of violin playing while playing video games.

Details of another prodigy's story are murky as well. It seems clear from the historical record that Mozart was musically precocious. There seems to be little doubt, for example, that he could play the piano at a very young age. However, accomplishments attributed to the young Mozart have been challenged. In particular, music historians have long suspected that Mozart's father, Leopold, ghost-wrote some of his son's early compositions. (Leopold Mozart was not only an accomplished composer in his own right, but also one of the best music *teachers* of his time and author of the first book in German on how to teach violin.) So, Mozart's story could as easily be held up as unassailable evidence for the nurture account of musical expertise as for the nature account—as could countless others. For example, when asked about how he developed his technique, Charlie Parker, the great jazz saxophonist, recalled in a 1954 radio interview, "I put quite a bit of study into the horn. . . . In fact the neighbors threatened to ask my mother to move once when we were living out West. She said I was driving them crazy with the horn. I used to put in at least 11 to 15 hours a day." Charlie Parker was also kicked out of his high school band—for lack of talent. The bottom line is that anecdotes can't be trusted to answer the question of whether talent plays a role in becoming an expert. Is there any better evidence?

The Importance of Basic Abilities

There is no single, agreed-upon definition of *talent*. However, as Howe, Davidson, and Sloboda (1998) discussed, there are three empirical qualifications that nearly all theorists agree on for designating a trait, or constellation of traits, as a component of talent. First, the trait must be *innate*. That is, it must be demonstrated that individual differences in the trait are substantially, if not entirely, due to genetic factors, as for example evidenced by stronger correlations between test scores for monozygotic (MZ) twins than dizygotic (DZ) twins. Second, the trait must contribute to the acquisition of skill in some domain. That is, it must be shown that people who possess a high level of the trait acquire a skill at a faster rate than people who possess a lower level of the trait, or reach a higher ultimate level of performance, or both. Finally, there must be variability in the trait across people. To acknowledge the idea of talent is to acknowledge that people are *not* all born alike, and so if a trait is said to be part of a talent, it must be the case that some people have more of it than others.

There is near universal agreement among intelligence theorists that cognitive abilities meet these qualifications for talent. First, cognitive abilities are substantially heritable. As revealed by twin and adoption studies, heritability estimates vary across samples, but are typically in the range from 50 percent to 75 percent for general intelligence, and just a bit lower for specific abilities such as spatial ability and verbal ability (Plomin, DeFries, McClearn, & McGuffin, 2008). Second, cognitive abilities predict acquisition of complex skills, with validities for specific abilities varying predictably depending on the nature of the domain. For example, in their longitudinal study of intellectual giftedness, Lubinski, Benbow, and colleagues found that visuo-spatial ability predicts achievement in the physical sciences whereas verbal ability predicts achievement in the humanities (see Robertson, Smeets, Lubinski, and Benbow, 2010). Finally, cognitive abilities are approximately normally distributed, which is to say that there is substantial variability in scores on tests deigned to measure them. What, then, do we know about the role of cognitive abilities in skilled performance?

The Organization of Cognitive Abilities

Over a century ago, Spearman (1904) observed that students' grades in academic courses—Classics, French, English, Mathematics, and so on—all tended to correlate positively with each other. Spearman also invented a statistical tool—factor analysis—to formally estimate the contribution of the general factor implied by this "positive manifold" to the variance in each of the measures. More than a century later, Spearman's g is one of the most replicated findings in psychological science. Given a reasonably large and representative sample of children, adolescents, or adults, a g factor nearly always emerges in a factor analysis of cognitive ability measures.

For nearly a century following Spearman's discovery, intelligence researchers squabbled over the question of whether g is all there is to human intelligence. The question was: Can intelligence be reduced to a single factor, or is it better to think of it as comprising multiple, specific abilities? L. L. Thurstone (1938) thought the latter, arguing for the existence of seven *primary mental abilities*—verbal comprehension, reasoning, perceptual speed, numerical ability, word fluency, associative memory, and spatial visualization (Thurstone, 1938). Around the same time, Raymond Cattell, a former student of Spearman, described a distinction between two general intelligences: *fluid* cognitive ability (Gf), reflecting the ability to solve novel problems, and a *crystallized* cognitive ability (Gc), reflecting knowledge acquired through experience (Cattell, 1971). Finally, in the early 1990s, Carroll (1993) did a great service to the field by putting the debate to rest. In his landmark survey of factor-analytic studies, Carroll re-analyzed more than 400 data sets, and concluded that cognitive abilities can be organized into three levels, or "strata." The first stratum includes a g factor, representing what diverse measures of cognitive ability have in common—which is to say, Spearman's g. The second stratum includes a small number of *broad cognitive abilities*, including fluid intelligence (Gf) and crystallized intelligence (Gc). The third stratum includes a much larger number of task specific abilities. There has been no serious challenge to Carroll's model over the past two decades.

A number of studies have investigated relationships between measures of music skill and cognitive abilities. Despite a few null findings (e.g., Shuter-Dyson, 1968), correlations between measures of general intelligence and musical skill have generally been found to be positive, significant, and sizable. Spearman (1904) himself reported a correlation of .70 between general intelligence and school marks for musical talent. More recently, Lynn, Wilson, and Gault (1989) had children perform conventional intelligence tests, as well as a test of musical ability with four subtests: pitch (compare successive tones), tunes (compare successive tunes), rhythm (compare successive rhythms), and chords (number of notes in chords). Loadings of the subtests on a g factor ranged from .45 to .59. Similarly, Phillips (1976) reported correlations of greater than .60 between scores on a cognitive ability test and a measure of musicality from two standardized tests of musical aptitude. There have also been reports of positive correlations between measures of musical skill and measures of more specific abilities. For example, Lynn, Wilson and Gault (1989) reported moderate positive correlations between measures of musical ability and scores on Raven's Progressive Matrices—a relatively pure measure of Gf—and Ruthsatz et al. (2008) reported a moderate positive correlation between Raven's scores and musical audition ratings in high school band members.

Working Memory Capacity: Four Decades of Evolution   So it seems that cognitive abilities may play at least some role in the acquisition of musical skill. Nevertheless, the question of what measures of cognitive abilities (e.g., Raven's) reflect at the level of information processing has never been satisfactorily answered. Indeed, since Spearman (1904), psychometric g has been derided as an atheoretical construct—yet another "black box" in psychology. One approach to answering this question has been termed the *cognitive correlates* approach. The basic idea of this approach is to design measures to capture "primitives" of the cognitive system, and then to see how these measures correlate with independent assessments of g (see Deary, 2011, for a review). *Working memory capacity* (WMC) has been conceptualized as one such component.

In the 1970s, Baddeley and Hitch (1974) reported a series of experiments in which they found that making participants perform secondary tasks designed to occupy short-term memory had surprisingly little effect on their performance in primary tasks such as reasoning and comprehension. For example, in one experiment, the only effect of secondary task load on performance in a grammatical reasoning task was to increase the amount of time participants required to solve the problems; there was no effect on accuracy. In light of this sort of finding— which was not easily reconcilable with the idea that short-term memory is a central bottleneck in information processing (Atkinson & Shiffrin, 1968)—Baddeley and Hitch proposed that short-term memory is a complex system that includes a *central executive*, which is responsible for control processes such as reasoning, and planning, and two "slave" systems for temporarily maintaining information—the *phonological loop* and the *visuospatial sketchpad*.

In the 1980s, Daneman and Carpenter (1980) developed a test of working memory capacity (WMC). Following Baddeley and Hitch's (1974) view of working memory as a system that can be devoted to both information storage and processing, Daneman and Carpenter designed their test—which they called *reading span*—to include interleaved storage and processing components. The participant was to read a series of sentences, remembering the final word of each sentence for later recall. Daneman and Carpenter found that reading span—the number of sentences a participant could read while maintaining perfect recall of the sentence-final words—correlated very strongly with various measures of reading comprehension. In a subsequent study, Turner and Engle (1989) replicated Daneman and Carpenter's finding of strong correlations between reading span and reading comprehension. But more important, Turner and Engle found that scores in another test of WMC—which they called *operation span*—correlated just as highly with reading comprehension. Turner and Engle concluded that whatever reading span and operation span captures, it is not task-dependent, but rather reflects a general capacity.

In the 1990s, Kyllonen and Christal (1990) carried out the first large-scale psychometric study of individual differences in WMC and psychometric intelligence—or "g." The take-home message of this study was that the two constructs are strongly correlated, and perhaps even the same. On the weight of this evidence, Kyllonen (1996) observed, "This finding of the centrality of the working memory capacity factor leads to the conclusion that working memory capacity may indeed be essentially Spearman's g" (p. 73). Later in the 1990s, Engle, Tuholski, Laughlin, and Conway (1999) proposed a more mechanistic account of individual differences in WMC. In this study, along with Gf tests, participants completed both simple span and complex span tasks. Engle et al. reasoned that simple span tasks require storage of information, whereas complex span tasks require storage but also *attention*, to coordinate the storage and processing requirements. There were two key findings. First, in a factor analysis, the complex span and simple span measures loaded on separate factors, which correlated positively though considerably less than unity. This finding wasn't particularly surprising, but was still important as the first factor-analytic demonstration of a distinction between working memory capacity and short-term memory. Second, when the variance common to the WMC and short-term memory factors was taken into account, the *residual* variance for WMC—that part of the variance which Engle et al. had argued reflects controlled attention—positively predicted Gf.

In the 2000s, there were more reports of strong relationships between WMC and Gf. Oberauer and colleagues found a near-perfect relationship between the *relational integration* function of working memory—reflecting the ability to make connects between elements in memory and thereby to create new represen-tations—and reasoning ability (e.g., Oberauer, Süß, Wilhelm, & Wittmann, 2008). This sort of evidence prompted Engle (2002) to suggest that WMC "is at least related to, maybe even isomorphic to, general fluid intelligence" (pp. 21–22). "Related to" turned out to be the true state of affairs. Kane et al. (2004) had participants complete both verbal and spatial complex span tasks to assess WMC, as well as verbal and spatial reasoning tests to assess Gf. Structural equation modeling revealed that it was possible to pull apart verbal and spatial WMC factors. However, these factors correlated strongly (> .80), implying the existence of a general WMC factor. And when modeled, this factor correlated strongly (r=.64) with Gf, but far less than 1. Subsequently, in a meta-analysis, Ackerman, Beier, and Boyle (2005) reported an average correlation of about .40 between Raven's and complex span, and thus suggested that the relationship between WMC and Gf was quite a bit weaker than Engle had supposed. However, in a commentary on Ackerman et al.'s meta-analysis, Kane, Hambrick, and Conway (2005) pointed out that Ackerman et al. underestimated the magnitude of the relationship between

WMC and Gf by focusing on the relationship at the manifest rather than latent variable level, and in a re-analysis of data from 12 studies found an average correlation of .72 between the constructs.

The 2000s also saw considerable progress toward identifying mechanisms that underlie variation in WMC (see Conway et al.'s 2007 edited volume). Engle, Kane, and colleagues reported a series of studies suggesting that WMC reflects the ability to use attention to maintain information in a highly active and accessible state, especially under conditions of distraction or interference. Two studies illustrate the flavor of this research. In the first (Kane, Bleckley, Conway, & Engle, 2001), subjects classified as either low-span or high-span performed a simple task. In one condition, the prosaccade condition, a flashing cue appeared in the same location on the screen as an upcoming stimulus—the letter B, P, or R—and the task was to press a key corresponding to the stimulus. In the other condition, the antisaccade condition, the target always appeared in the location opposite to that of the cue. For both reaction time and accuracy, Kane et al. found that advantage of high-spans over low-spans was larger in the antisaccade condition.

The second study requires a bit more background. In the 1950s, the British scientist Colin Cherry reported a series of experiments in which subjects were instructed to repeat a message presented in one ear—the "attended" ear—while ignoring a message presented in the other ear—the "unattended" ear (Cherry, 1953). Generally speaking, subjects had no problem with the task. Not only could subjects report little from the unattended message—they didn't even notice when, for example, the story changed or when the language changed from English to French. This sort of finding led Donald Broadbent, in his book *Perception and Communication* (1958), to propose that attention acts as an all-or-none filter, letting relevant information into working memory but blocking out irrelevant information. Nevertheless, Moray (1959) demonstrated that content from an unattended message is not completely rejected. A third of subjects heard their own names in the unattended ear, even though they failed to hear a word that was repeated 35 times. However, Conway, Cowan, and Bunting (2001) wondered why more of Moray's subjects didn't hear their own name. After all, as Dale Carnegie wrote, "A person's name is to that person, the sweetest, most important sound in any language." So why not 100 percent? Conway et al. reasoned that if complex span tasks do in fact capture the ability to control attention, then high-spans would be less likely to notice their names in the unattended ear. And this is what they found: In a replication of Moray's experiment, 65 percent of low-spans, *but only 20 percent of high-spans*, heard their name in the unattended ear. There was also a great deal of interest in the 2000s in trying to identify neurological underpinnings of WMC. Gray, Chabris, and Braver (2003), for example, found that a measure of prefrontal cortex activation, captured while subjects performed the n-back task, correlated positively and moderately with scores on Raven's.

Unresolved Issues: Construct and Predictive Validity   At the time of this writing, Daneman and Carpenter's (1980) original report of the reading span task has been cited well over a thousand times, and WMC has taken its place among the most researched topics in the field of psychology. WMC has also captured the popular imagination. Michael Kane and colleagues' research on WMC and mind-wandering has been the topic of a number of recent news articles (see, e.g., "Science paying attention to not paying attention" at msnbc.com), and in a recent *New York Times* Op-Ed, we discussed evidence for the role of WMC in music skill (Hambrick & Meinz, 2011b; more about this study in the next section). Nevertheless, there are a number of unresolved conceptual and psychometric issues concerning WMC. One is construct validity—whether WMC is empirically distinct from established ability constructs. Salthouse and colleagues have argued that because WMC and Gf correlate so highly it may not be meaningful to think of WMC as a distinct dimension of variation in cognition (see Salthouse, Pink, & Tucker-Drob, 2008). However, critics of this perspective have argued that to equate WMC with Gf is to gain no better understanding of either construct (Engle & Kane, 2004). Another unresolved issue is predictive validity—whether WMC predicts outcomes, independent of Gf and other abilities. There is some evidence that it does: in a study of Navy sailors, we found that WMC predicted performance in a multitasking paradigm, above and beyond Gf. Moreover, WMC accounted for more of the variance in multitasking after controlling for Gf than vice versa (Hambrick et al., 2010). However, there is not enough evidence at this point to argue that WMC adds to the prediction of complex task performance across a wide range of domains.

Working Memory Capacity and Musical Skill

It makes sense to think that WMC might be involved in playing music. Playing music is, after all, a highly complex cognitive task. The musician must decode symbols from a sheet of music, and maintain these representations for some period of time in order to execute the indicated actions. A simple test of the proposition of the idea that working memory is involved in all this would be to have novice musicians—let's say pianists—play music while doing a secondary task designed to tax WMC, such as random number generation. (We subjected the second author's husband—a novice pianist though expert trombonist—to exactly this torture, and he could barely play.) What is more interesting to us is whether individual differences in WMC translate into individual differences in musical skill.

A few studies have investigated individual differences in musical perception in children. Anvari, Trainor, Woodside, and Levy (2002) had four- and five-year-olds complete a test of musical perception, with rhythm, melody, and chord subtests, along with a digit span task. In the four-year-olds, a factor analysis of the subtest measures revealed a single factor, reflecting musical skill. This factor correlated very highly with digit span (r=.68). In the five-year-olds, two factors emerged—pitch perception and rhythm perception—both of which correlated highly with digit span (rs=.46 and .54, respectively). Carl Seashore (1938/1967), who developed the first test of musical aptitude, anticipated this sort of evidence in the design of his test:

> There are many vastly divergent aspects of musical memory in musical talent which may be measured, but if we shall select only one for the present purpose, that one will

undoubtedly be auditory memory span, that is, the capacity for grasping and retaining for a moment a group of musical sounds apart from melodic situations.

(p. 338)

There is also relevant evidence from studies of adults. We know of two studies of the role of WMC in sight-reading—playing music with little or no preparation, as when a pianist accompanies a soloist. In the first study, Kopiez and Lee (2006) had 52 university-level piano students complete a questionnaire to assess sight-reading practice, along with a sight-reading task and tests of cognitive abilities, including WMC (see Kopiez, Weihs, Ligges, & Lee, 2006, for a companion article). The sight-reading task included five levels of difficulty, and performance was objectively scored using software that compared the music to what the pianists actually played. The WMC task was a "mental counters" task, in which participants were required to keep track of changing values of digits displayed in cells of a 3×3 matrix. Not surprisingly, sight-reading practice correlated positively with sight-reading performance. However, this was not the whole story. The correlation between WMC and overall performance just missed conventional significance in a two-tailed test ($r = .26, p = .06$), and was thus significant in a one-tailed test, which would seem completely justified in this case.

In the second study, we had 57 pianists complete a deliberate practice questionnaire, a sight-reading task, and a battery of complex span tasks to measure WMC. The participants represented an extremely wide range of experience. For example, years playing the piano ranged from one to 57, and lifetime deliberate practice ranged from less than 200 hours to over 31,000 hours. Our specific goal was to test what we have recently referred to as the *circumvention-of-limits hypothesis*. The circumvention-of-limits hypothesis is the idea that acquisition of domain-specific knowledge reduces, and can even eliminate, the effect of cognitive abilities on complex task performance.

This idea has been mentioned, or implied, by a number of skill acquisition theorists. Extending Fitts and Posner's (1967) and Anderson's (1983) models of skill acquisition to an individual differences framework, Ackerman (1988) proposed that general intelligence is important for complex task performance early in training, but becomes less important as training continues and knowledge is proceduralized. Similarly, Ericsson and Charness (1994) argued that "[p]erformers can acquire skills that circumvent basic limits on working memory capacity and sequential processing" (p. 725).

Not surprisingly, we found that deliberate practice accounted for a large proportion of the variance in sight-reading performance—in fact, nearly half (44 percent). However, WMC accounted for an additional 7.4 percent of the variance—a much smaller but still sizable contribution—and there was no evidence for a WMC/deliberate practice interaction. In other words, as illustrated in Figure 7.3, WMC was as important as a predictor of sight-reading performance in beginners as in pianists with thousands of hours of deliberate practice. Based on this finding, we argued that deliberate practice is necessary for a high level of skill in sight-reading, but not always sufficient.

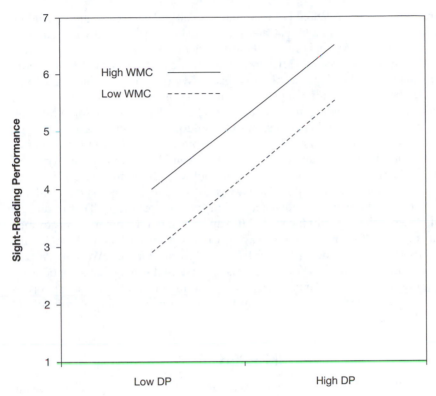

Figure 7.3   Sight-reading performance as a function of WMC and deliberate practice (DP). From Meinz and Hambrick (2010)

Training Studies.   Some reports have documented enhanced general cognitive abilities in musicians as compared to non-musicians. For example, musically trained children show enhanced verbal, mathematical, and visuospatial performance as compared to their untrained counterparts (see Schellenberg, 2001, for a review), although some have reported these effects to be temporary (Costa-Giomi, 1999). Most notably, Schellenberg (2004), using an experimental design, showed significantly larger gains in IQ in a group of children receiving music lessons than in control groups (no treatment or drama lessons) after only 36 weeks. Brandler and Rammsayer (2003) reported that adult musicians showed significantly higher verbal memory and significantly lower abstract reasoning scores than non-musicians.

FUTURE DIRECTIONS

Research has confirmed what most people would believe to be true about musical expertise: knowledge and skills acquired through years of practice are undeniably important. Musical expertise isn't acquired overnight. However, the evidence we have reviewed here suggests that this isn't the whole story. There have been a few reports of positive correlations between musical skill and basic capacities, including WMC. But we hasten to add that there is surprisingly little directly relevant evidence on this point. We believe that the first order of business where investigating the relationship between WMC and musical skill is concerned is to more convincingly establish that a relationship exists. We dream of conducting a study with musicians with a wide range of instruments—piano to piccolo—performing various tasks (sight-reading, memorized pieces) as well as a battery of WMC and ability tests. Our prediction is that WMC would predict sight-reading—playing without preparation—but not playing pieces from memory. Once there is better evidence of whether a relationship exists between WMC and various types of musical skill, the next step would be to figure out what drives the relationship. For example, we speculated that WMC impacts sight-reading by limiting the eye-hand span—how far the pianist is looking ahead in the piece of music. That is, all else equal, it seems that a pianist high in WMC can hold in mind more notes in advance of the one that they're currently playing than a pianist lower in WMC. This hypothesis could be investigated by tracking eye movements. We believe that research aimed at addressing these two goals—first establishing that a relationship exists between WMC and musical skill and then understanding the mechanisms behind that relationship—will significantly advance understanding of both WMC and skill.

REFERENCES

Ackerman, P. L. (1988). Determinants of individual differences during skill acquisition: Cognitive abilities and information processing. *Journal of Experimental Psychology: General, 117*, 288–318.

Ackerman, P. L., Beier, M. E., & Boyle, M. O. (2005). Working memory and intelligence: The same or different constructs? *Psychological Bulletin, 131*, 30–60.

Anderson, J. R. (1983). *The architecture of cognition.* Cambridge, MA: Harvard University Press.

Anvari, S. H., Trainor, L. J., Woodside, J., & Levy, B. A. (2002). Relations among musical skills, phonological processing, and early reading ability in preschool children. *Journal of Experimental Child Psychology, 83,* 111–130.

Atkinson, R. C., & Shiffrin, R. M. (1968). Human memory: A proposed system and its control processes. In K. W. Spence & J. T. Spence (Eds.), *The psychology of learning and motivation* (Vol. 2). New York: Academic Press.

Baddeley, A. D., & Hitch, G. (1974). Working memory. In G. H. Bower (Ed.), *The psychology of learning and motivation: Advances in research and theory* (Vol. 8). New York: Academic Press.

Brandler, S., & Rammsayer, T. H. (2003). Differences in mental abilities between musicians and non-musicians. *Psychology of Music, 31*, 123–138.

Broadbent, D. E. (1958). *Perception and communication.* New York: Pergamon.

Carroll, J. B. (1993). *Human cognitive abilities: A survey of factor-analytical studies.* New York: Cambridge University Press.

Cattell, R. B. (1971). *Abilities: Their structure, growth, and action.* Boston: Houghton Mifflin.

Charness, N., Reingold, E. M., Pomplun, M., & Stampe, D. M. (2001). The perceptual aspect of skilled performance in chess: Evidence from eye movements. *Memory and Cognition, 29*, 1146–1152.

Chase, W. G., & Simon, H. A. (1973). Perception in chess. *Cognitive Psychology, 4,* 55–81.

Cherry, E. C. (1953). Some experiments on the recognition of speech, with one and with two ears. *Journal of Acoustic Society of America, 25,* 975–979.

Conway, A. R. A., Cowan, N., & Bunting, M. F. (2001). The cocktail party phenomenon revisited: The importance of working memory capacity. *Psychonomic Bulletin & Review, 8,* 331–335.

Conway, A. R. A., Jarrold, C., Kane, M. J., Miyake, A., & Towse, J. (2007). *Variation in working memory.* Oxford: Oxford University Press.

Coolidge, F. L., & Wynn, T. (2009). *The rise of* Homo sapiens: *The evolution of modern thinking.* West Sussex, UK: Wiley-Blackwell.

Costa-Giomi, E. (1999). The effects of three years of piano instruction on children's cognitive development. *Journal of Research in Music Education, 47,* 198–212.

Daneman, M., & Carpenter, P. A. (1980). Individual differences in working memory and reading. *Journal of Verbal Learning and Verbal Behavior, 19,* 450–466.

Deary, I. J. (2011). Intelligence. *Annual Review of Psychology, 63,* 452–482.

de Groot, A. D. (1978). Thought and choice in chess (2nd ed.). The Hague: Mouton. (Original work published in 1946.)

Engle, R. W. (2002). Working memory capacity as executive attention. *Current Directions in Psychological Science, 11,* 19–23.

Engle, R. W., & Kane, M. J. (2004). Executive attention, working memory capacity, and a two-factor theory of cognitive control. In B. H. Ross (Ed.), *The psychology of learning and motivation,* volume 44 (pp. 145–199). New York: Academic Press.

Engle, R. W., Tuholski, S. W., Laughlin, J., & Conway, A. R. A. (1999). Working memory, short-term memory and general fluid intelligence: A latent variable model approach. *Journal of Experimental Psychology: General, 128,* 309–331.

Ericsson, K. A., & Charness, N. (1994). Expert performance: Its structure and acquisition. *American Psychologist, 49,* 725–747.

Ericsson, K. A., & Faivre, I. A. (1988). What's exceptional about exceptional abilities? The exceptional brain: Neuropsychology of talent and special abilities. In L. K. Obler & D. Fein (Eds.) *The exceptional brain: Neuropsychology of talent and special abilities* (pp. 436–473). New York: Guilford Press.

Ericsson, K. A., Krampe, R. T., & Tesch-Römer, C. (1993). The role of deliberate practice in the acquisition of expert performance. *Psychological Review, 100,* 363–406.

Ericsson, K. A., & Smith, J. (1991). Prospects and limits in the empirical study of expertise: An introduction. In K. A. Ericsson and J. Smith (Eds.), *Toward a general theory of expertise: Prospects and limits* (pp. 1–38). Cambridge: Cambridge University Press.

Fitts, P. M., & Posner, M. I. (1967). *Human performance.* Belmont, CA: Brooks Cole.

Furneaux, S., & Land, M. F. (1999). The effects of skill on the eye–hand span during music sight-reading. *Proceedings of the Royal Society of London, 266,* 2435–2440.

Galton, F. (1869). *Hereditary genius.* London: Macmillan.

Gilman, E., & Underwood, G. (2003). Restricting the field of view to investigate the perceptual spans of pianists. *Visual Cognition, 10,* 201–232.

Gobet, F., & Simon, H. A. (1996). The roles of recognition processes and look-ahead search in time-constrained expert problem solving: Evidence from grand-master-level chess. *Psychological Science, 7 (1),* 52–55.

Goolsby, T. W. (1994). Profiles of processing: Eye movements during sightreading. *Music Perception, 12,* 97–123.

Gray, J. R., Chabris, C. F., & Braver, T. S. (2003). Neural mechanisms of general fluid intelligence. *Nature Neuroscience, 6,* 316–322.

Halpern, A. R., & Bower, G. H. (1982). Musical expertise and melodic structure in memory for musical notation. *American Journal of Psychology, 95,* 31–50.

Hambrick, D. Z., Kane, M. J., & Engle, R. W. (2005). The role of working memory in higher-level cognition: Domain-specific versus domain-general perspectives. In R. Sternberg & J. E. Pretz (Eds.), *Cognition and intelligence: Identifying the mechanisms of the mind* (pp. 104–121). New York: Cambridge University Press.

Hambrick, D. Z., & Meinz, E. J. (2011a). Limits on the predictive power of domain-specific experience and knowledge in skilled performance. *Current Directions in Psychological Science, 20*, 275–279.

Hambrick, D. Z., & Meinz, E. J. (2011b). Sorry, strivers: Talent matters. *The New York Times*, Sunday Review, 11.

Hambrick, D. Z., Oswald, F. L., Darowski, E., Rench, T., & Brou, R. (2010). Determinants of success in multitasking: A synthetic work approach. *Applied Cognitive Psychology, 24*(8), 1149–1167.

Howe, M. J. A. (1990). *The origins of exceptional abilities*. Oxford: Basil Blackwell.

Howe, M. J. A., Davidson, J. W., & Sloboda, J. A. (1998). Innate talents: Reality or myth? *Behavioral and Brain Sciences, 21*, 399–407.

Kane, M. J., Bleckley, M. K., Conway, A. R. A., & Engle, R. W. (2001). A controlled-attention view of working memory capacity: Individual differences in memory span and the control of visual orienting. *Journal of Experimental Psychology: General, 130*, 169–183.

Kane, M. J., Hambrick, D. Z., & Conway, A. R. A. (2005). Working memory capacity and fluid intelligence are strongly related constructs: Comment on Ackerman, Beier, and Boyle (2004). *Psychological Bulletin, 131*, 66–71.

Kane, M. J., Hambrick, D. Z., Wilhelm, O., Payne, T., Tuholski, S., & Engle, R. W. (2004). The generality of working memory capacity: A latent variable approach to verbal and visuo-spatial memory span and reasoning. *Journal of Experimental Psychology: General, 133*, 189–217.

Kopiez, R., & Lee, J. I. (2006). Towards a dynamic model of skills involved in sight reading music. *Music Education Research, 8*, 97–120.

Kopiez, R., Weihs, C., Ligges, U., & Lee, J. I. (2006). Classification of high and low achievers in a music sight-reading task. *Psychology of Music, 34*, 15–26.

Kyllonen, P. C. (1996). Is working memory capacity Spearman's g? In I. Dennis and P. Tapsfield (Eds.), *Human abilities: Their nature and measurement* (pp. 49–75). Mahwah, NJ: Erlbaum.

Kyllonen, P. C., & Christal, R. E. (1990). Reasoning ability is (little more than) working-memory capacity?! *Intelligence, 14*, 389–433.

Lynn, R., Wilson, R. G., & Gault, A. (1989). Simple musical tests as measures of Spearman's g. *Personality and Individual Differences, 10*, 25–28.

Mechanic, M. (2011). Joshua Bell's virtuoso reality *Mother Jones*. May/June.

Meinz, E. J., & Hambrick, D. Z. (2010). Deliberate practice is necessary but not sufficient to explain individual differences in piano sight-reading skill: The role of working memory capacity. *Psychological Science, 21*, 914–919.

Meinz, E. J., & Salthouse, T. A. (1998). The effects of age and experience on memory for visually presented music. *Journals of Gerontology: Psychological Sciences, 53B*, 60–69.

Moray, N. (1959). Attention in dichotic listening: Affective cues and the influence of instructions. *The Quarterly Journal of Experimental Psychology, 11*, 56–60.

Oberauer, K., Süß, H.-M., Wilhelm, O., & Wittmann, W. W. (2008). Which working memory functions predict intelligence. *Intelligence, 36*, 641–652.

Phillips, D. (1976). An investigation of the relationship between musicality and intelligence. *Psychology of Music, 4*, 16–31.

Plomin, R., DeFries, J. C., McClearn, G. E., & McGuffin, P. (2008). *Behavioral Genetics* (5th ed.). New York: Worth Publishers.

Reingold, E. M., Charness, N., Pomplun, M., & Stampe, D. M. (2001). Visual span in expert chess players: Evidence from eye movements. *Psychological Science, 12*, 49–56.

Reingold, E. M., Charness, N., Schultetus, R. S., & Stampe, D. M. (2001). Perceptual automaticity in expert chess players: Parallel encoding of chess relations. *Psychonomic Bulletin and Review, 8,* 504–510.

Robertson, K., Smeets, S., Lubinski, D., & Benbow, C. P. (2010). Beyond the threshold hypothesis: Even among the gifted and top math/science graduate students, cognitive abilities, vocational interests, and lifestyle preferences matter for career choice, performance, and persistence. *Current Directions in Psychological Science, 19,* 346–351.

Ruthsatz, J., Detterman, D., Griscom, W. S., & Cirullo, B. A. (2008). Becoming an expert in the musical domain: It takes more than just practice. *Intelligence, 36,* 330–338.

Salthouse, T. A., Pink, J. E., & Tucker-Drob, E. M. (2008). Contextual analysis of fluid intelligence. *Intelligence, 36,* 464–486.

Schellenberg, E. G. (2001). Music and nonmusical abilities. *Annals of the New York Academy of Sciences, 930,* 355–371.

Schellenberg, E. G. (2004). Music lessons enhance IQ. *Psychological Science, 15,* 511–514.

Seashore, C. E. (1938/1967). *Psychology of music.* Mineola, NY: Dover.

Shuter-Dyson, R. (1968). *The psychology of musical ability.* Methuen: London.

Sloboda, J. A., Davidson, J. W., Howe, M. J. A., & Moore, D. G. (1996). The role of practice in the development of performing musicians. *British Journal of Psychology, 87,* 287–309.

Sosniak, L. A. (1985). Learning to be a concert pianist. In B. Bloom (Ed.), *Developing talent in young people* (pp. 19–67). New York: Ballantine Books.

Spearman, C. (1904). "General intelligence," objectively determined and measured. *American Journal of Psychology, 15,* 201–293.

Sternberg, R. J. (1996). Costs of expertise. In K. A. Ericsson (Ed.), *The road to excellence* (pp. 347–354). Mahwah, NJ: Erlbaum.

Thurstone, L. L. (1938). *Primary mental abilities.* Chicago: University of Chicago Press.

Truitt, F. E., Clifton, C., Pollatsek, A., & Rayner, K. (1997). The perceptual span and the eye–hand span in sight reading music. *Visual Cognition, 4,* 143–161.

Turner, M. L. & Engle, R. W. (1989). Is working memory capacity task dependent? *Journal of Memory and Language, 28,* 127–154.

Watson, J. B. (1970/1930). *Behaviorism.* New York: Norton. (Original work published 1930.)

Part IV

Working Memory and the Body

8

Working Memory and Diet

SCOTT E. KANOSKI

Department of Biological Sciences, University of Southern California,
Los Angeles, CA, USA

BACKGROUND INFORMATION

Working memory, the ability to actively store and manipulate information, is considered critical in normal everyday function and contributes significantly to other areas of cognition. Accumulating data show that learning and memory function, including some aspects of working memory, are influenced by diet and metabolic status. It has long been established that nutritional deficiency produces impairments in many domains of cognitive performance (for review, Del Parigi, Panza et al. 2006); however, modern Western cultures are no longer plagued by nutrient deficiency. Rather, the United States, the United Kingdom, and various other Western cultures appear to be facing an epidemic of *excessive* nutrient intake. In fact, obesity rates in the USA have increased by 75 percent since the early 1980s, with over one-third of adults now classified as obese (Ogden, Yanovski et al. 2007; CDC 2011) as defined by a body mass index (BMI) of greater than 30. In the UK, obesity rates have risen to now include approximately 25 percent of the adult population (Department of Health 2011). Obesity has recently been declared the second leading cause of preventable deaths in the USA, with average attributable annual healthcare costs nearly doubled since 1998 (Finkelstein, Trogdon et al. 2009). Given these alarming trends, a more relevant consideration of the influence of diet and metabolic status on cognition is what the effects of excessive energy intake and body weight gain are on memory function. Given how recently this "obesity epidemic" developed (within the past 20 years), researchers are only beginning to discover the effects of being overweight, obese, and consuming unhealthy high-calorie foods on cognition and neuropsychological function. The emerging picture is that while increased BMI and obesity are associated with impairments in working memory and other domains of cognitive function, certain dietary components that are commonly found in a Western diet, including saturated fat and simple carbohydrates (e.g., sugars), can have detrimental effects on brain substrates that control memory function, independent of the ability of these same dietary factors to contribute to obesity development. Further, both dietary factors and obesity are associated with the development of Alzheimer's disease and other forms of dementia (Kalmijn, Launer et al. 1997; Berrino 2002; Kanoski and Davidson 2011), which underscores the need for a better understanding of the relationships between diet, metabolic status, brain function, and cognition.

CURRENT EVIDENCE

This chapter first addresses the central nervous system controls of working memory, with a particular focus on two brain structures: the prefrontal cortex and the hippocampus. Next, evidence will be reviewed that links intake of a Western diet and obesity with impaired working memory and other types of memory dysfunction. Potential neurophysiological mechanisms mediating this type of dietary and metabolically induced cognitive impairment will then be addressed. Lastly, the implications of these findings will be discussed with regard to the growing obesity epidemic.

Brain Substrates of Working Memory

Complex behaviors are typically not mediated by processing in only one brain region, but rather involve a complex interplay between multiple brain areas. Working memory is no exception. Further, the necessity of neuronal processing in different brain regions has been shown to depend on the type of information (visuospatial, verbal, object, etc.) involved with the working memory demand (Honey and Fletcher 2006; Postle 2006). Here the focus will remain on two brain structures that are both linked with working memory function and have been shown to be altered by dietary and metabolic factors: the prefrontal cortex and the hippocampus.

The prefrontal cortex lies in front of the motor cortex at the front of the brain and is considered important for the implementation of various "higher-order" cognitive processes, including decision making and planning complex behaviors (Rushworth, Noonan et al. 2011). The prefrontal cortex is also necessary for working memory function, a notion that is largely credited to groundbreaking work from Goldman-Rakic and colleagues (Goldman-Rakic 1987). Goldman-Rakic demonstrated in non-human primates that neurons in the dorsolateral prefrontal cortex exhibited delay-related activity (e.g., neuronal firing) during a working memory task known as the delayed match to sample paradigm. Importantly, it was shown that either PFC-directed pharmacological disruption (Sawaguchi and Goldman-Rakic 1991) or selective lesions (Funahashi, Bruce et al. 1993) to the PFC impaired working memory function. The involvement of this brain region in working memory is also supported by several human imaging studies showing that the prefrontal cortex is activated during working memory tasks (e.g., Rama, Sala et al. 2001; Gruber and von Cramon 2003; Rama, Poremba et al. 2004). Whether prefrontal cortical involvement in working memory is based on storage of short-term memories, attention-based processing, or "gating" of sensory signals in working memory according to the behavioral relevance is not yet fully established and is a matter of debate (Postle 2006). Regardless, data from human and non-human animal models strongly support a critical role for this brain structure in the normal implementation of working memory function.

In 1957 Scoville and Milner initially reported memory loss in humans following damage to the hippocampus (Scoville and Milner 1957), a brain structure in the medial temporal lobe of the brain. Since that time the function of the hippocampus has been hotly debated. Two of the most influential theories of hippocampal function are: 1) the hippocampus is needed for declarative memory, or memory for facts and events (Squire 1992) [theory later revised, see (Cohen, Poldrack et al. 1997; Eichenbaum 2001; Squire 2004)], or 2) the hippocampus is critical for memory that requires processing of spatial information (O'Keefe and Dostrovsky 1971). While the hippocampus is not traditionally associated with working memory function, this brain structure is necessary for certain types of working memory, particularly working memory that requires the maintenance of spatial information. In rats, selective lesions to the hippocampus profoundly impair spatial working memory tasks in elevated mazes (Jarrard 1993; Jarrard, Davidson et al. 2004). In humans, a working memory task involving object-location associations produced neural activation in the hippocampus (Piekema, Kessels et al. 2006), and patients with brain damage that includes the hippocampus are impaired in the same spatial working memory task (Piekema, Fernandez et al. 2007). However, this is not to say that the hippocampal contribution to working memory is exclusive for spatial information, as deficits in working memory based on nonspatial information have also been reported following hippocampal damage in both humans (Piekema, Fernandez et al. 2007) and rodents (Jarrard, Davidson et al. 2004).

Western Diet Consumption, Obesity, and Memory Impairment

Increased adiposity and obesity have recently been linked with the development of cognitive impairment and the development of Alzheimer's disease and other forms of dementia (Naderali, Ratcliffe et al. 2009; Hassenstab, Sweat et al. 2010). Further, intake of dietary factors that are known to contribute to body weight gain and obesity development, such as saturated fat, are also linked with cognitive impairment and dementia. For instance, Morris and colleagues evaluated the relationship between intake of dietary fats and the development of cognitive decline and dementia in a series of human population-based studies (Morris, Evans et al. 2003; Morris, Evans et al. 2004; Morris, Evans et al. 2006). They reported that high intakes of saturated, but not unsaturated, fats across a period of about five years was linked with increased likelihood of developing both cognitive impairment and Alzheimer's disease (Morris, Evans et al. 2003; Morris, Evans et al. 2004). Another longitudinal study found a relationship between saturated fat intake and cognitive impairment over a 21-year period (Eskelinen, Ngandu et al. 2008). This latter study reported that prospective memory, which is memory to perform a planned action at a particular point in time, was negatively associated with saturated fat intake, whereas working memory for verbal information was not. This suggests that verbal working memory may be less susceptible to dietary factors compared to prospective memory. However, one limitation of these longitudinal human studies is that the food frequency questionnaires used to record dietary intake have been criticized for poor reliability and validity (Maffeis, Schutz et al. 1994; McNaughton, Hughes et al. 2007). In fact, one study reported that the reliability and validity of food frequency questionnaires are particularly low for individuals who have poor working memory skills (Jia, Craig et al. 2008). Thus, the ability to establish relationships between dietary factors and working memory ability in human populations is particularly challenging. Some of these concerns are greatly attenuated by using nonhuman animal models, which allow for a higher degree of control for dietary intake and reduce reliability and validity issues related to self-reporting measures.

Recent work using nonhuman animal models has shown that memory function, including certain types of working memory, is impaired following consumption of diets that are high in saturated fat, simple sugars (e.g., glucose, sucrose), or both. Similar to the human data described above, saturated fat appears to be linked with memory impairment in rodents, whereas intake of unsaturated fat is not (Greenwood and Winocur 1996). Other findings show that intake of simple sugars can also impair memory function in rodents compared to intake of complex carbohydrates (starches) (Jurdak and Kanarek 2009). In a series of studies, Kanoski, Davidson, and colleagues used a rat model to explore what types of memory function and what brain structures are susceptible to disruption by a Western diet (Kanoski, Meisel et al. 2007; Kanoski, Zhang et al. 2010). They used Pavlovian conditioning paradigms in which rats learn that stimuli, such as brief lights or tones, signal the delivery of a food reward. These studies found that relative to a healthy low-fat control diet, long-term intake (several months) of a diet similar to that commonly found in modern Western cultures (high in saturated fat and simple sugars) produced profound impairments in Pavlovian learning problems that rely on the integrity of the hippocampus. In fact, in some cases the magnitude of the observed impairments was comparable to what is found when the hippocampus is selectively removed (e.g., lesioned). On the other hand, Pavlovian learning problems that do not depend on the integrity of the hippocampus, including tasks that are of comparable difficulty, did not appear to be sensitive to disruption by the diet. These findings strongly suggest that excessive intake of a modern Western diet can lead to impaired function in memory problems that depend on the hippocampus. In fact, the hippocampus is a vulnerable brain structure to various types of insults, including environmental toxins, cardiovascular disease, and various types of dementia (Walsh and Emerich 1988). These findings show that this brain region is also particularly vulnerable to dietary and metabolic effects.

As discussed above, the hippocampus is necessary for the implementation of working memory, particularly that involving the utilization of visuospatial information. One way to assess this type of working memory problem in rats is via the radial arm maze paradigm. This paradigm uses an elevated maze with eight arms that radiate from a central platform. In one version of this paradigm (M'Harzi and Jarrard 1992) rats learn both a spatial and nonspatial task. For the spatial task, food-restricted rats learn which four of the eight arms are consistently baited with a food reward. The food is placed at the end of four of the arms in a recessed food cup that is not visible from the central platform, and the location of the food (which arms are baited with food) is based on the spatial location of the arm within the room that the maze is housed in. The spatial location is made more salient by the presence of spatial cues located outside the maze, like different posters and shapes on the walls. When trained on this task each day, rats will eventually learn over the course of several training days to go directly to the food-baited arms and consume the food, while ignoring the arms that are not baited with food. Performance is assessed based on two different types of errors: 1) a reference memory error, which is when the rat forgets the place (or arm) of the food location and enters an arm that is not one of the food-baited arms, and 2) a working memory error, which is when a rat returns to an arm that was previously visited on the same trial. Rats with selective neurotoxic lesions to the hippocampus are profoundly impaired in spatial reference and spatial working memory in this paradigm (Jarrard, Davidson et al. 2004).

The nonspatial radial arm maze task is similar, with one notable difference: visuospatial information is irrelevant to the location of the food. Instead, the locations of the four of the eight arms that are food-baited are based on the texture (wood, plastic, etc.) of inserts placed along the floor of each arm. The inserts are moved to different arms across trials to ensure that spatial information is not relevant to remembering food location. For the nonspatial version of the radial arm maze, rats with selective hippocampal lesions do not make more reference memory errors compared to controls. They do make more working memory errors; however, the magnitude of this impairment is reduced compared to the spatial version of this task (Jarrard, Davidson et al. 2004). Thus, while the hippocampus is critical for spatial working memory in both rats and humans, some evidence exists from the nonspatial radial arm maze task that the hippocampus also plays a role in working memory based on other types of information (nonspatial visual, tactile, etc.).

Kanoski and Davidson employed the spatial and nonspatial radial arm maze paradigms to examine the effects of varying lengths of Western diet consumption on reference and working memory in rats (Kanoski and Davidson 2010). Food-restricted rats consuming a healthy control diet were first trained to maximal performance on both the spatial and nonspatial tasks. Afterwards half of the rats were switched to unrestricted (*ad libitum*) access to a Western diet, whereas the other half of the rats were given *ad libitum* access to the control diet. Memory performance was then examined on several occasions following varying lengths of time of being maintained on the Western or control diet. Remarkably, the Western diet-fed rats exhibited significant impairments in spatial reference and spatial working memory after consuming the diet for only three days (see Figure 8.1), meaning that they committed more spatial reference and spatial working memory errors than the group that had been given unrestricted access to the control diet for three days. On the other hand, no impairments were observed after three days on the Western diet in the nonspatial radial arm maze task, which suggests that these effects may be based on impaired utilization of visuospatial information for memory demands.

One important implication of this outcome is that it suggests that dietary factors from a Western diet can impair memory processes independent of the ability of

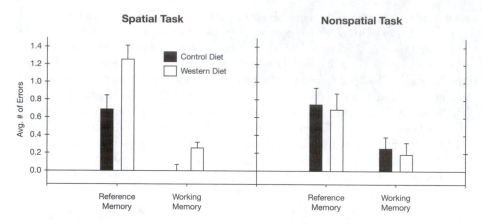

Figure 8.1   Only three days of Western diet consumption in rats impairs working memory and reference memory based on visuospatial information, but does not influence memory based on nonspatial information (modified from Kanoski and Davidson, 2011, *JEP:ABP*)

these dietary factors to promote obesity and related metabolic disorders (e.g., Type II diabetes, cardiovascular disease). As previously discussed, obesity and increased adiposity are associated with cognitive impairment in humans. Given that rats consuming diets high in saturated fat and simple sugars for a couple weeks will gain more weight and become obese relative to controls, a phenomenon known as "diet-induced obesity" (Levin and Dunn-Meynell 2002), it is difficult in many rodent studies to attribute learning impairments to obesity, or to dietary factors independent of obesity. However, in this study the rats consuming the Western diet for three days did not weigh more than the control rats consuming the healthy diet, yet they were impaired in spatial reference and working memory. These findings suggest that intake of Western diets induces rapid metabolic and physiological adaptations that can have a detrimental influence on memory function before the onset of obesity and related metabolic disorders.

The authors continued to assess memory performance in the same rats after increasing periods of Western or control diet consumption. Results revealed that the spatial reference and working memory impairments that arose after only three days on the Western diet remained relatively stable across five memory tests that were spread over a 90-day testing period. On the other hand, consistent reference and working memory impairments for the nonspatial task did not emerge until after a month of consuming the Western diet (see Figure 8.2). Notably, Western diet-induced body weight gain and increased adiposity arose after about two to three weeks on the diet, which suggests that deficits in the nonspatial task do not consistently emerge prior to obesity onset. Collectively, results from this study reveal the following about the effects of a Western diet on working memory function: 1) a very brief period of consuming Western diet (three days) can disrupt working memory function based on the utilization of visuospatial information, but not based on nonspatial information (e.g., tactile, nonspatial), 2) these spatial working memory impairments do not attenuate or augment with increasing

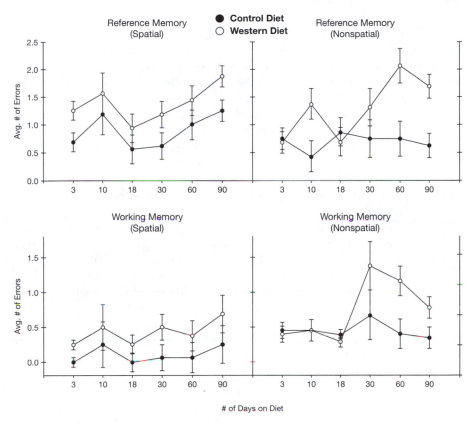

Figure 8.2   Working and reference memory impairments based on visuospatial information remain relatively stable across increased duration of Western diet consumption, whereas working and reference memory problems for nonspatial information develop only after a longer period consuming the diet (modified from Kanoski and Davidson, 2011, *JEP:ABP*)

durations of Western diet consumption, and 3) consistent working memory impairments involving nonspatial information arise after a longer period of Western diet consumption (30 or more days), which is after significant body weight gain has emerged relative to controls. It should be noted that the average life span of a rodent is approximately two to three years, which should be taken into account when considering the implications of these findings with regard to human consumption of a Western diet. Regardless, results imply that working memory function that relies on the hippocampus (e.g., spatial working memory) is more susceptible to dietary factors than working memory function that likely relies more on the prefrontal cortex and other brain regions (e.g., nonspatial working memory).

Other recent reports have also found that dietary factors common in a Western diet are associated with impaired spatial working memory performance. One study reported that two weeks' consumption of a high saturated fat and cholesterol diet produced impaired spatial working memory in rats in a water variation of the radial arm maze (Granholm, Bimonte-Nelson et al. 2008). In this version of the radial arm maze, rats learn about the location of a hidden escape platform (to escape swimming in the water), as opposed to the traditional radial arm maze where food-restricted rodents learn about the location of food. Results from this study show that spatial working memory impairments induced by dietary factors are not limited to memory processes related to food reinforcement, but also extend to other types of reinforcement, such as escape from stress. Another study reported spatial working memory deficits (using the standard food-reinforced version of the radial arm maze) in mice fed a high saturated fat diet (Valladolid-Acebes, Stucchi et al. 2011). Importantly, in this study the mice consuming the high saturated fat diet did not consume more calories than the mice consuming the control diet. These findings demonstrate that a diet high in saturated fat can impair spatial working memory independent of increased caloric intake of the high saturated fat compared to the control diet.

Many of the rodent studies discussed above used Western diets that differed from the control diet primarily in two important ways: 1) the Western diet contained increased levels of saturated and total fat, and 2) it contained higher levels of simple (sugars) compared to more complex carbohydrates (starches) compared to the control diet. While evidence from both human populations (Morris, Evans et al. 2004) and animal models (Greenwood and Winocur 1996) shows that it is the saturated, and not the total fat that contributes to cognitive impairment, the contribution of simple carbohydrates to memory impairment is less well established. A few recent findings suggest that simple sugars may contribute to memory dysfunction independent of whether they are combined with saturated fat. Jurdak and colleagues have shown that increased dietary sucrose in the absence of increased fat impairs spatial memory function in rats (Jurdak, Lichtenstein et al. 2008; Jurdak and Kanarek 2009). Dietary fructose has also been shown to impair spatial memory function in rats using diets that did not differ in fat content (Ross, Bartness et al. 2009). Another study reported that intake of a Western diet with saturated fat and glucose produced a greater degree of memory impairment in a hippocampal-dependent Pavlovian learning problem compared to intake of a similar diet with sucrose as the carbohydrate source (Kanoski, Meisel et al. 2007). These results were interpreted to mean that sugars with a higher glycemic load (the ability of a carbohydrate to rapidly increase blood sugar levels) can produce greater memory impairments given that glucose has a higher glycemic load than sucrose. Consistent with this interpretation, a study using adult human subjects found that intake of a meal with a higher vs. lower glycemic load produced impairments in memory, including working memory measured in a digit span task (Papanikolaou, Palmer et al. 2006). Similarly, verbal working memory was impaired in children who consumed a high glycemic vs. a low glycemic meal prior to memory testing (Benton, Maconie et al. 2007). Longitudinal studies are thus far lacking regarding whether longer-term intake of simple sugars is associated with working memory and other cognitive dysfunction in human populations.

Collectively the studies described above indicate that dietary factors commonly found in a Western diet (saturated fat and high glycemic sugars) impair memory function, particularly working memory for visuospatial information. These effects can in some cases occur independent of the development of obesity and metabolic syndrome, and do not require increased caloric intake compared to intake of a healthy control diet. The next section will address potential physiological and neurological mechanisms that may mediate these effects.

Mechanisms Underlying Memory Impairment by Western Diet Intake and Obesity

Excessive consumption of Western diet can produce multiple neurophysiological changes that can either directly or indirectly influence brain function. These changes include, but are not limited to, impaired glucoregulation (blood glucose regulation), reduced levels of central nervous system proteins and receptors, increased circulating triglycerides (a type of fat), increased inflammatory markers, and altered endothelial cell structure and function. This section will focus on how dietary and metabolic factors influence brain function through alterations in brain-derived neurotrophic factor and changes in glucoregulation.

Brain-derived neurotrophic factor, or BDNF, is a protein that plays an important role in learning and memory, particularly in memory function mediated by the hippocampus. Interference with BDNF can disrupt molecular processes that are believed to be the basis for memory formation, including synaptic plasticity and neurogenesis (Bergami, Rimondini et al. 2008; Danzer, Kotloski et al. 2008). It was reported that rats consuming a diet high in saturated fat and sucrose for a few months exhibited reduced levels of BDNF in the hippocampus; the same rats also demonstrated memory impairments in a hippocampal-dependent spatial memory problem (Molteni, Barnard et al. 2002). Another study reported that three months' consumption of a diet high in saturated fat and glucose reduced BDNF levels in rats both in the hippocampus and in the prefrontal cortex (Kanoski, Meisel et al. 2007). These BDNF reductions were associated with impaired learning performance in a Pavlovian conditioning task that is also impaired with damage to either the hippocampus or the prefrontal cortex. Given that dietary-induced alterations in BDNF levels occur in brain regions that mediate working memory function, it is possible that brain BDNF reductions mediate, in part, the effects of Western diet consumption on working memory impairment.

Consumption of saturated fat and simple sugars is linked with the development of metabolic syndrome (Hu, van Dam et al. 2001), which includes impaired blood glucose regulation as a primary characteristic. Impaired glucoregulation (i.e., glucose intolerance, or insulin resistance) is present in about 80 percent of obese individuals and is characterized by poor glycemic control due to reduced effectiveness of the pancreatic hormone insulin to regulate blood glucose levels (Martyn, Kaneki et al. 2008). Insulin resistance may be one mechanism through which longer-term intake of a Western diet impairs memory. In humans, there's a strong correlation between declining insulin sensitivity and cognitive dysfunction in otherwise healthy individuals (Kalmijn, Feskens et al. 1995; Kaplan, Greenwood et al. 2000). In subjects that have type II diabetes, cognitive function is improved following treatments that improve glucose regulation, and this cognitive improvement is particularly profound for tasks that involve working memory (Ryan, Freed et al. 2006).

Other convincing evidence that insulin resistance contributes to dietary effects on memory comes from animal studies. In one study (Pathan, Gaikwad et al. 2008) rats were fed a high saturated fat diet or a healthy control diet for one month. One week prior to assessment of memory function in a spatial task, rats were given daily administration of the insulin sensitizer rosiglitazone or a vehicle control. The rats fed the saturated fat diet were impaired in the spatial task, as previously shown by others. However, when these rats were given a one-week administration of the insulin sensitizer, which improved glucoregulation but did not influence body weight, these memory impairments were eliminated. Thus, it appears that for both humans and rodents, ameliorating insulin resistance can reduce memory impairments associated with glucose intolerance and Western diet intake.

How does insulin resistance contribute to memory impairment? Insulin and its receptor are abundant in the hippocampus, and brain administration of insulin improves hippocampal-dependent memory in rodents (Park, Seeley et al. 2000). The source of insulin in the brain is hypothesized to come from circulating insulin in the periphery (released from the pancreas), which is transported into the brain across the blood-brain barrier, as little or no insulin is produced in the brain itself (Woods, Chavez et al. 1996). In animals made obese from a high fat diet, the amount of insulin transported into the brain from the periphery is reduced relative to healthy weight controls (Kaiyala, Prigeon et al. 2000). Thus, the relationship between insulin resistance and working memory and other cognitive dysfunction may be based on reduced transport of insulin into the brain, and subsequent reduced activation of insulin receptors in the hippocampus and the prefrontal cortex. Alternatively, several studies have shown that in diet-induced obese rodents, insulin is less effective in engaging intracellular signaling pathways that are activated after the binding of insulin to its receptor in the brain (Mielke, Taghibiglou et al. 2005; McNay, Ong et al. 2010). It is likely that the relationship between insulin resistance and memory dysfunction is a combination of these two hypotheses: 1) transport of insulin from the periphery to the brain is reduced in diet-induced obesity, and 2) once in the brain, a type of brain insulin resistance is occurring at the receptor level, thus making insulin less effective in augmenting memory capabilities.

FUTURE DIRECTIONS

Implications of Western Diet-Induced Memory Dysfunction

One obvious implication of diet-induced working memory impairments is that such dysfunction may have negative impacts on quality of life for individuals affected. Working memory impairments can lead to failure in classroom learning activities (Gathercole, Lamont and Alloway 2006) and in acquiring general skills and knowledge. It is clear that working memory impairment negatively influences the ability to successfully manage demanding cognitive activities. Given that the number of children and adults in Western cultures that are considered obese is increasing at an alarming rate, particularly in the USA and the UK, and given the increasing availability of low-cost, unhealthy foods in Western cultures, more and more individuals may exhibit working memory impairments and other types of cognitive dysfunction as a result of consuming a Western diet and subsequently gaining excess body weight.

Another implication of diet-induced working memory impairment is that such an impairment may contribute to further intake of unhealthy foods and body weight gain; a type of "vicious cycle" model in which Western diet intake leads to memory impairment, and this impairment contributes to further consumption of the same dietary factors that caused the memory impairment in the first place (model first proposed in Davidson, Kanoski et al. 2007). In support of this idea, selective lesions to the hippocampus in rodents yield increased food intake and body weight gain relative to sham-lesioned controls (Davidson, Chan et al. 2009), a finding that underscores the importance of memory function to the regulation of food intake and body weight. Given that Western diet intake has negative effects on hippocampal function, the ability of the hippocampus to exert inhibitory control over excessive food intake may be compromised with Western diet intake and obesity. One mechanism through which this may occur is by disrupting a high-order type of hippocampal-dependent memory process known as "occasion setting" [reviewed in more detail elsewhere (Davidson, Kanoski et al. 2005; Davidson, Kanoski et al. 2007; Kanoski and Davidson 2011)]. Alternatively, Western diet intake may produce further excessive food intake by impairing working memory function. Higgs (2002) demonstrated in an eloquent study with human subjects that memory for a recent eating episode (e.g., a meal) reduces the amount of food consumed during a subsequent test meal. This effect was not based on differences in hunger or fullness, but rather on whether the subjects were cued prior to the test meal to remember the previous eating episode. It may be that working memory contributes to this phenomenon. When memory for food eaten in a previous meal is maintained in working memory, or alternatively when memory for food eaten earlier within the same meal is maintained in working memory, disruption of this working memory stream may contribute to excessive food intake. In other words, active working memory representation of recently consumed food may function to reduce ongoing and subsequent food intake. This hypothesis is supported by a study discussed above, which demonstrated that the reliability of self-reported dietary records is extremely low in individuals with poor working memory capabilities (Jia, Craig et al. 2008), suggesting working memory contributes to memory for recent eating episodes.

Conclusions

Obesity and intake of unhealthy foods commonly found in a Western diet (foods high in saturated fats and simple sugars) are associated with disruption of cognitive function, including impaired working memory function. Intake of these dietary factors can negatively impact memory function in rodents before the onset of obesity and related metabolic disturbances, which indicates a specific contribution of diet to memory disruption. Diet-induced memory impairment may be based on reduced levels of the protein brain-derived neurotrophic factor in the hippocampus and in the prefrontal cortex, two brain structures that are critical in the normal implementation of working memory function. Such impairment may also be based on the ability of Western diets to alter blood glucose regulation, as diet-induced memory impairments are ameliorated with drugs that improve glucoregulation. These findings have important implications for Western cultures given that intake of unhealthy, low-cost foods and rates of obesity and overweight are increasing at an alarming rate. It may be that the memory impairments produced by intake of foods high in saturated fats and high glycemic sugars contribute to further excessive food intake and body weight gain by disrupting memory functions that normally function to curb excessive food intake.

REFERENCES

Benton, D., A. Maconie, et al. (2007). "The influence of the glycaemic load of breakfast on the behaviour of children in school." *Physiol Behav* **92**(4): 717–724.

Bergami, M., R. Rimondini, et al. (2008). "Deletion of TrkB in adult progenitors alters newborn neuron integration into hippocampal circuits and increases anxiety-like behavior." *Proc Natl Acad Sci U S A* **105**(40): 15570–15575.

Berrino, F. (2002). "Western diet and Alzheimer's disease." *Epidemiol Prev* **26**(3): 107–115.

Centers for Disease Control and Prevention (CDC) (2011). "Overweight and obesity: Data and statistics." from http://www.cdc.gov/obesity/data/index.html (accessed June 9, 2012).

Cohen, N. J., R. A. Poldrack, et al. (1997). "Memory for items and memory for relations in the procedural/declarative memory framework." *Memory* **5**(1–2): 131–178.

Danzer, S., R. Kotloski, et al. (2008). "Altered morphology of hippocampal dentate granule cell presynaptic and postsynaptic terminals following conditional deletion of TrkB." *Hippocampus* **18**(7): 668–678.

Davidson, T. L., K. Chan, et al. (2009). "Contributions of the hippocampus and medial prefrontal cortex to energy and body weight regulation." *Hippocampus* **19**(3): 235–252.

Davidson, T. L., S. E. Kanoski, et al. (2005). "Memory inhibition and energy regulation." *Physiol Behav* **86**(5): 731–746.

Davidson, T. L., S. E. Kanoski, et al. (2007). "A potential role for the hippocampus in energy intake and body weight regulation." *Curr Opin Pharmacol* **7**(6): 613–616.

Del Parigi, A., F. Panza, et al. (2006). "Nutritional factors, cognitive decline, and dementia." *Brain Res Bull* **69**(1): 1–19.

Department of Health (2011). "Obesity." from http://www.dh.gov.uk/health/category/policy-areas/public-health/obesity-healthy-living/ (accessed June 26, 2012).

Eichenbaum, H. (2001). "The hippocampus and declarative memory: Cognitive mechanisms and neural codes." *Behav Brain Re* **127**(1–2): 199–207.

Eskelinen, M., T. Ngandu, et al. (2008). "Fat intake at midlife and cognitive impairment later in life: A population-based CAIDE study." *Int J Geriatr Psychiatry* **23**(7): 741–747.

Finkelstein, E. A., J. G. Trogdon, et al. (2009). "Annual medical spending attributable to obesity: Payer-and service-specific estimates." *Health Aff (Millwood)* **28**(5): w822–831.

Funahashi, S., C. J. Bruce, et al. (1993). "Dorsolateral prefrontal lesions and oculomotor delayed-response performance: Evidence for mnemonic 'scotomas'." *J Neurosci* **13**(4): 1479–1497.

Gathercole, S. E., E. Lamont, and T. P. Alloway (2006). Working memory in the classroom. *Working memory and education*. I. S. Pickering, Elsevier Press: 219–240.

Goldman-Rakic, P. (1987). Circuitry of primate prefrontal cortex and regulation of behaviour by representational memory. *Handbook of physiology: The nervous system*. P. F. Bethesda, American Physiological Society. **5**: 373–417.

Granholm, A., H. Bimonte-Nelson, et al. (2008). "Effects of a saturated fat and high cholesterol diet on memory and hippocampal morphology in the middle-aged rat." *J Alzheimers Dis* **14**(2): 133–145.

Greenwood, C. E. and G. Winocur (1996). "Cognitive impairment in rats fed high-fat diets: a specific effect of saturated fatty-acid intake." *Behav Neurosci* **110**(3): 451–459.

Gruber, O. and D. Y. von Cramon (2003). "The functional neuroanatomy of human working memory revisited. Evidence from 3-T fMRI studies using classical domain-specific interference tasks." *NeuroImage* **19**(3): 797–809.

Hassenstab, J. J., V. Sweat, et al. (2010). "Metabolic syndrome is associated with learning and recall impairment in middle age." *Dement Geriatr Cogn Disord* **29**(4): 356–362.

Higgs, S. (2002). "Memory for recent eating and its influence on subsequent food intake." *Appetite* **39**(2): 159–166.

Honey, G. D. and P. C. Fletcher (2006). "Investigating principles of human brain function underlying working memory: What insights from schizophrenia?" *Neuroscience* **139**(1): 59–71.

Hu, F., R. van Dam, et al. (2001). "Diet and risk of Type II diabetes: The role of types of fat and carbohydrate." *Diabetologia* **44**(7): 805–817.

Jarrard, L. E. (1993). "On the role of the hippocampus in learning and memory in the rat." *Behav Neural Biol* **60**(1): 9–26.

Jarrard, L. E., T. L. Davidson, et al. (2004). "Functional differentiation within the medial temporal lobe in the rat." *Hippocampus* **14**(4): 434–449.

Jia, X., L. C. Craig, et al. (2008). "Repeatability and validity of a food frequency questionnaire in free-living older people in relation to cognitive function." *J Nutr Health Aging* **12**(10): 735–741.

Jurdak, N. and R. Kanarek (2009). "Sucrose-induced obesity impairs novel object recognition learning in young rats." *Physiol Behav* **96**(1): 1–5.

Jurdak, N., A. Lichtenstein, et al. (2008). "Diet-induced obesity and spatial cognition in young male rats." *Nutr Neurosci* **11**(2): 48–54.

Kaiyala, K. J., R. L. Prigeon, et al. (2000). "Obesity induced by a high-fat diet is associated with reduced brain insulin transport in dogs." *Diabetes* **49**(9): 1525–1533.

Kalmijn, S., E. Feskens, et al. (1995). "Glucose intolerance, hyperinsulinaemia and cognitive function in a general population of elderly men." *Diabetologia* **38**(9): 1096–1102.

Kalmijn, S., L. J. Launer, et al. (1997). "Dietary fat intake and the risk of incident dementia in the Rotterdam Study." *Ann Neurol* **42**(5): 776–782.

Kanoski, S. E. and T. L. Davidson (2010). "Different patterns of memory impairments accompany short- and longer-term maintenance on a high-energy diet." *J Exp Psychol: Anim Behav Process* **36**(2): 313–319.

Kanoski, S. E. and T. L. Davidson (2011). "Western diet consumption and cognitive impairment: Links to hippocampal dysfunction and obesity." *Physiol Behav* **103**(1): 59–68.

Kanoski, S. E., R. L. Meisel, et al. (2007). "The effects of energy-rich diets on discrimination reversal learning and on BDNF in the hippocampus and prefrontal cortex of the rat." *Behav Brain Re* **182**(1): 57–66.

Kanoski, S. E., Y. Zhang, et al. (2010). "The effects of a high-energy diet on hippocampal function and blood–brain barrier integrity in the rat." *J Alzheimers Dis* **21**(1): 207–219.

Kaplan, R., C. Greenwood, et al. (2000). "Cognitive performance is associated with glucose regulation in healthy elderly persons and can be enhanced with glucose and dietary carbohydrates." *Am J Clin Nutr* **72**(3): 825–836.

Levin, B. E. and A. A. Dunn-Meynell (2002). "Defense of body weight depends on dietary composition and palatability in rats with diet-induced obesity." *Am J Physiol Regul Integr Comp Physiol* **282**(1): R46–54.

M'Harzi, M. and L. E. Jarrard (1992). "Effects of medial and lateral septal lesions on acquisition of a place and cue radial maze task." *Behav Brain Re* **49**(2): 159–165.

Maffeis, C., Y. Schutz, et al. (1994). "Elevated energy expenditure and reduced energy intake in obese prepubertal children: Paradox of poor dietary reliability in obesity?" *J Pediatr* **124**(3): 348–354.

Martyn, J., M. Kaneki, et al. (2008). "Obesity-induced insulin resistance and hyperglycemia: Etiologic factors and molecular mechanisms." *Anesthesiology* **109**(1): 137–148.

McNaughton, S. A., M. C. Hughes, et al. (2007). "Validation of a FFQ to estimate the intake of PUFA using plasma phospholipid fatty acids and weighed foods records." *Br J Nutr* **97**(3): 561–568.

McNay, E. C., C. T. Ong, et al. (2010). "Hippocampal memory processes are modulated by insulin and high-fat-induced insulin resistance." *Neurobiol Learn Mem* **93**(4): 546–553.

Mielke, J. G., C. Taghibiglou, et al. (2005). "A biochemical and functional characterization of diet-induced brain insulin resistance." *J Neurochem* **93**(6): 1568–1578.

Molteni, R., R. J. Barnard, et al. (2002). "A high-fat, refined sugar diet reduces hippocampal brain-derived neurotrophic factor, neuronal plasticity, and learning." *Neuroscience* **112**(4): 803–814.

Morris, M. C., D. A. Evans, et al. (2003). "Dietary fats and the risk of incident Alzheimer disease." *Arch Neurol* **60**(2): 194–200.

Morris, M. C., D. A. Evans, et al. (2004). "Dietary fat intake and 6-year cognitive change in an older biracial community population." *Neurology* **62**(9): 1573–1579.

Morris, M., D. A. Evans, et al. (2006). "Dietary copper and high saturated and trans fat intakes associated with cognitive decline." *Arch Neurol* **63**(8): 1085–1088.

Naderali, E. K., S. H. Ratcliffe, et al. (2009). "Obesity and Alzheimer's disease: A link between body weight and cognitive function in old age." *Am J Alzheimers Dis Other Demen* **24**(6): 445–449.

O'Keefe, J. and J. Dostrovsky (1971). "The hippocampus as a spatial map: Preliminary evidence from unit activity in the freely-moving rat." *Brain Res* **34**(1): 171–175.

Ogden, C. L., S. Z. Yanovski, et al. (2007). "The epidemiology of obesity." *Gastroenterology* **132**(6): 2087–2102.

Papanikolaou, Y., H. Palmer, et al. (2006). "Better cognitive performance following a low-glycaemic-index compared with a high-glycaemic-index carbohydrate meal in adults with type 2 diabetes." *Diabetologia* **49**(5): 855–862.

Park, C. R., R. J. Seeley, et al. (2000). "Intracerebroventricular insulin enhances memory in a passive-avoidance task." *Physiol Behav* **68**(4): 509–514.

Pathan, A., A. Gaikwad, et al. (2008). "Rosiglitazone attenuates the cognitive deficits induced by high fat diet feeding in rats." *Eur J Pharmacol* **589**(1–3): 176–179.

Piekema, C., G. Fernandez, et al. (2007). "Spatial and non-spatial contextual working memory in patients with diencephalic or hippocampal dysfunction." *Brain Res* **1172**: 103–109.

Piekema, C., R. P. Kessels, et al. (2006). "The right hippocampus participates in short-term memory maintenance of object-location associations." *NeuroImage* **33**(1): 374–382.

Postle, B. R. (2006). "Working memory as an emergent property of the mind and brain." *Neuroscience* **139**(1): 23–38.

Rama, P., A. Poremba, et al. (2004). "Dissociable functional cortical topographies for working memory maintenance of voice identity and location." *Cereb Cortex* **14**(7): 768–780.

Rama, P., J. B. Sala, et al. (2001). "Dissociation of the neural systems for working memory maintenance of verbal and nonspatial visual information." *Cogn Affect Behav Neurosci* **1**(2): 161–171.

Ross, A. P., T. J. Bartness, et al. (2009). "A high fructose diet impairs spatial memory in male rats." *Neurobiol Learn Mem* **92**(3): 410–416.

Rushworth, M. F., M. P. Noonan, et al. (2011). "Frontal cortex and reward-guided learning and decision-making." *Neuron* **70**(6): 1054–1069.

Ryan, C., M. Freed, et al. (2006). "Improving metabolic control leads to better working memory in adults with type 2 diabetes." *Diabetes Care* **29**(2): 345–351.

Sawaguchi, T. and P. S. Goldman-Rakic (1991). "D1 dopamine receptors in prefrontal cortex: Involvement in working memory." *Science* **251**(4996): 947–950.

Scoville, W. B. and B. Milner (1957). "Loss of recent memory after bilateral hippocampal lesions." *J Neurol Neurosurg Psychiatry* **20**: 11–21.

Squire, L. R. (1992). "Memory and the hippocampus: A synthesis from findings with rats, monkeys, and humans [erratum appears in *Psychol Rev* 1992 Jul; **99**(3): 582]." *Psychol Rev* **99**(2): 195–231.

Squire, L. R. (2004). "Memory systems of the brain: A brief history and current perspective." *Neurobiol Learn Mem* **82**(3): 171–177.

Valladolid-Acebes, I., P. Stucchi, et al. (2011). "High-fat diets impair spatial learning in the radial-arm maze in mice." *Neurobiol Learn Mem* **95**(1): 80–85.

Walsh, T. J. and D. F. Emerich (1988). "The hippocampus as a common target of neurotoxic agents." *Toxicology* **49**(1): 137–140.

Woods, S. C., M. Chavez, et al. (1996). "The evaluation of insulin as a metabolic signal influencing behavior via the brain." *Neurosci Biobehav Rev* **20**(1): 139–144.

9

Sleep Deprivation and Performance

The Role of Working Memory

PAUL WHITNEY
Department of Psychology, Washington State University, Pullman, WA, USA

PETER J. ROSEN
Department of Psychology, Washington State University, Pullman, WA, USA

BACKGROUND INFORMATION

Why Study Sleep Deprivation and Working Memory?

Studies of the effects of sleep loss on human performance and mental processing have deep roots in the history of experimental psychology, particularly in the domains of learning and memory (e.g., Feldman & Dement, 1968; Morris, Williams, & Lubin, 1960; Van Ormer, 1932). The early research was often intended not just to explore the practical questions of how and when fatigue leads to mental lapses, but also to use sleep as a manipulation that could be used to test basic theories, including the role of decay versus interference in forgetting. More recently, interest in what sleep research can tell us about fatigue effects on cognition has increased dramatically. As the length of work days has increased, along with irregular shifts and complaints of chronic fatigue and sleep disruptions (e.g., Alhola & Polo-Kantola, 2007; Golden & Figart, 2000), there is a clear need to understand fatigue effects and develop interventions to prevent mistakes that threaten health and safety (Dawson, Noy, Harma, Akerstedt, & Belenky, 2011). At the same time, advances in cognitive neuroscience have yielded new information about the nature of sleep and the sleep-cognition relationship (Kerkhof & Van Dongen, 2010).

One of the most important lessons of this growing body of research is that not all aspects of cognition are equally affected by sleep loss. Recent meta-analyses of studies using a wide range of cognitive tasks have shown that both total sleep deprivation and partial sleep restriction affect cognition, with particularly strong effects on vigilance and sustained attention, moderate to strong effects on working memory (WM), and, paradoxically, smaller effects on more complex decision making abilities (Koslowsky & Babkoff, 1992; Lim & Dinges, 2010). Fatigue effects on working memory (WM) are especially interesting to consider because, as the chapters in this volume demonstrate, WM is a hub of activity in almost any interesting cognitive task. Therefore, a greater understanding of how sleep deprivation affects WM may lead to insights about a wide range of fatigue effects in natural operational environments. In addition, research on sleep deprivation and WM may prove very important for coming to a better understanding of the WM system itself, and how it interfaces with other cognitive circuits. Just as dissociations produced by brain lesions have been very informative with regard to isolating subsystems involved in WM (Baddeley & Hitch, 1994; Gathercole, 1994), we are beginning to see evidence that sleep deprivation produces dissociations among different WM-related processes. Research on fatigue effects enjoy a particular advantage in comparison to lesion studies in that the compromised brain functions can be manipulated experimentally and the effects reversed.

CURRENT EVIDENCE

Selectivity in Sleep Deprivation Effects on Cognition

Central to the idea that sleep research can both be informed by, and inform, the study of cognition is the notion that sleep deprivation effects are selective. Although meta-analyses of fatigue effects on cognition converge on the notion that some cognitive systems are more affected by sleep deprivation than others, there are strong disagreements about how to characterize the nature of the most spared and most compromised functions (Harrison & Horne, 2000; Lim & Dinges, 2008; Pilcher, Band, Odle-Dusseau, & Muth, 2007). This controversy has important implications for studying fatigue effects on WM. One view holds that the prefrontal cortex (PFC) is especially vulnerable to the effects of sleep deprivation and thus tasks that load on cognitive abilities that are strongly PFC-associated show the strongest declines under fatigue (e.g., Harrison & Horne, 2000; Horne, 1993; Jones & Harrison, 2001). According to this hypothesis sleep deprivation has a selective and direct effect on WM and cognitive control functions. In contrast, Dinges and colleagues (Dinges et al., 1997; Lim & Dinges, 2008) have argued that the core cognitive deficit produced by sleep deprivation is difficulty maintaining sustained attention. According to this view, sleep deprivation effects on WM or other complex cognitive functions are an indirect consequence of problems with sustaining attention to the task at hand, which is a prerequisite for good performance across a range of tasks.

It is clear from the existing literature that not only are sleep deprivation effects on cognition not uniform, but even if we limit our focus to sleep deprivation effects on short-term memory and WM, results vary depending on the specific task used to assess performance as well as on the duration of sleep loss. Table 9.1 illustrates the range of tasks used and some of the typical results obtained. Although a number of studies have obtained small to moderate effects of sleep deprivation on WM, several other studies have not found such effects and the differences cut across manipulation of the hours of sleep deprivation. In addition, differences among the findings cannot be attributed simply to variations in task complexity. The largest effects are obtained on simple tests of the ability to detect the presence of stimuli presented at irregular intervals in vigilance tasks (see Lim & Dinges, 2010).

Overall the PFC-vulnerability hypothesis does not receive unequivocal support from studies of WM performance after sleep loss. Of course, although WM is typically thought of as a primarily frontal localized ability, the mapping between WM and the PFC is far from perfect. It is important then to determine whether studies of brain metabolism can shed light on the relationships among sleep loss, WM, and the PFC. In support for the view that sleep deprivation has an especially strong effect on the PFC, positron-emission tomography (PET) studies have found a specific decrease in glucose uptake occurs in the PFC and posterior parietal association cortices, corresponding to impairments in cognitive performance (Durmer & Dinges, 2005; Wu et al., 1991). Studies using functional magnetic resonance imagining (fMRI) have reported that sleep loss consistently decreases activation in all major brain regions associated with WM, and these activation patterns reliably correlate with the extent of WM performance decline (Chee & Chuah, 2007, 2008; Chee et al., 2006; Choo, Lee, Venkatraman, Sheu & Chee, 2005).

Other evidence, however, suggests that sleep deprivation effects on WM may be an indirect consequence of effects on sustained attention. For example, a decline in parietal activation following sleep deprivation was found to be correlated with behavioral decline on working memory tasks (Lim, Choo, & Chee, 2007), but the behavioral metric most clearly affected was within-subject response time variability.

Table 9.1 Typical Measures used to Assess Sleep Deprivation Effects on Short-Term and Working Memory

Task	Example Citations	Results	Hours Awake
Digit Span	Glenville et al. (1978)	No effect	30
	Quigley et al. (2000)	No effect	24
N-back task	Smith et al. (2002)	Moderate	21
	Choo et al. (2005)	Moderate	24
	Volkow et al. (2008)	No effect	24
Random Generation	Sagaspe et al. (2003)	No effect	36
	Heuer et al. (2005)	Moderate	24
	McMorris et al. (2007)	No effect	36
WM Scanning	Habeck et al. (2004)	Moderate to large	48
	Mu et al. (2005)	Moderate to large	30
	Tucker et al. (2010)	No effect	51

These variations in response time are consistent with lapses in sustained attention. A study by Chee and Chua (2007) supports a similar view. They varied WM load following sleep deprivation and found that decreases in parietal activation occurred in sleep-deprived participants well before WM capacity was saturated. The same study also found that activation of the ventral occipital extrastriate cortex, a region often associated with perceptual load (Todd & Marois, 2004), was decreased at these lower levels of load. Interestingly, Luber et al. (2008) found that performance by sleep-deprived subjects on a Sternberg-type WM task could be improved by transcranial magnetic stimulation of the upper medial *occipital* gyrus. However, stimulation of this region is likely to have improved visual processing of the stimulus encoding rather than affecting the efficiency of WM itself.

Electrophysiological studies of brain activity have also been conducted that are relevant to the debate on the locus of sleep deprivation effects. Stimulus-specific phasic electroencephalography (EEG) changes, or event-related potentials (ERPs), have been utilized in this research because of their strong association with individual mental operations (Bressler, 2002; Corsi-Cabrera, Arce, Del Río-Portilla, Pérez-Garci, & Guevara, 1999; Luck, 2005). The P2 and P3b are two ERP components commonly associated with WM and are theorized to index processes such as context updating in WM, and the comparison of target stimuli with the content of WM (Bressler, 2002; Donchin, 1981; Kok, 2001; Lenartowicz, Escobedo-Quiroz, & Cohen, 2010; Polich, 2007). Both total and partial sleep deprivation result in a significant decrease in amplitude and increase in latency for the P2 and P3b components (Corsi-Cabrera et al., 1999; Lee, Kim, & Suh, 2003; Morris, So, Lee, Lash, & Becker, 1992; Smith, McEvoy, & Gevins, 2002). The overall elongation of the latencies found in each of these ERP components represents the general cognitive slowing of the processes they are believed to index, and is expected considering the significant research describing this decline in overall processing speed due to sleep deprivation (Corsi-Cabrera et al., 1999; Horne, 1978, 1985). The decrease in ERP amplitude suggests a decrease in cortical activation required for proper information processing. This effect that sleep deprivation has on P2 and P3b amplitude can be interpreted in a number of ways. One possibility in support of the direct effect theory is that sleep deprivation is disrupting the normal processes involved in maintaining context representations in WM. In order to maintain context representations, continuous context updating must occur due to task switching (Monsell, 2003) and momentary lapses of attention (Lenartowicz et al., 2010). These ERP data may reflect an impairment in the ability to refocus and maintain context representations in WM due to a lack of sleep. Since sustained attention performance is severely handicapped by sleep deprivation (Lim & Dinges, 2008), this means that the inability to efficiently recover from these increased attentional lapses would essentially exacerbate the cognitive detriments already present in the sleep-deprived individual. In contrast, it is important to note that both P2 and P3b are highly attention-dependent components, and the effects observed could be due to direct effects of sleep deprivation on WM, or to downstream effects of sleep deprivation effects on attention.

Isolating the Effects of SD on Task Performance

Whether interpreting either the behavioral or physiological evidence relevant to the distinction between direct and indirect effects of sleep deprivation on WM, it is important to remember that caution should be exercised in interpreting impaired global performance on a given WM task (or other complex measure of cognitive ability). Consider a study by Mu and colleagues in which a Sternberg-type WM scanning task was administered to people before and after 30 hours of sleep deprivation (Mu et al., 2005). Mu et al. (2005) contrasted performance and functional neuroimaging across groups of subjects identified as either sleep-deprivation resilient or sleep-deprivation vulnerable. Subjects held a memory set of either zero or six items and responded whether a probe item was in the memory set. In the sleep-deprivation vulnerable group, reaction times (RTs) in the six-item condition were longer after sleep deprivation in comparison to their rested baseline performance. Comparisons of brain activation during WM scanning after sleep deprivation showed that the resilient group had *greater* activation of bilateral prefrontal and parietal circuits.

The Mu et al. results appear consistent with the hypothesis that the PFC is especially vulnerable to sleep deprivation and the most susceptible individuals are less able to recruit frontal circuits to perform WM tasks efficiently under conditions of fatigue. However, these same effects could be explained by the hypothesis that the vulnerable subjects, when fatigued, had poorer sustained attention to the stimulus sets, which increased time to encode information into WM. Neither the behavioral data nor the imaging data in Mu et al. are fine grained enough to distinguish between a compromised WM system and a normally functioning WM system that is starved for data.

By their very nature, WM tasks involve interactions among processes involved in stimulus encoding, maintenance and manipulation of information, and decision making and response outputs. Because overall performance on WM tasks reflects a mixture of different processes, some of which may be impaired by fatigue (or other sources of compromised brain functioning) while others are spared, addressing the problem of task specificity is a key to understanding how fatigue impairs cognitive performance. In order to specify the source, or sources, of fatigue effects on performance, measures of WM must be decomposed into component processes. A statistical approach to decomposing tasks into component processes has been successfully implemented in studies of executive control functions and WM (e.g., McCabe, Roediger, McDaniel, Balota, & Hambrick, 2010; Miyake, Friedman, Emerson, Witzki, Howerter, & Wager, 2000; Unsworth & Engle, 2007). For example, Miyake et al. examined the interrelationships among different executive functioning tests using latent variable analysis and found evidence for three dissociable executive abilities: shifting attention, updating of WM, and inhibition of activation. More recently, McCabe et al. administered a large battery of WM and executive function tasks and used factor analytic modeling to examine relations between the two domains. They found that: (1) these tasks strongly shared variance attributable to a common factor that they characterized as *executive attention*, and (2) executive attention is distinguishable from processing speed.

The studies that extract dissociable factors within WM and executive control tasks demonstrate the complex nature of these tasks and the danger of attributing performance declines under fatigue or other challenges to a single factor. What is less clear at present is whether there will be substantial convergence among studies regarding the cognitive components of WM and executive control tasks, and whether these factors will vary in their susceptibility to fatigue effects. Moreover, the use of the factor analytic strategy to dissociate cognitive processes would be very difficult to implement directly into research on the cognitive effects of sleep loss because sleep deprivation studies are typically expensive and labor intensive to conduct, and do not allow for the relatively large number of participants needed to perform statistical extraction of specific cognitive contributors to performance (see Kerkhof & Van Dongen, 2010, for an overview of sleep and cognition research strategies and designs).

Another approach to better specifying the particular cognitive abilities that contribute to performance of complex cognitive tasks that has been implemented in sleep deprivation studies is the use of tasks that are carefully designed to permit decomposition into different dependent measures. A recent study by Tucker and colleagues illustrates this strategy with regard to WM (Tucker, Whitney, Belenky, Hinson, & Van Dongen, 2010). Participants performed a Sternberg-type WM scanning task with memory sets of either two or four items. Compared to performance at rested baseline, participants who were kept awake for 51 hours showed large increases in overall RT on the task. However, by examining RT as a function of memory set size, RTs were decomposed into slopes, representing WM scanning, and intercepts, representing encoding, decision, and response processes. A striking pattern emerged. There were no sleep deprivation effects on WM scanning, only effects on the intercept, which reflects encoding, decision, and response components of the task. In light of the Luber et al. (2008) finding noted earlier, which showed improvement in performance on a Sternberg task with occipital stimulation of the brains of sleep-deprived subjects, it appears likely that the Tucker et al. results demonstrate problems with information encoding after sleep loss.

The version of the Sternberg task included in the Tucker et al. (2010) study also included a manipulation of the recency of foils used for the probe recognition task. Foils either came from the memory set on the preceding trial or had not been used for several trials. The difference in RTs between trials with recent and non-recent foils depends on the ability to overcome proactive interference in WM (e.g., Jonides, Smith, Marshuetz, Koeppe, & Reuter-Lorenz, 1998). Under both rested and sleep-deprived conditions, there was significant interference from recent negative probes, which replicates prior research using this manipulation. However, there was no indication of greater difficulty in overcoming proactive interference in the sleep-deprived condition. Since both WM scanning and resolution of interference in WM have been strongly associated with the PFC (Konishi, Chikazoe, Jimura, Asari, & Miyashita, 2005; Rypma & D'Esposito, 1999), the lack of fatigue effects on these processes, coupled with large fatigue effects on the non-WM components of the task, is problematic for the view that sleep deprivation has especially strong and direct effects on WM or other PFC functions.

Further evidence that WM is not especially or selectively vulnerable to sleep deprivation effects comes from a recent study by Tucker, Stern, Basner, and Rakitin (2011). They employed a Sternberg memory scanning task with young adults either in a rested or sleep-deprived state and compared their results with those of elderly rested participants. Because overall performance on tests of WM and executive function are impaired under sleep deprivation and among older adults, several investigators have claimed that the sleep-deprived brain is a model for the aging brain (e.g., Harrison, Horne, & Rothwell, 2000; Muzur, Pace-Schott, & Hobson, 2002). In the Tucker et al. (2011) study, both the sleep-deprived and the elderly groups showed impairment on the memory scanning task compared to rested young adults. However, the nature of the decline in performance was different for the two groups. As in Tucker et al. (2010), the effect of sleep deprivation was entirely in the intercept of the function relating RT to memory set size. In contrast, the aging effect was entirely in the memory scanning slope, suggesting a direct effect of aging on WM.

The Sternberg memory scanning task results show that sleep deprivation and aging produce dissociable cognitive effects, and it is risky to draw conclusions about WM tasks from global performance rather than from indices that target functions specific to WM. However, we still have not answered the question of what cognitive operations *are* particularly affected by sleep deprivation, nor have we fully explored the extent to which the affected cognitive operations have indirect effects on WM operations and global performance of complex tasks. These are active areas of inquiry in cognitive neuroscience and we do not have a complete answer to these questions. In the balance of this chapter we can, however, begin to chart the answers and highlight directions for future research that seem fruitful.

The Role of Working Memory in Avoiding Performance Decrements Caused by Sleep Loss

From the existing literature, it is difficult to sustain the hypothesis that WM is especially vulnerable to sleep deprivation (SD). Instead, research on the effects of SD on cognition reveals something of a paradox. Simple tests of vigilance and choice RT tend to show consistent and large effects of SD on performance, while in many complex cognitive tasks that involve decision making and reasoning, SD effects are often small and inconsistent (Lim & Dinges, 2008, 2010; Whitney & Hinson, 2010). Functionally, the WM system sits between early attention and encoding processes, which appear to be strongly affected by SD, and the complex cognitive operations of reasoning, which may or may not be disrupted by SD. So, a key question in trying to understand how SD leads to "real world" errors in performance is to trace the effects of SD on the throughput of information from encoding to WM, and map the throughput effects on performance. Understanding the flow of information through WM and its relation to complex task performance is also of theoretical interest because of the possibility that fatigued individuals may be using WM and executive control operations in a way that helps them compensate for inefficient lower level processing. If so, studies of SD and WM could help us better understand adaptive control of WM.

Several authors have called attention to the potential importance of top-down control mechanisms in explaining SD effects on performance. For example, Drummond, Brown, Salamat, and Gillin (2004; see also Drummond & Brown, 2001) had subjects perform Baddeley's logical reasoning task in which a sentence describing the order of sets of letters is compared to a letter set (*A does not precede B does not follow C; BCA*). Task difficulty was manipulated by varying the number of letters used. Performance did *not* differ depending on whether subjects had normal rest or 35 hours of SD. However, neuroimaging showed different patterns of cerebral reaction to increasing task difficulty depending on the sleep manipulation. Specifically, Drummond et al. found evidence for cerebral compensatory processing in which SD subjects showed increases with task difficulty in the same regions as subjects in the rested state; SD subjects also recruited new regions of the cortex not showing increased activation in rested subjects. These data suggest that processes for allocating attention, which have been attributed to the central executive in Baddeley's model of WM and to more distributed control processes in models like Cowan's (Cowan, 1995, 2005), play a key role in maintaining performance on complex tasks under SD even as the normal flow of information to WM is degraded.

At present, we do not know what initiates the attentional control operations that recruit additional brain circuits when performing complex tasks under sleep deprivation. A fruitful place to begin to answer this question may be embodied in the distinction between proactive and retroactive control (e.g., Braver & Barch, 2006). In proactive control, information about current goals is actively maintained in WM and that information guides the processing of new information in a top-down fashion. In reactive control, the processing of new information is not directed top-down, but goal-relevant information is retrieved and used as needed during task performance. One possibility is that as fatigue produced by sleep loss increases, a degraded flow of information to WM during performance leads to a shift toward greater use of proactive control mechanisms to guide task execution.

If WM control processes do play a role in compensatory processes that help maintain complex task performance under SD conditions, it is reasonable to assume that with extended sleep loss, or with a combination of sleep loss and other situational challenges that tax compensatory abilities, WM control processes will break down. Certainly, military personnel, emergency workers, and medical personnel, among others, commonly face stressful and complex decisions while also suffering from sleep loss. These situations sometimes produce calamitous outcomes. Controlled laboratory research on WM and SD has just begun to examine the processes that may underlie these kinds of scenarios. A recent study by Chuah, Dolcos, Chen, Zheng, Parimal, and Chee (2010) provides an interesting example. They tested the ability of rested and SD subjects to recognize pictures held in WM in a Sternberg-type task, but in the interval between presentation of the memory set and the recognition probe emotionally negative or neutral distracter pictures were presented. SD impaired people's ability to maintain the target pictures in WM in the presence of distracters, but the most interesting data came from imaging results in the condition that used emotionally negative distracters. The people most affected by negative emotional distracters when suffering from sleep loss also showed increased amygdala responses to negative distracters and reduced connectivity of the amygdala and the dorsolateral PFC. It would appear that for at least some people, an effect of SD is to increase emotional reactivity, which can in turn affect WM processing and probably the ability to use top-down control processes to maintain performance (cf., Yoo, Gujar, Hu, Jolesz, & Walker, 2007).

Two general implications of the Chuah et al. (2010) study and related work (e.g., Sterpenich, Albouy, & Boly, et al., 2007) should be kept in mind as further research on SD, WM, and complex task performance is pursued. First, SD effects are not limited to cold cognition. Emotional processing changes under SD may affect task performance directly, and it may spill over into the efficiency of cold cognitive mechanisms, particularly since WM is involved in the integration of affective and cold cognitive sources of information (Hinson, Jameson, & Whitney, 2002; Pessoa, 2008). One of the practical, and theoretically important, implications of further research on the relationship between SD and WM may be to contribute to our understanding of the combined role of both emotion and cognition in WM processes. Second, there were strong individual differences on the effects of SD observed in the Chuah et al. (2010) study. Such individual differences in reactions to SD are not limited to the effects of emotional distracters. Research by Van Dongen and colleagues has established that impairment from sleep loss varies significantly among individuals, yet is stable within individuals, suggesting a trait-like differential vulnerability exists (Van Dongen, Baynard, Maislin, & Dinges, 2004). However, it is important to note that *this differential vulnerability differs across task type as well*. So, there is not a single, general trait that reflects vulnerability to SD, but instead a given person may be more or less vulnerable depending on the criterial task. Thus, to answer the question of how WM is affected by SD we must not only perform a careful analysis of the specific task characteristics necessary to distinguish SD effects on WM versus non-WM task elements (Tucker et al., 2010), but we should also recognize that the answer to the question may depend on the particular processing strengths and weaknesses of a given individual. Perhaps the greatest benefit of continuing research on SD and WM will be to inform our understanding of the relationship between resilience to SD challenges and the ability to engage in compensatory control processing in a given complex task.

REFERENCES

Alhola, P., & Polo-Kantola, P. (2007). Sleep deprivation: Impact on cognitive performance. *Neuropsychiatric Disease and Treatment, 3*, 5, 553–567.

Baddeley, A. D., & Hitch, G. J. (1994). Developments in the concept of working memory. *Neuropsychology, 8*, 4, 485.

Braver, T. S., & Barch, D. M. (2006). Extracting core components of cognitive control. *Trends in Cognitive Sciences, 10*, 12, 529–532.

Bressler, S. L. (2002). Understanding cognition through large-scale cortical networks. *Current Directions in Psychological Science, 11*, 2, 58–61.

Chee, M. W., & Chuah, Y. M. L. (2007). Functional neuroimaging and behavioral correlates of capacity decline in visual short-term memory following sleep deprivation. *Proceedings of the National Academy of Sciences of the United States of America, 104*, 22, 9487–9492.

Chee, M. W., & Chuah, Y. M. L. (2008). Functional neuroimaging insights into how sleep and sleep deprivation affect memory and cognition. *Current Opinion in Neurology, 21*, 4, 417–423.

Chee, M. W. L., Chuah, Y. M. L., Venkatraman, V., Chan, W. Y., Philip, P., & Dinges, D. F. (2006). Functional imaging of working memory following normal sleep and after 24 and 35 h of sleep deprivation: Correlations of fronto-parietal activation with performance. *Neuroimage, 31,* 1, 419–428.

Choo, W. C., Lee, W. W., Venkatraman, V., Sheu, F. S., & Chee, M. W. (2005). Dissociation of cortical regions modulated by both working memory load and sleep deprivation and by sleep deprivation alone. *Neuroimage, 25,* 2, 579–587.

Chuah, L. Y. M., Chen, A. K., Zheng, H., Parimal, S., Chee, M. W. L., & Dolcos, F. (2010). Sleep deprivation and interference by emotional distracters. *Sleep, 33,* 10, 1305–1313.

Corsi-Cabrera, M., Arce, C., Del, R.-P. I. Y., Pérez-Garci, E., & Guevara, M. A. (1999). Amplitude reduction in visual event-related potentials as a function of sleep deprivation. *Sleep, 22,* 2, 181–189.

Cowan, N. (1995). *Attention and memory: An integrated framework.* New York, NY: Oxford University Press.

Cowan, N. (2005). *Working memory capacity.* New York, NY: Psychology Press

Dawson, D., Noy, Y. I., Harma, M., Akerstedt, T., & Belenky, G. (2011). Modeling fatigue and the use of fatigue models in work settings. *Accident Analysis and Prevention, 43,* 2, 549–564.

Dinges, D. F., Pack, F., Williams, K., Gillen, K. A., Powell, J. W., Ott, G. E., Aptowicz, C., … Pack, A. I. (1997). Cumulative sleepiness, mood disturbance, and psychomotor vigilance performance decrements during a week of sleep restricted to 4–5 hours per night. *Sleep, 20,* 4, 267–277.

Donchin, E. (1981). Presidential address, 1980. Surprise!…Surprise?. *Psychophysiology, 18,* 5, 493–513.

Drummond, S. P., & Brown, G. G. (2001). The effects of total sleep deprivation on cerebral responses to cognitive performance. *Neuropsychopharmacology New York, 25,* 5.

Drummond, S. P., Brown, G. G., Salamat, J. S., & Gillin, J. C. (2004). Increasing task difficulty facilitates the cerebral compensatory response to total sleep deprivation. *Sleep, 27,* 3, 445–451.

Durmer, J. S., & Dinges, D. F. (2005). Neurocognitive consequences of sleep deprivation. *Seminars in Neurology, 25,* 1, 117–129.

Feldman, R., & Dement, W. (1968). Possible relationships between REM sleep and memory consolidation. *Psychophysiology, 5,* 243–251.

Gathercole, S. E. (1994). Neuropsychology and working memory: A review. *Neuropsychology, 8,* 499–505.

Glenville, M., Broughton, R., Wing, A. M., & Wilkinson, R. T. (1978). Effects of sleep deprivation on short duration performance measures compared to the Wilkinson auditory vigilance task. *Sleep, 1,* 2, 169–176.

Golden, L., & Figart, D. (2000). Doing something about long hours. *Challenge, 43,* 6, 15–37.

Habeck, C., Rakitin, B. C., Moeller, J., Scarmeas, N., Zarahn, E., Brown, T., & Stern, Y. (2004). An event-related fMRI study of the neurobehavioral impact of sleep deprivation on performance of a delayed-match-to-sample task. *Brain Research: Cognitive Brain Research, 18,* 3, 306–321.

Harrison, Y., & Horne, J. (2000). Sleep loss and temporal memory. *The Quarterly Journal of Experimental Psychology A, 53,* 1, 271–279.

Harrison, Y., Horne, J. A., & Rothwell, A. (2000). Prefrontal neuropsychological effects of sleep deprivation in young adults: A model for healthy aging? *Sleep, 23,* 8, 1067–1073.

Heuer, H., Kohlisch, O., & Klein, W. (2005). The effects of total sleep deprivation on the generation of random sequences of key-presses, numbers and nouns. *The Quarterly Journal of Experimental Psychology, A: Human Experimental Psychology, 58,* 2, 275–307.

Hinson, J. M., Jameson, T. L., & Whitney, P. (2002). Somatic markers, working memory, and decision making. *Cognitive, Affective, and Behavioral Neuroscience, 2,* 4, 341–353.

Horne, J. A. (1978). A review of the biological effects of total sleep deprivation in man. *Biological Psychology, 7,* 1–2.

Horne, J. A. (1985). Sleep function, with particular reference to sleep deprivation. *Annals of Clinical Research, 17,* 5, 199–208.

Horne, J. A. (1993). Human sleep, sleep loss and behaviour. Implications for the prefrontal cortex and psychiatric disorder. *The British Journal of Psychiatry, 162,* 413–419.

Jones, K., & Harrison, Y. (2001). Frontal lobe function, sleep loss and fragmented sleep. *Sleep Medicine Reviews, 5,* 6, 463–475.

Jonides, J., Smith, E. E., Marshuetz, C., Koeppe, R. A., & Reuter-Lorenz, P. A. (1998). Inhibition in verbal working memory revealed by brain activation. *Proceedings of the National Academy of Sciences of the United States of America, 95,* 14, 8410–8413.

Kerkhof, G. A., & Van Dongen, H. P. A. (eds). (2010). *Human sleep and cognition, Part I: Basic research.* Progress in Brain Research, Vol. 185. Amsterdam, The Netherlands: Elsevier.

Kok, A. (2001). On the utility of P3 amplitude as a measure of processing capacity. *Psychophysiology, 38,* 3, 557–577.

Konishi, S., Chikazoe, J., Jimura, K., Asari, T., Miyashita, Y., & Mishkin, M. (2005). Neural mechanism in anterior prefrontal cortex for inhibition of prolonged set interference. *Proceedings of the National Academy of Sciences of the United States of America, 102,* 35, 12584–12588.

Koslowsky, M., & Babkoff, H. (1992). Meta-analysis of the relationship between total sleep deprivation and performance. *Chronobiology International, 9,* 2, 132–136.

Lee, H.-J., Kim, L., & Suh, K.-Y. (2003). Cognitive deterioration and changes of P300 during total sleep deprivation. *Psychiatry and Clinical Neurosciences, 57,* 5, 490–496.

Lenartowicz, A., Escobedo-Quiroz, R., & Cohen, J. D. (2010). Updating of context in working memory: An event-related potential study. *Cognitive, Affective and Behavioral Neuroscience, 10,* 2, 298–315.

Lim, J., Choo, W. C., & Chee, M. W. (2007). Reproducibility of changes in behaviour and fMRI activation associated with sleep deprivation in a working memory task. *Sleep, 30,* 1, 61–70.

Lim, J., & Dinges, D. F. (2008). Sleep deprivation and vigilant attention. *Annals of the New York Academy of Sciences, 1129,* 1, 305–322.

Lim, J., & Dinges, D. F. (2010). A meta-analysis of the impact of short-term sleep deprivation on cognitive variables. *Psychological Bulletin, 136,* 3, 375–389.

Luber, B., Stanford, A. D., Bulow, P., Nguyen, T., Rakitin, B. C., Habeck, C., Basner, R., ... Lisanby, S. H. (2008). Remediation of sleep-deprivation–induced working memory impairment with fMRI-guided transcranial magnetic stimulation. *Cerebral Cortex, 18,* 9, 2077–2085.

Luck, S. J. (2005). *An introduction to the event-related potential technique.* Cambridge, MA: MIT Press.

McCabe, D. P., Roediger, H. L., McDaniel, M. A., Balota, D. A., & Hambrick, D. Z. (2010). The relationship between working memory capacity and executive functioning: Evidence for a common executive attention construct. *Neuropsychology, 24,* 2, 222–243.

McMorris, T., Harris, R. C., Howard, A. N., Langridge, G., Hall, B., Corbett, J., Dicks, M., ... Hodgson, C. (2007). Creatine supplementation, sleep deprivation, cortisol, melatonin and behavior. *Physiology and Behavior, 90,* 1, 21–28.

Miyake, A., Friedman, N., Emerson, M., Witzki, A., Howerter, A., & Wager, T. (2000). The unity and diversity of executive functions and their contributions to complex "frontal lobe" tasks: A latent variable analysis. *Cognitive Psychology, 41,* 1, 49–100.

Monsell, S. (2003). Task switching. *Trends in Cognitive Sciences, 7,* 3.

Morris, A. M., So, Y., Lee, K. A., Lash, A. A., & Becker, C. E. (1992). The P300 event-related potential. The effects of sleep deprivation. *Journal of Occupational Medicine: Official Publication of the Industrial Medical Association, 34,* 12, 1143–1152.

Morris, G. O., Williams, H. L., & Lubin, A. (1960). Misperception and disorientation during sleep. *Archives of General Psychiatry, 2,* 247–254.

Mu, Q., Mishory, A., Johnson, K. A., Nahas, Z., Kozel, F. A., Yamanaka, K., Bohning, D. E.,

George, M. S. (2005). Decreased brain activation during a working memory task at rested baseline is associated with vulnerability to sleep deprivation. *Sleep, 28*, 4, 433–446.

Muzur, A., Pace-Schott, E. F., & Hobson, J. A. (2002). The prefrontal cortex in sleep. *Trends in Cognitive Sciences, 6*, 11.

Pessoa, L. (2008). On the relationship between emotion and cognition. *Nature Reviews Neuroscience, 9*, 148–158.

Pilcher, J. J., Band, D., Odle-Dusseau, H. N., & Muth, E. R. (2007). Human performance under sustained operations and acute sleep deprivation conditions: Toward a model of controlled attention. *Aviation, Space, and Environmental Medicine, 78*, 5, 15–24.

Polich, J. (2007). Updating P300: An integrative theory of P3a and P3b. *Clinical Neurophysiology, 118*, 10, 2128–2148.

Quigley, N., Green, J. F., Morgan, D., Idzikowski, C., & King, D. J. (2000). The effect of sleep deprivation on memory and psychomotor function in healthy volunteers. *Human Psychopharmacology: Clinical and Experimental, 15*, 3.

Rypma, B., & D'Esposito, M. (1999). The roles of prefrontal brain regions in components of working memory: Effects of memory load and individual differences. *Proceedings of the National Academy of Sciences of the United States of America, 96*, 11, 6558–6563.

Sagaspe, P., Charles, A., Taillard, J., Bioulac, B., & Philip, P. (2003). Inhibition et mémoire de travail: Effet d'une privation aiguë de sommeil sur une tâche de génération aléatoire. *Canadian Journal of Experimental Psychology = Revue Canadienne De Psychologie Expérimentale, 57*, 4, 265–273.

Smith, M. E., McEvoy, L. K., & Gevins, A. (2002). The impact of moderate sleep loss on neurophysiologic signals during working-memory task performance. *Sleep, 25*, 7, 784–794.

Sterpenich, V., Albouy, G., Boly, M., Vandewalle, G., Darsaud, A., Balteau, E., Dang-Vu, T. T., ... Maquet, P. (2007). Sleep-related hippocampo-cortical interplay during emotional memory recollection. *PLoS Biology, 5*, 11.

Todd, J. J., & Marois, R. (2004). Capacity limit of visual short-term memory in human posterior parietal cortex. *Nature, 428*, 6984, 751–754.

Tucker, A. M., Belenky, G., Whitney, P., Hinson, J. M., & Van Dongen, H. P. A. (2010). Effects of sleep deprivation on dissociated components of executive functioning. *Sleep, 33*, 1, 47–57.

Tucker, A. M., Stern, Y., Basner, R. C., & Rakitin, B. C. (2011). The prefrontal model revisited: Double dissociations between young sleep deprived and elderly subjects on cognitive components of performance. *Sleep, 34*, 8, 1039–1050.

Unsworth, N., & Engle, R. W. (2007). The nature of individual differences in working memory capacity: Active maintenance in primary memory and controlled search from secondary memory. *Psychological Review, 114*, 1.

Van Dongen, H. P. A., Baynard, M. D., Maislin, G., & Dinges, D. F. (2004). Systematic interindividual differences in neurobehavioral impairment from sleep loss: Evidence of trait-like differential vulnerability. *Sleep, 27*, 3, 423–433.

Van Ormer, E. B. (1932). Retention after intervals of sleep and of waking. *Archives of Psychology, 137*.

Volkow, N. D., Ferre, S., Telang, F., Ma, J., Thanos, P. K., Jayne, M., Wang, G.-J., ... Tomasi, D. (2008). Sleep deprivation decreases binding of [^{11}C]raclopride to dopamine D_2/D_3 receptors in the human brain. *Journal of Neuroscience, 28*, 34, 8454–8461.

Whitney, P., & Hinson, J. M. (2010). Measurement of cognition in studies of sleep deprivation. *Progress in Brain Research, 185*, 37–48.

Wu, J. C., Gillin, J. C., Buchsbaum, M. S., Hershey, T., Hazlett, E., Sicotte, N., & Bunney, W. E. J. (1991). The effect of sleep deprivation on cerebral glucose metabolic rate in normal humans assessed with positron emission tomography. *Sleep, 14*, 2, 155–162.

Yoo, S. S., Gujar, N., Hu, P., Jolesz, F. A., & Walker, M. P. (2007). The human emotional brain without sleep: A prefrontal amygdala disconnect. *Current Biology, 17*, 20.

10

Working Memory and Addictive Behavior

BONNIE J. NAGEL

Department of Psychiatry and Behavioral Neuroscience,
Oregon Health and Science University, Portland, OR, USA

MEGAN M. HERTING

Department of Behavioral Neuroscience,
Oregon Health and Science University, Portland, OR, USA

ANITA CSERVENKA

Department of Behavioral Neuroscience,
Oregon Health and Science University, Portland, OR, USA

As has hopefully been gleaned by the previous chapters in this book, working memory skills are critical to our success in many day-to-day behaviors. Working memory skills change across the lifespan, and can be altered, both positively and negatively, by numerous activities in which an individual engages. With this chapter, we hope to elucidate yet another daily process for which we use working memory, that is, decision-making, and how aberrations in working memory and decision-making processes may play a role in addictions, such as substance abuse and gambling behavior.

BACKGROUND INFORMATION

The Role of Working Memory in Decision-Making

Every day, individuals have to continually decide how to act on a second-to-second basis. When choosing how to act, it not only requires basic processing and discrimination of incoming stimuli, but also integrating this information with our current and future goals, values, and social norms. For example, as you are walking down the street you may have to detect an unfamiliar person approaching you. Despite this incoming stimulus (an unfamiliar person), your behavior may vary depending on your goal in that instance. If while walking your goal is to get to the bus stop quickly, as you walk, you may choose to move to the right in order to pass the oncoming stranger, whereas if you were out for a leisurely stroll, you may be more apt to make eye contact with the individual and say hello. In every instant, we decide how to act after integrating the situation and stimulus around us with our internal thoughts and goals. The process(es) by which we choose one course of action or behavior over other alternatives is known as *decision-making*.

As illustrated by the previous example of walking down the street, during decision-making, one must concurrently activate and integrate a number of pieces of information in order to make a final decision. Specifically, it is *working memory* that allows for this temporary storage and manipulation of information in order to regulate behavior and make optimal decisions. Thus, working memory processes are an essential component to decision-making. The interplay between working memory and decision-making can be seen in the following example:

Sam is sitting at his desk at work, and his stomach starts to growl. His clock says 12:15 pm, so he decides it is time to buy lunch. He decides he will buy a sandwich at the cafeteria. He gets up from his desk and heads towards the cafeteria. However, when he arrives, he sees that the sandwiches are sold out. He then quickly contemplates his next actions, which could be buying a salad instead, or heading over to the sandwich shop down the street. He weighs his options, deciding that he will have very little time to eat if he heads to the sandwich shop, so he orders a salad, pays the cashier, and gets his lunch to satisfy his hunger in a timely manner.

For Sam to get his lunch, he has to keep in mind his goals (e.g., getting to the cafeteria, ordering a sandwich, satisfying his hunger) while formulating his plan and accomplishing it. In addition, when he arrived at the cafeteria to find that the sandwiches were sold out, he had to actively consider alternative options, while estimating the cost-benefit of each choice (i.e., getting the sandwich he originally wanted may lead to less time to eat). Given that working memory processes are fundamental in decision-making, it is not surprising that limiting factors on working memory can compromise decision-making practices as well. For example, working memory capacity, the ability to mentally manipulate information and resist distractions, and the capability to maintain activation of the items in working memory over time, have all been implicated as important working memory properties for optimal decision-making (Finn, 2002). As the context and situation in which decisions must be made changes, these additional factors become instrumental in good decision-making practices.

Because working memory plays such an important role in one's ability to make good decisions, here we expand on the definitions of these working memory terms and explain how these distinct additional processes help to facilitate making decisions. Working memory capacity refers to the number of items that can be successfully held in mind at the same time and is important in situations where the options and their consequences must be considered to make a decision. We all have a limit to how many things we can keep track of mentally at one time. In fact, with every additional item, or an increase in our working memory load, more cognitive resources are consumed that are needed for keeping track of outcomes, which can deteriorate decision-making performance. This phenomenon can be exemplified by a commonly used laboratory decision-making task—the Iowa Gambling Task (IGT) (Bechara, Damasio, Damasio, & Anderson, 1994). The IGT involves four decks of cards in which you can win or lose money; unbeknownst to the participant, two of the decks are advantageous (they result in small gains, but also small losses) and two are disadvantageous decks (they result in large gains, but also large losses). The goal of the task is to earn as much money as possible, and thus avoid losses. Participants must learn through trial and error which decks result in greater future gains. Most individuals first choose from the disadvantageous decks, as they initially have large gains. However, with time, healthy adults will quickly switch to the advantageous decks, as over the long run, these decks win the participants the largest amount of money. For this and most types of gambling, there is an amount of reward associated with a probability of winning that reward. Consider the example of the following choices: Option 1: 10 percent probability of winning $50 and 90 percent probability of winning $0, OR Option 2: 90 percent probability of winning $10 and 10 percent probability of winning $0. With these two choices, there are different strategic features to which one might attend, with one being the amount of the possible win and the other being the probability of winning. For an optimal decision to be made, the integration of both of these features is necessary. With an increase in the complexity of these features or with additional features to be considered, increasing demands are placed on working memory. While a decision-making task, the IGT clearly challenges working memory. In addition to integrating the number and complexity of the task's features, gains and losses over each trial must be held in memory and then summed across different trials to allow the individual to determine which deck will result in the largest monetary amount. Therefore, if an individual is asked to retain additional information in mind during this task, he/she may have fewer resources to allocate to help remember and add the information together to determine which deck of cards is the best to choose from, and thus may choose poorly. In fact, this is exactly what happens when an increased working memory load is imposed on individuals. By challenging individuals to remember increasing numbers of random digits while they played, they were slower to switch from the disadvantageous to the advantageous decks, and thus made poorer gambling task choices (Dretsch & Tipples, 2008; Hinson, Jameson, & Whitney, 2002). This relationship between increased working memory and declining gambling performance is perhaps even more striking when complex analytic strategies are required in making the gambling choice (Gozzi, Cherubini, Papagno, & Bricolo, 2011).

A similar relationship between working memory ability and impulsive decision-making can also be seen using another laboratory decision-making procedure, known as the delay discounting task (Green, Fry, & Myerson, 1994). In this task, individuals are asked to make a number of choices between smaller, immediate amounts of money, or larger, delayed amounts of money. For example, an individual may be asked, "Which would you prefer to have: $100 now or $100 in a month?" Not surprisingly, almost everyone would choose $100 now. However, the decision may not be as straightforward when asked, "Which would you prefer to have: $80 now or $100 in one month? How about $80 now or $100 in one year, or $20 now or $100 in a year?" Most individuals will usually prefer the smaller variable amount of money immediately if the value is high, but the delayed option when the immediate value is low. As you can see from the latter examples, these decisions can become increasingly complex by varying the amount of money to be received, as well as the timeline. By using a number of delay and monetary reward options, impulsive decision-making—or a preference for small, immediate rewards over delayed, larger rewards—can be assessed. Like the IGT, this laboratory task of decision-making also places demands on working memory. Similar to the real-world instance of making a decision about immediate and future consequences, this task utilizes working memory processes to hold the reward options in mind as the individual manipulates and integrates the information to allow them to choose between the two options. Impairments in working memory could lead to suboptimal and more impulsive decisions, such as picking the immediate outcome in preference to others. As with the IGT, an increased working memory load can interfere with making optimal decisions. For example, in a study of 44 healthy adults, Hinson and colleagues demonstrated that having individuals hold extra information in mind during this task, such as increasing numbers of random digits (i.e., increasing their working memory load), results in greater impulsive decision-making compared to what the individual would choose under basal, lower working memory load conditions (Hinson, Jameson, & Whitney, 2003). Furthermore, besides inducing greater impulsive decision-making by increasing memory load, the intrinsic capability of working memory processes can influence discounting performance. Specifically, poorer working memory performance on classic working memory paradigms, such as a verbal n-back task or span tasks, is associated with greater impulsive decision-making on the delay discounting task (Bobova, Finn, Rickert, & Lucas, 2009; Shamosh et al., 2008). While this relationship between working memory and decision-making is also partially accounted for by the relationship between working memory abilities and overall intelligence (Shamosh et al., 2008), clearly both intrinsic working memory ability, as well as environmentally induced reductions in working memory capacity, readily affect our ability to make good decisions.

In addition to one's ability to hold a number of things in mind, the capability to resist distraction and maintain activation of items held in working memory are important functions, and can also contribute to advantageous decision-making. The capacity to resist distractions and mentally manipulate information refers to how well we can inhibit unnecessary items from interfering with our current working memory store. This also depends on our ability to control the focus of our attention between active items while making a decision. It is easy to understand that if you have a large number of items you are trying to process and manipulate, as during a time of high working memory load, the items that aren't especially useful may take additional resources away from the more important items, and thus interfere with the current processing stream. But what determines which items may be more likely to be maintained and which lost to interference? It turns out that the capability to maintain activation of the items in working memory over time can vary as a function of the saliency of the item, with more salient items being easier to keep in mind than less salient ones (Fine & Minnery, 2009). Furthermore, when it comes to distractions, more salient information is more likely to interfere with working memory processes at hand. This notion has been substantiated by a neuroimaging study suggesting that presentation of distracting emotionally salient stimuli disrupts healthy working memory-related brain response and, in turn, impairs working memory performance (Dolcos & McCarthy, 2006). One could easily imagine how this might be the case. For example, it isn't surprising that if you overheard your name being said in the other room (your name being a very salient item for you), you would be more inclined to devote some of your cognitive resources to that stimulus (e.g., identify who is calling, deciding if the call could wait until the end of the paragraph, etc.) compared to overhearing another individual's name being spoken, which you may be able to ignore altogether. While highly salient items can be important in facilitating working memory processes (e.g., it is unlikely for Sam to ignore his hunger pains and forget about lunch), they can also pose a challenge when attempting to maintain an item in working memory that is less salient. In fact, the ability to maintain items in working memory, despite their saliency, becomes increasingly important when making decisions. For example, during decision-making on the delay discounting task, more salient information, such as the immediate outcomes or rewards, need to be compared to less salient information, like expected future consequences. However, this can only be done if both out-comes, despite their saliency, are maintained and updated in working memory for manipulation (i.e., through comparisons). Given this, it is not surprising that impos-ing a high working memory load while performing the delay discounting task results in individuals showing a greater preference for the immediate rather than the delayed rewards (Hinson et al., 2003). In this case, the working memory resources are taxed, leaving the more salient stimuli to dominate remaining cognitive resources, and ultimately leaving individuals to pick the smaller, immediate reward, which is often a less optimal decision on the task.

In summary, working memory plays an important role in our ability to make everyday decisions. Increased working memory capacity allows for greater acti-vation of items, and also decreases the likelihood of interference of activated items. Furthermore, given that more salient items are easier to keep activated, having a larger working memory capacity allows for the activation, maintenance, and manipulation of lower salient items during the decision-making process. Thus, having a lower working memory capacity can result in suboptimal and impulsive decision-making.

CURRENT EVIDENCE

Decision-Making, Working Memory, and Addiction

Above, we demonstrated that working memory skills are imperative to being able to weigh options and alternatives and ultimately make optimal decisions. Many of the decisions that we make throughout the day involve whether or not to engage in a particular activity. Importantly, although many of those possible choices and activities are adaptive and necessary, others are not, or may become maladaptive if performed repeatedly. An *addiction* can be defined as any activity, substance, or object that consumes a large portion of an individual's time, and significantly impairs one's physical, mental, or psychological well-being. Individuals can become addicted to a number of things, including drugs and alcohol, as well as to non-substance related behaviors, such as gambling. Thus, while some addictions are psychologically based, others also involve a physical dependence, such as those involving substances of abuse. Both types of addictions, however, are thought to share similar behavioral characteristics and neurobiological profiles, many of which may reflect deficits in impulse control and decision-making (Grant, Potenza, Weinstein, & Gorelick, 2010). Specifically, key components to addictive behaviors include the following:

1. Apparent loss of control; engaging in the behavior to a greater extent than intended
2. Repeated, and unsuccessful attempts to cut back or quit
3. A large amount of daily life is spent in activities related to the behavior or trying to recover from its effects
4. Craving; preoccupation with the behavior or activities that relate to that behavior
5. The behavior is continued despite its negative consequences
6. Tolerance; need to increase the intensity or frequency of the behavior to achieve the desired effect, or diminished effect with continued behavior of the same intensity
7. Withdrawal; restlessness or irritability if unable to engage in the behavior.

From the above list, it is clear that a number of key behavioral characteristics of addiction may reflect impairments in decision-making, such as loss of control and continuing the behavior despite facing a number of negative consequences. Unfortunately, according to the Substance Abuse and Mental Health Services Administration (2011), poor decision-making associated with addiction affects millions of Americans, with 7 percent affected with alcoholism and 2.8 percent with illicit substance dependence, and 0.5–1 percent with gambling addictions (Wareham & Potenza, 2010). Furthermore, given the similarities in poor decision-making between substance and non-substance addictions, a high level of co-morbidity can also be seen between these disorders. For example, among pathological gamblers, there are elevated rates of alcohol and drug abuse. Individually, as well as combined, these disorders pose a large psychological burden for the individual and their families, as well as being a costly expense to society, exceeding $600 trillion annually. Thus, there has been a great interest in improving our understanding of addictive behaviors to better aid in the prevention and treatment of these disorders. For example, a number of people have gambled or consumed an alcoholic beverage in their life, but why do some individuals become addicted to those behaviors and others do not? Is poor decision-making or working memory to blame? The answers to these questions are complex and not completely understood, but through years of research on this topic, it has become increasingly clear that individuals with addictions have a number of differences in their working memory capacity that may help to explain poor decision-making.

Evidence for Both Poor Working Memory and Atypical Decision-making in Addiction

Both non-substance and substance-related addictions are associated with working memory deficits. In the case of substance addiction, both the acute and chronic use of drugs can impair working memory behavior. For example, acute alcohol consumption has been shown to reduce working memory performance on a number of auditory and visual tasks by impairing the strategies for holding information in mind (Saults, Cowan, Sher, & Moreno, 2007). Other results suggest that the acute intoxication effects of alcohol on working memory are most apparent during declining blood alcohol concentrations (Schweizer et al., 2006). In addition to the deficits seen when the drug is on board, chronic exposure can lead to poor working memory, even during times of abstinence. These effects can be particularly pronounced with drugs that are associated with physiological withdrawal. Although the impact of acute nicotine administration on working memory performance has been difficult to determine (Greenstein et al., 2010; Heishman, Kleykamp, & Singleton, 2010), the detriment that can occur with increasing withdrawal was clearly demonstrated with a study by Mendrek and colleagues examining the performance of nicotine smokers after less than one or more than thirteen hours of abstinence on a 2-back working memory task (Mendrek et al., 2006). They found that smokers took longer to respond and made more errors when they had not smoked for over thirteen hours compared to when they performed the task following a more recent cigarette break (<1 hour condition). Findings such as this have been shown for other drugs of abuse as well, and suggest that impairments exist in working memory in substance-dependent individuals even after ceasing drug use. Early abstinent individuals with opioid dependence show decrements in complex working memory performance, which negatively correlated with days of withdrawal (i.e., the more time since use, the better the performance) (Rapeli et al., 2006). In a study of heavy, but recently abstinent, methylenedioxymethamphetamine (MDMA) and marijuana users, verbal working memory skills were impaired compared to non-using controls (Gouzoulis-Mayfrank et al., 2000). Interestingly, this effect appeared to be related more to marijuana use, as no group difference was seen between combined MDMA and marijuana users compared to those who used comparable amounts of marijuana alone. Given these findings, it may not be surprising that even after several weeks of abstinence, heavy marijuana using adolescents show impaired verbal working memory (Hanson et al., 2010). Certainly, preoccupation with using a substance, particularly when in withdrawal, can absorb cognitive resources, rendering fewer resources available to complete other tasks. Using the lunchtime example from the first section of this chapter, imagine that Sam is also a cigarette smoker, and that while he is trying to weigh his alternative lunch options in an effort to make a good decision, cognitive and attentional resources are also being recruited by his nicotine craving and the fact that it has been several hours since his last cigarette. The increasing demands that are made on his working memory system, namely maintaining activation of several relevant stimuli (e.g., what to have for lunch) while resisting distracters (e.g., his desire for a cigarette), is likely to have a deleterious effect on his ability to make an optimal decision (e.g., he forgoes lunch all together in order to have a cigarette, or is unable to maintain all of the information in working memory, and thus is late returning to work). While this phenomenon helps to explain why working memory deficits can be seen immediately following abstinence (particularly during the phase of withdrawal—either psychological, physiological, or both), prolonged chronic exposure to substances can also result in long-term impairments in working memory.

Chronic alcohol abuse has been associated with persisting deficits in working memory. In a study of one-month detoxified alcoholic men, compared to controls, abstinent male alcoholics showed impaired executive functioning, including impaired visual working memory skills (Sullivan, Rosenbloom, & Pfefferbaum, 2000). Similarly, in a study of neuropsychological functioning in alcoholic women, with an average abstinence period of approximately three and a half months, persisting deficits in verbal and nonverbal working memory skills were apparent (Sullivan, Fama, Rosenbloom, & Pfefferbaum, 2002). Substances of abuse, beyond alcohol, also show persisting deleterious effects on working memory abilities. For instance, abstinent substance users, including those in remission from cocaine, alcohol, marijuana, and heroin, who had a median abstinence duration of eight months, have shown poorer working memory than healthy controls on tasks of spatial span and letter and number sequencing (Fernandez-Serrano, Perez-Garcia, Schmidt Rio-Valle, & Verdejo-Garcia, 2010; Hildebrandt, Brokate, Eling, & Lanz, 2004). Although abstinent at the time of the assessment, the greater duration and quantity of drugs used throughout an individual's lifetime was significantly associated with poorer working memory performance, suggesting that substances can have long-lasting and dose-related consequences on cognition and behavior. Similar to drug addiction, non-substance abusing addicts, such as problem gamblers, also exhibit impaired performance on working memory tasks compared to age-matched controls (Leiserson & Pihl, 2007), suggesting that working memory may be a central feature contributing to addiction behaviors. As previously discussed, working memory is essential for good decision-making, and may contribute to suboptimal decision-making, such as the loss of control and persistence of behaviors despite associated negative consequences, often seen in addiction. While impairments in one or all of the subcomponents in working memory may contribute to poor decision-making related to addiction, such as reduced working memory capacity, the inability to resist distraction, and difficulty maintaining strong activation over time, it is the influence of the saliency of addiction-related choices and distractions that likely affect working memory and decision-making in addiction.

For those individuals with a behavioral addiction, the addictive behavior itself, as well as the cues and contexts surrounding that behavior, become increasingly more rewarding and salient to the addicted individual than to a non-addict. Based on the fact that highly salient information can take precedence over other items in working memory and also can be more successful in interfering, the addictive item may bias working memory processes and influence one's decisions. Take for example the following situation where an individual with alcoholism is faced with the decision to go out to the pub to watch a sporting event or go home to watch the game. The decision requires the individual to consider a number of choices, as well as the immediate and future consequences associated with each of the alternatives. The options are influenced by their temporal immediacy (e.g., more immediate outcomes are more salient), their importance to the individual, and the expected outcome. The most salient aspects for an individual with alcohol abuse may be the immediate physiological and psychological rewards of having a drink (relaxation) and social reward related to the joy of being with others at the bar. Furthermore, as previously mentioned, an individual with low working memory capacity is less likely to consider the less salient options, that are often of a delayed nature, such as the negative consequences of drinking (hangover), or even the positive, but less salient, consequences of watching the game at home (family, well-being). Therefore, the increased saliency of addictive behaviors, associated immediate rewards, and low working memory capacity in individuals may contribute to poor decision-making.

Consistent with the idea of poor working memory resulting in suboptimal decision-making in addiction, impaired decision-making alone has been seen in individuals with addiction. Both pathological gamblers and alcohol-dependent individuals show greater impulsive and risky decision-making in the laboratory compared to persons who do not exhibit these addictive behaviors (Lawrence, Luty, Bogdan, Sahakian, & Clark, 2009). For example, using the IGT, pathological gamblers and current and abstinent alcoholics have been shown to select fewer advantageous cards compared to controls. Again, for those with substance dependence, longer duration and increased quantity of use related to poorer performance. After long-term abstinence, the magnitude of the number of choices taken from the disadvantageous decks was related to the duration of peak alcohol use; those who drank large quantities of alcohol for longer were worse at picking the most advantageous cards (Fein, Klein, & Finn, 2004). These findings suggest that similar to working memory, long-term substance use is also associated with deficits in decision-making. Furthermore, greater neurocognitive deficits in inhibitory control and decision-making have been shown to predict relapse in substance users (Bowden-Jones, McPhillips, & Joyce, 2006) and problem gamblers (Goudriaan, Oosterlaan, De Beurs, & Van Den Brink, 2008). Thus, it is possible that impaired working memory may interfere with acquisition of new information or strategies to reduce or abstain from addiction-related behaviors.

In addition to suboptimal decision-making on the IGT, addicts show more impulsive decision-making—a behavioral trait that has been recognized as a potential factor contributing to multiple phases of addiction, including acquisition, escalation, and relapse. A current theory is that addiction may result from an individual choosing the immediate reward (i.e., drugs) over the later more rewarding consequences (life goals, family, well-being, etc.). Evidence for this theory lies in the finding that adolescent and adult substance abusers repeatedly show robust discounting of delayed rewards compared to age-matched controls. In fact, an increased preference for choosing those immediate, smaller rewards, despite options for larger, future rewards is consistently seen in individuals who use alcohol, methamphetamine, cocaine, heroin, and nicotine. A similar discounting profile is also seen in non-substance addictive behaviors, such as in pathological gambling (Dixon, Marley, & Jacobs, 2003). Interestingly, in a study by Petry and colleagues (Petry & Casarella, 1999), discounting behavior was examined in substance abusers with and without problem gambling to see if there were additive effects of these two addictive behaviors on impulsive decision-making. They found that substance abusers without gambling problems preferred more immediate rewards than healthy controls, but that substance abusers who were also pathological gamblers were even more impulsive and prone to choose smaller, but immediate rewards, than the group of non-gambling substance abusers. These findings further suggest that impulsive decision-making may be a key component of addiction, and again, based on the argument that intact working memory is inherent to optimal decision-making, suggests a strong interplay between working memory and addictive behavior.

The above studies provide strong evidence that individuals with behavioral addictions show both poor working memory and poor decision-making, but more recently it has been shown that these two cognitive deficiencies are related in addicts. For example, Lawrence and colleagues (2009) found that alcohol-dependent individuals showed impairments in risky decision-making and working memory deficits compared to a non-using control population. Similarly, in a sample of substance abusing individuals with a wide spectrum of drug of choice, including alcohol, methamphetamine, and cocaine, both working memory and decision-making performance were well below that seen in a demographically matched control group (Bechara & Martin, 2004). These experiments are especially important, as they show that both cognitive deficits are seen within the same individuals, and further support that poor working memory may lead to poor decision-making. Interestingly, however, there has been much less research supporting this idea in non-substance users. In fact, Lawrence et al. showed that while gamblers also showed increased risky decisions compared to controls, similar to alcohol abusers, working memory deficits were only specific to the alcohol-dependent group. The finding that pathological gamblers did not have impairments in this cognitive domain are in contrast to the findings of others, but may suggest that working memory deficits play a larger role in substance-related addictions. By performing similar studies comparing and contrasting specific substance and non-substance disorders, we will be able to better understand some of the core working memory features of addiction.

In addition to both working memory and decision-making deficits present within addicted individuals, it is important to know if this relationship is in fact asymmetrical and/or causal. That is, does poor working memory directly influence poor decision-making in these individuals? Until this year, the answer to this question was unclear. However, more recently, Bickel and colleagues set out to examine if deficits in decision-making in substance abusers could be diminished by increasing their working memory ability (Bickel, Yi, Landes, Hill, & Baxter, 2011). Specifically,

Bickel and colleagues had one group of treatment-seeking abstinent cocaine and methamphetamine users undergo working memory training, and another group of abstinent drug users that did not undergo this training, as part of their treatment regimen. Interestingly, those individuals who underwent working memory training made significantly fewer impulsive decisions on the delay discounting task compared to those abusers who did not undergo working memory training as part of their treatment. In fact, those who were trained on working memory skills decreased their preference for immediate, smaller rewards compared to larger, delayed rewards by 50 percent. These results provide strong evidence for a causal relationship between working memory processes and evaluating past and future options in addiction. There are, however, a number of remaining questions to be answered. For example, is this change in discounting rewards and impulsive decision-making long lasting? Also, is there a ceiling to how much training can result in less impulsive decision-making? Future research is necessary to address these questions. Nonetheless, these recent findings suggest that working memory can influence decision-making, and that poor working memory is at least one neurocognitive factor that may help us to understand poor decision-making accompanied by addictive behaviors.

Neuroimaging Studies of Working Memory in Addiction

Many studies to date have reported working memory dysfunction in those who are addicted to alcohol or other substances. These investigations have shown that behavioral deficits related to working memory can lead to disadvantageous decision-making with regard to alcohol and substance use. However, the brain basis of these behaviors has only recently begun to be discovered. There are many questions to consider: How does brain activity relate to working memory performance? What brain areas are important for optimal working memory? How might the brain function differently during maintenance of working memory in someone who suffers from addiction compared to a healthy individual? Uncovering the neural phenotypes associated with poor working memory functioning is a major goal of recent research aimed at advancing the understanding of the underlying neurobiology of addiction.

Neuroimaging of the brain in the last 20 years has provided increasing evidence to suggest that addiction is associated with various abnormalities in working memory-related brain response. One technology used in brain imaging research is known as functional magnetic resonance imaging (fMRI), a non-invasive tool that allows for the investigation of brain functioning by examining changes in blood oxygen level-dependent response. Specifically, fMRI examines changes in blood oxygenation in the brain, which is used as an indirect measure of neural activity. For example, data collected from fMRI tasks can reveal which parts of the brain are significantly activated while an individual performs tasks in an MRI scanner. Thus, this tool can be very useful in comparing clinical populations with healthy controls to understand the impact of psychiatric disorders on brain areas involved in working memory functioning. Addiction research has also been using fMRI to advance the understanding of differences in brain activity between substance abusing individuals and healthy controls. Similar to behavioral studies, the use of drugs of addiction can influence working memory-related brain response during both the acute, intoxicated phase, as well as with more long-term chronic use patterns. Thus, when examining the relationships between addiction and the neural bases of working memory, it is important to consider each of these scenarios in turn.

Intact working memory for verbal information, objects, and spatial relationships is mediated by multiple brain areas that are essential for higher-order executive control, including regions of the dorsolateral, ventral, and superior prefrontal cortex, as well posterior parietal brain regions (Wager & Smith, 2003; Walter et al., 2003). As previously suggested, poor working memory functioning may lead to a reduced capacity to maintain goal-directed information and less use of sophisticated analytic decision-making strategies, thereby leading to poor choices with regard to alcohol and/or drug use. In addition to its contributions to working memory functioning, the frontal lobe, and in particularly the prefrontal cortex, plays a major role in the ability to make advantageous decisions, show good judgment, and engage proper inhibitory control, and has often been implicated in executive functioning deficits seen in addicted individuals. Thus, not surprisingly, there has been ample evidence to suggest that frontal lobe activity may be aberrant in both alcohol- and substance-dependent patients, as well as during acute intoxication, and this can be exemplified with tasks examining working memory during fMRI.

Given the behavioral working memory deficits seen among actively intoxicated individuals, one might expect that acute alcohol intoxication would also be associated with abnormal brain response during working memory tasks. This is, in fact, the case. In an fMRI study of healthy adult males, Gundersen and colleagues showed reduced brain response in prefrontal and dorsal anterior cingulate cortical brain regions during a verbal, numeric n-back working memory task with acute alcohol intoxication (Gundersen, Specht, Gruner, Ersland, & Hugdahl, 2008). Another study of acute alcohol effect in both males and females demonstrated that alcohol intoxication resulted in attenuated brain response in the dorsolateral prefrontal cortex during a visual working memory span task (Paulus, Tapert, Pulido, & Schuckit, 2006). Similarly, a follow-up study by Gunderson and colleagues demonstrated load-related reductions in fronto-cerebellar brain regions during working memory, despite intoxicated individuals maintaining task performance comparable to non-affected peers (Gundersen, Gruner, Specht, & Hugdahl, 2008). These results parallel the behavioral findings of impaired working memory functioning in individuals acutely under the influence of alcohol and provide a plausible neurobiological correlate for these functional deficits.

Not only are the influences of substances on the neural substrates visible during acute intoxication, but more commonly, and perhaps more importantly, we see these effects after chronic use, even following a period of abstinence. For example, chronic alcoholism is also associated with many neural abnormalities, which impair cognition and result in poor performance on neuropsychological tests that examine executive functioning. Neuroimaging studies have revealed that the prefrontal cortex is especially vulnerable to the effects of chronic alcohol consumption (Cadete-Leite, Alves, Tavares, & Paula-Barbosa, 1990). Therefore, deficits in frontal lobe-mediated capacities, such as working memory, are often aberrant in alcohol-dependent individuals. One of the first studies to examine working memory performance in chronic alcoholics was conducted by Pfefferbaum and colleagues (2001), who investigated fMRI brain activity during a spatial working memory task in alcohol abusers who had been abstinent for an average of four months. In this task, participants were asked to remember whether the location of a letter that was displayed on the screen was the same location of another letter they saw two screens before. Despite equivalent performance on the task between the alcohol abusers and healthy controls, alcoholics showed weaker cortical brain activity in multiple prefrontal brain regions, required for attention and spatial working memory, compared to their peers. In contrast, chronic alcohol users showed greater activity in more inferior portions of the frontal lobe compared to controls. Very recently, functional connectivity of the brain during a spatial working memory task was examined in alcoholics and controls, and results suggested that, despite comparable task performance, alcoholics showed atypical functional connectivity between posterior brain networks, including the posterior cingulate cortex and the cerebellum (Chanraud, Pitel, Pfefferbaum, & Sullivan, 2011). These results suggest that alcohol dependence may lead to a change in strategy to complete working memory tasks and/or functional reorganization of the brain, which may be a way to compensate for damage to the affected brain areas implicated in working memory functioning. This type of brain functioning could lead to suboptimal decision-making with regard to alcohol use, particularly if brain areas required for working memory maintenance are performing less efficiently in these individuals.

It is important to mention that the working memory deficits seen in alcohol abusers are present on a wide variety of working memory tasks, not limited to those involving spatial information, as seen in the studies described above. For example, more recently, similar frontal lobe abnormalities were seen on a verbal working memory task in those who suffer from an alcohol use disorder. In a verbal working memory n-back task, individuals were required to remember a letter that appeared two screens before. Even in this relatively simple task, alcoholics had significantly weaker frontal lobe response (Park et al., 2011). However, it should be noted that mixed evidence exists in many fMRI studies examining working memory functioning among individuals with alcohol use disorders. Studies that have found *increased* brain activity in fronto-cerebellar circuitry in alcoholics, suggest that greater and more widespread frontal activity in alcoholics is related to compensatory mechanisms in which other brain areas are activated to allow alcoholics to remain on par in performance to healthy controls (Desmond et al., 2003). These mixed results may relate to the brain's ability to compensate up to a point (i.e., up to a certain level of alcohol abuse), beyond which decrements in brain activity prevail.

An intriguing question is whether individuals who suffer from substance dependence, other than alcoholism, also show similar differences in brain activity compared to healthy controls. In other words, are these differences in neural activity common across multiple types of substance addiction? The answer to this question, for the most part, is yes. While there are certainly some differences, even across studies examining alcohol-dependent individuals, very similar patterns emerge in studies of working memory that have examined both alcohol and other substance addicted individuals. For example, cocaine-dependent individuals exhibit similar patterns of brain activity during working memory tasks to those of alcoholics. Working memory has been examined in cocaine addicts by looking at attention-shifting abilities and associated brain activity. Attention shifting involves switching to an item in working memory to re-activate the memory of that item or switching away from an item in working memory to suppress the memory of that item. These functions are mediated by fronto-parietal brain regions involved in executive control and attention, and it is believed that dysfunction in attention-shifting may be one of the hallmarks of addiction. For example, a deficit in attention shifting might be seen in an individual who may not be able to re-activate thoughts that are not drug-related or may have difficulty suppressing drug-related thoughts in favor of switching to those that are task-relevant. Kubler and colleagues (Kubler, Murphy, & Garavan, 2005) examined attention shifting in a verbal working memory task, on which cocaine-dependent individuals and controls did not differ in performance. During this task, participants were required to switch between keeping the number of red versus blue circles in their head, as they were presented consecutively on a screen. Analysis of the imaging data indicated that cocaine-dependent participants showed hypoactivity in many of the regions necessary for executive functioning, including prefrontal and parietal cortical areas. This type of atypical brain functioning during attention shifting in cocaine abusers may result in poor decisions with regard to drug use, particularly if they are having difficulties suppressing thoughts of drug craving or re-activating non-drug related thoughts.

Similarly, in a study of recently abstinent cocaine abusers, hypoactivity of brain regions was found in the prefrontal cortex, thalamus, and striatum (Moeller et al., 2010). As these brain regions are part of the cortico-thalamo-striatal loops that play a prominent role in addiction, alterations in dopaminergic functioning due to years of chronic cocaine use is plausible. These circuits also play a role in motor and cognitive functioning, indicating that these systems may be compromised in cocaine users during working memory tasks. Participants in this study were required to perform a delayed match to sample task, during which individuals were presented with a string of numbers followed by a distracter stimulus. Subsequently, during the appearance of a probe stimulus, an individual had to confirm whether the string of numbers exactly matched the ones they saw a couple of seconds before the distracter item. Again, cocaine-dependent participants were no different from non-users on accuracy during the task, but differences in brain functioning in cortico-thalamo-striatal loops suggested that reduced activity of this circuit might be associated with weaker cognitive functioning in the presence of distracters. One might hypothesize that drug-related stimuli, which serve as distracters from every-day functioning in addicted individuals, might lead to weaker brain activity in cognitive and motor circuits that could result in poor decisions with regard to drug use.

In addition to studies of cocaine abuse, other drugs of abuse, less thought to have physiological addictive properties and be more associated with psychologically based addiction, have been connected to abnormal brain response during working memory. In particular, chronic marijuana use has been associated with increased prefrontal brain response, specifically in inferior and middle frontal gyri, during 2-back spatial working memory (Smith, Longo, Fried, Hogan, & Cameron, 2010). In addition, they show more widespread neural activity during spatial working memory in both working memory-related brain regions (e.g., prefrontal and anterior cingulate cortex) and those not commonly seen activated during spatial working memory (e.g., basal ganglia) (Kanayama, Rogowska, Pope, Gruber, & Yurgelun-Todd, 2004), which again suggests a compensatory neural response needed to achieve adequate task performance. Notably, this type of compensatory brain response during working memory has also been shown to persist even after a one-month period of abstinence (Padula, Schweinsburg, & Tapert, 2007).

Given the results described above, why is it important to examine working memory brain functioning in addicted individuals? How do brain differences in working memory functioning result in poor decisions with regard to substance use? One commonly used fMRI task (discussed previously) is the IGT, which assesses decision-making by asking participants to pick cards from decks that are either associated with monetary reward or punishment. A study by Tanabe and colleagues (2007) investigated brain response during decision-making in the IGT in substance-dependent individuals with and without gambling problems. Both of these groups had weaker brain activity in the ventromedial prefrontal cortex, a brain region that has been associated with affective decision-making. Weaker brain activity during decision-making in this task may indicate that substance-dependent individuals have greater difficulty maintaining information related to reward and punishment as the task progresses, which could mean that they are less sensitive to feedback regarding their decisions. Perhaps observed poor working memory capacity and attention skills seen in individuals who suffer from addiction relates to weaker decision-making-related brain activity. For example, while behavioral performance was no different between substance-dependent participants and controls in this task, weaker prefrontal brain activity may relate to poor decision-making seen in addicts when presented with more heated, real-life decisions and situations. One can imagine that the combination of working memory deficits and weaker decision-making-related brain response might result in poorer choices in an addict who is deciding between spending money on their next high and/or their next spin of the roulette wheel, or who is, alternatively, contemplating refraining from such behavior.

While many neuroimaging studies are being conducted to examine working memory functioning in individuals addicted to alcohol or other substances, it is often difficult to make comparisons between studies. These limitations are due to differences in the type of substance being abused, the duration of abuse, the age of the participants, the history of treatment, and the length of abstinence from the drug of abuse. Furthermore, beyond these differences in participant demographics, different types of working memory tasks with various loads of working memory difficulty are administered across studies. For example, spatial and verbal working memory tasks, attention shifting tasks, and delayed match to sample tasks are a few of the tasks that are commonly administered in fMRI studies. Beyond this, differences in analytic strategies for examining imaging data may also produce different results across studies. Despite all of these possible differences that may make interpretation of results difficult, it appears that the common theme indicates that addiction is associated with atypical brain activity in many areas of the frontal and parietal lobes—regions necessary for cognitive control, working memory, and attention (Smith & Jonides, 1998). Furthermore, the cortico-thalamo-striatal loops involved in executive processing, motor control, and reward are also altered in substance-dependent individuals (Belin, Jonkman, Dickinson, Robbins, & Everitt, 2009).

FUTURE DIRECTIONS

Altered Working Memory and Decision-making in Those At-risk for Addiction

The studies and examples presented thus far have emphasized that the last decade of neuroimaging studies has resulted in outstanding advancements in the understanding of brain and behavior relationships in working memory functioning in the field of addiction. These studies confirm that numerous addictive substances and behaviors, such as gambling, are associated with aberrant working memory functioning, both during acute intoxication and after prolonged abstinence, and suggest that even when task performance is not compromised, abnormalities in the underlying neurobiological substrates of working memory are present. While many of the differences in brain activity seen in addicted individuals are common across studies and have been, at times, related to substance abuse characteristics (e.g., duration or amount of use), one very important question should be raised. Are these differences in behavior and neurobiology in addicts a result of years of heavy alcohol/substance use or addictive behavior, or were they present even prior to abuse, thereby indicating potential neural markers of risk in individuals who suffer from addiction? Recently, studies have begun to explore this "chicken-or-the-egg" question by examining working memory functioning in individuals who are at risk for addiction, based on a family history of alcohol or substance use disorders. Importantly, however, at the time of the study, these youth have never used alcohol or drugs heavily, which removes the possibility that differences in brain activity seen in at-risk youth and their peers are due to the effects of heavy alcohol or substance use. In addition, none of these youth were prenatally exposed to heavy alcohol or drugs. Behaviorally, a study of non-substance abusing adults with a family history of alcoholism demonstrated aberrant executive working memory and decision-making processes in this population (Lovallo, Yechiam, Sorocco, Vincent, & Collins, 2006). In addition, our lab has demonstrated that adolescents with a family history of alcoholism display slowed decision-making speed on the delay discounting task compared to youth with no familial alcoholism, although discounting behavior was comparable (Herting, Schwartz, Mitchell, & Nagel, 2010). This slowed decision response time could be attributable to deficits in working memory or the ability to concurrently weigh the outcomes associated with each alternative, though this is speculative since delay discounting behavior was not examined in relation to working memory skills in this study. At a neural level, one recent fMRI study in adolescents with a family history of alcoholism used a spatial working memory task to examine brain activity compared to teens without such family history (Spadoni, Norman, Schweinsburg, & Tapert, 2008). Interestingly, findings from this study indicated that family history of alcoholism was not related to any differences in brain response during spatial working memory. However, brain activity differences in a simple vigilance condition did differ between at-risk youth and their peers. Specifically, increased brain response was observed in midline structures that normally deactivate during low cognitive demand, such as the vigilance condition. The authors proposed that this type of atypical brain activity may be related to mind wandering, which could result in deficits in adaptive decision-making, thereby putting youth with a family history of alcoholism at risk for poor decisions with regards to alcohol consumption. In addition to the above findings, recent findings from our own lab suggest that, during a verbal 2-back working memory task, largely substance-naïve youth with a family history of alcoholism show atypical superior and dorsolateral prefrontal brain response compared to adolescents without familial alcoholism (Cservenka, Herting, & Nagel, 2012). These abnormalities in brain response were also associated with slower reaction time on the task in family history-positive youth. However, these differences in reaction time did not fully explain the differences in brain response between the groups. Together, these findings suggest that many of the abnormalities in working memory behavior thought to be associated with substances or behaviors of abuse may, in fact, be associated with premorbid risk factors for addiction. This work provides an exciting starting point for developing prevention and intervention strategies.

CONCLUSIONS

Behavioral and neuroimaging studies of addiction have shown atypical perform-ance and brain functioning during a variety of tasks of working memory and decision-making in both alcohol- and substance-dependent individuals, as well as in non-substance-related addictions, such as gambling. Further, important emerg-ing research is beginning to investigate whether these differences are present in individuals at risk for addictive behaviors, so as to identify neural markers and behavioral phenotypes that may be associated with subsequent alcohol and/or substance abuse or excessive gambling behavior. These advancements in the field will better inform treatment and prevention strategies aimed at reducing the prevalence of addiction in hopes of ultimately reducing the overwhelming burden at the individual and societal level.

REFERENCES

Bechara, A., Damasio, A. R., Damasio, H., & Anderson, S. W. (1994). Insensitivity to future consequences following damage to human prefrontal cortex. *Cognition, 50*(1–3), 7–15.

Bechara, A., & Martin, E. M. (2004). Impaired decision making related to working memory deficits in individuals with substance addictions. *Neuropsychology, 18*(1), 152–162.

Belin, D., Jonkman, S., Dickinson, A., Robbins, T. W., & Everitt, B. J. (2009). Parallel and interactive learning processes within the basal ganglia: Relevance for the understanding of addiction. *Behavioural Brain Research, 199*(1), 89–102.

Bickel, W. K., Yi, R., Landes, R. D., Hill, P. F., & Baxter, C. (2011). Remember the future:

Working memory training decreases delay discounting among stimulant addicts. *Biological Psychiatry, 69*(3), 260–265.

Bobova, L., Finn, P. R., Rickert, M. E., & Lucas, J. (2009). Disinhibitory psychopathology and delay discounting in alcohol dependence: Personality and cognitive correlates. *Experimental and Clinical Psychopharmacology, 17*(1), 51–61.

Bowden-Jones, H., McPhillips, M., & Joyce, E. M. (2006). Neurobehavioural characteristics and relapse in addiction. *British Journal of Psychiatry, 188,* 494; author reply 494.

Cadete-Leite, A., Alves, M. C., Tavares, M. A., & Paula-Barbosa, M. M. (1990). Effects of chronic alcohol intake and withdrawal on the prefrontal neurons and synapses. *Alcohol, 7*(2), 145–152.

Chanraud, S., Pitel, A. L., Pfefferbaum, A., & Sullivan, E. V. (2011). Disruption of functional connectivity of the default-mode network in alcoholism. *Cerebral Cortex, 21,* 2272–2281.

Cservenka, A., Herting, M. M., & Nagel, B. J. (2012). Atypical frontal lobe activity during verbal working memory in youth with a family history of alcoholism. *Drug and Alcohol Dependence, 123,* 98–104.

Desmond, J. E., Chen, S. H., DeRosa, E., Pryor, M. R., Pfefferbaum, A., & Sullivan, E. V. (2003). Increased frontocerebellar activation in alcoholics during verbal working memory: An fMRI study. *Neuroimage, 19*(4), 1510–1520.

Dixon, M. R., Marley, J., & Jacobs, E. A. (2003). Delay discounting by pathological gamblers. *Journal of Applied Behavioral Analysis, 36*(4), 449–458.

Dolcos, F., & McCarthy, G. (2006). Brain systems mediating cognitive interference by emotional distraction. *Journal of Neuroscience, 26*(7), 2072–2079.

Dretsch, M. N., & Tipples, J. (2008). Working memory involved in predicting future outcomes based on past experiences. *Brain and Cognition, 66*(1), 83–90.

Fein, G., Klein, L., & Finn, P. (2004). Impairment on a simulated gambling task in long-term abstinent alcoholics. *Alcoholism: Clinical and Experimental Research, 28*(10), 1487–1491.

Fernandez-Serrano, M. J., Perez-Garcia, M., Schmidt Rio-Valle, J., & Verdejo-Garcia, A. (2010). Neuropsychological consequences of alcohol and drug abuse on different components of executive functions. *Journal of Psychopharmacology, 24*(9), 1317–1332.

Fine, M. S., & Minnery, B. S. (2009). Visual salience affects performance in a working memory task. *Journal of Neuroscience, 29*(25), 8016–8021.

Finn, P. R. (2002). Motivation, working memory, and decision making: A cognitive-motivational theory of personality vulnerability to alcoholism. *Behavioral and Cognitive Neuroscience Reviews, 1*(3), 183–205.

Goudriaan, A. E., Oosterlaan, J., De Beurs, E., & Van Den Brink, W. (2008). The role of self-reported impulsivity and reward sensitivity versus neurocognitive measures of disinhibition and decision-making in the prediction of relapse in pathological gamblers. *Psychological Medicine, 38*(1), 41–50.

Gouzoulis-Mayfrank, E., Daumann, J., Tuchtenhagen, F., Pelz, S., Becker, S., Kunert, H. J., et al. (2000). Impaired cognitive performance in drug free users of recreational ecstasy (MDMA). *Journal of Neurology, Neurosurgery, and Psychiatry, 68*(6), 719–725.

Gozzi, M., Cherubini, P., Papagno, C., & Bricolo, E. (2011). Recruitment of intuitive versus analytic thinking strategies affects the role of working memory in a gambling task. *Psychological Research, 75*(3), 188–201.

Grant, J. E., Potenza, M. N., Weinstein, A., & Gorelick, D. A. (2010). Introduction to behavioral addictions. *American Journal of Drug and Alcohol Abuse, 36*(5), 233–241.

Green, L., Fry, A. F., & Myerson, J. (1994). Discounting of delayed rewards: A life-span comparison. *Psychological Science, 5,* 33–36.

Greenstein, J. E., Kassel, J. D., Wardle, M. C., Veilleux, J. C., Evatt, D. P., Heinz, A. J., et al. (2010). The separate and combined effects of nicotine and alcohol on working memory capacity in nonabstinent smokers. *Experimental and Clinical Psychopharmacology, 18*(2), 120–128.

Gundersen, H., Gruner, R., Specht, K., & Hugdahl, K. (2008). The effects of alcohol intoxication on neuronal activation at different levels of cognitive load. *Open Neuroimaging Journal, 2*, 65–72.

Gundersen, H., Specht, K., Gruner, R., Ersland, L., & Hugdahl, K. (2008). Separating the effects of alcohol and expectancy on brain activation: An fMRI working memory study. *Neuroimage, 42*(4), 1587–1596.

Hanson, K. L., Winward, J. L., Schweinsburg, A. D., Medina, K. L., Brown, S. A., & Tapert, S. F. (2010). Longitudinal study of cognition among adolescent marijuana users over three weeks of abstinence. *Addictive Behavior, 35*(11), 970–976.

Heishman, S. J., Kleykamp, B. A., & Singleton, E. G. (2010). Meta-analysis of the acute effects of nicotine and smoking on human performance. *Psychopharmacology, 210*(4), 453–469.

Herting, M. M., Schwartz, D., Mitchell, S. H., & Nagel, B. J. (2010). Delay discounting behavior and white matter microstructure abnormalities in youth with a family history of alcoholism. *Alcoholism: Clinical and Experimental Research, 34*(9), 1590–1602.

Hildebrandt, H., Brokate, B., Eling, P., & Lanz, M. (2004). Response shifting and inhibition, but not working memory, are impaired after long-term heavy alcohol consumption. *Neuropsychology, 18*(2), 203–211.

Hinson, J. M., Jameson, T. L., & Whitney, P. (2002). Somatic markers, working memory, and decision making. *Cognitive and Affective Behavioral Neuroscience, 2*(4), 341–353.

Hinson, J. M., Jameson, T. L., & Whitney, P. (2003). Impulsive decision making and working memory. *Journal of Experimental Psychology: Learning, Memory, and Cognition, 29*(2), 298–306.

Kanayama, G., Rogowska, J., Pope, H. G., Gruber, S. A., & Yurgelun-Todd, D. A. (2004). Spatial working memory in heavy cannabis users: A functional magnetic resonance imaging study. *Psychopharmacology, 176*(3–4), 239–247.

Kubler, A., Murphy, K., & Garavan, H. (2005). Cocaine dependence and attention switching within and between verbal and visuospatial working memory. *European Journal of Neuroscience, 21*(7), 1984–1992.

Lawrence, A. J., Luty, J., Bogdan, N. A., Sahakian, B. J., & Clark, L. (2009). Problem gamblers share deficits in impulsive decision-making with alcohol-dependent individuals. *Addiction, 104*(6), 1006–1015.

Leiserson, V., & Pihl, R. O. (2007). Reward-sensitivity, inhibition of reward-seeking, and dorsolateral prefrontal working memory function in problem gamblers not in treatment. *Journal of Gambling Studies, 23*(4), 435–455.

Lovallo, W. R., Yechiam, E., Sorocco, K. H., Vincent, A. S., & Collins, F. L. (2006). Working memory and decision-making biases in young adults with a family history of alcoholism: Studies from the Oklahoma family health patterns project. *Alcoholism: Clinical and Experimental Research, 30*(5), 763–773.

Mendrek, A., Monterosso, J., Simon, S. L., Jarvik, M., Brody, A., Olmstead, R., et al. (2006). Working memory in cigarette smokers: Comparison to non-smokers and effects of abstinence. *Addictive Behavior, 31*(5), 833–844.

Moeller, F. G., Steinberg, J. L., Schmitz, J. M., Ma, L., Liu, S., Kjome, K. L., et al. (2010). Working memory fMRI activation in cocaine-dependent subjects: Association with treatment response. *Psychiatry Research, 181*(3), 174–182.

Padula, C. B., Schweinsburg, A. D., & Tapert, S. F. (2007). Spatial working memory performance and fMRI activation interaction in abstinent adolescent marijuana users. *Psychology of Addictive Behaviors, 21*(4), 478–487.

Park, M. S., Sohn, S., Park, J. E., Kim, S. H., Yu, I. K., & Sohn, J. H. (2011). Brain functions associated with verbal working memory tasks among young males with alcohol use disorders. *Scandinavian Journal of Psychology, 52*(1), 1–7.

Paulus, M. P., Tapert, S. F., Pulido, C., & Schuckit, M. A. (2006). Alcohol attenuates load-related activation during a working memory task: Relation to level of response to alcohol. *Alcoholism: Clinical and Experimental Research, 30*(8), 1363–1371.

Petry, N. M., & Casarella, T. (1999). Excessive discounting of delayed rewards in substance abusers with gambling problems. *Drug and Alcohol Dependence, 56*(1), 25–32.

Pfefferbaum, A., Desmond, J. E., Galloway, C., Menon, V., Glover, G. H., & Sullivan, E. V. (2001). Reorganization of frontal systems used by alcoholics for spatial working memory: An fMRI study. *Neuroimage, 14*(1 Pt 1), 7–20.

Rapeli, P., Kivisaari, R., Autti, T., Kahkonen, S., Puuskari, V., Jokela, O., et al. (2006). Cognitive function during early abstinence from opioid dependence: A comparison to age, gender, and verbal intelligence matched controls. *BioMedCentral Psychiatry, 6*, 9.

Saults, J. S., Cowan, N., Sher, K. J., & Moreno, M. V. (2007). Differential effects of alcohol on working memory: Distinguishing multiple processes. *Experimental and Clinical Psychopharmacology, 15*(6), 576–587.

Schweizer, T. A., Vogel-Sprott, M., Danckert, J., Roy, E. A., Skakum, A., & Broderick, C. E. (2006). Neuropsychological profile of acute alcohol intoxication during ascending and descending blood alcohol concentrations. *Neuropsychopharmacology, 31*(6), 1301–1309.

Shamosh, N. A., Deyoung, C. G., Green, A. E., Reis, D. L., Johnson, M. R., Conway, A. R., et al. (2008). Individual differences in delay discounting: Relation to intelligence, working memory, and anterior prefrontal cortex. *Psychological Science, 19*(9), 904–911.

Smith, A. M., Longo, C. A., Fried, P. A., Hogan, M. J., & Cameron, I. (2010). Effects of marijuana on visuospatial working memory: An fMRI study in young adults. *Psychopharmacology, 210*(3), 429–438.

Smith, E. E., & Jonides, J. (1998). Neuroimaging analyses of human working memory. *Proceedings from the National Academy of Sciences of the United States of America, 95*(20), 12061–12068.

Spadoni, A. D., Norman, A. L., Schweinsburg, A. D., & Tapert, S. F. (2008). Effects of family history of alcohol use disorders on spatial working memory BOLD response in adolescents. *Alcoholism: Clinical and Experimental Research, 32*(7), 1135–1145.

Substance Abuse and Mental Health Services Administration (2011). *Results from the 2010 National Survey on Drug Use and Health: Summary of National Findings*, NSDUH Series H-41, HHS Publication No. (SMA) 11-4658. Rockville, MD: Substance Abuse and Mental Health Services Administration.

Sullivan, E. V., Fama, R., Rosenbloom, M. J., & Pfefferbaum, A. (2002). A profile of neuropsychological deficits in alcoholic women. *Neuropsychology, 16*(1), 74–83.

Sullivan, E. V., Rosenbloom, M. J., & Pfefferbaum, A. (2000). Pattern of motor and cognitive deficits in detoxified alcoholic men. *Alcoholism: Clinical and Experimental Research, 24*(5), 611–621.

Tanabe, J., Thompson, L., Claus, E., Dalwani, M., Hutchison, K., & Banich, M. T. (2007). Prefrontal cortex activity is reduced in gambling and nongambling substance users during decision-making. *Human Brain Mapping, 28*(12), 1276–1286.

Wager, T. D., & Smith, E. E. (2003). Neuroimaging studies of working memory: a meta-analysis. *Cognitive, Affective and Behavioral Neuroscience, 3*(4), 255–274.

Walter, H., Bretschneider, V., Gron, G., Zurowski, B., Wunderlich, A. P., Tomczak, R., et al. (2003). Evidence for quantitative domain dominance for verbal and spatial working memory in frontal and parietal cortex. *Cortex, 39*(4–5), 897–911.

Wareham, J. D., & Potenza, M. N. (2010). Pathological gambling and substance use disorders. *American Journal of Drug and Alcohol Abuse, 36*(5), 242–247.

Part V

Working Memory
and Decision Making

11

Working Memory and Anxiety

Exploring the Interplay of Individual Differences across Development

LAURA VISU-PETRA

Developmental Psychology Lab, Department of Psychology,
Babeş-Bolyai University, Romania

LAVINIA CHEIE

Developmental Psychology Lab, Department of Psychology,
Babeş-Bolyai University, Romania

ANDREI C. MIU

Cognitive Neuroscience Laboratory, Department of Psychology,
Babeş-Bolyai University, Romania

*E*motion and cognition are inextricably linked in human mental life and the study of their interaction represents a hallmark of contemporary research in cognitive sciences (Gray, 2004). The study of anxiety offers an ideal framework for this type of investigation, since one of its distinctive features is the preferential processing of threat-related information (see Bar-Haim, Lamy, Pergamin, Bakermans-Kranenburg, van Ijzendoorn, 2007, for a recent meta-analysis), which influences individual's somatic, emotional, cognitive, and behavioral functioning (Eysenck, 1992). In the cognitive domain, despite the widely acknowledged impact of anxiety on the preferential allocation of *attention* to threat, the presence of an analogous *memory* bias has been a matter of controversy. Although there is consensus with regard to the importance of memory processes for the establishment and maintenance of an anxious cognitive style, and to the emerging implications for psychotherapy (Williams, 1996), both theoretical and empirical work provided mixed support for anxiety–memory interactions

(MacLeod & Mathews, 2004). The present chapter aims to review these findings, following several directions that offer promising avenues for their integration, and revealing their implications for cognitive and developmental models of anxiety, and for academic and therapeutic interventions.

The first topic of interest relates to what type of *working memory* (WM) is measured across investigations approaching potential anxiety-related effects. As noted by some researchers (e.g., Banich et al., 2009) rather different "flavors" of this construct have been considered. In an integrative attempt to relate different types of memory, Cowan (2008) remarks that WM has been defined in three slightly divergent ways: as short-term memory applied to cognitive tasks, as a multi-component system that stores and processes information in short-term memory, and as the attentional control deployed to manage short-term memory. Not surprisingly, these different conceptualizations are reflected in studies focusing on anxiety-related effects, although there is seldom any explicit mention of the type of WM being investigated. Studies have initially focused on anxiety-related disruptions of WM capacity and processing (Processing Efficiency Theory; PET, Eysenck & Calvo, 1992), and more recently on the impact of anxiety upon attentional control (Attentional Control Theory; ACT, Eysenck, Derakshan, Santos, & Calvo, 2007). The first approach was supported by a large body of—mostly behavioral—evidence, revealing that, especially on difficult and demanding memory tests, performance deficits arise due to anxious individuals' tendency to process task-irrelevant information associated with their worries (Eysenck & Calvo, 1992). The second approach focuses on the functions of the central executive and on goal-related patterns of performance, relying on convergent behavioral, electro-physiological, and neuroimaging data (Eysenck et al., 2007) to reveal attentional control failures in high-anxious participants.

Aside from performance deficits on WM tasks with emotionally neutral stimuli, researchers have focused on the contents of the memoranda, investigating whether the introduction of *emotionally relevant* (especially threat-related) information generated anxiety-related memory biases. In order for a memory bias to be ascertained, one would have to look for both between-group differences (between low-anxious and high-anxious participants) and within-group differences between processing of neutral versus threat-related information (Mitte, 2008). Evidence revealing such a memory bias has been rather inconsistent (see recent reviews by Coles & Heimberg, 2002; MacLeod & Mathews, 2004; Mitte, 2008; Miu & Visu-Petra, 2010), with results highly dependent upon the population and the anxiety dimension being investigated (clinical, non-clinical, state vs. trait), the memory system (explicit vs. implicit), the experimental paradigm (recall vs. recognition), or even the procedural details (stimulus modality, encoding procedure, retention interval). This chapter will focus on studies with non-clinical, *high-anxious participants*, and on *explicit memory biases*, revealed by both recall and recognition paradigms (but see Coles & Heimberg, 2002 for a review of explicit and implicit biases in clinical anxiety).

Although the number of studies dealing with the impact of anxiety on memory (either short-term memory, WM, or long-term memory) is still disproportionately small compared to the literature on attentional biases, there are more and more investigations claiming that the dynamics of cognitive biases should be studied longitudinally. From this developmental perspective, memory processes are bound to play an important role in the translation of the emotional "capture" of attention into the long-lasting, "looming" cognitive style (Riskind & Williams, 2005) characterizing anxious individuals.

Despite the focus on non-clinical populations, we subscribe to a continuum model of anxiety (see Endler & Kocovski, 2001, for a discussion of categorical versus continuum approaches to anxiety), whereby temperamental predispositions (e.g., behavioral inhibition), dimensional manifestations (state-trait anxiety), and anxiety disorders all represent phenotypic outcomes of lifelong gene–environment interactions that lead an underlying diathesis to be manifested or remain silent (Pine, 2007). This perspective emphasizes the paramount importance of memory processes in the generation and maintenance of *developmental trajectories* of anxiety, a direction that will be consistently pursued throughout the chapter.

BACKGROUND INFORMATION

There has been a long-standing intuition that anxiety is associated with cognitive performance decrements. "No passion so effectually robs the mind of all its powers of acting and reasoning as fear," stated the philosopher and political theorist Edmund Burke (1756). Empirical support for this intuition extends back several decades, identifying negative associations between the stable tendency to respond with anxiety in the anticipation of threatening situations (e.g., evaluative), and intelligence (Calvin, Koons, Bingham, & Fink, 1955; but see Kraus, 1965; Kanekar, Neelakantan, & D'Souza, 1976, for negative findings), learning (Spence & Spence, 1966; Weinstein, Cubberly, & Richardson, 1982), or problem solving skills (Deffenbacher, 1978; Sinclair, 1974).

In order to explain the negative association between anxiety and cognitive performance, Sarason (1984) proposed a *cognitive interference* theory, suggesting that worrisome thoughts interfere with the efficient allocation of attention to task-relevant information, reducing the cognitive resources available for task performance. The influential *Processing Efficiency Theory* (Eysenck & Calvo, 1992) adds two major clarifications to this explanation. First, the theory places anxiety-related effects in the context of Baddeley and Hitch's (1974) WM model, and proposes that "Anxious subjects engage in task-irrelevant processing which preempts processing resources and some of the available capacity of working memory" (Eysenck, 1979, p. 363). Therefore, anxiety is thought to exert most of its impact on WM tasks that involve the processing and storage capacity of the central executive. Second, the theory introduces an important distinction between performance effectiveness (quality, accuracy), and efficiency (effort or resources spent on task). Negative effects of anxiety are predicted to be greater on measures of efficiency, rather than of effectiveness, considering the motivational function of anxiety. More specifically, when faced with performance deterioration, anxious individuals invest greater effort (hence the reduced cognitive efficiency) in order to compensate for their worry-induced capacity limitations. There is extensive empirical support for these predictions, across distinct developmental periods and experimental contexts. First, anxiety has been shown to negatively affect WM performance on executive-demanding tasks by introducing higher processing demands (Ashcraft & Kirk, 2001; Darke, 1988; Eysenck, 1985; Richards, French, Keogh, & Carter, 2000; Tohill & Holyoak, 2000), or dual-task paradigms (Calvo & Ramos, 1989; Derakshan & Eysenck, 1998; Eysenck, Payne, & Derakshan, 2005; MacLeod & Donnellan, 1993; Visu-Petra, Cheie, Benga, & Alloway, 2011). Past and recent research supported the assumption that worry in a verbal form is the critical ingredient responsible for anxiety-induced WM impairments (Crowe, Matthews, & Walkenhorst, 2007; Hayes, Hirsch, & Mathews, 2008; Leigh & Hirsch, 2011; Rapee, 1993). This accounts for the larger interference between anxiety and performance on verbal, rather than on visual-spatial WM tasks (Ikeda, Iwanaga, & Seiwa, 1996; Markham & Darke, 1991; Rapee, 1993; but see Shackman et al., 2006, for threat-of-shock induced state anxiety, which selectively disrupts spatial WM). Second, anxiety has been shown to affect efficiency measures (response time, mental effort), leaving unaltered performance effectiveness (Darke, 1988; Derakshan & Eysenck, 1998; Elliman, Green, Rogers, & Finch, 1997; Eysenck, 1989; Eysenck, Payne, & Santos, 2006; Hadwin, Brogan, & Stevenson, 2005; Ikeda, et al., 1996; Murray & Janelle, 2003; Visu-Petra, Miclea, Cheie, & Benga, 2009).

All of the abovementioned effects have been documented using stimuli that did not include threat-explicit material. However, some studies did manipulate the degree of experienced threat (e.g., via ego-threatening instructions), revealing amplified WM impairments in high-anxious participants faced with stressful contexts (Beilock, 2008; Ng & Lee, 2010; Sorg & Whitney, 1992). When *threatening* information was incorporated in the to-be-remembered items, traditional theories varied in their expectations regarding potential anxiety-related memory impairments. Some theoretical positions have been skeptical regarding the existence of an anxiety-related explicit memory bias altogether. Williams, Watts, MacLeod, and Matthews proposed a complex model (1988, revised in 1997), emphasizing the automatic (integration) and strategic (elaboration) stages of information processing in anxiety. According to this theory, anxiety is characterized by emotionally congruent integrative processing, affecting the early encoding stages. However, it is not characterized by emotionally congruent elaborative processing, which would strengthen associative connections between new and existing mental representations, favoring their subsequent recall. An important clarification of the theory is that threatening stimuli, which are attended selectively in high-anxious subjects, are encoded perceptually, and not further elaborated conceptually, due to (1) their evolutionary relevance and biological preparedness, and (2) the deliberate avoidance of elaborative thought about aversive events (Mathews, Mackintosh, & Fulcher, 1997). Therefore, high-anxious persons are expected to present an implicit (especially on perceptually demanding tasks), but not an explicit memory bias (on conceptually based recall tasks). Despite the elegance of this conceptualization, the evidence for the implicit memory bias has been just as inconsistent as the one for the explicit memory bias. In a recent review (MacLeod & Mathews, 2004) the authors contended that, although sometimes inconclusive, measures of implicit memory, especially involving perceptually driven processes, detected an anxiety-linked memory advantage better than measures of explicit memory (recall or recognition). However, this conclusion was not supported by a more recent meta-analysis (Mitte, 2008), which found no solid support for an implicit memory bias in high-anxious individuals.

Most theorists, however, acknowledged the high probability of an explicit memory bias toward threat, which would be accentuated in high-anxious participants beyond its adaptive, evolutionary value (Nairne, Thompson, & Pandeirada, 2007). However, different explanations were proposed for this selective advantage of threat-related information. *Schema theories* suggested that the threat schemata that anxious individuals acquire from a very young age (Kendall & Ingram, 1987) favor the processing and retrieval of schema-congruent information (Beck & Emery, 1985), affecting both automatic and strategic information processing (Beck & Clark, 1997). Bower's semantic network theory of emotions (1981) also acknowledged emotion-congruent processing biases, which arise from the increased activation of multiple representations associated with an emotion node, which become active during the presentation of a potential threat.

Other approaches made an explicit distinction between proximal and distal anxiety-related memory effects. Research regarding the *arousal-memory* relationship revealed the detrimental impact of arousal for short-term recall, and its facilitative effect for long-term recall (Kleinsmith & Kaplan, 1964). It has been presumed that the greater arousal experienced by high-anxious participants when confronted with threat-related stimuli generates similar temporary memory deficits, but a longer-term memory enhancement for those specific stimuli (Eysenck, 1977; Mitte, 2008). However, emotional arousal has been shown to represent a double-edged sword for memory (Strange, Hurlemann, & Dolan, 2003), generating an emotion-induced enhanced memory for the emotional stimulus, coupled with an emotion-induced retrograde amnesia for the preceding items. Moreover, it has been shown that individual levels of trait anxiety significantly interacted with both of these memory biases (Miu, Heilman, Opre, & Miclea, 2005).

Cloitre and Leibowitz (1991) analyzed the type of processing being involved: perceptual or conceptual. According to these authors, anxiety facilitates the immediate perceptual processing of threat, increasing its activation. However, a cognitive avoidance mechanism inhibits the subsequent conceptual, elaborative processing, of threat-related material, limiting its accessibility. Therefore, high-anxious individuals are expected to show enhanced perceptual, but diminished conceptual memory for threatening information (although the expected results were not validated in a sample with panic disorder; Cloitre & Leibowitz, 1991). Finally, perceptual and conceptual memory biases, both immediate and delayed, can be expected based on high-anxious individuals' difficulty in *disengaging attention* from negative cues (Derryberry & Reed, 2002; Fox, Russo, Bowles, & Dutton, 2001; Koster, Crombez, Verschuere, & De Houwer, 2004; Yiend & Mathews, 2001), leading to a deeper encoding and subsequent recall of these items (Daleiden, 1998; Reed & Derryberry, 1995).

To summarize, a seminal line of research has identified anxiety-related WM impairments, especially on tasks that make heavy demands on the central executive (and, to a lesser degree, the phonological loop). Although high-anxious individuals often display comparable performance with low-anxious ones, they invest additional resources to compensate for the capacity and processing limitations induced by their task-irrelevant worries. Considering the large body of evidence documenting the preferential allocation of attention to threatening information in high-anxious individuals, a corresponding memory bias was to be expected. However, evidence in this direction has been mixed and inconclusive. Besides the several comprehensive reviews acknowledging this conundrum, an integrative theoretical framework and, accordingly, a more formal systematization of the accumulating evidence was needed.

CURRENT EVIDENCE

Within the last decade, a substantial increase in the number of studies targeting anxiety influences on cognitive performance has been noted. This surge of interest can be tracked down to at least three factors: (1) the theoretical advances promoted by a unifying theory, focusing on attentional control mechanisms, responsible for anxiety-related effects across neutral and emotionally relevant contexts; (2) the methodological advances offered by neuroimaging techniques; and (3) the therapeutic advances, consisting of an incorporation of the latest findings into treatment packages targeting cognitive biases, such as the Attentional Bias Modification paradigm (see Bar-Haim, 2010; Mathews & MacLeod, 2002, for reviews). We will review how the first two directions have influenced research targeting the specific influence of anxiety on WM processes. Unfortunately, intervention studies designed specifically to diminish memory biases in anxiety are scarce, probably due to the controversy still surrounding the very presence of such a bias. Finally, we will present two directions that we consider highly relevant (although still under-investigated) for research in this field: the role of memory processes in establishing and maintaining the developmental trajectory of anxiety, and the role of individual differences in WM capacity in modulating the impact of anxiety on memory functions.

A Unifying Theory

While incorporating the general framework of PET, the Attentional Control Theory (Derakshan & Eysenck, 2009; Eysenck et al., 2007) extends it in (at least) two significant directions. First, a more precise description of the *mechanism* through which anxiety interferes with cognitive performance is provided, by placing this interaction in the context of goal-directed (top-down) and stimulus-directed (bottom-up) attentional systems (Corbetta & Shulman, 2002). The key assumption is that anxiety disrupts attentional control, an essential function of the central executive component of the WM system. Anxiety is thereby conceptualized as "a state in which an individual is unable to instigate a clear pattern of behaviour to remove or alter the event / object / interpretation that is threatening an existing goal" (Power & Dalgleish, 1997, pp. 206–207, as cited in Derakshan & Eysenck, 2009). By increasing attention to such task-irrelevant stimuli (especially threat-related), anxiety disrupts the balance between the goal-directed and stimulus-directed systems in favor of the latter.

This prediction allows for the incorporation of the literature regarding stimulus emotional valence, with anxious individuals showing enhanced distractibility and difficulties disengaging from threat-related stimuli, either external, present in the task itself, or internally generated by the subjective interpretation of the (evaluative) context. As a corollary, anxiety is also expected to enhance performance when the required responses primarily involve the stimulus-driven attentional system and not the goal-directed attentional system. Support for these predictions is beginning to accumulate (see Derakshan & Eysenck, 2009; Eysenck et al., 2007; Eysenck & Derakshan, 2011, for reviews). The meta-analysis by Mitte (2008) provided a comprehensive systematization of the existing evidence of memory enhancement for threat-related information, affecting both recognition and recall processes in high-anxious individuals. It found support for: a within-group trend toward preferred recognition of threat-related pictorial (but not verbal) compared to neutral material; a between-group difference indicating better recall of verbal threatening material and poorer recall of positive material compared to low-anxious individuals; no consistent evidence for an implicit memory bias. Some studies show that there is a degree of content-specificity in the preferential processing of threat, so that the specific worries that an individual has are also the ones most likely to be remembered when found in memory tasks (Calvo, Avero, Dolores Castillo, & Miguel-Tobal, 2003; Reidy, 2004). Ignoring the personal relevance of threat items could be an important explanation for divergent findings, in addition to the methodological diversity characterizing the studies (Mitte, 2008).

Second, the homuncular (Cowan, 1988) perspective on the central executive is replaced with a more *functional* approach, provided by the executive functions model of Miyake and collaborators (2000). This model identifies three independent (yet interdependent) executive functions: shifting (flexibly switching between multiple tasks, operations, or mental sets), updating (using and monitoring, and refreshing the representations in WM), and inhibition (the ability to deliberately inhibit dominant, automatic, or prepotent responses when necessary). ACT predicts that anxiety mainly disrupts the functions of *inhibition* ("negative" attentional control) and *shifting* ("positive" attentional control), and, to a lesser degree, the updating function. Support for the negative effect of anxiety on inhibition is drawn from multiple behavioral, electrophysiological, and neuroimaging studies (see Eysenck & Derakshan, 2011, for a recent review). The typical finding is that high-anxious individuals are more susceptible to (especially threat-related) distraction than low-anxious individuals. It is important to stress the fact that several neuro-imaging investigations have supported the existence of a general (not just threat-related) impairment of attentional control in high-anxious individuals (Basten, Stelzel, & Fiebach, 2011; Bishop, 2009; Fales et al., 2008). Similar to the documented inhibitory failures, high-anxious individuals have also been shown to present more difficulties in flexibly shifting between different mental/task sets (see Eysenck & Derakshan, 2011, for a recent review).

Given our focus on memory functioning, it is of relevance to explore ACT's prediction of a limited effect of anxiety on the *updating* function. There appears to be some discrepancy between the ACT conceptualization of updating as "concerned with the transient storage of information, and so involv[ing] short-term memory rather than attentional control per se" (Derakshan & Eysenck, 2009, p. 12), and the original view of this function, since "the essence of Updating lies in the requirement to actively manipulate relevant information in working memory, rather than passively store information" (Miyake et al., 2000, p. 57). Considering that in its traditional sense updating is an executive process (Smith & Jonides, 1999) that requires attentional control in order to monitor, code, substitute, and update incoming information in response to task goals (see Ecker, Lewandowsky, Oberauer, & Chee, 2010, for an experimental decomposition of its sub-processes), presumably anxiety will also affect its functioning, especially in updating contexts that include threat-related distracters. Although not focused on anxiety effects, Schmeichel (2007) investigated the hypothesis that initial efforts at executive control temporarily undermine subsequent efforts at executive control. Using tasks involving simple information storage, or updating, he showed that attempts to maintain and update information in memory were impaired by prior efforts at executive control, whereas attempts simply to maintain information in memory remained relatively unaffected. In our view, the resource depletion approach proposed by this complex investigation is similar to the ACT approach, and could provide a fruitful strategy for analyzing anxiety-related effects on the updating function, in contexts containing neutral or threat-explicit material. Presumably anxious individuals' attempts to exert executive control in order to attenuate their task-irrelevant worries could deplete subsequent executive resources required by the updating task itself (see Fales et al., 2008, Fales, Becerril, Luking, & Barch, 2010; or Visu-Petra et al., 2009, 2011, for preliminary evidence). However, further research in this direction is necessary.

Functional Neuroimaging of Anxiety and WM

The neural mechanisms of the relationship between anxiety and executive functions have started to be investigated in humans using event-related potentials (e.g., Ansari & Derakshan, 2011) and functional neuroimaging methods (for reviews, see Banich et al., 2009; Bishop, 2007; Braver, Cole, & Yarkoni, 2010). As a popular complement of experimental manipulation, functional neuroimaging allows one to analyze how a brain region, which is presumably involved in the type of information processing that is studied (e.g., emotion, executive function), shows within-subject sensitivity to manipulation (e.g., high vs. low interference) and correlates with task performance between subjects (Braver et al., 2010). This section will illustrate how functional magnetic resonance imaging (fMRI) studies have not only contributed to testing psychological theories on anxiety and executive functions, but also generated new hypotheses that extended these theories.

Neuroimaging results have converged on showing that the increased suscep-tibility to emotional (threat) distraction in anxiety is reflected by enhanced activity in emotion processing brain regions such as the amygdala and the ventromedial prefrontal cortex. Two fMRI studies have recently supported this hypothesis in relation to WM. In one of these studies (Denkova et al., 2010), the participants had to encode and maintain in WM three emotionally neutral faces during a delay interval that preceded the memory test. During this five-second delay, the participants were presented with neutral or angry faces with mouth open (that were morphed from scrambled or neutral faces with mouth closed), after which a probe face was displayed and they rated on a three-point scale their confidence on whether the probe had been presented during encoding or was new. Angry face distracters activated regions associated with emotion (i.e., amygdala, ventromedial prefrontal cortex) and face processing (i.e., fusiform gyrus). Trait anxiety was positively correlated with activity in all these brain regions. The fusiform gyrus was a special case because its activation in trials with angry face distracters was related to both trait anxiety (left hemisphere) and WM performance (right hemisphere) (Denkova et al., 2010). Another study (Fales et al., 2010) used a 2-back WM task in which participants had to decide whether a certain face was the same as or different from the one that had been displayed two trials back. Trait anxiety positively correlated with activation of the left amygdala during fearful face relative to neutral face trials, and negatively correlated with activation of the left inferior frontal gyrus and left insula during happy face relative to neutral face trials (Fales et al., 2010). Both studies found no significant impact of trait anxiety on WM performance, although Denkova et al. (2010) reported a partial enhancing effect of trait anxiety on WM, but only for the trials with emotional distracters, in which the participants reported high levels of confidence in the recognition of probes. Overall, these results support the idea that trait anxiety facilitates the neural activity associated with the bottom-up processing of emotional distracters in WM, without affecting WM performance.

Anxiety has not only been related to increased bottom-up emotional distraction, but also with differences in top-down attentional control mechanisms such as inhibition or shifting (Eysenck et al., 2007). Rather than altering performance per se, this would result in reduced cognitive efficiency. But how would low cognitive efficiency in attentional control be reflected at the neural level? Some studies have suggested that anxiety is associated with reduced activation of brain regions involved in cognitive control, such as the dorsolateral prefrontal cortex, even in the absence of emotional distracters that might trigger amygdala hyperactivation (for a review, see Bishop, 2007). Neuroimaging data from WM studies partially support this view. For instance, trait anxiety negatively correlated with activity in the dorsolateral and dorsomedial prefrontal cortex in a delayed-response WM task with distraction (Denkova et al., 2010). The activation of the right superior frontal gyrus in fearful face trials from a 2-back WM task was also negatively correlated with trait anxiety (Fales et al., 2010). However, based on results from neuroimaging studies of other executive functions (e.g., planning, action selection), Fales et al. (2008) drew attention to the fact that *increased* activation of these regions could also be expected. In contrast with underactivation (interpreted as deficient recruitment) of cognitive control regions, hyperactivation of these regions might mirror the reduced cognitive efficiency associated with anxiety. At any rate, simply analyzing the degree of activation of a brain region without describing the temporal dynamic of activity changes and their relation with task demands does not offer specific information about the psychological mechanisms (Eysenck & Derakshan, 2011). Reduced or increased neural recruitment can reflect differences in efficiency, motivation, effort, or in the capacity to activate brain regions when needed (Fales et al., 2008). A finer-grained neural definition of cognitive efficiency is therefore desirable.

The processes underlying cognitive efficiency can be distinguished based on the dynamics of cognitive control, contrasting sustained and transient representations of task goals depending on task demands. The *Dual Mechanisms of Control* theory (DMC, Braver, Gray, & Burgess, 2007; Fales et al., 2008), which emerged from neuroimaging research, argues that there are two types of cognitive control: proactive control, which involves early attentional selection and a sustained representation of task requirements or goals throughout periods of high control demand; and reactive control, which involves only weaker preparatory attentional biases and transient representation of task requirements only when a task-relevant stimulus is encountered or conflict occurs in processing. The sustained representation of task goals in WM allows more effective top-down control of information processing because the preparatory attentional biases promote the prevention or rapid resolution of conflict during ongoing information processing. In the reactive control mode, bottom-up influences are stronger since the task goal representations are only transiently activated when conflict occurs. However, the latter type of cognitive control is adaptive when unpredictable threats are possible in the environment or one must respond to changing task contingencies.

The DMC theory posits that although all people use both types of cognitive control depending on task requirements, anxious people may be more prone to reactive control because of their increased arousal and environmental vigilance (Braver et al., 2007; Fales et al., 2008). Two predictions were thus put forward in an fMRI study of WM in anxiety: (1) trait anxiety would involve greater transient, and less sustained activation in cognitive control regions such as the dorsolateral prefrontal cortex; and (2) trait anxiety would also involve difficulty in transiently reducing the tonic activation of default regions (e.g., ventromedial prefrontal cortex), which would be necessary in difficult trials (Fales et al., 2008). Difficulties in default network deactivation were previously associated with momentary lapses in attention (Weissman, Roberts, Visscher, & Woldorff, 2006), as well as increased anxiety in the absence of a cognitive task (Simpson, Drevets, Snyder, Gusnard, & Raichle, 2001). The emotional modulation of default network activity might thus be critical for optimal activation in cognitive control regions. Using a verbal 3-back WM task, Fales et al. (2008) found that high trait anxiety was associated with reduced sustained activation and increased transient activation in a cognitive control network (e.g., right inferior frontal cortex). This suggested that anxious participants may increase reactive control in order to compensate for reductions in proactive control. In addition, high trait anxiety was also related to greater sustained deactivation of the default network (e.g., left inferior parietal cortex) (Fales et al., 2008). This might indicate an active inhibitory process by which regions associated with spontaneous mental activity are deactivated in order to reduce awareness of anxious arousal and rumination. This may be a compensatory strategy for dealing with increased arousal in anxiety. Fales and colleagues (2008) emphasized that if one only focused on the transient activation of cognitive control regions, one would conclude that high trait anxiety is indeed associated with reduced cognitive efficiency. However, since there were no differences in WM performance between anxiety groups, one may describe the pattern of results found in this important neuroimaging study (Fales et al., 2008) as two alternative routes to the same behavioral performance: increased sustained activation of cognitive control regions in low trait anxiety vs. increased transient activation of cognitive control regions and increased sustained deactivation of default network regions in high trait anxiety.

In summary, these functional neuroimaging studies that used WM tasks showed that anxiety facilitates activity in regions associated with the perception of social and emotional stimuli. This offers support for the idea that anxiety is related to increased bottom-up interference by emotional distracters, in line with ACT (Eysenck et al., 2007). In addition, neuroimaging results in the framework of the dual mechanisms of control underscored that the differences in WM-related neural activity observed in anxiety may be viewed as an alternate route to cognitive efficacy, rather than reduced cognitive efficiency. Future studies along this line are warranted.

Memory and the Developmental Trajectory of Anxiety

Most of the research concerning the anxiety–WM relationship has been conducted with adults, and research regarding anxiety's potential detrimental effect upon WM functioning in children has remained rather limited. A possible explanation could be given by the inconsistency of results obtained from studies investigating emotional memory biases in adults (see Miu & Visu-Petra, 2010, for a review). However, in recent years, more researchers turned their attention toward this under-investigated area. The main reasons for this recent interest would be accounted for by (1) the need to investigate high-anxious children's poor academic performance (e.g., Aronen, Vuontela, Steenari, Salmi, & Carlson, 2005; Owens, Stevenson, Norgate, & Hadwin, 2008); and (2) the need to investigate the early precursors of anxiety-related memory impairments (e.g., Visu-Petra et al., 2011). We will review the current evidence regarding children's performance deficits on WM tasks with emotionally neutral stimuli, as well as performance particularities on tasks involving emotionally relevant information.

In the developmental context, the research line focusing on the link between anxiety and WM for *emotionally neutral* information seems to be better documented than the one concerning a content-specific memory bias in anxiety. Yet, the existing studies conducted with both clinical and non-clinical high-anxious children have yielded mixed evidence of impaired memory for neutral information (see also Miu & Visu-Petra, 2010). The first set of evidence can be derived from studies conducted with clinical populations, in which most of the findings imply a link between anxiety symptomatology and poor WM performance (Aronen et al., 2005; Pine, Wasserman, & Workman, 1999; Toren et al., 2000; Vasa et al., 2007; but see also Günther, Holtkamp, Jolles, Herpertz-Dahlmann, & Konrad, 2004 for contradictory results). Although evidence of a memory impairment in clinically anxious children clearly exists, the results of these studies are rather inconsistent with regard to stimulus modality effects (verbal vs. visual-spatial). However, some of these inconsistencies are probably accounted for by methodological differences such as investigating different or restrictive anxiety diagnoses (e.g., Günther et al.,

2004; Toren et al., 2000; Vasa et al., 2007), using a large age range (e.g., 8–17 years in Günther et al., 2004; 9–20 years in Vasa et al., 2007), or the various experimental paradigms and procedural details.

Few studies have attempted to validate the existence of a general WM impairment in non-clinical, *high-anxious children*. All of these studies explored this relationship by directly addressing ACT's (Eysenck et al., 2007) main predictions considering anxiety's detrimental effect on both efficiency and accuracy of performance. The first of such developmental studies were carried out with *school-age children*. Hadwin et al. (2005) directly tested PET assumptions (i.e., the detrimental effects of state anxiety, affecting the phonological loop and central executive components of WM on the one hand, and processing efficiency on the other hand) in a sample of school-age children (9 to 10 years old). WM performance was evaluated using forward digit span, backward digit span, and a spatial WM test, while time taken to complete the task and self-reports of subjective mental effort were considered measures of performance efficiency. The results revealed that while state anxiety was not related to the accuracy of performance on any WM test, high-anxious children took longer to complete the backward digit span task, and more effort to complete the forward digit span task, compared to low-anxious children. The findings thus confirmed the above-mentioned hypotheses. Moreover, processing efficiency impairments were also reported in a study that compared the performance of high and low trait test anxiety groups of ten-year-olds on a mental arithmetic task, varying in WM demands (Ng & Lee, 2010). Consistent with the PET/ACT's predictions and Hadwin et al.'s previous findings (2005), the adverse effects of anxiety were found on the memory load task efficiency. However, some results were inconsistent with ACT predictions, as the detrimental effects of test anxiety did not increase as the WM demands increased. Owens et al. (2008) also directly tested ACT's predictions, investigating the relationship between trait anxiety, WM, and academic performance in a sample of school-age children (11 to 12 years old). WM was evaluated using the backward digit recall test and a computerized version of the Corsi block test. Consistent with the abovementioned results and ACT's predictions, trait anxiety was again found to be negatively associated with verbal WM performance, and no association was found between trait anxiety and visuo-spatial WM.

More recently, the trait anxiety–short-term memory relationship was also investigated in *preschoolers*. Visu-Petra et al. (2009) investigated the effects of trait anxiety on simple span accuracy and performance efficiency (response timing) in a sample of three- to six-year-olds. At the first time point, WM was assessed using a digit span task and a word span task, and eight months later, children were assessed with the same tasks and a newly introduced nonword span task. As predicted by the ACT, the results showed that trait anxiety was a negative predictor of span effectiveness over time, as well as a concurrent negative predictor for efficiency (in the case of word and non-word span). The micro-analysis of response timing (measuring the duration taken to prepare the response, to produce each word, and the pauses between words) indicated that children with high trait anxiety took longer to prepare their answers, as they had longer pauses between words and longer preparatory intervals. In another study, Visu-Petra et al. (2011) investigated both short-term memory and WM performance in relation to trait anxiety in two samples of preschoolers (three to seven years old). In Study 1, children's short-term memory was assessed using two verbal tasks (word and digit span) and two visuo-spatial tasks (color, object, and Corsi span). In Study 2, WM was tested using the Automated Working Memory Assessment (AWMA, Alloway, 2007) battery. Results revealed that while both the visual-spatial storage and updating performance did not differ between the two anxiety groups, their performance differed on the verbal measures. In this respect, when simple verbal storage was required, high-anxious preschoolers displayed efficiency deficits only, but when executive demands were higher (i.e., verbal updating), both efficiency and accuracy of response were impaired.

To sum up, although the number of studies exploring the relationship between non-clinical anxiety and WM in children is limited, a consistent pattern of results, confirming ACT's (Eysenck et al., 2007) predictions, is notable. Findings suggest that (1) there are comparable levels of both accuracy and efficiency of performance between the two anxiety groups on the visuo-spatial short-term memory and WM tasks (see Hadwin et al., 2005; Owens et al., 2008; Visu-Petra et al., 2011); (2) higher levels of anxiety mainly disrupt children's verbal performance efficiency on both WM tests (see Hadwin et al., 2005; Ng & Lee, 2010; Owens et al., 2008; Visu-Petra et al., 2011), as well as on simple storage tasks (see Visu-Petra et al., 2009; Visu-Petra et al., 2011); (3) high levels of anxiety can also disrupt children's performance effectiveness, mainly as a function of the increase in executive load involved in the memory task (see Visu-Petra et al., 2011).

Next, we will turn our attention to studies investigating memory for *emotional* information across development. Although symptoms of subclinical and clinical anxiety are common even in the preschool period (Cartwright-Hatton, McNicol, & Doubleday, 2006; Egger & Angold, 2006) and persist through the childhood years and into adulthood (Hadwin & Field, 2010a; Weems, 2008), research analyzing the onset of children's anxiety-related cognitive biases has been scarce and often contradictory. In recent years, researchers have struggled to organize evidence supporting the existence of cognitive biases in high-anxious children's processing of emotional information by adopting an information-processing perspective (e.g., Daleiden & Vasey, 1997; Field & Lester, 2010a; Hadwin, Garner, & Perez-Olivas, 2006; Hadwin & Field, 2010a; Pine, 2007). This integrative perspective is essential for investigating both distal and proximal vulnerability markers that contribute to the development and maintenance of child and adolescent anxiety (Ingram & Price, 2010; Muris, 2006).

Anxious children display distinctive patterns of information processing biases (see Hadwin & Field, 2010b; Field & Lester, 2010a, 2010b; Pine, 2007). In one of the most comprehensive developmental models of cognitive biases in early information processing in anxiety, Pine (2007) argues that genetic and environmental influences operate directly at the level of the neural circuitry that shapes threat responses, influencing information processing mechanisms. It is hypothesized that there is an interaction between attentional biases that occur in the early stages of information processing and subsequent learning processes that lead children to classify a broad range of stimuli as dangerous. Providing a similar explanation,

Weems and Watts (2005) argued that selective attention, memory biases, and negative cognitive errors could have a very important role in the generation and maintenance of childhood anxiety symptoms.

Existing evidence of early memory biases toward negative information would support the *developmental continuity* framework (Weems, 2008), acknowledging the early onset of information processing biases in high-anxious children. In favor of this perspective, Pine (2007) conjectures that the information processing biases could be even stronger in young children due to the enhanced plasticity of their threat-processing circuitry. Moreover, based on developmental cognitive research findings, Field & Lester (2010a) argue that early childhood (four to seven years old) could be an important developmental period in learning interpretational biases to threat, while attentional biases could develop during early childhood (Pérez-Edgar et al., 2010). The *developmental discontinuity* perspective (Kindt & Van den Hout, 2001), however, theorizes that it is highly unlikely that an information processing bias would occur earlier than the age of 10 to 12 years. It is argued that the trajectories of high- and low-anxious children diverge later on the developmental pathway because only older high-anxious children present a threat-related inhibitory deficiency (as a result of repeated exposure to aversive stimuli), not visible in low-anxious children. Early or late, it is evident that information processing biases play an important role in fostering and maintaining anxiety-related symptomatology, and understanding child anxiety is essential considering that the symptoms often persist beyond childhood (Weems, 2008). We will review the existent evidence regarding anxiety-related cognitive bias in remembering emotional information encountered in WM tasks.

To date, most of the developmental researchers studying cognitive vulnerability factors in high-anxious children, have been interested in investigating attentional biases toward threat and threat appraisal distortions. Results revealed that, compared to their low-anxious counterparts, high-anxious children display an attentional bias toward threatening information (see Malcarne, Hansdottir, & Merz, 2010; Miu & Visu-Petra, 2010, for recent reviews). However, data regarding high-anxious children's cognitive vulnerability factors, especially with respect to remembering emotional information, remain scarce and inconsistent (see Hadwin, Garner, & Perez-Olivas, 2006, for a review). Developmental research with *clinical populations* has yielded mixed results in terms of *verbal* short-term memory recall. An overall poorer memory performance, as well as a bias favoring negative information recall were found in children and adolescents with PTSD (Moradi, Taghavi, Neshat-Doost, Yule, & Dalgleish, 2000; but see Dagleish et al., 2003 for no significant effects in samples of PTSD and GAD patients). In the *visual* domain, no significant interference of negative task-irrelevant images (backgrounds) was found on memory performance in the anxiety-only group (Ladouceur et al., 2005). Again, the scarcity of the existing literature and the inconsistency of the existing results prevent us from drawing any conclusions.

Again, few studies have investigated WM or short-term memory for emotional information in *non-clinical* samples. In the *verbal WM* domain, the first data derived from studies conducted with *school-age* children. Daleiden (1998) investigated the effects of trait anxiety on a conceptual and perceptual verbal memory task in a sample of school-age children (11 to 13 years old). The children were presented with two lists of 30 emotional words (positive, negative, and neutral). Results revealed that the recall of negative words (relative to positive and neutral) was better in the high-anxious group when recall reflected conceptual (relative to perceptual) memory. Another study conducted by Reid, Salmon, and Lovibond (2006) investigated cognitive biases in a nonclinical sample of school-age children (8 to 14 years old) assessed for anxiety, depression, and aggression symptoms. Regarding memory biases, the authors used a verbal memory task involving self-descriptors (44 positive and negative adjectives) and varied the depth of processing in the encoding stage, from a superficial level (the child had to decide if it was a long or a short word) to a deeper, self-referential level. Their findings revealed a memory bias toward negative information, present only when scores from all types of symptomatology were combined, and no specific association with anxiety.

More recently, WM for emotional information was also investigated in high and low trait anxiety *preschoolers*. Using a task modified from the List Learning task (NEPSY battery; Korkman, Kirk, & Kemp, 1998) containing words with different emotional valences (negative, positive, neutral), Cheie and Visu-Petra (2012) investigated emotional biases in verbal short-term memory in a sample of three- to seven-year-olds. The results surprisingly revealed immediate memory avoidance of negative information in young high-anxious children, as they showed poorer short-term recall for negative words compared to low-anxious preschoolers, although this tendency disappeared in the delayed memory test. Thus, although the majority of results suggest that there might be biases for high-anxious children's recall of verbal information, the findings are inconsistent, stressing the need for replication and broadening this research domain.

As for the relationship between non-clinical anxiety and emotional biases in *visual WM*, to our knowledge, there is just one published study. Using a memory updating task in a sample of preschoolers (59 to 88 months), Visu-Petra, Țincaș, Cheie, and Benga (2010) found that, compared to their low-anxious counterparts, high-anxious children were both less efficient and less accurate in recognizing happy faces, but more accurate in identifying previously seen angry faces. Also, high-anxious children were less accurate in recognizing happy (relative to neutral) facial expressions, while low-anxious children were less accurate in response to angry (relative to happy and neutral) faces. The results confirm previous findings from research with adults (Moser, Huppert, Duval, & Simons, 2008; Silvia, Alan, Beauchamp, Maschauer, & Workman, 2006), revealing a negative bias favoring the recognition of threatening faces in children with high levels of anxiety, as well the absence of a positive bias toward positive visual information, for high-anxious participants only.

An Individual Differences Perspective

The studies presented above have followed only the direction of reciprocal connection between anxiety and WM. More specifically, they all investigated how elevated levels of anxiety interfere with WM functioning, affecting performance accuracy or efficiency. However, the opposite direction has also been investigated, in (the few) investigations looking at how individual differences in WM capacity can modulate anxiety's disruptive effects on cognitive functioning. The reasoning behind this prediction is that although anxiety results in a general restriction in individuals' WM resources, having a higher WM capacity should serve as a buffer against this effect. In the non-clinical population, participants with higher WM have been shown to be more proficient in terms of general cognitive control (see Ilkowska & Engle, 2010, for a review), showing increased resistance to interference (Kane & Engle, 2003), better control of visual attention (Kane, Bleckley, Conway, & Engle, 2001), or better capacity to ignore distracting auditory information (Colflesh & Conway, 2007; Conway, Cowan, & Bunting, 2001). Last, but not least, people with higher WM capacity have also been shown to be better at self-regulating their emotional experience (Schmeichel, Volokov, & Demaree, 2008), which could also represent a key factor in diminishing anxiety's negative impact upon WM performance.

The relationship between trait anxiety and individual differences in WM capacity has been investigated in a few studies that covered different portions of the developmental trajectory. Studying ten-year-olds' performance on tasks with high and low memory load, under evaluative or non-evaluative conditions, Ng and Lee (2010) used individual differences in WM capacity as a covariate. They did not find a significant effect of this covariate in altering participants' performance, irrespective of anxiety group (high or low).

Working with undergraduates, Johnson and Gronlund (2009) found that trait anxiety correlated negatively with task accuracy at low and average levels of WM capacity, but not at high levels of WM capacity. Therefore, individuals with low WM capacity appear particularly vulnerable to anxiety's disruptive effect on perform-ance. Importantly, anxiety and WM capacity did not correlate; it was only when attentional control processes were overloaded that the disruptive effects of anxiety were noted, mediated by individual levels of WM capacity. A different possibility resulted from the studies of Beilock and collaborators (Beilock & Carr, 2005; Beilock, Kulp, Holt, & Carr, 2004) who found that state anxiety (due to induced situational pressure) only disrupted performance for those high in WM capacity. The authors suggested that these individuals rely on attentional-control intensive strategies to solve the (demanding) WM task, and that these processes are selectively disrupted by anxiety (Beilock & DeCaro, 2007). However, the impact of trait anxiety was not explicitly evaluated and could still moderate the relationship between WM capacity and performance (Johnson & Gronlund, 2009).

These results suggest that individual WM capacity might be indicative for the impact of anxiety on WM-challenging evaluations, and that the conjunction between low WM and high trait anxiety could be responsible for the deleterious effects of anxiety on academic achievement.

FUTURE DIRECTIONS

WM is of paramount importance for every aspect of human mental life, from attention (Huang & Pashler, 2007), to language comprehension (Lewis, Vasishth, & Van Dyke, 2006), cognitive style (Alloway, Banner, & Smith, 2010), or long-term memory formation (Ranganath, Cohen, & Brozinsky, 2005). Therefore, the study of its interplay with enduring personality characteristics such as trait anxiety is of relevance for research and interventions targeting the optimization of cognitive performance and individual well-being. While the preceding sections have dealt with implications for research into cognition–emotion interactions, vulnerability to psychopathology, and developmental trajectories, we will now turn to relevance for applied settings, considering the impact of the anxiety–memory link on academic outcomes and on therapeutic approaches to anxiety.

Implications for Academic Performance

The relationship between anxiety and neurocognitive functioning in children has been mainly investigated at the level of the consequences, as it has been well documented that a higher level of anxiety is related to poorer academic achievement (see Ashcraft, 2002; Crozier & Hostettler, 2003; Kessler, Foster, Saunders, & Stang, 1995; Woodward & Fergusson, 2001). A less documented area concerns the neurocognitive mechanisms underlying this relationship. Within the ACT (Eysenck et al., 2007) framework, the interference between anxiety and WM functioning represents a potential mechanism that may account for anxiety's detrimental effect on academic performance. Some indirect evidence derives from studies showing that a poorer academic achievement and learning difficulties are also associated with a poorer WM capacity (e.g., Alloway & Gathercole, 2005; Alloway et al., 2005; Gathercole & Baddeley, 1990; Gathercole & Pickering, 2000; Gathercole, Pickering, Knight, & Stegmann, 2004; Henry, 2001; Jarrold, Baddeley, & Hewes, 1999; McLean & Hitch, 1999; Swanson & Sachse-Lee, 2001).

However, there are few studies specifically focusing on the association between anxiety, WM, and academic performance. In their study, Aronen and his collaborators (2005) concluded that teacher-rated anxiety/depression symptoms were negatively related to WM functioning and the ability to concentrate, an outcome that would lead to having a poorer academic performance in school. Nevertheless, the children's academic performance per se was not evaluated, so the authors' conclusions relied solely on teachers' reports.

Directly testing ACT's predictions, Owens et al. (2008) investigated the relationship between trait anxiety, WM, and academic performance in a sample of school-age children. The authors evaluated academic achievement through measures of verbal, nonverbal, and quantitative reasoning, as well as the national curriculum-based Standardized Assessment Tests (SATs) in mathematics, English, and science. As mentioned earlier, trait anxiety was found to be negatively associated with verbal WM. Most importantly, verbal WM was also found to partially mediate the relationship between trait anxiety and academic performance, accounting for 51 percent of the association. Given these results and the fact that visuospatial WM accounted for only 9 percent of the anxiety–academic performance relationship, this study not only confirms ACT's predictions with regard to the detrimental effects of anxiety on the phonological loop and central executive components, but it also demonstrates that verbal WM is an important neurocognitive mechanism underlying anxiety's negative effect on school outcomes. Moreover, similar results have been recently obtained in independent samples of school-age children (Owens, Stevenson, Norgate, & Hadwin, submitted; as described in Curtis, 2009; Yousefi et al., 2009).

In sum, even though the neurocognitive underpinnings of the anxiety–academic performance relationship have been largely overlooked, given the evidence from recent developmental studies, there are reasons to believe that WM functioning represents a specific mechanism that accounts for anxiety's detrimental effect on academic achievement, in line with the individual differences approach presented above. The implications of targeting WM as a mediator in the relation between anxiety and school performance are great, as WM could represent an important factor to be considered in developing educational interventions for underachieving children with higher levels of anxiety. Several interventions targeting various aspects of WM functioning have been validated (Alloway, in press; Klingberg et al., 2005; Holmes, Gathercole, & Dunning, 2009; Loosli, Buschkuehl, Perrig, & Jaeggi, 2011). Aside from improving cognition and school performance, such interventions could provide high-anxious children with a more efficient buffer against anxiety's detrimental effects on academic achievement.

Implications for Therapy

Current research into the cognitive and neurobiological underpinnings of anxiety has led to a recent refinement of therapeutic goals and methods, as well as to a re-conceptualization of the mechanisms through which traditional therapies such as Cognitive Therapy (CT) elicit and maintain significant change. In a recent review of these advances, Clark and Beck (2009) state that "treatment process research that elucidates the mechanisms of therapeutic change in CT has lagged behind the advances attained in the outcome research" (2009, p. 422). CT or Cognitive Behavioral Therapy (CBT) has been shown to significantly reduce information processing biases, especially attentional (see Tobon, Ouimet, & Dozois, 2011, for a recent review). However, there is little intervention research targeting memory functioning in high-anxious or clinically anxious individuals. One of the few proposals of memory modification as an outcome variable in clinical anxiety treatments is provided by Tryon and McKay (2009), suggesting that therapeutic outcome should also be measured via memory change. However, this analysis applies more to long-term memory and learning processes, rather than to "online" WM processes. In a more focused intervention, Bomyea and Amir (2011) trained non-clinical participants with an inhibition task and showed that participants in the training group presented an enhanced WM capacity and experienced fewer intrusions during a thought suppression task, suggesting a potential common underlying mechanism responsible for these changes.

Other studies provide valuable suggestions for future research targeting the improvement of memory functioning in anxiety. Amir and Bomyea (2011) found that socially phobic individuals present a better WM capacity for threat than for neutral words; they suggested that programs designed to train WM toward non-threat information (similar to the programs designed to reduce attentional biases) could enhance the processing of benign information in these individuals. Mindfulness interventions have been shown to promote several executive functioning dimensions, including WM (Zeidan, Johnson, Diamond, David, & Goolkasian, 2010), along with their benefits for mood and affective processes (Nyklicek & Kuijpers, 2008) or for emotional regulation (Nielsen & Kaszniak, 2006). It would be interesting to investigate whether the mechanisms that allow an enhanced attentional control and reduction of attentional lapses through the use of such techniques also provide a buffer against anxiety's disruptive effects on WM, minimizing the impact of internally generated distracters (worries). There is one study that actually shows that mindfulness training applied to military cohorts prepared for deployment to Iraq protected against the degradation of their WM capacity over the predeployment interval and reduced the negative affect they experienced (Jha, Stanley, Kiyonaga, Wong, & Gelfand, 2010).

To summarize, to our knowledge, there are virtually no interventions directly targeting WM processes for neutral or threat-related information in high-anxious or clinically anxious participants. However, considering that WM processes play an essential role in self-regulation and cognitive control over affect (Hofman, Schmeichel, Friese, & Baddeley, 2011), it is to be expected that such programs will arise in the near future.

CONCLUSION

The main research question investigated throughout the chapter focused on the cognitive outcomes of the interaction between individual differences in trait anxiety and WM functioning. Most of the reviewed literature focused on one direction of this interaction, analyzing whether there is a disruptive effect of trait anxiety (further amplified by anxious state) on cognitive performance, in general, and on WM, in particular. As emphasized throughout the chapter, this rather straight-forward prediction should be nuanced in several directions. First, one major distinction relates to the contents of the memory task. Would anxiety interfere with WM processes even when the to-be-remembered contents do not involve an explicit threat? Apparently, the answer is yes, but not without reserve. When the executive demands of the task are low, and there is ample time to process and to invest additional resources, the performance (accuracy) of high-anxious individuals cannot be reliably distinguished from that of their low-anxious counterparts. However, if additional measures of invested resources are collected (reaction time, mental effort, sensitivity to reward), the effects of anxiety become visible, high-anxious individuals presenting reduced processing efficiency. However, further investigations are required to reveal the dynamics of this (allegedly) diminished efficiency and its neural correlates (see Ansari & Derakshan, 2011; Bishop, 2009; Fales et al., 2008 for preliminary evidence). Rather than reflecting a true reduction in cognitive efficiency, the pattern of activation (and de-activation) of brain areas specific to high-anxious individuals could offer an alternative pathway to optimize behavioral performance (Fales et al., 2008) in the presence of internally generated distracters such as worrying thoughts. However, when the executive demands of the tasks overload a person's WM system, reductions in both effectiveness and efficiency are more visible considering that anxiety is associated with depletion of central executive (and phonological loop) resources.

But what happens when information with emotional valence is introduced? The answer needs to be calibrated according to the relevance of this information for the task at hand, and to the level of threat being experienced, both influencing how motivation and emotion interact to enhance or impair executive control (Pessoa, 2009). When (negative) emotional information is relevant for the goals of the individual, anxiety can enhance cognitive performance by favoring a more rapid detection and encoding of threat-related information. When emotional valence is task-irrelevant, anxiety acts as a distracter and impairs performance by allocating resources in a stimulus-driven mode toward (task-irrelevant) threatening information. However, evidence for the translation of this well-documented attentional bias into a memory bias for threat-related information is still inconclusive. When positive information is provided, there is some preliminary evidence that high-anxious individuals (especially socially anxious) fail to show an attentional bias toward positive (social) stimuli (e.g., Moser et al., 2008). Again, how this lack of an attentional positive bias affects memory processes remains unknown (but see Visu-Petra et al., 2010, for developmental evidence). As for the second factor (i.e., level of threat), further empirical support from studies in which this variable is explicitly manipulated is required to support the existing theoretical proposals. Most of them (see Pessoa, 2009, for a discussion) converge on proposing that stimuli with a low level of threat benefit from sensory enhancement, leading to an "emotional capture" of attention, and to further preferential information processing. However, high threat value, despite benefiting from the same enhanced sensory processing, actually diverts resources away from the central executive; this is visible to a greater degree in high-anxious individuals than in their low-anxious counterparts (Bishop, 2007).

Two important areas of investigation warrant further attention: the developmental trajectory of the anxiety–memory interaction, and the importance of individual differences in WM capacity and processing. Along these lines, further (preferably longitudinal) individual differences research can be advocated for understanding the neural and behavioral mechanisms of executive control and the underlying sources of individual variation (Braver, Cole, & Yarkoni, 2010).

The practical implications of an individual difference approach to emotion–cognition interactions during development are extremely relevant. Most of the literature reviewed above found relevant proofs for anxiety–memory interactions; however, we were unable to identify research documenting how interventions targeting one of the two variables also influence and shape the other. Interventions targeting attention and interpretation biases have been linked to overall reductions in state and trait anxiety (Brosan, Hoppitt, Shelfer, Sillence, & Mackintosh, 2011). Memory outcomes for negative versus positive information could be monitored and actively targeted as part of these intervention protocols (Amir & Bomyea, 2011). However, training WM per se could be beneficial for the reduction of anxiety. Hofman et al. (2011) convincingly demonstrate the centrality of WM processes for everyday attempts at cognitive control and self-regulation of thought and action. Recent WM training programs claim that benefits extend over other aspects of human cognition and affect, leading to documented amelioration in disorders of self-regulation, such as hyperactivity or addictions (Houben, Wiers, & Jansen, 2011; Mezzacappa & Buckner, 2010). Although it is not a self-regulatory disorder per se, anxiety has been associated with attentional control failures, so the introduction of WM training programs could be beneficial in reducing anxiety symptoms by promoting enhancements in cognitive control.

However, Hofman et al. (2011) also stress the importance of establishing self-regulatory goals and being motivated to follow them in order to benefit from the existing WM resources. Any attempts to reduce anxiety in order to optimize educational and professional performance or for therapeutic purposes should take into account this *motivational function* of anxiety, since "the study of neural mechanisms suggests that anxiety is not simply a distraction to the cognitive apparatus; it may be fundamental to motivating cognition adaptively" (Luu, Tucker, & Derryberry, 1998, p. 577). Cognitive researchers and cognitive-behavioral therapists have acknowledged the adaptive function of anxiety, suggesting that mild to moderate anticipatory anxiety about realistic threats is necessary for the development of adaptive coping responses with stressors (Borkovec, 1994; Mathews, 1990), especially in environments in which threats are subtle or disguised, requiring a degree of "hypervigilance" to be identified (Matthews & Dorn, 1995). However, when this response is exacerbated, or is present in the absence of realistic threats, anxiety becomes a burden on the cognitive system. Efforts directed toward reducing or altering these maladaptive responses, supported by individual strengths in WM resources required to actively implement plans of change (Matthews & Wells, 1999), are most likely to recalibrate emotion–cognition interactions and to promote an optimal executive control.

ACKNOWLEDGMENTS

This work was partially supported by the National University Research Council of Romania (grants PD427/2010 awarded to L. Visu-Petra, and PD411/2010 awarded to A. C. Miu), and by an "Invest in people" POSDRU/6/1.5/S/4 grant from the Sectorial Operational Programme for Human Resources Development awarded to L. Cheie.

REFERENCES

Alloway, T. P. (2007). *Automated working memory assessment*. London: Harcourt.

Alloway, T. P. (in press). Can interactive working memory training improving learning? *Journal of Interactive Learning Research*.

Alloway, T. P., Banner, G., & Smith, P. (2010). Working memory and cognitive styles in adolescents' attainment. *British Journal of Educational Psychology*, 80, 567–581.

Alloway, T. P., & Gathercole, S. E. (2005). The role of sentence recall in reading and language skills of children with learning difficulties. *Learning and Individual Differences, 15*, 271–282.

Alloway, T. P., Gathercole, S. E., Adams, A. M., Willis, C. S., Eaglen, R., & Lamont, E. (2005). Working memory and phonological awareness as predictors of progress towards early learning goals at school entry. *British Journal of Developmental Psychology, 23,* 417–426.

Amir, N., & Bomyea, J. (2011). Working memory capacity in generalized social phobia. *Journal of Abnormal Psychology, 120*(2), 504–509.

Ansari, T. L., & Derakshan, N. (2011). The neural correlates of impaired inhibitory control in anxiety. *Neuropsychologia, 49*(5), 1146–1153.

Aronen, E. T., Vuontela, V., Steenari, M.-R., Salmi, J., & Carlson, S. (2005). Working memory, psychiatric symptoms, and academic performance at school. *Neurobiology of Learning and Memory, 83*(1), 33–42.

Ashcraft, M. H. (2002). Math anxiety: Personal, educational and cognitive consequences. *Current Directions in Psychological Science, 11,* 181–185.

Ashcraft, M. H., & Kirk, E. P. (2001). The relationships among working memory, math anxiety and performance. *Journal of Experimental Psychology: General, 2,* 224–237.

Baddeley, A. D., & Hitch, G. J. (1974). Working memory. In G. A. Bower (Ed.), *The psychology of learning and motivation: Advances in research and theory* (Vol. 8, pp. 47–89). New York: Academic Press.

Banich, M. T., Mackiewicz, K. L., Depue, B. E., Whitmer, A. J., Miller, G. A., & Heller, W. (2009). Cognitive control mechanisms, emotion and memory: A neural perspective with implications for psychopathology. *Neuroscience and Biobehavioral Reviews, 33*(5), 613–630.

Bar-Haim, Y. (2010). Research review: Attention bias modification (ABM): A novel treatment for anxiety disorders. *Journal of Child Psychology and Psychiatry 51*(8), 859–870.

Bar-Haim, Y., Lamy, D., Pergamin, L., Bakermans-Kranenburg, M. J., & van Ijzendoorn, M. H. (2007). Threat-related attentional bias in anxious and nonanxious individuals: A meta-analytic study. *Psychological Bulletin, 133,* 1–24.

Basten, U., Stelzel, C., & Fiebach, C. J. (2011). Trait anxiety modulates the efficiency of inhibitory control. *Journal of Cognitive Neuroscience, 23*(10), 3132–3145. epub.

Beck, A. T., & Clark, D. H. (1997). An information processing model of anxiety: Automatic and strategic processes. *Behaviour Research and Therapy, 35,* 49–58.

Beck, A. T., & Emery, G. (1985). *Anxiety disorders and phobias: A cognitive perspective.* New York: Basic Books.

Beilock, S. L. (2008). Math performance in stressful situations. *Current Directions in Psychological Science, 17,* 339–343.

Beilock, S. L., & Carr, T. H. (2005). When high-powered people fail: Working memory and "choking under pressure" in math. *Psychological Science, 16,* 101–105.

Beilock, S. L., & DeCaro, M. S. (2007). From poor performance to success under stress: Working memory, strategy selection, and mathematical problem solving under pressure. *Journal of Experimental Psychology: Learning, Memory, and Cognition, 33,* 983–998.

Beilock, S. L., Kulp, C. A., Holt, L. E., & Carr, T. H. (2004). More on the fragility of performance: Choking under pressure in mathematical problem solving. *Journal of Experimental Psychology: General, 133,* 584–600.

Bishop, S. J. (2007). Neurocognitive mechanisms of anxiety: An integrative account. *Trends in Cognitive Science, 11*(7), 307–316.

Bishop, S. J. (2009). Trait anxiety and impoverished prefrontal control of attention. *Nature Neuroscience, 12,* 92–98.

Bomyea, J., & Amir, N. (2011). The effect of an executive functioning training program on working memory capacity and intrusive thoughts. *Cognitive Therapy and Research, 5,* 1–7

Borkovec, T. D. (1994). The nature, functions and origins of worry. In G. Davey & F. Tallis (Eds.), *Worrying: Perspectives on theory, assessment and treatment* (pp. 5–33). Chichester, UK: Wiley.

Bower, G. H. (1981). Mood and memory. *American Psychologist, 36*, 129–148.

Braver, T. S., Cole, M. W., & Yarkoni, T. (2010). Vive les differences! Individual variation in neural mechanisms of executive control. *Current Opinion in Neurobiology, 20*(2), 242–250.

Braver, T. S., Gray, J. R., & Burgess, G. C. (2007). Explaining the many varieties of working memory variation: Dual mechanisms of cognitive control. In A. R. A. Conway, C. Jarrold, M. J. Kane, A. Miyake, & J. N. Towse (Eds.), *Variation in working memory* (pp. 76–106). Oxford: Oxford University Press.

Brosan, L., Hoppitt, L., Sillence, A., Shelfer, L., & Mackintosh, B. (2011). Cognitive Bias Modification for attention and interpretation reduces trait and state anxiety study in a clinically anxious population. *Journal of Behavior Therapy and Experimental Psychiatry, 42*(3), 258–264.

Burke, E. (1756). *A philosophical inquiry into the origin of our ideas of the sublime and beautiful.* London.

Calvin, A. D., Koons, P. B., Bingham, J. L., & Fink, H. H. (1955). A further investigation of the relationship between manifest anxiety and intelligence. *Journal of Consulting Psychology, 19*, 280–282.

Calvo, M. G., & Ramos, P. M. (1989). Effects of test anxiety on motor learning: The processing efficiency hypothesis. *Anxiety Research, 2*, 45–55.

Calvo, M. G., Avero, P., Castillo, M. D., & Miguel Tobal, J. J. (2003). Multidimensional anxiety and content-specificity effects in preferential processing of threat. *European Psychologist, 8*, 252–265.

Cartwright-Hatton, S., McNicol, K., & Doubleday, E. (2006). Anxiety in a neglected population: Prevalence of anxiety disorders in pre-adolescent children. *Clinical Psychology Review, 26*, 817–833.

Cheie, L., & Visu-Petra, L. (2012). Relating individual differences in anxiety to memory for emotional information in young children. *Journal of Individual Differences, 33*(2), 109–118.

Clark, D. A., & Beck, A. T. (2009). *Cognitive therapy of anxiety disorders: Science and practice.* New York: Guilford Press.

Cloitre, M., & Leibowitz, M. R. (1991). Memory bias in panic disorder: An investigation of the cognitive avoidance hypothesis. *Cognitive Therapy and Research, 15*, 371–386.

Coles, M. E., & Heimberg, R. G. (2002). Memory biases in the anxiety disorders: Current status. *Clinical Psychology Review, 22*, 587–627.

Colflesh, G. J. H., & Conway, A. R. A. (2007). Individual differences in working memory capacity and divided attention in dichotic listening. *Psychonomic Bulletin and Review, 14*, 699–703.

Conway, A. R. A., Cowan, N., & Bunting, M. F. (2001). The cocktail party phenomenon revisited: The importance of working memory capacity. *Psychonomic Bulletin and Review, 8*, 331–335.

Corbetta, M., & Shulman, G. L. (2002). Control of goal-directed and stimulus-driven attention in the brain. *Nature Review Neuroscience, 3*, 201–215.

Cowan, N. (1988). Evolving concepts for memory storage, selective attention, and their mutual constraints within the human information processing system. *Psychological Bulletin, 104*, 163–191.

Cowan, N. (2008). What are the differences between long-term, short-term, and working memory? *Progress in Brain Research, 169*, 323–338.

Crowe, S. F., Matthews, C., & Walkenhorst, E. (2007). The relationship between worry, anxiety and thought suppression and the components of working memory in a non-clinical sample. *Australian Psychologist, 42*(3), 170–177.

Crozier, W. R., & Hostettler, K. (2003). The influence of shyness on children's test performance. *British Journal of Educational Psychology, 73*, 317–328.

Curtis, C. A. (2009). The relationship between anxiety, working memory and academic performance among secondary school pupils with social, emotional and behavioural difficulties: A test of Processing Efficiency Theory. Doctoral Thesis, University of Southampton, UK.

Daleiden, E. L. (1998). Childhood anxiety and memory functioning: A comparison of systemic and processing accounts. *Journal of Experimental Child Psychology, 68*(3), 216–235.

Daleiden, E. L., & Vasey, M. W. (1997). An information-processing perspective on childhood anxiety. *Clinical Psychology Review, 17,* 407–429.

Dalgleish, T., Taghavi, R., Neshat-Doost, H., Moradi, A., Canterbury, R., & Yule., W. (2003). Differences in patterns of processing bias for emotional information across disorders: An investigation of attention, memory and prospective cognition in children and adolescents with depression, generalized anxiety and Posttraumatic Stress Disorder (PTSD). *Journal of Clinical Child and Adolescent Psychology, 32,* 10–21.

Darke, S. (1988). Anxiety and working memory capacity. *Cognition and Emotion, 2,* 145–154.

Deffenbacher, J. L. (1978). Worry, emotionality and task generated interference: An empirical test of attentional theory. *Journal of Educational Psychology, 70,* 248–254.

Denkova, E., Wong, G., Dolcos, S., Sung, K., Wang, L., Coupland, N., et al. (2010). The impact of anxiety-inducing distraction on cognitive performance: A combined brain imaging and personality investigation. *PLoS One, 5*(11), e14150.

Derakshan, N., & Eysenck, M. W. (1998). Working memory capacity in high trait-anxious and repressor groups. *Cognition and Emotion, 12,* 697–713.

Derakshan, N., & Eysenck, M. W. (2009). Anxiety, processing efficiency and cognitive performance: New developments from attentional control theory. *European Psychologist, 14*(2), 168–176.

Derryberry, D., & Reed, M. A. (2002). Anxiety-related attentional biases and their regulation by attentional control. *Journal of Abnormal Psychology, 111,* 225–236.

Ecker, U. K. H., Lewandowsky, S., Oberauer, K., & Chee, A. E. H. (2010). The components of working memory updating: An experimental decomposition and individual differences. *Journal of Experimental Psychology: Learning, Memory, and Cognition, 36,* 170–189.

Egger, H. L., & Angold, A. (2006). Anxiety disorders. In J. Luby (Ed.), *Handbook of preschool mental health: Development, disorders, and treatment* (pp. 137–164). New York: Guilford Press.

Elliman, N. A., Green, M. W., Rogers, P. J., & Finch, G. M. (1997). Processing efficiency theory and the working memory system; Impairments associated with sub-clinical anxiety. *Personality and Individual Differences, 23,* 31–35.

Endler, N. S., & Kocovski, N. L. (2001). State and trait anxiety revisited. *Journal of Anxiety Disorders, 15*(3), 231–245.

Eysenck, M. W. (1977). Arousal, learning, and memory. *Psychological Bulletin, 83,* 389–404.

Eysenck, M. W. (1979). Anxiety, learning, and memory: A reconceptualization. *Journal of Research in Personality, 13,* 363–385.

Eysenck, M. W. (1985). Anxiety and cognitive-task performance. *Personality and Individual Differences, 6,* 574–586.

Eysenck, M. W. (1989) Anxiety and cognition: Theory and research. In T. Archer and L.-G Nilsson (Eds.), *Aversion, avoidance and anxiety: Perceptives on aversively motivated behaviour.* London: Erlbaum.

Eysenck, M. W. (1992) The nature of anxiety. In A. Gale and M. W. Eysenck (Eds.), *Handbook of individual differences: Biological perspectives.* Chichester: Wiley.

Eysenck, M. W., & Calvo, M. G. (1992). Anxiety and performance: The Processing Efficiency Theory. *Cognition and Emotion, 6,* 409–434.

Eysenck, M. W., & Derakshan, N. (2011). New perspectives in attentional control theory. *Personality and Individual Differences, 50,* 955–960.

Eysenck, M. W., Derakshan, N., Santos, R., & Calvo, M. G. (2007). Anxiety and cognitive performance: Attentional control theory. *Emotion, 7*(2), 336–353.

Eysenck, M. W., Payne, S., & Derakshan, N. (2005). Trait anxiety, visuospatial processing, and working memory. *Cognition and Emotion, 19*(8), 1214–1228.

Eysenck, M. W., Payne, S., & Santos, R. (2006). Anxiety and depression: Past, present, and future events. *Cognition and Emotion, 20*(2), 274– 294.

Fales, C. L., Barch, D. M., Burgess, G. C., Schaefer, A., Mennin, D. S., Gray, J. R., et al. (2008). Anxiety and cognitive efficiency: Differential modulation of transient and sustained neural activity during a working memory task. *Cognitive, Affective, and Behavioral Neuroscience, 8*(3), 239–253.

Fales, C. L., Becerril, K. E., Luking, K. R., & Barch, D. M. (2010). Emotional-stimulus processing in trait anxiety is modulated by stimulus valence during neuroimaging of a working-memory task. *Cognition and Emotion, 24*(2), 200–222.

Field, A. P., & Lester, K. J. (2010a). Learning of information processing biases in anxious children and adolescents. In J. Hadwin and A. P. Field (Eds.), *Information processing biases and anxiety: a developmental perspective* (pp. 253–278). Chichester: Wiley.

Field, A. P., & Lester, K. J. (2010b). Is there room for "development" in models of information processing biases to threat in children and adolescents? *Clinical Child and Family Psychology Review, 13*, 315–332.

Fox, E., Russo, R., Bowles, R. J., & Dutton, K. (2001). Do threatening stimuli draw or hold visual attention in sub-clinical anxiety? *Journal of Experimental Psychology: General, 130* (4), 681–700.

Gathercole, S. E., & Baddeley, A. (1990). Phonological memory deficits in language disordered children: Is there a causal connection? *Journal of Memory and Language, 29*, 336–360.

Gathercole, S. E., & Pickering, S. J. (2000). Working memory deficits in children with low achievements in the national curriculum at seven years of age. *British Journal of Educational Psychology, 70*, 177–194.

Gathercole, S. E., Pickering, S. J., Knight, C., & Stegmann, Z. (2004). Working memory skills and educational attainment: Evidence from National Curriculum assessments at 7 and 14 years of age. *Applied Cognitive Psychology, 40*, 1–16.

Gray, J. R. (2004). Integration of emotion and cognitive control. *Current Directions in Psychological Science, 13*(2), 46–48.

Günther, T., Holtkamp, K., Jolles, J., Herpertz-Dahlmann, B., & Konrad, K. (2004). The influence of sertraline on attention and verbal memory in children and adolescents with anxiety disorders. *Journal of Child and Adolescent Psychopharmacology, 15*(4), 608–618.

Hadwin, J. A., & Field, A. P. (Eds.) (2010a). *Information processing biases and anxiety: A developmental perspective.* Chichester: Wiley.

Hadwin, J. A., & Field, A. P. (2010b). An introduction to the study of information processing biases in childhood anxiety: Theoretical and methodological issues. In J. A. Hadwin & A. P. Field (Eds.), *Information processing biases and anxiety: A developmental perspective* (pp. 1–18). Chichester: Wiley.

Hadwin, J. A., Brogan, J., & Stevenson, J. (2005). State anxiety and working memory in children: A test of processing efficiency theory. *Educational Psychology, 25*(4), 379–393.

Hadwin, J. A., Garner, M., & Perez-Olivas, G. (2006). The development of information processing biases in childhood anxiety: A review and exploration of its origins in parenting. *Clinical Psychology Review, 26*, 876–894.

Hayes, S., Hirsch, C., & Mathews, A. (2008). Restriction of working memory capacity during worry. *Journal of Abnormal Psychology, 117*, 712–717.

Henry, L. A. (2001). How does the severity of a learning disability affect working memory performance? *Memory, 9*, 233–247.

Hofmann, W., Friese, M., Schmeichel, B. J., & Baddeley, A. D. (2011). Working memory and self-regulation. In K. D. Vohs & R. F. Baumeister (Eds.), *Handbook of self-regulation: Research, theory, and applications* (2nd ed.), vol. 2, pp. 204–225. New York: Guilford Press.

Holmes, J., Gathercole, S. E., & Dunning, D. (2009). Adaptive training leads to sustained enhancement of poor working memory in children. *Developmental Science, 12,* 9–15.

Houben, K., Wiers, R. W., & Jansen, A. (2011). Getting a grip on drinking behavior: Training working memory to reduce alcohol abuse. *Psychological Science, 22*(7), 968–975.

Huang, L., & Pashler, H. (2007). Working memory and the guidance of visual attention: Consonance-driven orienting. *Psychonomic Bulletin and Review, 14,* 148–153.

Ikeda, M., Iwanaga, M., & Seiwa, H. (1996). Test anxiety and working memory system. *Perceptual and Motor Skills, 82,* 1223–1231.

Ilkowska, M., & Engle, R. W. (2010). Trait and state differences in working memory capacity. In A. Gruszka, G. Matthews, & B. Szymura (Eds.), *Handbook of individual differences in cognition: Attention, memory, and executive control.* New York: Springer.

Ingram, R. E., & Price, J. M. (2010). *Vulnerability to psychopathology: Risk across the lifespan* (2nd ed.). New York: Guilford Press.

Jarrold, C., Baddeley, A. D., & Hewes, A. K. (1999). Genetically dissociated components of working memory: Evidence from Down's and Williams syndrome. *Neuropsychologia, 37*(6), 637–651.

Jha, A. P., Stanley, E. A., Kiyonaga, A., Wong, L., & Gelfand, L. (2010). Examining the protective effects of mindfulness training on working memory capacity and affective experience in a military cohort. *Emotion, 10,* 54–64.

Johnson, D. R., & Gronlund, S. D. (2009). Individuals lower in working memory capacity are particularly vulnerable to anxiety's disruptive effect on performance. *Anxiety, Stress, and Coping, 22,* 201–213.

Kane, M. J., & Engle, R. W. (2003). Working memory capacity and the control of attention: The contributions of goal neglect, response competition, and task set to Stroop interference. *Journal of Experimental Psychology: General, 132,* 47–70.

Kane, M. J., Bleckley, M. K., Conway, A. R. A., & Engle, R. W. (2001). A controlled-attention view of working-memory capacity. *Journal of Experimental Psychology: General, 130*(2), 169–183.

Kanekar, S., Neelakantan, P., & D'Souza, M. (1976). Anxiety, intelligence and academic performance. *Psychological Records, 38,* 938.

Kendall, P. C. & Ingram, R. E. (1987). Anxiety: Cognitive factors and the anxiety disorders. *Cognitive Therapy and Research, 11,* 521–523.

Kessler, R. C., Foster, C. L., Saunders, W. B., & Stang, P. E. (1995). Social consequences of psychiatric disorders: Educational attainment. *American Journal of Psychiatry, 152,* 1026–1032.

Kindt, M., & van den Hout, M. (2001). Selective attention and anxiety: A perspective on developmental issues and the causal status. *Journal of Psychopathology and Behavioral Assessment, 23,* 193–202.

Kleinsmith, L. J., & Kaplan, S. (1964). The interaction of arousal and recall interval in nonsense syllable paired associate learning. *Journal of Experimental Psychology, 67,* 124–126.

Klingberg, T., Fernell, E., Olesen, P., Johnson, M., Gustafsson, P., Dahlstrom, K., et al. (2005). Computerized training of working memory in children with ADHD: a randomized, controlled trial. *Journal of the American Academy of Child and Adolescent Psychiatry, 44,* 177–186.

Korkman, M., Kirk, U., & Kemp, S. (1998). *NEPSY: A developmental neuropsychological assessment.* New York: The Psychological Corporation.

Koster, E. H. W., Crombez, G., Verschuere, B., & De Houwer, J. (2004). Selective attention to threat in the dot probe paradigm: Differentiating vigilance and difficulty to disengage. *Behaviour Research and Therapy, 42,* 1183–1192.

Kraus, J. (1965). Cattell anxiety scale scores and WAIS attainment in three groups of psychiatric patients. *Australian Journal of Psychology, 17*, 229–232.

Ladouceur, C. D., Dahl, R. E., Williamson, D. E., Birmaher, B., Ryan, N. D., & Casey, B. J. (2005). Altered emotional processing in pediatric anxiety, depression, and comorbid anxiety-depression. *Journal of Abnormal Child Psychology, 33*(2), 165–177.

Leigh, E., & Hirsch, C. (2011). Worrying in imagery and verbal-linguistic form: Impact on residual working memory capacity. *Behaviour Research and Therapy, 49*, 99–105.

Lewis, R. L., Vasishth, S., & Van Dyke, J. A. (2006). Computational principles of working memory in sentence comprehension. *Trends in Cognitive Science, 10*(10), 447–454.

Loosli, S. V., Buschkuehl, M., Perrig, W. J., & Jaeggi, S. M. (2011). Working memory training improves reading processes in typically developing children. *Child Neuropsychology*, May 27, 1–17. [Epub ahead of print.]

Luu, P., Tucker, D. M., & Derryberry, D. (1998). Anxiety and the motivational basis of working memory. *Cognitive Therapy and Research Special Issue: Cognition and Anxiety, 22*(6), 577–594.

MacLeod, C., & Donnellan, A. M. (1993). Individual differences in anxiety and the restriction of working memory capacity. *Personality and Individual Differences, 15*, 163–173.

MacLeod, C., & Mathews, A. (2004). *Selective memory effects in anxiety disorders: An overview of research findings and their implications in memory and emotion.* Oxford: Oxford University Press.

Malcarne, V. L., Hansdottir, I., & Merz, E. L. (2010). Vulnerability to anxiety disorders in childhood and adolescence. In R. E. Ingram & J. M. Price (Eds.), *Vulnerability to psychopathology: Risk across the lifespan.* New York: Guilford Publications.

Markham, R., & Darke, S. (1991). The effects of anxiety on verbal and spatial task performance. *Australian Journal of Psychology, 43*, 107–111.

Mathews, A. (1990). Why worry? The cognitive function of anxiety. *Behaviour Research and Therapy, 28*, 455–468.

Mathews, A., & MacLeod, C. (2002). Induced emotional biases have causal effects on anxiety. *Cognition and Emotion, 16*, 310–315.

Mathews, A., Mackintosh, B., & Fulcher, E. P. (1997). Cognitive biases in anxiety and attention to threat. *Trends in Cognitive Sciences, 1*, 340–345.

Matthews, G., & Dorn, L. (1995). Personality and intelligence: Cognitive and attentional processes. In D. Saklofske & M. Zeidner (Eds.), *International handbook of personality and intelligence* (pp. 367–396). New York: Plenum.

Matthews, G., & Wells, A. (1999). The cognitive science of emotion and attention. In M. Power & T. Dalgleish (Eds.), *Handbook of cognition and emotion.* Hove, UK: Erlbaum.

McLean, J. F., & Hitch, G. J. (1999). Working memory impairments in children with specific arithmetic learning difficulties. *Journal of Experimental Child Psychology, 74*, 240–260.

Mezzacappa, E., & Buckner, J. (2010). Working memory training for children with attention problems or hyperactivity: A school-based pilot study. *School Mental Health, 2*(4), 202–208.

Mitte, K. (2008). Memory bias for threatening information in anxiety and anxiety disorders. *Psychological Bulletin, 134*, 886–911.

Miu, A. C., Heilman, R. M., Opre, A., & Miclea, M. (2005). Emotion-induced retrograde amnesia and trait anxiety. *Journal of Experimental Psychology: Learning, Memory and Cognition, 31*, 1250–1257.

Miu, A. C., & Visu-Petra, L. (2010). Anxiety disorders in children and adults: A cognitive, neurophysiological and genetic characterization. In R. Carlstedt (Ed.), *Handbook of integrative clinical psychology, psychiatry, and behavioral medicine: Perspectives, practices, and research* (pp. 309–351). New York: Springer.

Miyake, A., Friedman, N. P., Emerson, M. J., Witzki, A. H., Howerter, A., & Wager, T. D.

(2000). The unity and diversity of executive functions and their contributions to complex "frontal lobe" tasks: A latent variable analysis. *Cognitive Psychology, 41*, 49–100.

Moradi, A., Taghavi, R., Neshat-Doost, H., Yule, W., & Dalgleish, T. (2000). Memory bias for emotional information in children and adolescents with Posttraumatic Stress Disorder: A preliminary study. *Journal of Anxiety Disorder, 14*(5), 521–534.

Moser, J. S., Huppert, J. D., Duval, E., & Simons, R. F. (2008). Face processing biases in social anxiety: An electrophysiological study. *Biological Psychology, 78*, 93–103.

Muris, P. (2006). The pathogenesis of childhood anxiety disorders: Considerations from a developmental psychopathology perspective. *International Journal of Behavioral Development, 30*, 5–11.

Murray, N. P., & Janelle, C. M. (2003). Anxiety and performance: A visual search examination of the Processing Efficiency Theory. *Journal of Sport and Exercise Psychology, 25*, 171–187.

Nairne, J. S., Thompson, S. R., & Pandeirada, J. N. S. (2007). Adaptive memory: Survival processing enhances retention. *Journal of Experimental Psychology: Learning, Memory, and Cognition, 33*, 263–273.

Ng, E. L., & Lee, K. (2010). Children's task performance under stress and non-stress conditions. *Cognition and Emotion, 24*(7), 1229–1238.

Nielsen, L., & Kaszniak, A. W. (2006). Awareness of subtle emotional feelings: A comparison of long-term meditators and non-meditators. *Emotion, 6*, 392–405.

Nyklicek, I., & Kuijpers, K. F. (2008). Effects of mindfulness-based stress reduction intervention on psychological well-being and quality of life: Is increased mindfulness indeed the mechanism? *Annals of Behavioral Medicine, 35*(3), 331–340.

Owens, M., Stevenson, J., Norgate, R., & Hadwin, J. A. (2008). Working memory partially mediates the relationship between trait anxiety and academic performance. *Anxiety, Stress, and Coping, 21*, 417–430.

Owens, M., Stevenson, J., Norgate, R., & Hadwin, J. A. (submitted). Emotion, working memory and stress reactivity in academic performance.

Pérez-Edgar, K., Bar-Haim, Y., McDermott, J. M., Chronis-Tuscano, A., Pine, D. S., & Fox, N. A. (2010). Attention biases to threat and behavioral inhibition in early childhood shape adolescent social withdrawal. *Emotion, 10*, 349–357.

Pessoa, L. (2009). How do emotion and motivation direct executive function? *Trends in Cognitive Science, 13*, 160–166.

Pine, D. S. (2007). Research review: A neuroscience framework for pediatric anxiety disorders. *Journal of Child Psychology and Psychiatry, 48*, 631–648.

Pine, D. S., Wasserman, G. A., & Workman, S. B. (1999). Memory and anxiety in prepubertal boys at risk for delinquency. *Journal of the American Academy of Child and Adolescent Psychiatry, 38*, 1024–1031.

Power, M. J., & Dalgleish, T. (1997). *Cognition and emotion: From order to disorder*. Hove: Erlbaum.

Ranganath, C., Cohen, M. X., & Brozinsky, C. J. (2005). Working memory maintenance contributes to long-term memory formation: Neural and behavioral evidence. *Journal of Cognitive Neuroscience, 17*, 994–1010.

Rapee, R. M. (1993). The utilization of working memory by worry. *Behavior Research and Therapy, 31*, 617–620.

Reed, M. A., & Derryberry, D. (1995). Temperament and attention to positive and negative trait information. *Personality and Individual Differences, 18*, 135–147.

Reid, S-C., Salmon, K., & Lovibond, P. (2006). Cognitive biases in childhood anxiety, depression, and aggression: Are they pervasive or specific? *Cognitive Therapy and Research, 30*, 531–549.

Reidy, J. (2004). Trait anxiety, trait depression, worry and memory. *Behaviour Research and Therapy, 42*, 937–948.

Richards, A., French, C. C., Keogh, E., & Carter, C. (2000). Test anxiety, inferential reasoning and working memory load. *Anxiety, Stress and Coping, 13*, 87–109.

Riskind, J. H., & Williams, N. L. (2005). The looming cognitive style and generalized anxiety disorder: Distinctive danger schemas and cognitive phenomenology. *Cognitive Therapy and Research, 29*, 7–27.

Sarason, I. G. (1984). Stress, anxiety and cognitive interference: Reactions to tests. *Journal of Personality and Social Psychology, 46*(4), 929–938.

Schmeichel, B. J. (2007). Attention control, memory updating, and emotion regulation temporarily reduce the capacity for executive control. *Journal of Experimental Psychology: General, 136*, 241–255.

Schmeichel, B. J., Volokhov, R., & Demaree, H. A. (2008). Working memory capacity and the self-regulation of emotional expression and experience. *Journal of Personality and Social Psychology, 95*, 1526–1540.

Shackman, A. J., Sarinopoulos, I., Maxwell, J. S., Pizzagalli, D. A., Lavric, A., & Davidson, R. J. (2006). Anxiety selectively disrupts visuospatial working memory. *Emotion, 6*, 40–61.

Silvia, P. J., Allan, W. D., Beauchamp, D. L., Maschauer, E. L., & Workman, J. O. (2006). Biased recognition of happy facial expressions in social anxiety. *Journal of Social and Clinical Psychology, 25*(6), 585–602.

Simpson, J. R., Jr., Drevets, W. C., Snyder, A. Z., Gusnard, D. A., & Raichle, M. E. (2001). Emotion-induced changes in human medial prefrontal cortex: II. During anticipatory anxiety. *Proceedings of National Academy of Sciences USA, 98*(2), 688–693.

Sinclair, K. E. (1974). Anxiety and cognitive processes in problem solving. *Australian Journal of Education, 18*(3), 239–254.

Smith, E. E., & Jonides, J. (1999). Storage and executive processes in the frontal lobes. *Science, 283*, 1657–1661.

Sorg, B. A., & Whitney, P. (1992). The effect of trait anxiety and situational stress on working memory capacity. *Journal of Research in Personality, 26*, 235–241.

Spence, J. T., & Spence, K. W. (1966). The motivational components of manifest anxiety: Drive and drive stimuli. In C. Spielberger (Ed.), *Anxiety and behavior* (pp. 291–326). New York: Academic Press.

Strange, B. A., Hurlemann, R., & Dolan, R. J. (2003). An emotion-induced retrograde amnesia in humans is amygdala- and beta-adrenergic-dependent. *Proceedings of the National Academy of Sciences of the United States of America, 100*, 13626–13631.

Swanson, H. L., & Sachse-Lee, C. (2001). Mathematical problem solving and working memory in children with learning disabilities: Both executive and phonological processes are important. *Journal of Experimental Child Psychology, 79*, 294–321.

Tobon, J. I., Ouimet, A. J., & Dozois, D. J. A. (2011). Attentional bias in anxiety disorders following cognitive behavioral treatment. *Journal of Cognitive Psychotherapy: An International Quarterly, 25*, 114–131.

Tohill, J. M., & Holyoak, K. J. (2000). The impact of anxiety on analogical reasoning. *Thinking and Reasoning, 6*, 27–40.

Toren, P., Sadeh, M., Wolmer, L., Eldar, S., Koren, S., Weizman, R., & Laor, N. (2000). Neurocognitive correlates of anxiety disorders in children: A preliminary report. *Journal of Anxiety Disorders, 14*(3), 239–247.

Tryon, W. W., & McKay, D. (2009). Memory modification as an outcome variable in anxiety disorder treatment. *Journal of Anxiety Disorders, 23*, 546–556.

Vasa, R. A., Roberson-Nay, R., Klein, R. G., Mannuzza, S., Moulton, J. L., Guardino, M., et al. (2007). Memory deficits in children with and at risk for anxiety disorders. *Depression and Anxiety, 24*, 85–94.

Visu-Petra, L., Cheie, L., Benga, O., & Alloway, T. P. (2011). Effects of trait anxiety on memory storage and updating in young children. *International Journal of Behavioral Development, 35*(1), 38–47.

Visu-Petra, L., Miclea, M., Cheie, L., & Benga, O. (2009). Processing efficiency in preschoolers' memory span: Individual differences related to age and anxiety. *Journal of Experimental Child Psychology, 103*(1), 30–48.

Visu-Petra, L., Țincaș, I., Cheie, L., & Benga, O. (2010). Anxiety and visual-spatial memory updating in young children: An investigation using emotional facial expressions. *Cognition and Emotion, 24*(2), 223–240.

Weems, C. F. (2008). Developmental trajectories of childhood anxiety: Identifying continuity and change in anxious emotion. *Developmental Review, 28,* 488–502.

Weems, C. F., & Watts, S. E. (2005). Cognitive models of childhood anxiety. In F. Columbus (Ed.), *Progress in anxiety disorder research*. Hauppauge, NY: Nova Science Publishers, Inc.

Weinstein, C. E., Cubberly, W. E., & Richardson, F. C. (1982). The effects of test anxiety on learning at superficial and deep levels of processing. *Contemporary Educational Psychology, 7*(2), 107–112.

Weissman, D. H., Roberts, K. C., Visscher, K. M., & Woldorff, M. G. (2006). The neural bases of momentary lapses in attention. *Nature Neuroscience, 9*(7), 971–978.

Williams, J. M. G. (1996). Memory processes in psychotherapy. In P. M. Salkovskis (Ed.), *Frontiers of cognitive therapy* (pp. 97–113). New York: Guilford Press.

Williams, J. M., Watts, F. N., MacLeod, C., & Mathews, A. (1988). *Cognitive psychology and emotional disorders*. Chichester, UK: John Wiley & Sons.

Williams, J. M., Watts, F. N., MacLeod, C., & Mathews, A. (1997). *Cognitive psychology and emotional disorders* (2nd ed.) Chichester, UK: John Wiley & Sons.

Woodward, L. J., & Fergusson, D. M. (2001). Life course outcomes of young people with anxiety disorders in adolescence. *Journal of the American Academy of Child and Adolescent Psychiatry, 40,* 1086–1093.

Yiend, J., & Mathews, A. (2001). Anxiety and attention to threatening pictures. *Quarterly Journal of Experimental Psychology: Human Experimental Psychology, 54*(3), 665–681.

Yousefi, F., Mansor, M. B., Juhari, R. B., Redzuan, F., Talib, M. A., Kumar, V., & Naderi, H. (2009). Memory as a mediator between test-anxiety and academic achievement in high school students. *European Journal of Scientific Research, 35*(2), 274–280.

Zeidan, F., Johnson, S. K., Diamond, B. J., David, Z., & Goolkasian, P. (2010). Mindfulness meditation improves cognition: Evidence of brief mental training. *Consciousness and Cognition, 19*(2), 597–605.

12

The Integration of Emotion and Cognitive Control

ANDREW MATTARELLA-MICKE

Department of Psychology, University of Chicago, Chicago, IL, USA

SIAN L. BEILOCK

Department of Psychology, University of Chicago, Chicago, IL, USA

Working memory is studied not simply because it relates to elementary cognitive tasks measured in the lab (Engle, 2002), but because it is extremely good at predicting how people will perform on a wide range of real-world tasks such as reasoning (Kyllonen & Christal, 1990), problem solving (Carpenter, Just, & Shell, 1990), and language comprehension (MacDonald, Just, & Carpenter, 1992). Despite working memory's predictive power in the laboratory, the real world itself is not composed of subjects toiling away dispassionately at abstract cognitive puzzles. Rather, it contains real challenges, stacked with significant material and affective consequences for the people that engage them.

As anyone who has ever fumbled for words during a public speech or stared anxiously at a blank test knows, the emotional response evoked by a stressful situation carries profound implications for cognitive performance. In these situations, it is not only one's cognitive capacity that dictates success, but his or her ability to perform at a high level when it is most important. In the current chapter, we argue that whether an individual will succeed in an emotion-inducing situation depends more on the intensity and nature of their emotional response than on how many words they normally recall on the reading span.

We review evidence that intense emotional reactions impair cognitive performance by disrupting working memory—thereby making individual differences in working memory a less-than-perfect predictor of performance in high-stakes situations. But, while the predictive power of working memory might wane at these emotional boundary conditions, its explanatory power becomes highly apparent.

Across the domains of math anxiety, stereotype threat, and high-stakes choking, we show how the basic science of working memory has been applied to characterize the relationship between emotion and cold cognition and—ultimately—to predict how individuals will perform. We consider mechanisms at both the cognitive and neuroscientific level that might help to explain performance and unite these disparate research programs. Finally, we conclude by highlighting important issues in the field, and considering potential future directions.

BACKGROUND INFORMATION

Math Anxiety

For math anxious individuals, mathematical materials and contexts elicit an adverse emotional reaction. This reaction can be intense, leading to shaky hands, a pounding heart, even breathlessness. Because this emotional reaction is both potent and selective, and because mathematical cognition is such a well studied intellectual domain (Ashcraft, 1992; Campbell, 2005), math anxiety provides an ideal test bed to study the effects of emotion on cognitive performance.

This relationship is complicated, however, by potential differences in math skill across different math anxiety groups. Individuals high in math anxiety avoid math classes and have lower grades in those classes they do attend (Ashcraft & Kirk, 2001). Still, interventions that treat the emotional component associated with math anxiety (rather than training math skills) have been shown to improve the math performance of highly math anxious individuals (Hembree, 1990). This supports an alternative explanation for how math anxiety compromises performance, namely, that the anxiety itself causes an online deficit in math problem solving (Ashcraft, Kirk, & Hopko, 1998).

The claim that the performance deficits characteristic of math anxiety are caused by anxiety and not based in skill or ability alone developed from the work of Ashcraft and colleagues (Ashcraft & Faust, 1994; Faust, 1996). Ashcraft and Faust (1994) observed that although math anxious individuals exhibit poor performance on standardized tests, they do not show consistent deficits in the fundamental operations of mental arithmetic. For example, when participants completed simple single-digit addition and multiplication problems, high math-anxious individuals differed only marginally from their low math-anxious counterparts. However, when high math-anxious individuals completed complicated two-digit problems they showed substantial deficits. Problems with a carry were particularly impaired. While the fundamental operations underlying these two classes of arithmetic are identical, they differ on one dimension: reliance on working memory. This led Ashcraft and colleagues to hypothesize that the effects of math anxiety on performance had their basis in the operation of working memory.

To investigate this hypothesis further, Ashcraft and Kirk (2001) designed an experimental paradigm to explicitly manipulate working memory demands during math problem solving. They asked low and high math-anxious individuals to perform a mental arithmetic task while simultaneously maintaining random letter strings in working memory. Within subjects, they manipulated the demands of both the primary math task (by including a carry or not) and the secondary memory task (by varying the number of letters to maintain).

Relative to low math-anxious individuals, participants high in math anxiety showed an exaggerated increase in performance errors when both the math and memory tasks placed high demands on working memory. The authors concluded that performance deficits under demanding dual-task conditions were most pronounced in high math-anxious individuals because their emotional reaction diverted attention away from the content of the task. Similar to a demanding secondary task, the emotional processes co-opted the working memory capacity that might have otherwise been available for math performance.

In the decade following this research, the online disruption of working memory by anxiety has become a central thesis in math anxiety research (Ashcraft & Krause, 2007). Nevertheless, whether poor performance in math anxious individuals can be solely attributed to this online deficit is still a matter of debate. For example, in a longitudinal study of adolescent math anxiety, Ma and Xu (2004) found that poor mathematics performance preceded math anxiety over time. However, Beilock and colleagues (2010) have shown that the math anxiety of female elementary school teachers is communicated to their female students, which in turn affects math test performance. Thus, although the findings of Ma and Xu are consistent with the claim that struggling in math can lead to math anxiety, there is an element to math anxiety that is separable from math ability, can be communicated socially, and impacts math performance. The tension between these studies typifies the confusion between math anxiety and math aptitude that is an inescapable part of math anxiety research. This tension also underscores the gains that can be made from a comprehensive view of the effects of emotion on cognition.

Stereotype Threat

High math-anxious students are not the only group that shows a characteristic deficit in performance for a particular domain. Achievement gaps are not just common, they are common knowledge. Because members of a disadvantaged group are aware of their achievement gap, and fear confirming it, they often suffer the same kind of crippling anxiety that disrupts the performance of math anxious individuals. "Stereotype threat" refers to this claim, that knowledge of an achievement gap can actually perpetuate it. Similar to the claim that deficits from math anxiety are caused by differences in affect rather than skill or ability, instances of an achievement gap may be attributable to stereotype threat.

The stereotype threat phenomenon was first established in a pioneering study by Steele and Aronson (1995), which showed that the poor performance of African American participants on standardized tests could in part be accounted for by whether or not a negative stereotype about their performance was made salient. In this study, participants were administered a series of SAT problems, described as either "a genuine test of verbal abilities" or merely as "research to better understand psychological factors in solving verbal problems." When the SAT problems were described as indicative of verbal ability, African American participants performed worse than European American participants that were tested concurrently.

This performance difference was reduced when problems were framed as a non-diagnostic research challenge. The study established that at least part of the achievement gap in African American SAT performance is derived from an online effect of the situation on performance.

The basic stereotype threat effect has been replicated with a number of populations and stereotypes. When a task is characterized as a test of intelligence, children with low socioeconomic (SES) status underperform relative to high SES children (Croizet & Claire, 1998) and Latinos perform more poorly than Whites (Gonzales, Blanton, & Williams, 2002). When stereotypes about mathematical ability are emphasized, women underperform relative to men (Spencer, Steele, & Quinn, 1999), and Whites underperform relative to Asians (Aronson, Lustina, Good, Keough, & Steele, 1999). The effects of stereotype threat on performance extend even to undergraduate majors with different reputations for intelligence (Croizet et al., 2004). This effect is not only general, it is substantial. In one study, marking one's gender after an advanced placement calculus test led to a 33 percent reduction in the gender gap in performance compared to the standard practice of marking it prior to testing (Danaer & Crandall, 2008).

Despite the pervasiveness and social significance of stereotype threat, the cognitive mechanism through which these achievement gaps are perpetuated reduces to the same disruption underlying mathematics anxiety: a disruption of working memory. Schmader and Johns (2003) provide compelling evidence for this mechanism. In a series of three experiments, they asked women (Experiment 1) and Latinos (Experiment 2) to complete a math-based working memory span task under either a stereotype threat or a control condition. In the control condition, neither group differed in performance from their respective Caucasian male control groups. In the stereotype threat condition, both groups exhibited a marked drop in their estimated span, suggesting that stereotype threat might have a particular effect on working memory.

Though these first studies are consistent with a working memory mechanism, the final experiment (Experiment 3) provides a particularly strong causal argument. In this experiment, a verbal working memory task was selected in order to dissociate the stereotype threat task (a math task) from the span measure. The authors conjectured that a working memory task immediately following the stereotype threat manipulation might suffer the same anxiety that normally interferes with the threatened task. This unrelated span task could therefore act as a measure of working memory disruption, while remaining uncontaminated by performance expectations or aptitude differences related to the negative math stereotype.

As expected, in the stereotype threat condition, participants exhibited a significant drop in performance on both the threatened task and on the unrelated working memory task. Critically, the drop in span performance statistically mediated (or accounted for) the relationship between stereotype threat and performance on the primary task. Individuals that suffered most from stereotype threat on the math task showed an equivalent deficit in working memory. This mediation substantiates the causal links between stereotype threat, working memory, and performance.

Since Schmader and Johns (2003), the claim that stereotype threat disrupts working memory has been reinforced in a number of studies. Stereotype threat has induced performance deficits in the antisaccade task (Jamieson & Harkins, 2007), the Stroop task (Inzlicht, McKay, & Aronson, 2006), and on the n-back (Beilock, Rydell, & McConnell, 2007). Each of these tasks exhibits a positive relationship between individual differences in working memory and performance (Kane, Bleckley, Conway, & Engle, 2001; Kane & Engle, 2003; Schmiedek, Hildebrandt, Lövdén, Wilhelm, & Lindenberger, 2009), and is closely tied to the operation of executive attention.

High-Pressure Situations

A significant challenge to studying the relationship between emotion and cognition is that the emotional component of performance is often confounded with the population under study. One cannot completely rule out the alternative explanation that differences in performance are not about emotion, but instead are the result of intrinsic differences (in ability or otherwise) across the observed groups. This challenge is particularly salient in math anxiety research, but is also a factor in stereotype threat research where comparisons are often made indirectly, only after differences across the stereotype and control groups have been statistically equated (e.g., by controlling for prior SAT scores of participants).

One way to tackle this fundamental impasse is to experimentally manipulate the affective conditions under investigation. By randomly assigning participants to either an emotional or control situation, this alternative approach ensures that any difference measured across the groups is a function of the experimental inter-vention rather than intrinsic to a particular group. In one such experiment, Beilock and colleagues (2004) placed participants into either a high-pressure or control group while they completed math problems that placed either high or low demands on working memory. Participants in the control condition completed two blocks of problems under standard performance instructions. These participants were simply told to complete the problems as quickly and accurately as possible. Unremarkably, performance in the control condition remained the same across the two math problem blocks.

Participants in the high-pressure condition completed the first block of problems under identical instructions. However, for the second block of problems, high-pressure participants received a set of significant social and monetary incentives. High-pressure participants were instructed that if they met a difficult performance criterion (improving by 20 percent in accuracy and reaction time from the first block) they could double their compensation. High-pressure participants were also instructed that their reward was tied to another participant (a "partner"). In order for either partner to receive the added compensation, both had to meet the performance criterion. Finally, each participant was told that their partner had already completed the experiment and met the performance criterion. Thus, in the high-pressure scenario, participants were entirely responsible for winning (or losing) the added compensation for themselves and their partner.

As a result of these overwhelming performance incentives, participants in the high-pressure condition significantly dropped in accuracy across the two blocks. Critically, this reduction in the high-pressure group's performance was restricted to problems that placed high demands on working memory. Because participants were randomly assigned to a condition and because both conditions performed equally well on the first problem block, this high-pressure experiment ruled out the possibility that population-related differences in aptitude could account for the effect of anxiety on performance. Instead, an online disruption of working memory remains the only plausible account. Further, by dissociating performance of high and low demanding problems, the Beilock et al. (2004) experiment contains an important, often overlooked control. In order to demonstrate that working memory is the mechanism of choking under pressure, investigators must show not only that working memory reliant processes suffer as a function of anxiety, but also that *non-*working memory reliant processes do not.

The dissociation between tasks that place significant demand on working memory and those that do not is central to the thesis that anxiety disrupts working memory. Unfortunately, one cannot rule out the possibility that changes to a task designed to recruit different levels of working memory might also change a second unknown psychological dimension. To exclude this alternative explanation, Beilock and colleagues (2004) exposed a second group of participants to the same high-pressure situation. However, instead of varying problem type, they relied on degree of practice to modulate working memory demand. Through massive repetition (50 trials), a selection of problems was practiced until performance became automatized. When a cognitive task is automatized, the working memory demanding operations of the task become circumvented by retrieval from memory (Logan, 1988). In the case of mathematics, instead of performing the cognitively demanding process of computing and maintaining intermediate calculations, the answer to the entire problem is recalled directly from long-term memory.

Instead of exhibiting differences in choking as a function of problem type, performance depended on the degree of practice that a particular problem had received. Highly practiced problems were reduced in their engagement of working memory and therefore did not suffer the effects of pressure. Participants did show the prior pattern of choking on unpracticed problems. This experiment provides explicit evidence that it is not the choice of problem per se (particular problems selected for training were counterbalanced across participants), but the demands that these problems place on working memory that makes them sensitive to choking under pressure.

High-pressure situations also provide an ideal test bed for one counterintuitive prediction of the working memory mechanism. Specifically, while the effect of intense emotion typically impairs performance, this need not be the case. If a cognitive task could be identified that actually *improves* when working memory is taxed, this improvement should generalize to high-pressure performance. Markman, Maddox, and Worthy (2006) provided just such a demonstration. Similar to previous research, they found that pressure significantly disrupted performance when participants were asked to complete a working memory-demanding categorization task. Surprisingly, however, participants improved under pressure when asked to complete a categorization task based on proceduralized learning. This type of category learning, referred to as "information integration," is most effectively acquired by implicit processing, which places little demand on working memory. Explicit processing, a working memory-dependent process, can actually impede information integration category learning (DeCaro, Thomas, & Beilock, 2008). Thus, when Markman et al. (2006) placed participants in a high-stakes situation their reduced working memory paradoxically improved proceduralized category learning.

Individual differences in working memory and choking   At the outset of this chapter, we proposed that individual differences in working memory can fail to predict performance in a highly emotional situation. Indeed, one's affective reaction to the situation will play a large role in determining the extent to which working memory will be impaired. On the other hand, while span tasks may fail to predict anxious *performance*, basic research in working memory capacity suggests that individual differences in working memory should predict *choking*.

This inference is drawn from previous working memory studies that have shown that although high-span individuals excel on such tasks as category recall (Rosen & Engle, 1997), visual attention (Bleckley, 2001), and the inhibition of proactive interference (Kane & Engle, 2000), a secondary task selectively impairs performance for these very same high-span individuals. This is because low-spans either lack the excess working memory resources to expend on performing these tasks, or rely on heuristics that minimize this expenditure. Thus, while a secondary task consumes the working memory capacity that high-spans use to improve their performance, it has little effect on low spans. This same pattern of results holds for high pressure situations. When anxiety consumes working memory, individual differences in this capacity predict which individuals will suffer the most (Beilock & Carr, 2005).

In sum, studies of high-pressure performance support and extend the evidence from math anxiety and stereotype threat that anxiety disrupts working memory performance. By dissociating emotional reactions from a particular task or group, high-pressure scenarios have been used to test novel and counterintuitive predictions of the mechanism. This research program is also closely tied to basic research in working memory. As we discuss later, we anticipate that new and exciting directions in the area of emotion research will come from a close dialogue with contemporary working memory research.

Other Sources of Anxiety

Both common and scientific definitions of anxiety are highly broad in nature. Thus, it is important to note that our review necessarily neglects phenomena that are often characterized as anxiety, but which deviate from the acute, aversive reactions to performance situations that we focus on. Still, research on these related anxieties yields results that are surprisingly consistent with our approach. One method that has been applied to induce anticipatory anxiety is to repeatedly perturb participants with a mild shock. In one such study (Shackman et al., 2006), participants exhibited significant impairments on a 3-back working memory task as a consequence of shock anticipation, even in trials when the actual shock was withheld. A similar disruption of 2-back performance has been elicited through the presentation of a video designed to induce a negative withdrawal state (Gray, 2001). These results suggest that even loosely related forms of anxiety provide evidence in line with a disruption of performance related to working memory.

There is also a significant program of research, based in the Attentional Control Theory (ACT), devoted to the chronic effects of anxiety exhibited by individuals that score highly on trait anxiety inventories (Eysenck & Calvo, 1992; Eysenck, Derakshan, Santos, & Calvo, 2007). Despite the potential differences between a brief and intense affective response and a chronic predisposition toward anxiety, the theoretical and empirical bases of these approaches share substantial similarities with our own. Both frameworks propose that working memory is disrupted due to anxiety, though ACT makes specific claims about the subcomponents of working memory that are affected.

These claims rely on a framework of working memory provided by Miyake and colleagues (2000). This framework divides the central executive of working memory into three subcomponents: Inhibition ("One's ability to deliberately inhibit dominant, automatic, or prepotent responses when necessary"), Shifting ("Shifting back and forth between multiple tasks, operations, or mental sets") and Updating ("Updating and monitoring of working memory representations"). According to ACT, anxiety selectively affects the inhibition and shifting components of the central executive.

Evidence that the inhibition component of the central executive is selectively impaired as a function of anxiety comes from poor performance of high trait-anxious individuals on incongruent (Pallak, Pittman, Heller, & Munson, 1975) and anxiety (Mogg, Mathews, Bird, & Macgregor-Morris, 1990) related words in the Stroop task. High anxiety individuals also show difficulty inhibiting semantically related lures when determining whether a probe word is related to the meaning of a preceding sentence (e.g., Ace following "He dug with a spade"; Wood, Mathews, & Dalgleish, 2001). Shifting impairment in high-anxious individuals is evidenced by poor task-switching performance (Derakshan, Smyth, & Eysenck, 2009), and prospective memory failure (a putative shifting process; Cockburn & Smith, 1994).

While the above approaches are highly consistent with a dysfunction in working memory capacity, there are important empirical departures across these instances of anxiety. In particular, the anticipation of shock (Shackman et al., 2006) disrupts spatial working memory selectively over verbal working memory. This result diverges from recent findings in high stakes pressure (DeCaro, Rotar, Kendra, & Beilock, 2010) and stereotype threat (Beilock et al., 2007; Schmader & Johns, 2003) of a selective disruption of verbal working memory described in detail below. Additionally, ACT proposes the updating function of working memory is relatively spared in high trait anxious individuals. This approach therefore makes the specific prediction that working memory span tasks (which recruit primarily updating) should not be affected by anxiety. While this prediction differs from evidence reviewed above (Schmader & Johns, 2003) and in acute test anxiety (Calvo, Ramos, & Estevez, 1992), it is a common finding in the trait anxiety research (Calvo & Eysenck, 1996; Eysenck et al., 2007).

The strong commonalities across these types of anxiety suggest that there may be a common framework that can accommodate each aspect of anxiety. In almost all cases, executive function is impacted by anxiety. Nevertheless, current empirical disparities suggest that, while it is useful to consider evidence from all sources, no current framework is sufficiently elaborated to incorporate each perspective into a single approach.

CURRENT EVIDENCE

Cognitive Mechanisms

The previously reviewed evidence supports the claim that emotionally charged situations hamper complex thinking through their impact on working memory. However, this explanation lacks a causal link—it's not clear *why* emotion impacts working memory. In the current section, we will discuss potential explanations for the link between emotion and working memory. In general, these accounts fall into two classes of explanation: verbal rumination theories and emotion regulation theories.

Verbal Rumination Theories According to verbal rumination theories, the online worries elicited by an emotional situation are the principal source of decrements to working memory. Indeed, individuals that suffer from high pressure (DeCaro et al., 2010), stereotype threat (Beilock et al., 2007), or math-anxiety (Dew, Galassi, & Galassi, 1984) report more worry-related thoughts than their respective controls. The question remains, however, whether these verbal ruminations cause decrements in working memory, or if they are merely a byproduct of emotional situations.

Indirect evidence for the competitive relationship between working memory resources and verbal rumination comes from studies that measure the effect of a dual task on reports of worry. In one such study by Rapee (1993), participants were asked to complete a demanding secondary task immediately prior to reporting their thoughts. While a visuospatial task had no effect, when the secondary task recruited resources of both the phonological loop and central executive, participants reported significantly fewer worry-related thoughts. This finding was replicated and extended to include overall mood by Van Dillen and Koole (2007). Thus, behavioral evidence is consistent with the claim that negative ruminations and working memory share a common resource.

Evidence for a direct causal link between verbal ruminations and performance loss is, however, sparse. In one study, Osborne (2001) used an archival dataset consisting of achievement test scores and anxiety self-reports measured immediately afterward. Osborne found that reported anxiety levels partially mediated the gender and racial gap in test score performance. Still, the effect size reported in this study was small and causal claims are weak due to its observational nature.

In a more systematic laboratory study, Cadinu and colleagues (2005) experimentally manipulated stereotype threat and recorded negative thoughts prior to performance. They found that increases in negative thoughts associated with the stereotype threat condition mediated the decrement to performance on a math test. As would be expected, this relationship did not hold for participants in the control (no-threat) condition. Thus, previous work in the stereotype threat literature is consistent with the role of negative thoughts in disrupting task performance.

Verbal rumination theories predict not only that working memory will be taxed in a highly emotional situation, but also make a specific claim about the nature of this cognitive load: that it will be selectively verbal in nature. Math anxiety research is broadly consistent with this claim, as most arithmetic tasks have a verbal component to their working memory demands (DeStefano & LeFevre, 2004). Reading span, a verbal working memory task, is also a commonly impaired task (Schmader & Johns, 2003) in stereotype threat.

More selective experiments, however, have explicitly manipulated the modality of working memory demands. For example, Beilock and colleagues (2007) show that emotion-related decrements to performance are selective for math tasks that rely heavily on verbal working memory resources. This research relies on the finding that arithmetic problems presented horizontally place more demands on verbal working memory than problems presented vertically, which rely on spatial capacity (Trbovich & LeFevre, 2003). Applying this knowledge to both high-stakes (DeCaro et al., 2010) and stereotype threat situations (Beilock et al., 2007), Beilock and colleagues show that emotion-related performance loss is selective for horizontally oriented (verbally demanding) as opposed to vertically oriented (more spatially demanding) arithmetic problems.

In the high-pressure experiment, Beilock and colleagues (DeCaro et al., 2010) also asked participants to engage in a talk-aloud condition where they reported their internal mental state. The frequency of negative thoughts and worries predicted performance on the horizontal problems (the more worries, the worse the problem performance), but not on the vertical problems. Moreover, being asked to talk aloud about steps of the math problems shifted the negative thoughts to on-task thoughts, and eliminated the effects of the high-pressure scenario on performance.

Emotion Regulation Theories   Although self-report measures of verbal rumination correlate with emotion-related performance, it is difficult to demonstrate that this relationship is causal. Simply because higher anxiety (and worse performance) is evidenced by greater frequency of reported negative thoughts, this does not mean that negative thoughts are the true *cause* of performance deficits. An alternative explanation for this coincidence has been proposed, that the active suppression of emotion and verbal rumination is the true source of working memory disruption in this equation (Schmader, Johns, & Forbes, 2008). Under this account, the report of negative ruminations does not carry direct implications for performance, but indirectly indicates a performance scenario likely to engage resource consuming emotion regulation.

Indeed, emotion regulation is engaged spontaneously during emotional situations such as the ones described above (Volokhov & Demaree, 2010). While this process is not always effective in reducing the perceived degree of negative affect (Wegner, Erber, & Zanakos, 1993), it does place significant demands on working memory (Schmeichel, 2007). Consistent with the demanding role of emotion regulation, the efficacy of negative emotion suppression depends on individual differences in working memory. Individuals higher in working memory capacity suppress both emotional experiences and facial expressions to evocative stimuli more effectively (Schmeichel, Volokhov, & Demaree, 2008). Thus, emotion regulation is spontaneously initiated during emotional contexts and is cognitively draining when in operation, making it a plausible mechanism for anxiety-related decrements. Further evidence is required, however, to cement the causal argument that emotion regulation underlies performance decrements seen in emotional situations. A study by Johns, Inzlicht and Schmader (2008) provides a significant step in this direction.

Johns and colleagues placed women in either a control or stereotype threat situation related to the gender gap in math performance. In between blocks of the math task, these women engaged in two tasks: a working memory span task and a dot probe task. As in previous studies (Schmader & Johns, 2003), the span task acted as an online measure of the disruption of working memory caused by stereotype threat, using content unrelated to the stereotype threat manipulation to avoid contamination by stereotype-related performance expectations.

The dot probe task is a reaction time task designed to measure the allocation of spatial attention. In the dot probe task, participants are instructed to indicate whether a dot is located above or below fixation as rapidly as possible. Prior to the onset of the dot, orienting stimuli are presented in positions corresponding to the two possible locations of the dot. These orienting stimuli are designed to attract attention to their location. In the Johns et al. (2008) adaptation of this task, the orienting stimuli consisted of a word placed in each of the two potential dot locations. On filler trials, both words were affectively neutral and unrelated to task; however, on critical trials, one of the two words was related to anxiety. A comparison of reaction times when the dot is preceded by an anxiety-related word relative to when it is preceded by neutral words provides an index of attentional allocation to anxiety-related content.

As one might expect, participants in the stereotype threat condition exhibited significant attentional biases towards the anxiety-related content, as indicated by a facilitated response to anxiety-related words relative to neutral words. This facilitation was not exhibited in the non-threat control condition. This supports the assertion that stereotype threat participants are in an anxiety-inducing situation. As expected, participants in the stereotype threat condition showed performance decrements on the working memory task. Individual differences in working memory performance predicted degree of facilitation on the dot probe task. That is, the more participants showed an anxiety-related orienting of visual attention, the lower a participant's recorded working memory.

A critical second manipulation provides evidence that emotional regulation may be at work in stereotype threat situations. In the previously described conditions, the dot probe task was described as a measure of perceptual focus. As a part of a second manipulation, another set of participants was explicitly informed that the dot probe task measured anxiety. This manipulation was designed to investigate whether stereotype threat individuals would spontaneously engage in defensive suppression of this display of anxiety (i.e., by trying to manage their orienting to the anxiety-related content) and whether this regulation would be tied to working memory performance.

Participants in the non-threat condition of this second, "anxiety measurement" version of the experiment showed a pattern of results similar to the original "neutral description" version described before. However, results for the new stereotype threat condition differed from the initial stereotype threat results in two ways. First, the facilitation for anxiety-related words disappeared. According to Johns et al. (2008), when participants were made aware that the dot probe task was sensitive to their anxiety they engaged in emotion regulation to conceal their anxiety, thus eliminating their anxiety-biases. As a result, in the "anxiety measurement" condition, a reduced dot probe bias was indicative of active attempts to regulate the anxious reaction to the stereotype situation.

Assuming that emotion regulation is indeed the cause of working memory disruption, a reduced dot probe bias should not only indicate anxiety suppression, it should also relate to lower working memory capacity, caused by the impact of emotion regulation. This leads us to the second difference in the "anxiety measurement" stereotype-condition results: The original negative relationship between anxiety-related orienting on the dot probe task and working memory reversed. Now, the degree of anxiety-bias was positively related to performance on the working memory task, with more bias (*less suppression*) relating to greater working memory performance. In other words, to hide their emotional reaction to the stereotype threat condition, anxious participants were motivated to suppress their dot probe bias. The index of emotion suppression (dot probe *un*bias) thus became the key predictor of working memory performance: The more emotion suppression, the more depleted their working memory and the lower their working memory performance.

While individuals in an anxiety-inducing situation (particularly one with an evaluative component) may be predisposed to directly suppress their anxious reaction, this is not the only means of emotion regulation available. Reappraisal is another mechanism of emotion regulation discussed in the literature (Gross, 2002). Instead of inhibiting an emotion, reappraisal consists of changing the way a situation is construed in order to decrease its emotional impact. Unlike emotion suppression, reappraisal is thought not to draw heavily on working memory resources.

The positive effects of reappraisal on working memory-related performance are evident in several studies that have intervened to affect participant construal of the situation. For example, in a study by Ben-Zeev, Fein, and Inzlicht (2005), women encouraged to misattribute their anxiety to a "subliminal noise generator" were insulated in part from the negative effects of stereotype threat. Similarly, merely telling participants that anxiety does not harm test performance has been found to eliminate stereotype threat deficits (Johns et al., 2008).

While these predictions follow most directly from an emotion regulation mechanism, the reduction in negative emotion caused by these interventions is also consistent with a verbal rumination mechanism. Perhaps the most persuasive evidence that emotion regulation is a key cognitive mechanism underlying the effects of anxiety on performance is manifest in interventions that uncouple the relationship between indices of anxiety and performance. In one such study, Ramirez and Beilock (2011) asked participants to either expressively (Klein & Boals, 2001) write down their worries about a high-pressure performance scenario, to write about an unrelated emotional event, or to sit for a time-matched control.

Although both the unrelated writing and control groups substantially dropped in performance due to the high pressure situation, the expressive writing group actually improved in performance in the high-pressure situation. This result is consistent with the claim that participants engaged in some type of reappraisal process that improved performance through either reduced worry, or reduced suppression of worry. Critically, participants recorded their state anxiety after the performance situation. While reported anxiety increased as a function of pressure, it did not differ depending on the writing condition. Emotional regulation processes and not anxiety itself seem to be tied to performance in this study. These results are therefore most consistent with a cognitive reappraisal mechanism.

Yet, though experiments may dissociate self-reports of anxiety from performance, this does not rule out verbal rumination as a potential mechanism for working memory impairment. This dissociation may simply be an artifact of a poor measure of verbal rumination. Moreover, emotion regulation theories fail to account for modality-specific results predicted by verbal rumination theories. Thus, both theories seem to explain their specialized phenomena particularly well, while stretching somewhat to account for all the data. As long as both mechanisms yield unique, testable hypotheses, they will both remain viable characterizations of the interaction between emotion and working memory.

Neural Mechanisms

Another means of tackling the relationship between emotion and working memory is to approach the issue at the implementational level, asking whether measures of neural function can contribute an understanding of how working memory is compromised in stereotype threat, math anxiety, and high-pressure situations. Studies of human performance using neuroimaging methods are surprisingly sparse in this regard. Our own work (Mattarella-Micke & Beilock, 2012), however, provides preliminary neural support for the claim that working memory systems are disrupted as a function of pressure.

In this study we investigated whether the blood oxygenation level-dependent (BOLD) signal could predict performance outcomes in a high-stakes situation. Relying on the logic that the underlying mechanism of choking is a disruption of working memory, we proposed that fMRI could measure the online operation of working memory and therefore the online process of choking. Participants in the scanner were asked to complete math problems prior to and following a high-stakes scenario containing the same strong financial and social incentives described in previous studies conducted in our lab (Beilock & Carr, 2005; Beilock et al., 2004).

As in previous studies, participants choked as a result of the high stakes, becoming less accurate after the introduction of pressure, but only on WM demanding math problems. Critically, neural activity in two working memory regions, the intraparietal sulcus (IPS) and the inferior frontal junction (IFJ) also predicted performance outcomes. Participants who choked under pressure exhibited less activation in these regions, suggesting that the high pressure situation disrupted the normal operation of working memory.

We also investigated changes in connectivity as a function of pressure to see whether choking under pressure might be related to shifts in communication across the working memory network. For those who performed the best under pressure (i.e., "choked" the least), the ventromedial prefrontal cortex (vmPFC), a region that has been implicated in the processing of anxiety (Wager et al., 2009) and emotional processing (Hornak et al., 2003) was more likely to uncouple (decrease in connectivity) from the IPS and IFJ after the addition of pressure. When the vmPFC uncouples from the IFJ and IPS, the ability of affective reactions to interfere with the normal operation of working memory is limited and choking under pressure is reduced.

This work provides the first functional neuroimaging evidence that choking under pressure is mediated by an online disruption of working memory. But, while fMRI is well suited to a broad characterization of the functional networks underlying human performance, it cannot provide the spatial and temporal resolution needed to propose a detailed neuronal model of working memory's role in anxiety-induced performance failure. On the other hand, there is a robust animal literature that attempts just this.

One research program has tackled the issue of anxiety in animal performance by characterizing the effects of the hormone cortisol on the prefrontal cortex. In a series of experiments using rats, Roozendaal, McReynolds, and McGaugh (2004) have shown that the stress hormone corticosterone interferes with performance on a working memory task. During acute anxiety, corticosterone is released as a result of increasing sympathetic activation. Roozendaal and colleagues show that corticosterone causes the rats to fail on a delayed alternation T-maze, a task that measures the rat equivalent of working memory. Eliciting corticosterone-induced failure depends on the normal operation of the amygdala, a key region in emotion processing. When the basolateral complex of the amygdala is ablated or its receptors blocked, performance of the rats becomes unaffected by increasing cortisol. Taken together, these findings suggest a potential mechanism for the physiological effects of anxiety: working memory is disturbed by the effects of both corticosteroids and emotional input from the amygdala on the prefrontal cortex.

Of course, a delayed alternation T-maze in rats is a poor substitute for complex human cognition. On the other hand, this basic science has motivated tests of a similar neural mechanism in humans. For example, Elzinga and Roelofs (2005) found that salivary cortisol reactivity correlated with digit span when participants performed the span task in front of a live, high-pressure audience. Participants were divided into groups based on whether they exhibited a robust cortisol reaction. Individuals that exhibited a robust cortisol response due to the high-stakes scenario showed substantially lower digit spans relative to individuals that did not show a similar response.

Importantly, the observed decrement to digit span was not due to cortisol alone. Although high responders exhibited a reduction in digit span, this reduction occurred only during the live audience performance. These same high responders did not exhibit a deficit when they completed the same digit span after leaving the performance situation, even though their salivary cortisol levels were the same. The authors proposed that, similar to the mechanism of Roozendaal et al., deficits to working memory operation required not only cortisol, but also a negative emotional reaction and interpretation of the situation at hand.

Work in our lab has also been motivated by the animal research of Roozendaal and colleagues. In one study we tested the hypothesis that a similar interaction between cortisol response and emotional interpretation might provide an explanation for the effects of math anxiety on performance. We expected the effects of cortisol on math performance would depend on each participant's math anxiety, which acted as a proxy for their emotional reaction. Further, we expected this effect of cortisol and math anxiety on performance would be due to a disruption of working memory. Thus, based on research in our lab showing that individual differences in working memory can capture the effect of anxiety on performance (Beilock & Carr, 2005), we also administered the reading span.

We predicted that, while low working memory individuals would be less affected by an online decrement to working memory, high working memory individuals would be especially sensitive to the effects of cortisol and math anxiety on performance. This is precisely what we found. Performance on the math problems was predicted by a three-way interaction between working memory span, math anxiety, and cortisol concentration. While low working memory individuals did not vary in performance as a function of cortisol, high working memory individuals did differ. For high working memory individuals, when cortisol was low, differences in math anxiety had little effect on performance. However, when cortisol was high, high math-anxious individuals higher in working memory performed substantially worse than their low math-anxious counterparts.

Thus, the claim that cortisol disrupts working memory only when paired with an adverse emotional reaction was supported by our data. The work of Roozendaal et al. (2004) provides a useful framework for characterizing the effects of emotion on performance. By drawing on an understanding of the factors that contribute to cortisol release, one can predict situations that might also affect the interaction of emotion and working memory. However, while this work informs our understanding of anxious performance, its application is limited by the slow time frame of cortisol release (it peaks around 20 minutes; Dickerson & Kemeny, 2004), which may not match the timeline of many behavioral phenomena. The use of rats in this animal model also begs the question of whether this cortisol mechanism will fully generalize to primate neurobiology.

A second biological account of choking under pressure comes from the work of Arnsten and colleagues (Arnsten 2009). This work proposes that the interruption of working memory in a high-anxiety environment is caused by excessive release of the catecholamines dopamine and norepinephrine into the prefrontal cortex. According to this account, dopamine and norepinephrine each independently maintain a delicate balance in the prefrontal cortex. This balance, best characterized by an "inverted U"-shaped function for each neurotransmitter, has been studied most explicitly in the dorsolateral prefrontal cortex (DLPFC).

The DLPFC is thought to be a key component of the working memory network (Wager & Smith, 2003). Primate research has shown that neurons in the DLPFC maintain active firing during the period between the encoding of an item and its subsequent retrieval from working memory (Goldman-Rakic, 1995). Importantly, each neuron is tuned for a particular item or class of items during the maintenance phase. That is, the neuron fires for certain types of content, but not others. Neurons differ in their degree of selective tuning—highly tuned neurons fire only when maintaining a specific class of content, whereas less tuned neurons exhibit tonic activity for a wide range of content.

The DLPFC maintains working memory content in a distributed code that is represented by net activity of the selectively tuned neurons in its neural population. Dopamine and norepinephrine play an important role in this process. Dopamine appears to "reduce noise" in this neural population (Vijayraghavan, Wang, Birnbaum, Williams, & Arnsten, 2007). When administered in low doses, dopamine sharpens the tuning of neurons by suppressing non-selective spontaneous activity. However, when dopamine concentration reaches levels that are too high in the synapse, it can suppress even stimulus-selective activity. Thus, the level of dopamine in the DLPFC maintains a delicate balance between too little suppression (increasing noise) and too much suppression (reducing signal in addition to noise).

Norepinephrine acts in a reciprocal manner to dopamine. Instead of reducing noise as dopamine does, norepinephrine acts to "amplify signal" by increasing tuned neural activity during delay (Arnsten, 2000). Too little norepinephrine, and neurons in the DLPFC respond only weakly during maintenance of their selective content (reduced signal). Too much norepinephrine increases activity in a non-selective manner (increasing not only signal, but also noise).

The delicate balance in the DLPFC is disrupted by a highly stressful situation. Both dopamine and norepinephrine release is increased in the PFC during exposure to stress (Finlay, Zigmond, & Abercrombie, 1995; Roth, Tam, Ida, Yang, & Deutch, 1988). This excessive catecholaminergic release coincides with a disruption of selective firing in DLPFC neurons and impaired performance on working memory tasks. Finally, this impaired working memory elicited by stress is blocked by selective norepinephrine (Birnbaum, Gobeske, Auerbach, Taylor, & Arnsten, 1999) and dopamine (Murphy, Arnsten, Goldman-Rakic, & Roth, 1996) antagonists.

Arnsten's model has several advantages. Because it is specified at the neuronal level, the timescale of the model could potentially match any behavioral intervention. Further, because of the extensive research on causes of catecholamine release in primates, this model provides researchers with an independent metric for situations and factors that contribute to emotion-related decrements. Finally, Arnsten's model can also accommodate the role of cortisol in the disruption of prefrontal function. It is possible for glucocorticoids such as cortisol to exaggerate catecholaminergic actions in the PFC, thus making the PFC more sensitive to extreme levels of either dopamine or norepinephrine (Gründemann, Schechinger, Rappold, & Schömig, 1998).

Despite all its advantages, a challenge remains for Arnsten's model to be reconciled with cognitive models of emotion and working memory. In particular, while

Arnsten's model does suggest that negative affect could have a direct effect on working memory performance, it does not make any modality-specific predictions consistent with a verbal rumination mechanism. This approach is yet more difficult to reconcile with an emotion regulation mechanism, as processes like suppression and reappraisal have no obvious counterpart in primate models.

CONCLUSIONS AND FUTURE DIRECTIONS

Based on the above evidence, we have outlined a general framework that unites disparate social and affective phenomena (i.e., stereotype threat, math anxiety, and choking under pressure) under a common mechanism. At the foundation of this framework is the working memory construct. Indeed, a disruption of working memory successfully accounts for the bulk of anxiety-effects on performance. The strength of the working memory mechanism, however, is that it generates novel predictions for the effects of anxiety on cognition.

For example, work by Kane et al. (Moore, Clark, & Kane, 2008) has shown that individuals high in working memory exhibit more utilitarian biases in their moral reasoning. That is, high working memory individuals are more likely to espouse killing one person in order to save others—especially if the act of killing must be carried out in a personal and affectively unpleasant manner. According to a dual process account of moral reasoning, this is because the negative affect engaged by the utilitarian act must be actively suppressed by limited, working memory-dependent resources. This novel finding yields immediate predictions within the current framework: In an affectively charged situation—one in which moral reasoning may play an important role—the ability of individuals to properly activate the working memory-dependent component of their moral reasoning capacity should be impaired. As a result, higher working memory individuals should not show more of a utilitarian bias as found in Moore et al. (2008). This untested prediction is a direct consequence of the predictive capacity of the working memory framework, and carries theoretical and practical implications for moral reasoning. Similar relationships exist between working memory and real-world tasks such as eyewitness testimony (Jaschinski & Wentura, 2002), delay discounting (Shamosh et al., 2008), and mind wandering (McVay & Kane, 2009). The interruption of cognition caused by anxiety should be present on any task that recruits working memory.

The picture becomes less clear, however, as we move beyond the broad claim that anxiety disrupts working memory and try to carve out more specific cognitive mechanisms. In particular, no current model can incorporate the effects of not only math anxiety (Ashcraft & Krause, 2007), stereotype threat (Schmader et al., 2008), and performance pressure (Beilock et al., 2004), but also trait anxiety (Eysenck et al., 2007), shock anticipation (Shackman et al., 2006), and mood induction (Gray, 2001). These disparate research programs would benefit from more cross-fertilization, common materials, and procedures.

Finally, greater input from basic neuroscientific research on anxiety is a critical ingredient in this endeavor (Arnsten, 2009; Roozendaal et al., 2004). While the tools and technical expertise of animal research are outside the reach of many cognitive and social researchers, the basic science of these approaches can yield novel, testable hypotheses (Elzinga & Roelofs, 2005; Mattarella-Micke, Mateo, Kozak,Foster, & Beilock, 2011).

ACKNOWLEDGMENT

This research is supported by the NSF Spatial Intelligence and Learning Center, SBE-0541957 and SBE-1041707.

REFERENCES

Arnsten, A. F. T. (2000). Through the looking glass: Differential noradrenergic modulation of prefrontal cortical function. *Neural Plasticity, 7*(1), 33–146.

Arnsten, A. F. T. (2009). Stress signalling pathways that impair prefrontal cortex structure and function. *Nature reviews. Neuroscience, 10*(6), 410–422. doi: 10.1038/nrn2648

Aronson, J., Lustina, M. J., Good, C., Keough, K., & Steele, C. M. (1999). When white men can't do math: Necessary and sufficient factors in stereotype threat. *Journal of Experimental Social Psychology, 35*(1), 29–46.

Ashcraft, M. H. (1992). Cognitive arithmetic: A review of data and theory. *Cognition, 44*(1–2), 75–106.

Ashcraft, M. H., & Faust, M. W. (1994). Mathematics anxiety and mental arithmetic performance: An exploratory investigation. *Cognition and Emotion, 8*(2), 97–125.

Ashcraft, M. H., & Kirk, E. P. (2001). The relationships among working memory, math anxiety, and performance. *Journal of Experimental Psychology: General, 130*(2), 224–237.

Ashcraft, M. H., Kirk, E. P., & Hopko, D. (1998). On the cognitive consequences of mathematics anxiety. In C. Dolan (Ed.), *The development of mathematical skills*. Hove, England: Psychology Press.

Ashcraft, M. H., & Krause, J. A. (2007). Working memory, math performance, and math anxiety. *Psychonomic Bulletin and Review, 14*(2), 243–248.

Beilock, S. L., & Carr, T. H. (2005). When high-powered people fail: Working memory and "choking under pressure" in math. *Psychological Science, 16*(2), 101–105.

Beilock, S. L., Gunderson, E. A., Ramirez, G., & Levine, S. C. (2010). Female teachers' math anxiety affects girls' math achievement. *Proceedings of the National Academy of Sciences of the United States of America, 107*(5), 1860–1863. doi: DOI 10.1073/pnas.0910967107

Beilock, S. L., Kulp, C. A., Holt, L. E., & Carr, T. H. (2004). More on the fragility of performance: Choking under pressure in mathematical problem solving. *Journal of Experimental Psychology: General, 133*(4), 584–600.

Beilock, S. L., Rydell, R. J., & McConnell, A. R. (2007). Stereotype threat and working memory: Mechanisms, alleviation, and spillover. *Journal of Experimental Psychology: General, 136*(2), 256–276. doi: 10.1037/0096-3445.136.2.256

Ben-Zeev, T., Fein, S., & Inzlicht, M. (2005). Arousal and stereotype threat. *Journal of Experimental Social Psychology, 41*(2), 174–181.

Birnbaum, S., Gobeske, K. T., Auerbach, J., Taylor, J. R., & Arnsten, A. F. (1999). A role for norepinephrine in stress-induced cognitive deficits: Alpha-1-Adrenoceptor mediation in the prefrontal cortex. *Biological Psychiatry, 46*(9), 1266–1274.

Bleckley, M. K. (2001). *Working memory capacity as controlled attention: Implications for visual selective attention*. Unpublished doctoral dissertation, Georgia Institute of Technology.

Cadinu, M., Maass, A., Rosabianca, A., & Kiesner, J. (2005). Why do women underperform under stereotype threat? Evidence for the role of negative thinking. *Psychological Science, 16*(7), 572–578.

Calvo, M. G., & Eysenck, M. W. (1996). Phonological working memory and reading in test anxiety. *Memory, 4*(3), 289–305. doi: 10.1080/096582196388960

Calvo, M. G., Ramos, P. M., & Estevez, A. (1992). Test anxiety and comprehension efficiency: The role of prior knowledge and working memory deficits. *Anxiety, Stress and Coping: An International Journal, 5*(2), 125–138. doi: 10.1080/10615809208250492

Campbell, J. (2005). *The handbook of mathematical cognition.* London: Psychology Press.

Carpenter, P. A., Just, M. A., & Shell, P. (1990). What one intelligence test measures: A theoretical account of the processing in the Raven Progressive Matrices Test. *Psychological Review, 97*(3), 404.

Cockburn, J., & Smith, P. T. (1994). Anxiety and errors of prospective memory among elderly people. *British Journal of Psychology, 85*(2), 273–282.

Croizet, J. C., & Claire, T. (1998). Extending the concept of stereotype threat to social class: The intellectual underperformance of students from low socioeconomic backgrounds. *Personality and Social Psychology Bulletin, 24*(6), 588–594.

Croizet, J. C., Despres, G., Gauzins, M. E., Huguet, P., Leyens, J. P., & Meot, A. (2004). Stereotype threat undermines intellectual performance by triggering a disruptive mental load. *Personality and Social Psychology Bulletin, 30*(6), 721–731.

Danaer, K., & Crandall, C. S. (2008). Stereotype threat in applied settings re-examined. *Journal of Applied Social Psychology, 38*(6), 1639–1655.

DeCaro, M. S., Rotar, K. E., Kendra, M. S., & Beilock, S. L. (2010). Diagnosing and alleviating the impact of performance pressure on mathematical problem solving. *Quarterly Journal of Experimental Psychology, 63*(8), 1619–1630. doi: 10.1080/1747021 0903474286

DeCaro, M. S., Thomas, R. D., & Beilock, S. L. (2008). Individual differences in category learning: Sometimes less working memory capacity is better than more. *Cognition, 107*(1), 284–294.

Derakshan, N., Smyth, S., & Eysenck, M. W. (2009). Effects of state anxiety on performance using a task-switching paradigm: An investigation of attentional control theory. *Psychonomic Bulletin and Review, 16*(6), 1112–1117. doi: 16/6/1112 [pii] 10.3758/PBR. 16.6.1112 [doi]

DeStefano, D., & LeFevre, J.-A. (2004). The role of working memory in mental arithmetic. *European Journal of Cognitive Psychology, 16*(3), 353–386. doi: 10.1080/09541440244000328

Dew, K. H., Galassi, J. P., & Galassi, M. D. (1984). Math anxiety: Relation with situational test anxiety, performance, physiological arousal, and math avoidance behavior. *Journal of Counseling Psychology, 31*(4), 580–583. doi: 10.1037/0022-0167.31.4.580

Dickerson, S. S., & Kemeny, M. E. (2004). Acute stressors and cortisol responses: A theoretical integration and synthesis of laboratory research. *Psychological Bulletin, 130*(3), 355–391.

Elzinga, B. M., & Roelofs, K. (2005). Cortisol-induced impairments of working memory require acute sympathetic activation. *Behavioral Neuroscience, 119*(1), 98–103. doi: 10.1037/0735-7044.119.1.98

Engle, R. W. (2002). Working memory capacity as executive attention. *Current Directions in Psychological Science, 11*, 19–23.

Eysenck, M. W., & Calvo, M. G. (1992). Anxiety and performance: The processing efficiency theory. *Cognition and Emotion, 6*, 409–434.

Eysenck, M. W., Derakshan, N., Santos, R., & Calvo, M. G. (2007). Anxiety and cognitive performance: Attentional control theory. *Emotion, 7*(2), 336–353. doi: 10.1037/1528-3542.7.2.336

Faust, M. W. (1996). Mathematics anxiety effects in simple and complex addition. *Mathematical Cognition, 2*(1), 25–62.

Finlay, J. M., Zigmond, M. J., & Abercrombie, E. D. (1995). Increased dopamine and norepinephrine release in medial prefrontal cortex induced by acute and chronic stress: Effects of diazepam. *Neuroscience, 64*(3), 619–628.

Goldman-Rakic, P. S. (1995). Architecture of the prefrontal cortex and the central executive. *Annals of the New York Academy of Sciences, 769,* 71–84.

Gonzales, P. M., Blanton, H., & Williams, K. J. (2002). The effects of stereotype threat and double-minority status on the test performance of Latino women. *Personality and Social Psychology Bulletin, 28*(5), 659–670.

Gray, J. R. (2001). Emotional modulation of cognitive control: Approach-withdrawal states double-dissociate spatial from verbal two-back task performance. *Journal of Experimental Psychology: General, 130*(3), 436–452.

Gross, J. J. (2002). Emotion regulation: Affective, cognitive, and social consequences. *Psychophysiology, 39*(3), 281–291. doi: 10.1017.s0048577201393198

Gründemann, D., Schechinger, B., Rappold, G. A., & Schömig, E. (1998). Molecular identification of the corticosterone-sensitive extraneuronal catecholamine transporter. *Nature Neuroscience, 1*(5), 349–351. doi: 10.1038/1557

Hembree, R. (1990). The nature, effects, and relief of mathematics anxiety. *Journal for Research in Mathematics Education, 21*(1), 33–46. doi: 10.2307/749455

Hornak, J., Bramham, J., Rolls, E. T., Morris, R. G., O'Doherty, J., & Bullock, P. R. (2003). Changes in emotion after circumscribed surgical lesions of the orbitofrontal and cingulate cortices. *Brain, 126*(7), 1691–1712.

Inzlicht, M., McKay, L., & Aronson, J. (2006). Stigma as ego depletion: How being the target of prejudice affects self-control. *Psychological Science, 17*(3), 262–269.

Jamieson, J. P., & Harkins, S. G. (2007). Mere effort and stereotype threat performance effects. *Journal of Personality and Social Psychology, 93*(4), 544–564.

Jaschinski, U., & Wentura, D. (2002). Misleading postevent information and working memory capacity: An individual differences approach to eyewitness memory. *Applied Cognitive Psychology, 16*(2), 223–231. doi: 10.1002/acp.783

Johns, M., Inzlicht, M., & Schmader, T. (2008). Stereotype threat and executive resource depletion: Examining the influence of emotion regulation. *Journal of Experimental Psychology: General, 137*(4), 691–705. doi: 10.1037/a0013834

Kane, M. J., Bleckley, M. K., Conway, A. R., & Engle, R. W. (2001). A controlled-attention view of working-memory capacity. *Journal of Experimental Psychology: General, 130*(2), 169–183.

Kane, M. J., & Engle, R. W. (2000). Working-memory capacity, proactive interference, and divided attention: Limits on long-term memory retrieval. *Journal of Experimental Psychology: Learning, Memory, and Cognition, 26*(2), 336–358.

Kane, M. J., & Engle, R. W. (2003). Working-memory capacity and the control of attention: The contributions of goal neglect, response competition, and task set to Stroop interference. *Journal of Experimental Psychology: General, 132*(1), 47–70.

Klein, K., & Boals, A. (2001). The relationship of life event stress and working memory capacity. *Applied Cognitive Psychology, 15*(5), 565–579.

Kyllonen, P. C., & Christal, R. E. (1990). Reasoning ability is (little more than) working-memory capacity?! *Intelligence, 14*(4), 389–433.

Logan, G. D. (1988). Toward an instance theory of automatization. *Psychological Review, 95*(4), 492–527. doi: 10.1037/0033-295x.95.4.492

Ma, X., & Xu, J. (2004). The causal ordering of mathematics anxiety and mathematics achievement: A longitudinal panel analysis. *Journal of Adolescence, 27*(2), 165–179. doi: 10.1016/j.adolescence.2003.11.003

MacDonald, M. C., Just, M. A., & Carpenter, P. A. (1992). Working memory constraints on the processing of syntactic ambiguity. *Cognitive Psychology, 24*(1), 56–98.

Markman, A. B., Maddox, W. T., & Worthy, D. A. (2006). Choking and excelling under pressure. *Psychological Science, 17*(11), 944–948. doi: 10.1111/j.1467-9280.2006.01809.x

Mattarella-Micke, A., & Beilock, S. L. (2012). Individual differences in frontoparietal activity predict high-stakes choking. Poster presented at the nineteenth Annual Convention of the Cognitive Neuroscience Society.

Mattarella-Micke, A., Mateo, J., Kozak, M. N., Foster, K., & Beilock, S. L. (2011). Choke or thrive? The relation between salivary cortisol and math performance depends on individual differences in working memory and math anxiety. *Emotion, 11*(4), 1000–1005.

McVay, J. C., & Kane, M. J. (2009). Conducting the train of thought: Working memory capacity, goal neglect, and mind wandering in an executive-control task. *Journal of Experimental Psychology: Learning, Memory, and Cognition, 35*(1), 196–204. doi: 10.1037/a0014104

Miyake, A., Friedman, N. P., Emerson, M. J., Witzki, A. H., Howerter, A., & Wager, T. D. (2000). The unity and diversity of executive functions and their contributions to complex "frontal lobe" tasks: A latent variable analysis. *Cognitive Psychology, 41*(1), 49–100.

Mogg, K., Mathews, A., Bird, C., & Macgregor-Morris, R. (1990). Effects of stress and anxiety on the processing of threat stimuli. *Journal of Personality and Social Psychology, 59*(6), 1230–1237.

Moore, A. B., Clark, B. A., & Kane, M. J. (2008). Who shalt not kill? Individual differences in working memory capacity, executive control, and moral judgment. *Psychological Science, 19*(6), 549–557.

Murphy, B. L., Arnsten, A. F. T., Goldman-Rakic, P. S., & Roth, R. H. (1996). Increased dopamine turnover in the prefrontal cortex impairs spatial working memory performance in rats and monkeys. *Proceedings of the National Academy of Sciences of the United States of America, 93*(3), 1325–1329.

Osborne, J. W. (2001). Testing stereotype threat: Does anxiety explain race and sex differences in achievement? *Contemporary Educational Psychology, 26*(3), 291–310.

Pallak, M. S., Pittman, T. S., Heller, J. F., & Munson, P. (1975). The effect of arousal on Stroop color-word task performance. *Bulletin of the Psychonomic Society, 6*(3), 248–250.

Ramirez, G., & Beilock, S. L. (2011). Writing about testing worries boosts exam performance in the classroom. *Science, 331*(6014), 211–213.

Rapee, R. M. (1993). The utilisation of working memory by worry. *Behaviour Research and Therapy, 31*(6), 617–620.

Roozendaal, B., McReynolds, J. R., & McGaugh, J. L. (2004). The basolateral amygdala interacts with the medial prefrontal cortex in regulating glucocorticoid effects on working memory impairment. *Journal of Neuroscience, 24*(6), 1385–1392.

Rosen, V. M., & Engle, R. W. (1997). The role of working memory capacity in retrieval. *Journal of Experimental Psychology: General, 126*(3), 211–227. doi: 10.1037/0096-3445.126.3.211

Roth, R. H., Tam, S. Y., Ida, Y., Yang, J. X., & Deutch, A. Y. (1988). Stress and the mesocorticolimbic dopamine systems. *Annals of the New York Academy of Sciences, 537*, 138–147.

Schmader, T., & Johns, M. (2003). Converging evidence that stereotype threat reduces working memory capacity. *Journal of Personality and Social Psychology, 85*(3), 440–452.

Schmader, T., Johns, M., & Forbes, C. (2008). An integrated process model of stereotype threat effects on performance. *Psychological Review, 115*(2), 336–356. doi: 10.1037/0033-295x.115.2.336

Schmeichel, B. J. (2007). Attention control, memory updating, and emotion regulation temporarily reduce the capacity for executive control. *Journal of Experimental Psychology: General, 136*(2), 241–255. doi: 2007-06470-006 [pii] 10.1037/0096-3445.136.2.241

Schmeichel, B. J., Volokhov, R. N., & Demaree, H. A. (2008). Working memory capacity and the self-regulation of emotional expression and experience. *Journal of Personality and Social Psychology, 95*(6), 1526–1540. doi: 10.1037/a0013345

Schmiedek, F., Hildebrandt, A., Lövdén, M., Wilhelm, O., & Lindenberger, U. (2009). Complex span versus updating tasks of working memory: The gap is not that deep. *Journal of Experimental Psychology: Learning, Memory, and Cognition, 35*(4), 1089–1096. doi: 10.1037/a0015730

Shackman, A. J., Sarinopoulos, I., Maxwell, J. S., Pizzagalli, D. A., Lavric, A., & Davidson, R. J. (2006). Anxiety selectively disrupts visuospatial working memory. *Emotion, 6*(1), 40–61. doi: 10.1037/1528-3542.6.1.40

Shamosh, N. A., Deyoung, C. G., Green, A. E., Reis, D. L., Johnson, M. R., & Conway, A. R. (2008). Individual differences in delay discounting: Relation to intelligence, working memory, and anterior prefrontal cortex. *Psychological Science, 19*(9), 904–911. doi: 10.1111/j.1467-9280.2008.02175.x

Spencer, S. J., Steele, C. M., & Quinn, D. M. (1999). Stereotype threat and women's math performance. *Journal of Experimental Social Psychology, 35*(1), 4–28.

Steele, C. M., & Aronson, J. (1995). Stereotype threat and the intellectual test performance of African Americans. *Journal of Personality and Social Psychology, 69*, 797–811.

Trbovich, P. L., & LeFevre, J. A. (2003). Phonological and visual working memory in mental addition. *Memory and Cognition, 31*(5), 738–745.

Van Dillen, L. F., & Koole, S. L. (2007). Clearing the mind: A working memory model of distraction from negative mood. *Emotion, 7*(4), 715–723. doi: 10.1037/1528-3542.7.4.715

Vijayraghavan, S., Wang, M., Birnbaum, S. G., Williams, G. V., & Arnsten, A. F. T. (2007). Inverted-U dopamine D1 receptor actions on prefrontal neurons engaged in working memory. *Nature Neuroscience, 10*(3), 376–384. doi: 10.1038/nn1846

Volokhov, R. N., & Demaree, H. A. (2010). Spontaneous emotion regulation to positive and negative stimuli. *Brain and Cognition, 73*(1), 1–6. doi: 10.1016/j.bandc.2009.10.015

Wager, T. D., & Smith, E. E. (2003). Neuroimaging studies of working memory: A meta-analysis. *Cognitive, Affective, and Behavioral Neuroscience, 3*(4), 255–274.

Wager, T. D., van Ast, V. A., Hughes, B. L., Davidson, M. L., Lindquist, M. A., & Ochsner, K. N. (2009). Brain mediators of cardiovascular responses to social threat, Part II: Prefrontal-subcortical pathways and relationship with anxiety. *Neuroimage, 47*(3), 836–851.

Wegner, D. M., Erber, R., & Zanakos, S. (1993). Ironic processes in the mental control of mood and mood-related thought. *Journal of Personality and Social Psychology, 65*(6), 1093–1104.

Wood, J., Mathews, A., & Dalgleish, T. (2001). Anxiety and cognitive inhibition. *Emotion, 1*(2), 166–181. doi: 10.1037/1528-3542.1.2.166

13

Working Memory and Meditation

ALEEZÉ SATTAR MOSS
*Jefferson-Myrna Brind Center of Integrative Medicine,
Thomas Jefferson University, Philadelphia, PA, USA*

DANIEL A. MONTI
*Jefferson-Myrna Brind Center of Integrative Medicine,
Thomas Jefferson University, Philadelphia, PA, USA*

ANDREW NEWBERG
*Jefferson-Myrna Brind Center of Integrative Medicine,
Thomas Jefferson University, Philadelphia, PA, USA*

BACKGROUND INFORMATION

*M*editation has been an integral part of many spiritual and healing traditions for over 5,000 years. It has become increasingly popular in many countries and there has been a burgeoning of research on the potential benefits of meditation for reducing stress and anxiety, and improving physical health and well-being. More recently researchers have started to examine the cognitive benefits of various meditation practices and to study the impact of meditation on the brain. Research findings suggest that even short periods of meditation can change brain structure and function and lead to improvements in cognitive function. Preliminary evidence indicates that meditation training can specifically enhance working memory as well as protect working memory capacity from deteriorating during periods of high stress. In this chapter we review recent findings of research on the relationship between meditation, attention, and memory. We also examine the neural correlates of meditation and review findings from neuroscientific studies.

CURRENT EVIDENCE

Meditation, Attention, and Memory

The term meditation refers to a wide range of practices arising out of different religious, spiritual, and secular traditions. Depending on the tradition, meditation may be a way to establish a sense of calm and serenity; a way to reduce stress and alleviate depression; a way to reduce anxieties and deal with panic disorders; a way to improve health; or a way to deal with chronic illness. Meditation may also be a way to cultivate greater self-awareness, a spiritual path, a way to be in touch with peak spiritual experiences. This divergence in forms and understandings of meditation corresponds to studies of meditation, with different meditation practices showing different outcomes (for example see Fell et al., 2010 for a comparison of studies of Indian Yogis and Japanese Buddhist monks). Given the variety of meditation practices and traditions, an all-encompassing definition of meditation is not possible. However, it is helpful for the scientific study of meditation to have some basic way to categorize the different types of meditation. In general, most forms of meditation involve the regulation of attention or emotion. Recently, meditation practices have been divided into two broad categories—focused attention and open awareness meditation. A brief discussion of attention will be helpful in elaborating this broad categorization of meditation.

The most consistent theoretical model of attention suggests that it consists of three distinct networks: alerting (also referred to as vigilance or sustained attention), orienting (selective attention or concentration), and conflict monitoring (executive attention) (McDowd, 2007; Posner and Petersen, 1990; Posner and Rothbart, 2007). Alerting is involved in achieving and maintaining an attentive state; orienting is involved in selectively focusing on a subset of space or available information; and conflict monitoring is involved in the management of goal-directed behavior, target and error detection, conflict resolution, and the inhibition of automatic responses. These three networks are behaviorally and neurally distinct and dissociable (Fan et al., 2002, 2005). In addition to these subsets of attention, there is also "attention switching," referred to as an ability to change attentive focus in a flexible manner (Chiesa et al., 2011; Mirsky et al., 1991).

Neuroimaging studies of attention have systematically shown activation in three different neural networks using spatial cuing and flanker tasks. While attention "sources" have been identified in frontal and parietal subregions for all the different attention networks, "sites" have been localized to considerably different subregions across these networks. Alerting primarily activates the prefrontal cortex (PFC), the premotor cortex, intraparietal sulcus, the locus coeruleus, and thalamic regions (Coull et al., 1999). Orienting activates the cortical areas including dorsolateral PFC, medial PFC, and anterior and posterior cingulate cortex, and specific subregions of parietal cortex (Astafiev et al., 2003; Corbetta et al., 1998; Gitelman et al., 1999; Small et al., 2003; Vandenberghe et al., 2001). Collectively, engagement of attention for relevant stimuli, disengagement of attention from task irrelevant stimuli, and movement of attention are described as the "shift" operation. It has been suggested that distinct subregions of the parietal cortex (including the superior parietal lobule, the temporal parietal junction, and the intraparietal sulcus) are involved in the engagement of attention, which varies under different perceptual load conditions (Corbetta et al., 1995), the disengagement of attention (Posner et al., 1987), and covert and overt movement of attention (Yantis et al., 2002). Finally, conflict monitoring activates the anterior cingulate (ACC) cortex, PFC, and IPS. Having briefly discussed the attention networks and their neural correlates we can now return to the discussion of meditation.

Given this description of attention, meditative practices have been categorized into the two general styles mentioned above depending on how the meditator deploys his/her attention (Cahn and Polich 2006; Fell et al., 2010; Lutz et al., 2008). If attention is focused on a single object, whether the object is abstract (such as an imagined picture or a feeling) or concrete (such as a mantra, the breath, or a body sensation, or an external object), then the style is categorized as focused attention meditation or concentration practice (Lutz et al., 2007, 2008). To sustain this focus, the practitioner has to constantly monitor and regulate the quality of attention toward that object. When attention wanders the practitioner is to notice that without judgment, let go of whatever the attention has become engaged with, and return to the object of focus.

Thus, focused attention is thought to not only train one's ability to sustain attention, but also to develop three other regulative attentional skills. One is the monitoring faculty that remains vigilant to distraction while maintaining the intended focus. Another skill is the ability to disengage from a distracting object without further involvement (attention switching). The third skill involves the ability to promptly redirect focus to the chosen object (selective attention) (Lutz et al., 2008). Slagter and colleagues (2011) highlight the parallels between the processes involved in focused attention meditation and the recent neuroscientific conceptualizations of attention. The ability to focus and sustain attention on an intended object or task requires skills involved in the monitoring focus of attention and detecting distraction, disengaging attention from the source of distraction, and (re)directing and engaging attention to the intended object (Posner and Peterson, 1990).

The second general category of meditation is open monitoring meditation, sometimes referred to as mindfulness meditation, where the meditator maintains an open awareness of whatever arises in the field of attention (whether it is a sound, a body sensation, a thought) moment by moment, and without judgment. Open monitoring meditation involves non-reactively monitoring the content of experience, without focusing on any explicit object (Lutz et al., 2007, 2008). The distinction between focused attention (concentration practice) and open awareness (mindfulness practice) is used and commonly accepted within the meditation literature and teaching practices. However, it is important to note that they are not exclusive—mindfulness training for instance usually begins with training in focused attention to build concentration, progressing eventually to open awareness meditation practices. Even during a particular open meditation practice, the practitioner usually starts by calming the mind and reducing distractions with focused attention. The practitioner then gradually reduces focus on a single object and opens up the field of awareness.

In mindfulness or open monitoring meditation the monitoring faculty of attention is emphasized. Open monitoring meditation is thought to enhance non-reactive, meta-cognitive monitoring, as well as increase awareness of automatic cognitive and emotional interpretations of sensory, perceptual, and endogenous stimuli, and through this enhance cognitive flexibility and reappraisal (Bishop et al., 2004; Chambers et al. 2009; Lutz et al. 2008; Slagter et al., 2011).

Like attention, memory is also not a single process. Several types of partially independent memory processes modulated by different brain regions have been identified (Budson 2009; Chiesa et al. 2011; Henke 2010). The memory types include, among others, semantic and episodic memory, procedural memory, and working memory. While semantic, episodic, and procedural memory belong to long-term memory, working memory brings together the fields of short-term memory and attention. Working memory and attention are interconnected such that when a person attends to an object, information about that object enters working memory. Working memory is assumed to be necessary for the maintenance of information in the mind while performing complex tasks such as reasoning, comprehension, and learning (Baddeley, 2010). Working memory can be divided into three distinct components, which also have separate neural networks: processing and storing phonologic information; processing and storing visual information; and an executive system allocating attentional resources (Baddeley, 1998). Some studies suggest that working memory consists of focused attention governed by a limited-capacity search function (Verhaeghen et al., 2004). Working memory deficits have been associated with a range of psychological conditions, including anxiety and depression, attention deficit hyperactivity disorder (Koschack et al., 2003), borderline personality disorder (Stevens et al., 2004), and post-traumatic stress disorder (Clark et al., 2003). Promisingly, studies are beginning to show that mental training and relaxation techniques can increase the capacity of the working memory search function (Verhaeghen et al., 2004).

Meditation and Attention

Neurocognitive studies have shown that meditation may improve attention and cognitive function (for review see Chiesa et al., 2011: Lutz et al., 2007, 2008). Meditation practice and increased mindfulness appear to be related to improved attentional functions and cognitive flexibility (Carter et al., 2005; Chan and Woollacott, 2007; Jha et al., 2007; Moore and Malinowski, 2009; Pagnoni and Cekic, 2007; Slagter et al., 2007; Valentine and Sweet, 1999).

Three studies that compared long-term meditators with matched controls (Josefsson and Broberg, 2011; Pagnoni and Cekic, 2007; Valentine and Sweet, 1999) observed significantly higher performances in tasks involving sustained attention in meditators as compared to controls. Pagnoni and Cekic (2007) used a rapid visual presentation task to investigate age-related effects of meditation practice in meditators and non-meditators. While the control subjects displayed the expected decrease in attentional performance with age, no such decrease was found in meditators. Valentine and Sweet (1999) found that meditation practitioners scored significantly higher on a test of sustained attention (Wilkins' counting test) than non-meditators. Furthermore, the authors found that long-term meditators (more than 24 months of meditation experience) scored significantly higher than short-term meditators (less than 24 months), suggesting perhaps the development of a more distributed attentional focus in long-term practice of mindfulness meditation as compared with concentrative practices.

Another study by Jha and colleagues (2007) compared expert meditators after a one-month intensive Vipassana meditation (Buddhist insight meditation in which mindfulness is a key element) retreat with novices with no prior meditation practice assigned to either an eight-week Mindfulness-Based Stress Reduction (MBSR) course (a standardized and secular form of mindfulness training) or to a waiting list. The study found a significant reduction of response time (RT) scores as measured by the attentional network task (ANT) in the intensive retreat group as compared with novices. Interestingly study results also showed that those in the MBSR group had significant improvements on selective attention compared with the one-month intensive retreat and control group, as measured with the ANT. This may reflect an enhancement in the ability to exclude unwanted stimuli following early stages of practice (MBSR in novice meditators) but not in expert meditators who were more concerned with training their open monitoring faculty (see Chiesa et al., 2011).

Other studies show higher levels of selective attention in long-term meditators compared with controls (Chan and Woollacott, 2007; Hodgins and Adair, 2010; Van den Hurk et al., 2010; Moore and Malinowski, 2009). Chan and Woollacott (2007) compared the effects of meditation practice on the Stroop (measures executive network) and Global-Local Letters (measures orientation network) tasks. They found that meditation practice was associated with increased efficiency of the executive attentional network although it did not have an effect on the orienting network. Moore and Malinowski (2009) compared meditators with a meditation-naïve control group on tasks that measure cognitive flexibility and the speed of processing visual information. They found that meditators outperformed non-meditators on all measures and that performance was positively correlated to participants' self-reported scores on mindfulness measures.

In a longitudinal study comparing individuals randomly assigned to a meditation retreat group or a waiting-list control, three months of focused awareness meditation practice (five hours a day) was found to improve sustained visual attention (MacLean et al., 2010). Compared to the control group, meditation retreat participants showed enhanced perceptual discrimination and vigilance on a sustained visual attention task. Notably, the enhancements in sustained attention ability were still observed three months after the end of the retreat, demonstrating enduring changes in sustained attention.

Slagter et al. (2007) investigated the effects of a three-month Vipassana retreat on "attentional blink." In attentional blink paradigms, stimuli such as letters or numbers are presented in rapid succession (50 images per second), and the task is to identify target stimuli (e.g., a particular number or letter) from the flow of non-targets. Attentional blink is the process whereby a second target stimulus (T2) presented within 500ms of a first stimulus (T1) in a rapid sequence of distractors, is often not detected (Raymond et al., 1992). This is possibly the result of a deficit in the ability to process two temporally close, meaningful stimuli. This is taken to mean that additional time is needed for attentional resource allocation for T1. The results of the study by Slagter and colleagues found that compared to an age-matched control group, the meditation retreat group showed a significantly smaller attentional blink. Additionally, the reduction in the attentional blink was associated with a reduction in brain resource allocation (measured by EEG) to T1 (Slagter et al., 2007). The study findings thus suggest a more efficient allocation of resources as a result of meditation training. These results were replicated in a case-control study that compared expert mindfulness meditators with age-matched and younger controls (van Leeuwen et al., 2009). Not only did the meditation group show a much smaller attentional blink, but stemming from an older population they performed even better than the young control group, even though performance on the attentional blink has been shown to drop with age.

Collectively, these findings suggest that even brief periods of meditation training, such as an eight-week MBSR program or short intensive training, can improve cognitive function. However, studies suggest that the beneficial effects of meditation are moderated by intensity and length of training. Significantly higher attentional abilities was found in long-term meditators as compared with matched controls on different domains of attention (Chan and Woollacott, 2007; Hodgins and Adair, 2010; Pagnoni and Cekic, 2007; Valentine and Sweet, 1999). A significant positive relationship was observed between the amount of meditation experience and enhanced cognitive abilities and brain structural changes (Pagnoni and Cekic, 2007). Furthermore, meditation appears to protect the brain from age-related cognitive decline (Van Leeuwen et al., 2009).

Meditation and Memory

There have been fewer studies investigating the effects of meditation practices on memory. However, these studies suggest that there are meditation-related improvements in working memory and sustained attention measures in novice meditators who underwent meditation training compared to non-meditators (Chambers, Lo and Allen, 2008; Jha et al., 2010; Tang et al., 2007). Chambers et al. (2008) examined the impact of a ten-day Vipassana (mindfulness) meditation retreat on novice meditators' working memory capacity, measured by response time (RT) on a novel attention task that required participants to attend and update information between two categories, and five self-report measures of cognitive processes and affect. They found that meditation training increased mindfulness, enhanced working memory capacity, and reduced switch costs in the attention task. In addition, mindfulness training reduced anxiety, negative affect, and depression. Zeidan et al. (2010) studied the effects of a four-day mindfulness retreat in novice meditators and found a significant improvement in working memory capacity as measured by the digit span backward and forward of the Wechsler Adult Intelligence Scale.

Another study by Jha and colleagues (2010) examined the protective effects of a mindfulness-based mental fitness training modeled on MBSR on working memory capacity and mood states in the military service members preparing for deployment (Jha et al., 2010). This is a period of intense stress, which can lead to decreases in cognitive function and increases in emotional disturbances (Stanley and Jha, 2009). Working memory capacity was assessed by the Operation span (Ospan) task. Ospan scores showed a trend in improvement in the mindfulness training group with high practice, whereas they deteriorated over time in the control group and in the meditation group with low practice. Study results also suggest that improvements in working memory capacity may mitigate negative affect such as stress or anxiety (Jha et al., 2010).

Newberg et al. (2010) studied the effects of meditation on memory in a group of older subjects with memory problems, ranging from age-associated memory loss, mild-cognitive impairment, and early Alzheimer's Disease. An eight-week (12 minutes a day) practice of Kirtan Kriya (a form of mantra meditation) led to improvements on neuropsychological tests of verbal fluency, Trails B, and logical memory in the meditation group compared to controls. These improvements in cognitive function were correlated with changes in the brain that will be discussed more fully below. The findings from this preliminary study are noteworthy because it is one of the few studies to look at the effects of meditation in an elderly population with age-related cognitive decline, mild-cognitive impairment, and early Alzheimer's Disease (Newberg et al., 2010). The results suggest that there is improvement in memory and changes in cerebral blood flow associated with meditation practice.

Neuroimaging Studies of Meditation

The results of neuroimaging (PET, SPECT, and fMRI) studies indicate a number of changes that support the mechanism by which meditation may help with memory and cognition. For example, Herzog et al. (1990) utilized FDG PET to measure regional glucose metabolism in subjects undergoing Yoga Meditative Relaxation. Findings from the study showed a significant increase in the frontal:occipital ratio of cerebral metabolism in the meditators. Specifically, there was only a mild increase in the frontal lobe, but marked decreases in metabolism in the occipital and superior parietal lobes. Other studies utilizing functional magnetic resonance imaging (fMRI) in subjects performing a similar yoga relaxation technique designed to bring about the "relaxation response" demonstrate relative increases in cerebral blood flow in the frontal lobes as well as the limbic system (Lazar et al., 2000; Lou et al., 1999).

A single photon emission computed tomography (SPECT) imaging study of Tibetan Buddhist meditation demonstrated a number of complex changes including relatively increased cerebral blood flow (CBF) in the prefrontal cortex and cingulate gyrus (Newberg et al., 2001). The regional CBF ratio of long-term meditators was higher than non-meditators in the prefrontal cortex, amygdala, thalamus, and brainstem regions. Together, the results of these studies suggest that meditation may lead to increased activity in the structures underlying attention and memory processes.

A study by Holzel et al. (2007) found that Vipassana meditation activated the rostral anterior cingulated cortex (ACC) and the dorsal medial prefrontal cortex in both hemispheres. In addition, these investigators found that Vipassana meditation might enhance cerebral activity in brain areas related to interoception and attention, such as the PFC, the right anterior insula, and the right hippocampus (Holzel et al., 2008). These findings suggest that mindfulness meditation may enhance attentional abilities.

A study by Lazar et al. (2003) compared individuals with extensive training in Kundalini (mantra-based) or Vipassana meditation using fMRI. Subjects were studied during meditation and several control tasks. Similar but non-overlapping frontal and parietal cortices and subcortical structures were engaged during meditation by both groups, and these patterns differed from those observed during control tasks. The main area of common activation was the dorsal cingulate cortex.

Lazar et al. (2005) used MRI to investigate individual differences in cerebral cortical thickness and found that brain regions associated with attention and sensory processing, including the prefrontal cortex and right anterior insula, were thicker in meditators than matched controls. The differences in cortical thickness were specific to areas relevant to meditation, as the groups did not differ in mean thickness across the entire cortex. Holzel et al. (2011) used MRI to study the effect of MBSR on gray matter concentration. Changes in gray matter concentration were investigated using voxel-based morphometry, and compared with a waiting list control group. Results show increases in gray matter concentration within the left hippocampus. Whole brain analyses identified increases in the posterior cingulate cortex, the temporo-parietal junction, and the cerebellum in the MBSR group compared with the controls. The authors conclude that the results of their study suggest that an eight-week mindfulness training is associated with changes in gray matter concentration in brain regions involved in learning and memory processes, emotion regulation, self-referential processing, and perspective taking.

Pagnoni and Cekic (2007), using MRI to examine age-related decline of cerebral gray matter volume and attentional performance (using a computerized sustained attention task) in meditators and matched controls, found a reliable negative correlation of both gray matter volume and attentional performance with age in non-meditators. However, meditators did not show a significant correlation of either measure with age. Further, the effect of meditation on gray matter volume was most prominent in the putamen, a structure strongly implicated in attentional processing.

Tang and colleagues have performed several studies with integrative body–mind training (IBMT), which incorporates mindfulness, body relaxation, and mental imagery, and showed increased CBF associated with a five-day training program in the right anterior cingulated, putamen, and caudate, implying changes in self-regulation, executive function, and reward networks (Tang et al., 2009). This same group also found improvements in the performance on the ANT and levels of anxiety, fatigue, depression, and anger as measured by the Profile of Mood States scale (Tang et al., 2007). Finally, Tang and colleagues performed diffusion tensor imaging before and after IBMT training and found changes in fractional anisotropy in the corona radiata associated with the anterior cingulate, which is a central structure involved in the self-regulation network (Tang et al., 2010).

Several fMRI studies of meditation have specifically shown activation of a larger distributed network of attention-related brain regions, including frontal parietal regions, insula, thalamus, basal ganglia, and cerebellar regions. Individuals with greater levels of meditation experience show greater activation in these regions compared to novices, which is suggestive of a training effect. It also demonstrates long-term structural changes produced by meditation. Holzel et al. (2008) found greater gray matter concentration in the anterior insula, a brain region that is important for awareness of internal experience, in experienced Vipassana meditators (with a mean practice of 8.6 years, two hours daily). In another study, more than 10,000 hours of Zen meditation was associated with increased cortical thickness in the dorsal anterior cingulate cortex. A study by Brefczynski-Lewis et al. (2007) using fMRI found that there are overlapping activation regions for expert meditators with over 10,000 hours of practice and novice meditators in attention-related brain regions, including frontal parietal regions, lateral occipital, insula, multiple thalamic nuclei, basal ganglia, and cerebellar regions. Despite these similarities, expert meditators showed greater activation than novice meditators in multiple brain regions implicated in attentional processing, including the superior frontal sulcus and the intraparietal sulcus, attention-related and other frontoparietal regions. In contrast, novice meditators had greater activation in regions shown to negatively correlate with performance in a sustained attention task.

A previously mentioned SPECT study by Newberg et al. (2010) that examined changes in CBF after an eight-week Kirtan Kriya (mantra meditation) practice in elderly subjects with memory problems found that compared to controls the meditation group showed significantly higher CBF in the frontal lobe regions and right superior parietal lobe. Further, there was some correlation between improvements in cognitive function and increased CBF. The increased baseline CBF in the frontal cortex for the meditation group is particularly interesting since these frontal lobe structures are not only important mediators of attention and executive function, but also appear to be affected in patients with various dementia disorders and mild cognitive impairment.

Together the results of these studies show that the mental training of attention and cognitive skills as cultivated through focused attention and open monitoring meditation is associated with changes in brain structure and function, as well as improved attention and memory task performance. Moreover, neuroimaging work suggests that both types of meditation not only activate brain regions during meditation, but may produce long-lasting changes in brain and mental function that translate into tasks that are not associated with meditation (Slagter et al., 2011). Meditation seems to have a neuroprotective effect and may reduce the cognitive decline associated with normal aging.

FUTURE DIRECTIONS

The research on meditation and memory is still in its nascent stages. More detailed study of the clinical and physiological effects are needed. Such studies should include much larger population sizes so that a variety of demographic variables including age, gender, education, and socioeconomic status can be factored in. Furthermore, individuals with a variety of different cognitive problems ranging from age-related cognitive decline to Alzheimer's disease and other dementias should be included to determine if meditation will work in each of these groups.

The literature certainly requires more brain imaging studies that include imaging of more subjects and more detailed image analysis. Structural changes including volumetric analysis of MRI scans can help demonstrate the effects of meditation on the morphology of the brain. Functional studies that include fMRI, PET, and SPECT will also be highly useful for the further investigation of meditation practices on memory. In addition, it will be important to apply imaging studies to a broad array of meditation practices to determine if and how they might provide a benefit to memory processes in the brain. Such studies should eventually focus on longitudinal data in order to fully assess long-term changes in the brain and memory associated with meditation practices.

Finally, an area that has had very limited exploration is the evaluation of various neurotransmitter systems as they relate to meditation practices. There is evidence that many different neurotransmitter systems may be associated with meditation practices (Newberg and Iversen, 2003). Such systems include dopamine, serotonin, and glutamate, which may have a significant relationship to memory processes in the brain. Correlating changes in these neurotransmitter systems with clinical changes in memory may further contribute to our understanding of how meditation may affect memory and cognition.

CONCLUSIONS

In this chapter we discussed the relationship between meditation and attention, and examined the literature on meditation effects on attention and working memory. We then reviewed neuroscientific studies to understand meditation effects on the brain. While the neuroscientific literature is difficult to parse, with different imaging techniques and differential impact of an array of meditation practices complicating the picture, studies generally indicate that even short-term meditation training can improve various attentional networks and working memory capacity. The findings do suggest that meditation effects are moderated by length and intensity of training. Meditation may have a neuroprotective effect and appears to prevent age-related cognitive decline as well as reductions in cortical thickness. The neuroimaging studies demonstrate that not only are particular areas of the brain activated during meditation, but also that meditation practice leads to long-term changes in brain structure and function. All of this is extremely encouraging and has many clinical implications for improving working memory capacity in those with disorders associated with working memory deficits; in preventing working memory capacity decline for those in high-stress professions, such as the military in active duty; as well as improving memory and cognitive function in elderly individuals with memory loss or mild-cognitive impairment.

REFERENCES

Astafiev SV, Shulman GL, Stanley CM, et al. (2003). Functional organization of human intraparietal and frontal cortex for attending, looking, and pointing. *Journal of Neuroscience* 23:4689–99.

Baddeley A (1998). Recent developments in working memory. *Current Opinion in Neurobiology* 8:234–8.

Baddeley A (2010). Working memory. *Current Biology* 20:R136–40.

Bishop SR, Lau M, Shapiro S (2004). Mindfulness: A proposed operational definition. *Clinical Psychology* 11:230–41.

Brefczynski-Lewis JA, Lutz A, Schaefer HS, Levinson DB, Davidson RJ (2007). Neural correlates of attention expertise in long-term meditation practitioners. *Proceedings of the Natural Academy of Sciences of the USA* 104(27):11483–8.

Budson AE (2009). Understanding memory dysfunction. *Neurologist* 15:71–9.

Cahn BR, Polich J (2006). Meditation states and traits: EEG, ERP, and neuroimaging studies. *Psychological Bulletin* 132:180–211.

Carter OL, Presti DE, Callistemon C, Ungerer Y, Liu GB, Pettigrew JD (2005). Meditation alters perceptual rivalry in Tibetan Buddhist monks. *Current Biology* Jun 7; 15(11):R412–3.

Chambers R, Gullone E, Allen NB (2009). Mindful emotion regulation: An integrative review. *Clinical Psychological Review* 29(6):560–72.

Chambers R, Lo BCY, Allen NB (2008). The impact of intensive mindfulness training on attentional control, cognitive style and affect. *Cognitive Therapy and Research* 32:303–22.

Chan D, Woollacott M (2007). Effects of level of meditation experience on attentional focus: Is the efficiency of executive or orientation networks improved? *Journal of Alternative and Complementary Medicine* 13:651–7.

Clark CR, McFarlane AC, Morris P et al. (2003). Cerebral function in post-traumatic stress disorder during verbal working memory updating: A positron emission tomography study. *Biological Psychiatry* 53:474–81.

Chiesa A, Calati R, Serretti A (2011). Does mindfulness training improve cognitive abilities? A systematic review of neuropsychological findings. *Clinical Psychology Review* 31:449–64.

Corbetta M, Akbudak E, Conturo TE, et al. (1998). A common network of functional areas for attention and eye movements. *Neuron* 21:761–73.

Corbetta M, Shulman GL, Miezin FM, Petersen SE (1995). Superior parietal cortex activation during spatial attention shifts and visual feature conjunction. *Science* 270:802–5.

Coull JT, Buchel C, Friston KJ, Frith CD (1999). Noradrenergically mediated plasticity in a human attentional neuronal network. *Neuroimage* 10:705–15.

Fan J, McCandliss BD, Fossella J, Flombaum JI, Posner MI (2005). The activation of attentional networks. *NeuroImage* 26:471–9.

Fan J, McCandliss B, Sommer T, Raz A, Posner M (2002). Testing the efficiency and independence of attention networks. *Journal of Cognitive Neuroscience* 14:340–7.

Fell J, Axmacher N, Haupt S (2010). From alpha to gamma: Electrophysiological correlates of meditation-related states of consciousness. *Medical Hypotheses* 75:218–24.

Gitelman DR, Nobre AC, Parrish TB, et al. (1999). A large-scale distributed network for covert spatial attention: Further anatomical delineation based on stringent behavioural and cognitive controls. *Brain* 122:1093–106.

Henke K (2010). A model for memory systems based on processing modes rather than consciousness. *Nature Reviews Neuroscience* 11:523–32.

Herzog H, Lele VR, Kuwert T, Langen KJ, Rota Kops E, Feinendegen LE (1990). Changed pattern of regional glucose metabolism during yoga meditative relaxation. *Neuropsychobiology* 23(4):182–7.

Hodgins HS, Adair KC (2010). Attentional processes and meditation. *Consciousness and Cognition* 19(4):872–8.

Holzel BK, Carmody J, Vangel M, Congleton C, Yerramsetti SM, Gard T, Lazar SW (2011). Mindfulness practice leads to increases in regional brain gray matter density. *Psychiatry Research* 191(1):36–43.

Holzel BK, Ott U, Gard T, Hempel H, Weygandt M, Morgen K, Vaitl D (2008). Investigation of mindfulness meditation practitioners with voxel-based morphometry. *Social Cognitive and Affective Neuroscience* 3:55–61.

Holzel BK, Ott U, Hempel H, Hackl A, Wolf K, Stark R, Vaitl D (2007). Differential engagement of anterior cingulate and adjacent medial frontal cortex in adept meditators and non-meditators. *Neuroscience Letters* 421:16–21.

Jha AP, Krompinger J, Baime MJ (2007). Mindfulness training modifies subsystems of attention. *Cognitive, Affective and Behavioral Neuroscience* 7:109–19.

Jha AP, Stanley EA, Kiyonaga A, Wong L, Gelfand L (2010). Examining the protective effects of mindfulness training on working memory capacity and affective experience. *Emotion* 10:54–64.

Josefsson T, Broberg A (2011). Meditators and non-meditators on sustained and executive attentional performance. *Mental Health, Religion, and Culture* 14:291–309.

Koschack J, Kunert HJ, Derichs G, Weniger G, Irle E (2003). Impaired and enhanced attentional function in children with attention deficit/hyperactivity disorder. *Psychological Medicine* 33:481–9.

Lazar SW, Bush G, Gollub RL, et al. (2000). Functional brain mapping of the relaxation response and meditation. *Neuroreport* 11:1581–5.

Lazar SW, Bush G, Gollub RL, Fricchione GL, Khalsa G, Benson H (2003). Functional brain imaging of mindfulness and mantra-based meditation. Paper presented at the meeting of the Society for Neuroscience. New Orleans, LA.

Lazar SW, Kerr CE, Wasserman RH, et al. (2005). Meditation experience is associated with increased cortical thickness. *Neuroreport* 16(17):1893–7.

Lou HC, Kjaer TW, Friberg L, Wildschiodtz G, Holm S, Nowak M (1999). A 15O-H2O PET study of meditation and the resting state of normal consciousness. *Human Brain Mapping* 7: 98–105.

Lutz A, Dunne JD, Davidson RJ (2007). Meditation and the neuroscience of consciousness: An introduction. In P. Zelazo, M. Moscovitch, & E. Thompson (Eds.), *Cambridge handbook of consciousness* (pp. 499–554). New York: Cambridge University Press.

Lutz A, Slagter HA, Dunne JD, Davidson RJ (2008). Attention regulation and monitoring in meditation. *Trends in Cognitive Science* 12(4):163–9.

McDowd JM (2007). An overview of attention: Behavior and brain. *Journal of Neurologic Physical Therapy* 12:17–125.

MacLean KA, Ferrer E, Aichele SR et al. (2010). Intensive meditation training improves perceptual discrimination and sustained attention. *Psychological Science* 21:829–39.

Mirsky AF, Anthony BJ, Duncan CC, Ahearn MB, Kellam SG (1991). Analysis of the elements of attention: A neuropsychological approach. *Neuropsychology Review* 2:109–45.

Moore A, Malinowski P (2009). Meditation, mindfulness and cognitive flexibility. *Consciousness and Cognition* 18:176–86.

Newberg AB, Alavi A, Baime M, et al. (2001). The measurement of regional cerebral blood flow during the complex cognitive task of meditation: A preliminary SPECT study. *Psychiatry Research: Neuroimaging* 106:113–22.

Newberg AB, Iversen J (2003). The neural basis of the complex mental task of meditation: Neurotransmitter and neurochemical considerations. *Medical Hypothesis* 61(2): 282–91.

Newberg AB, Wintering N, Khalsa DS, Roggenkamp H, Waldman MR (2010). Meditation effects on cognitive function and cerebral blood flow in subjects with memory loss: A preliminary study. *Journal of Alzheimer's Disease* 20(2):517–26.

Pagnoni C, Cekic M (2007). Age effects on gray matter volume and attentional performance in Zen meditation. *Neurobiology of Aging* 28:1623–7.

Posner MI, Petersen SE (1990). The attention system of the human brain. *Annual Review of Neuroscience* 13:25–42.

Posner MI, Rothbart MK (2007). Research on attention networks as a model for the integration of psychological science. *Annual Review of Psychology* 58:1–23.

Posner MI, Walker JA, Friedrich FA, Rafal RD (1987). How do the parietal lobes direct covert attention? *Neuropsychologia* 25:135–45.

Raymond JE, Shapiro KL, Arnell KM (1992). Temporary suppression of visual processing in an RSVP task: An attentional blink? *Journal of Experimental Psychology: Human Perception and Performance* 18:849–60.

Slagter HA, Davidson RJ, Lutz A (2011). Mental training as a tool in the neuroscientific study of brain and cognitive plasticity. *Frontiers of Human Neuroscience* 5.

Slagter HA, Lutz A, Greischar LL, Francis AD, Nieuwenhuis S, Davis JM, Davidson RJ (2007). Mental training affects distribution of limited brain resources. *PLoS Biology* 5(6):1228–35.

Small DM, Gitelman DR, Gregory MD, Nobre AC, Parrish TB, Mesulam MM (2003). The posterior cingulate and medial prefrontal cortex mediate the anticipatory allocation of spatial attention. *Neuroimage* 18:633–41.

Stanley EA, Jha AP (2009). Mind fitness: Improving operational effectiveness and building warrior resilience. *Joint Force Quarterly* 55, 144–51.

Stevens A, Burkhardt M, Hautzinger M, Schwarz J, Unckel C (2004). Borderline personality disorder: Impaired visual perception and working memory. *Psychiatry Research* 125:257–67.

Tang Y-Y., Lu Q, Geng X, et al. (2010). Short-term meditation induces white matter changes in the anterior cingulate. *Proceedings of the National Academy of Sciences* 107:15649–52.

Tang Y-Y, Ma Y, Fan Y, et al. (2009). Central and autonomic nervous system interaction is altered by short-term meditation. *Proceedings of the National Academy of Sciences* 106:8865–70.

Tang Y-Y, Ma Y, Wang J, et al. (2007). Short-term meditation training improves attention and self-regulation. *Proceedings of the National Academy of Sciences* 104:17152–6.

Valentine ER, Sweet PLG (1999). Meditation and attention: A comparison of the effects of concentrative versus mindfulness meditation on sustained attention. *Mental Health, Religion and Culture* 2:59–70.

Van den Hurk PA, Giommi F, Gielen SC, et al. (2010). Greater efficiency in attentional processing related to mindfulness meditation. *Quarterly Journal of Experimental Psychology* 44:405–15.

Van Leeuwen S, Muller NG, Melloni L (2009). Age effects on attentional blink performance in meditation. *Consciousness and Cognition* 18:593–9.

Vandenberghe R, Gitelman DR, Parrish TB, Mesulam MM (2001). Functional specificity of superior parietal mediation of spatial shifting. *Neuroimage* 14:661–73.

Verhaeghen P, Cerella J, Basak C (2004). A working memory workout: How to expand the focus of serial attention from one to four items in 10 hours or less. *Journal of Experimental Psychology: Learning, Memory, and Cognition* 30:1322–37.

Yantis S, Schwarzbach J, Serences JT, et al. (2002). Transient neural activity in human parietal cortex during spatial attention shifts. *Nature Neuroscience* 5:995–1002.

Zeidan F, Johnson SK, Diamond BJ, et al. (2010). Mindfulness meditation improves cognition: Evidence of brief mental training. *Consciousness and Cognition* 19:597–605.

Part VI

The Future of
Working Memory

Training

14

Training Working Memory

SUSANNE M. JAEGGI
Department of Psychology, University of Maryland, College Park, MD, USA

MARTIN BUSCHKUEHL
Department of Psychology, The University of Michigan, Ann Arbor, MI, USA

HISTORICAL PERSPECTIVE

Background Information

Working memory (WM) is an essential system that underlies the performance of virtually all complex cognitive activities (cf. previous chapters in this book). Consider mentally multiplying 33 x 21, reading a complex paragraph, or following a lecture while simultaneously keeping up with the latest posts on social network communities. All of those tasks rely on deliberate WM processes in that they require multiple processing steps and temporary storage of intermediate results to accomplish the tasks at hand. Thus, WM can be seen as the cognitive mechanism that supports active maintenance of task-relevant information during the performance of a cognitive task. It has been shown that WM is predictive for a wide range of complex cognitive tasks such as planning or problem solving (Shah & Miyake, 1999), but also school-relevant tasks such as reading comprehension and math. In general, WM capacity is crucial for our general ability to acquire knowledge and learn new skills (Pickering, 2006).

There are large individual differences in WM capacity, that is, people differ in terms of how much information they can hold in WM, and also, how easily they can hold that information in the face of distraction (Engle, Kane, & Tuholski, 1999; Jonides, et al., 2008). Those individual differences are related to the fact that the functioning of the WM system is highly predictive of scholastic achievement and educational success (Pickering, 2006). It has been shown that WM is even better at predicting scholastic achievement than measures of intelligence, at least at an early age (Alloway & Alloway, 2010). Deficits in WM are considered as the primary source of cognitive impairment in numerous special needs populations ranging from attention deficit hyperactivity disorder (ADHD) to mathematics disability (Minear & Shah, 2006). Furthermore, it is one of the cognitive skills particularly affected by socioeconomic status (Noble, McCandliss, & Farah, 2007). And not only that, WM also has significant effects on classroom behavior. For example, children with lower WM capacity often forget teacher instructions, have difficulties staying on track with classroom tasks, and are easily distracted (Alloway et al., 2009). Teachers were more likely to rate children with poor WM capacity as more disruptive and inattentive (Gathercole, Lamont, & Alloway, 2006). In sum, WM is a crucial cognitive skill that is relevant for success in and out of schools.

Given the relevance of WM to daily life and educational settings, it is not surprising that a current major topic in Cognitive Science is the development of WM interventions (see Buschkuehl & Jaeggi, 2010; Klingberg, 2010; Lustig, Shah, Seidler, & Reuter-Lorenz, 2009; Shipstead, Redick, & Engle, 2010 for reviews). One of the aims in those interventions is not only to train participants' WM skills, but also to obtain generalizing effects that go beyond the trained domain, an effect which is termed "transfer."

In order to get a sense of what is meant by transfer, consider the following analogy: Physical training not only has an effect on trained activities, but also on activities that are not explicitly trained. For example, running on a regular basis can increase biking performance (Suter, Marti, & Gutzwiller, 1994), but more generally, running will improve performance on any activity that benefits from an efficient cardiovascular system and strong leg muscles, such as climbing stairs or swimming. This *transfer* from a trained to an untrained physical activity is, of course, very desirable as we do not have to perform a large variety of different physical activities in order to improve general fitness (Buschkuehl, Jaeggi, Shah, & Jonides, 2012). Although the existence of transfer in the physical domain is not surprising to anyone, demonstrating transfer from *cognitive* training has been difficult (see, e.g., Detterman, 1993; Owen et al., 2010; Salomon & Perkins, 1989; Singley & Anderson, 1989). This failure to demonstrate transfer in the cognitive domain is astonishing, given the fact that the study of transfer has been a central issue in learning theory and can be traced back to the beginning of the last century (Judd, 1908; Thorndike, 1906; Thorndike & Woodworth, 1901). Some authors conceptually divide transfer into the categories of "near" and "far" (e.g., Salomon & Perkins, 1989; Singley & Anderson, 1989; Willis, 2001). Near transfer refers to an effect of the trained task on a non-trained task that is closely related to it, perhaps only different on few features; far transfer refers to an effect of the trained task on a non-trained task that is quite different, perhaps sharing very few features. Unfortunately, as Salomon and Perkins (1989) point out, there is neither a formal definition nor an operational method to measure the distance of transfer although there are some attempts to do so (Barnett & Ceci, 2002). Nevertheless, it may be most useful to understand near and far transfer effects as two points on a continuum and to loosely use the distinction as a means to describe the intervention's impact (Woltz, Gardner, & Gyll, 2000). Although there is ample evidence for very near transfer effects, only a handful of studies provide evidence for far transfer effects (e.g., Zelinski, 2009). The common feature of many of these successful far transfer studies is that training has focused on improving WM. It might be easier to understand why those WM interventions should work if we refer back to the analogy in the physical domain we described earlier: If it can be assumed that WM takes the place of the cardiovascular system in the physical domain as an underlying entity of the cognitive system, then, as in physical training, training this underlying entity might lead to benefits in those tasks that rely on the functioning of this WM system.

In the following, we will review the state of the art of WM training and transfer, and further, discuss some of the possible underlying mechanisms that might drive transfer effects if they are found.

CURRENT EVIDENCE

How is The Field Changing?

Two of the first articles that focused on WM training were published by Klingberg and colleagues (Klingberg et al., 2005; Klingberg, Forssberg, & Westerberg, 2002). In their studies, they trained children with ADHD by means of a battery of computerized tasks targeting mainly WM processes. Since WM deficits are a central issue in children with ADHD, the rationale was to train WM in order to improve not only ADHD symptoms, but also to achieve transfer to other tasks which rely on WM. Indeed, both studies demonstrated that a five-week intervention resulted in transfer effects to non-trained WM tasks, and, most interestingly, to a test of matrix reasoning, a common proxy to measure fluid intelligence (Gf). In addition, they reported improvements in executive control (Stroop) and ADHD symptoms; however, those results were inconsistent between the two studies (but see Beck, Hanson, Puffenberger, Benninger, & Benninger, 2010 for a recent replication of ADHD symptom reductions).

However, the far transfer effects reported above do not seem to be easily replicated. For example, Holmes and collaborators were not able to replicate the far transfer effects in children with ADHD and with low WM capacity, respectively, even by using Klingberg et al.'s intervention (Holmes, Gathercole, & Dunning, 2009; Holmes et al., 2010). That is, although improvements in non-trained WM tasks were found consistently, there were no improvements in intelligence or scholastic achievement measures. In addition, Klingberg's group conducted two studies with typically developing preschoolers (Bergman Nutley et al., 2011: WM only group; Thorell, Lindqvist, Bergman Nutley, Bohlin, & Klingberg, 2009: WM group), but again, while both studies found benefits within the trained domain, there was no transfer to intelligence. Taken together, it seems that the training regimen developed by Klingberg and colleagues has some benefits, but those are most consistently expressed within the trained domain of WM and are therefore best described as near transfer effects.

Although somewhat promising, one drawback of the aforementioned approach is that it is hard to get at the underlying mechanisms of transfer, given the fact that the intervention relies on more than one training task. From an applied point of view, such a kitchen-sink approach is very useful since, first of all, it takes the notion of training variability into account, which increases learning (Schmidt & Bjork, 1992), and second, it increases the chances for a processing overlap between training and transfer tasks (Dahlin, Neely, Larsson, Backman, & Nyberg, 2008), and finally, task alternations might help to maintain motivation to train over a longer period of time. There are also other WM training batteries, i.e., interventions consisting of multiple training tasks, used in the literature, some of which are also successfully resulting in transfer, e.g., in the context of schizophrenia (see McGurk, Twamley, Sitzer, McHugo, & Mueser, 2007 for a meta-analysis), but also in healthy young and old adults (Schmiedek, Lövdén, & Lindenberger, 2010). On the other hand, there has been a recent large-scale study in which virtually no transfer was found (Owen et al., 2010).

Thus, in order to learn more about underlying mechanisms, the field needs more intervention studies in which only one training task is used. Of course, the drawback of such an approach might be that effect sizes are smaller and consequently transfer effects might be harder to detect. Nevertheless, there have been several studies using such an approach. For example, in two studies focusing on training young adults, we used an adaptive n-back task as a training vehicle and observed improvements in matrix reasoning tasks related to Gf (Jaeggi, Buschkuehl, Jonides, & Perrig, 2008; Jaeggi et al., 2010). Li and colleagues used a non-adaptive version of the n-back task to train old adults; however, they only found improvement within the trained domain (Li et al., 2008); and Dahlin and colleagues used a WM updating task and also only found transfer to non-trained WM tasks (Dahlin et al., 2008: young adults only). Others have used WM span-like training tasks and trained children, young adults, and old adults (Borella, Carretti, Riboldi, & De Beni, 2010; Buschkuehl et al., 2008; Chein & Morrison, 2010; Loosli, Buschkuehl, Perrig, & Jaeggi, 2012; Van der Molen, Van Luit, Van der Molen, Klugkist, & Jongmans, 2010); all of them found transfer within the trained WM domain, and some even reported far transfer effects, e.g., to reading-related processes (Chein & Morrison, 2010; Loosli et al., 2012). However, none of these studies has found improvements in measures of intelligence, except for one study, which differs from the others in terms of an extremely short training time (Borella et al., 2010; but see also Karbach & Kray, 2009).

What have we learned from intervention studies targeting WM? First of all, WM training is promising in that there are clear indications for generalizing effects. It seems that the most consistent domains in which transfer can be expected is in related, but non-trained WM tasks, a fact which is nevertheless astonishing in itself given the common assumption that WM capacity is rather fixed (e.g., Cowan, 2005; Oberauer, 2006). There is also accumulating evidence for far transfer effects, for example in the domain of executive control (Klingberg et al., 2005; Klingberg et al., 2002; Thorell et al., 2009), reading (Chein & Morrison, 2010; Loosli et al., 2012), and even Gf (Borella et al., 2010; Jaeggi et al., 2008; Jaeggi et al., 2010; Klingberg et al., 2005; Klingberg et al., 2002; Schmiedek et al., 2010). Unfortunately, until now, there has been no evidence that WM training extends beyond laboratory tasks such as to direct measures of scholastic achievement or real-world tasks (notable exceptions might be symptom reductions in ADHD and psychosocial functioning in schizophrenia; e.g., Beck et al., 2010; Klingberg et al., 2005; Klingberg et al.,

2002; McGurk et al., 2007). In sum, at the current state of knowledge, little is known about the extent of generalization, and whether there are differential effects as a function of the various intervention approaches used.

Another open question concerns the optimal scheduling and duration of training. We have shown that there is a dose-response effect of training suggesting larger transfer effects with longer training time (Jaeggi et al., 2008). Further, it seems that interventions that last about a month are most frequently used; however, there are shorter WM interventions that have benefits as well (e.g., Borella et al., 2010; Loosli et al., 2012), and there are interventions that even last as much as a couple of months (Schmiedek et al., 2010). Nevertheless, the optimal duration of a successful intervention is still largely unknown, and also, whether certain spacing intervals might boost the training effect (Cepeda, Pashler, Vul, Wixted, & Rohrer, 2006), and finally, whether there is an upper limit that participants might achieve.

Further, it is still unresolved whether and which transfer effects last beyond the training period, and if so, for how long. Only a handful of studies have tested the long-term effects of training by re-testing the experimental and control groups some time after training completion (Borella et al., 2010; Buschkuehl et al., 2008; Klingberg et al., 2005; Van der Molen et al., 2010). There is some evidence for long-term effects of the training, but other effects, such as transfer effects that are only present at follow-up but not at post-test ("sleeper effects"), are hard to interpret (Van der Molen et al., 2010). However, in order to achieve any or stronger long-term effects, it might be that as in physical exercise, behavior therapy, or learning processes in general, occasional practice or booster sessions might be necessary in order to maximize retention (e.g., Ball et al., 2002; Bell et al., 2008; Cepeda et al., 2006; Haskell et al., 2007; Whisman, 1990).

FOR WHOM WORKING MEMORY TRAINING WORKS AND WHY

In Search of Mechanisms

Concluding from the literature reviewed above, generalizing effects following WM training are observed over a wide population range, from typically developing pre-schoolers (Bergman Nutley et al., 2011; Thorell et al., 2009), school-aged children (Loosli et al., 2012), to young adults (Chein & Morrison, 2010; Jaeggi et al., 2008; Jaeggi et al., 2010), and old adults (Borella et al., 2010; Buschkuehl et al., 2008; Dahlin et al., 2008; Li et al., 2008; Schmiedek, et al., 2010). Further, there is evidence that WM training is also effective in special needs populations with pre-existing WM deficits, such as ADHD (Holmes et al., 2010; Klingberg et al., 2005), learning disabilities (Holmes et al., 2009; Van der Molen et al., 2010), and even schizophrenia (McGurk et al., 2007). The question is now for whom the training works best. By directly comparing young and old adults, it seems harder to demonstrate transfer in old adults (Dahlin et al., 2008; Li et al., 2008; Schmiedek et al., 2010). That is, advanced age and thus, limitations in plasticity might be a restricting factor for training and transfer. Consequently, it might be that transfer is more likely for those participants who are already high functioning. However, the successful training studies with special needs populations proved otherwise, and further, our own research has shown that it is those individuals who start off with lowest scores who profit the most, presumably because they have more room to improve (Jaeggi et al., 2008).

Despite the accumulating evidence that there are generalizing effects, we only have a very vague idea *why* those transfer effects occur, a stage that is very similar to where psychotherapy research was at some years ago (Kopta, Lueger, Saunders, & Howard, 1999). Thus, with the current knowledge, we can only speculate about the possible underlying mechanisms of training and transfer. As Chein and Morrison (2010) pointed out, there are many reasons why participants could perform better after training, such as, for example, changes in strategies, improved executive control or speed of processing, pre-existing individual differences and motivational factors, or simply familiarity with the stimuli and improved test-taking skills. The question is now whether we can derive some general principles from the existing literature that might shed some light on the underlying mechanisms, and with that, provide some guidelines as to how to make an intervention most effective.

In general, it seems that in order to obtain transfer, the intervention should minimize the development of explicit strategies and skills that are specific to the task in question because the object of training must be changes in the information processing system, not changes in the way one particular task is performed. Indeed, it has been shown that strategy training usually only leads to very narrow transfer (Ericsson & Delaney, 1998; Neely & Backman, 1993, 1995; but see Carretti, Borella, & De Beni, 2007; St Clair-Thompson, Stevens, Hunt, & Bolder, 2010). A related principle is also that there should be variability in training tasks so individuals may develop more flexible strategies rather than strategies that are only applicable to the trained task alone (Schmidt & Bjork, 1992). This principle probably accounts for some of the success of intervention studies that combine different tasks and types of training interventions (such as Bergman Nutley et al., 2011; Klingberg et al., 2005, 2002; McGurk et al., 2007; Schmiedek et al., 2010; Thorell et al., 2009).

Another approach to induce task variability within the same task is to incorporate various difficulty levels (Jaeggi et al., 2008, 2010), as well as varying material and contexts to the same training task. This can be achieved by using an adaptive training method that continuously adjusts the current training difficulty to the actual performance of each subject (see Tallal et al., 1996 for a pioneering study). This principle may be critically important for WM training in that it also adds to the motivational features of the task in that it is never too challenging and thus, overwhelming, but at the same time not too easy so that participants get bored and disengage from the task. Indeed, studies that have not utilized adaptive training programs failed to show transfer (cf. Craik et al., 2007; Klingberg et al., 2005, 2002: control groups).

Another important mechanism might be that training and transfer tasks need to share a common processing basis (Jaeggi et al., 2008; Jonides, 2004), which might apply to both the cognitive as well as the neural domain. Indeed, it has been shown that transfer occurs if the training and the transfer task engage overlapping brain regions, but not if they engage different regions (Dahlin et al., 2008; see Lustig & Reuter-Lorenz, Chapter 15 in this volume, for more about underlying brain mechanisms of training).

To conclude, in order to advance the field, it is important to increase the current knowledge by conducting studies using well-defined training tasks, broad transfer assessments, as well as follow-up measurements in the experimental and control groups. Ideally, those control groups should engage in activities that are as similar as possible to the experimental group (also in terms of motivational features), except for the process of interest, although no-contact control groups might be useful in some instances as well (Chein & Morrison, 2010; Shipstead et al., 2010; Willis, 2001). In those future studies, more fine-grained and nuanced analyses are needed in order to determine and disentangle possible predictors and moderators for training and transfer success. However, one has to keep in mind that the logistics for running intervention studies are usually very challenging, expensive, and time consuming. Therefore, progress may not take place as quickly in this field as it does in others. Nevertheless, despite some prominent null-effects (Owen et al., 2010), some of the studies reviewed here are clearly promising. But future researchers and users should keep in mind what probably applies to both researchers and participants, in particular that it needs persistence in order to be successful (Ericsson, 2003).

REFERENCES

Alloway, T. P., & Alloway, R. G. (2010). Investigating the predictive roles of working memory and IQ in academic attainment. *Journal of Experimental Child Psychology, 106*(1), 20–29.

Alloway, T. P., Gathercole, S. E., Kirkwood, H., & Elliott, J. (2009). The cognitive and behavioral characteristics of children with low working memory. *Child Development, 80*(2), 606–621.

Ball, K., Berch, D. B., Helmers, K. F., Jobe, J. B., Leveck, M. D., Marsiske, M., et al. (2002). Effects of cognitive training interventions with older adults: A randomized controlled trial. *JAMA, 288*(18), 2271–2281.

Barnett, S. M., & Ceci, S. J. (2002). When and where do we apply what we learn? A taxonomy for far transfer. *Psychological Bulletin, 128*(4), 612–637.

Beck, S. J., Hanson, C. A., Puffenberger, S. S., Benninger, K. L., & Benninger, W. B. (2010). A controlled trial of working memory training for children and adolescents with ADHD. *Journal of Clinical Child and Adolescent Psychology, 39*(6), 825–836.

Bell, D. S., Harless, C. E., Higa, J. K., Bjork, E. L., Bjork, R. A., Bazargan, M., et al. (2008). Knowledge retention after an online tutorial: A randomized educational experiment among resident physicians. *Journal of General Internal Medicine, 23*(8), 1164–1171.

Bergman Nutley, S., Soderqvist, S., Bryde, S., Thorell, L. B., Humphreys, K., & Klingberg, T. (2011). Gains in fluid intelligence after training non-verbal reasoning in 4-year-old children: A controlled, randomized study. *Developmental Science, 14*(3), 591–601.

Borella, E., Carretti, B., Riboldi, F., & De Beni, R. (2010). Working memory training in older adults: Evidence of transfer and maintenance effects. *Psychology and Aging, 25*(4), 767–778.

Buschkuehl, M., & Jaeggi, S. M. (2010). Improving intelligence: A literature review. *Swiss Medical Weekly, 140*(19–20), 266–272.

Buschkuehl, M., Jaeggi, S. M., Hutchison, S., Perrig-Chiello, P., Dapp, C., Muller, M., et al. (2008). Impact of working memory training on memory performance in old-old adults. *Psychology and Aging, 23*(4), 743–753.

Buschkuehl, M., Jaeggi, S. M., Shah, P., & Jonides, J. (2012). Working memory training and transfer. In R. Subotnik, A. Robinson, C. Callahan & E. J. Gubbins (Eds.), *Malleable minds: Translating insights from psychology and neuroscience to gifted education* (pp. 101–115). Storrs, ST: National Center for Research on Giftedness and Talent, University of Connecticut.

Carretti, B., Borella, E., & De Beni, R. (2007). Does strategic memory training improve the working memory performance of younger and older adults? *Experimental Psychology, 54*(4), 311–320.

Cepeda, N. J., Pashler, H., Vul, E., Wixted, J. T., & Rohrer, D. (2006). Distributed practice in verbal recall tasks: A review and quantitative synthesis. *Psychological Bulletin, 132*(3), 354–380.

Chein, J. M., & Morrison, A. B. (2010). Expanding the mind's workspace: Training and transfer effects with a complex working memory span task. *Psychonomic Bulletin and Review, 17*(2), 193–199.

Cowan, N. (2005). *Working memory capacity*. New York: Psychology Press.

Craik, F. I., Winocur, G., Palmer, H., Binns, M. A., Edwards, M., Bridges, K., et al. (2007). Cognitive rehabilitation in the elderly: Effects on memory. *Journal of the International Neuropsychological Society, 13*(1), 132–142.

Dahlin, E., Neely, A. S., Larsson, A., Backman, L., & Nyberg, L. (2008). Transfer of learning after updating training mediated by the striatum. *Science, 320*(5882), 1510–1512.

Detterman, D. K. (1993). The case for prosecution: Transfer as an epiphenomenon. In D. K. Detterman & R. J. Sternberg (Eds.), *Transfer on trial: Intelligence, cognition, and instruction* (pp. 1–24). Norwood, NJ: Ablex Publishing Corporation.

Engle, R. W., Kane, M. J., & Tuholski, S. W. (1999). Individual differences in working memory capacity and what they tell us about controlled attention, general fluid intelligence, and functions of the prefrontal cortex. In A. Miyake & P. Shah (Eds.), *Models of working memory: Mechanisms of active maintenance and executive control* (pp. 102–134). Cambridge: Cambridge University Press.

Ericsson, K. A. (2003). Deliberate practice and the acquisition and maintenance of expert performance in medicine and related domains. *Academic Medicine, 79*(10), S70–S81.

Ericsson, K. A., & Delaney, P. F. (1998). Working memory and expert performance. In R. Logie & K. J. Gilhooly (Eds.), *Working memory and thinking* (pp. 93–114). Hillsdale, NJ: Erlbaum.

Gathercole, S. E., Lamont, E., & Alloway, T. P. (2006). Working memory in the classroom. In S. Pickering (Ed.), *Working memory and education* (pp. 219–240). Oxford, UK: Elsevier Press.

Haskell, W. L., Lee, I. M., Pate, R. R., Powell, K. E., Blair, S. N., Franklin, B. A., et al. (2007). Physical activity and public health: Updated recommendation for adults from the American college of sports medicine and the American heart association. *Circulation, 116*(9), 1081–1093.

Holmes, J., Gathercole, S. E., & Dunning, D. L. (2009). Adaptive training leads to sustained enhancement of poor working memory in children. *Developmental Science, 12*(4), F9–F15.

Holmes, J., Gathercole, S. E., Place, M., Dunning, D. L., Hilton, K. A., & Elliott, J. G. (2010). Working memory deficits can be overcome: Impacts of training and medication on working memory in children with ADHD. *Applied Cognitive Psychology, 24*(6), 827–836.

Jaeggi, S. M., Buschkuehl, M., Jonides, J., & Perrig, W. J. (2008). Improving fluid intelligence with training on working memory. *Proceedings of the Natural Academy of Sciences of the USA, 105*(19), 6829–6833.

Jaeggi, S. M., Studer-Luethi, B., Buschkuehl, M., Su, Y.-F., Jonides, J., & Perrig, W. J. (2010). The relationship between n-back performance and matrix reasoning: Implications for training and transfer. *Intelligence, 38*(6), 625–635.

Jonides, J. (2004). How does practice makes perfect? *Nature Neuroscience, 7*(1), 10–11.

Jonides, J., Lewis, R. L., Nee, D. E., Lustig, C., Berman, M. G., & Moore, K. S. (2008). The mind and brain of short-term memory. *Annual Review of Psychology, 59*, 193–224.

Judd, C. H. (1908). The relation of special training and general intelligence. *Educational Review, 36*, 28–42.

Karbach, J., & Kray, J. (2009). How useful is executive control training? Age differences in near and far transfer of task-switching training. *Developmental Science, 12*(6), 978–990.

Klingberg, T. (2010). Training and plasticity of working memory. *Trends in Cognitive Sciences, 14*(7), 317–324.

Klingberg, T., Fernell, E., Olesen, P. J., Johnson, M., Gustafsson, P., Dahlstrom, K., et al. (2005). Computerized training of working memory in children with ADHD: A randomized, controlled trial. *Journal of the American Academy of Child and Adolescent Psychiatry, 44*(2), 177–186.

Klingberg, T., Forssberg, H., & Westerberg, H. (2002). Training of working memory in children with ADHD. *Journal of Clinical and Experimental Neuropsychology, 24*(6), 781–791.

Kopta, S. M., Lueger, R. J., Saunders, S. M., & Howard, K. I. (1999). Individual psychotherapy outcome and process research: Challenges leading to greater turmoil or a positive transition? *Annual Review of Psychology, 50*, 441–469.

Li, S. C., Schmiedek, F., Huxhold, O., Rocke, C., Smith, J., & Lindenberger, U. (2008). Working memory plasticity in old age: Practice gain, transfer, and maintenance. *Psychology and Aging, 23*(4), 731–742.

Loosli, S. V., Buschkuehl, M., Perrig, W. J., & Jaeggi, S. M. (2012). Working memory training improves reading processes in typically developing children. *Child Neuropsychology, 18*(1), 62–78.

Lustig, C., Shah, P., Seidler, R., & Reuter-Lorenz, P. A. (2009). Aging, training, and the brain: A review and future directions. *Neuropsychology Review, 19*(4), 504–522.

McGurk, S. R., Twamley, E. W., Sitzer, D. I., McHugo, G. J., & Mueser, K. T. (2007). A meta-analysis of cognitive remediation in schizophrenia. *American Journal of Psychiatry, 164*(12), 1791–1802.

Minear, M., & Shah, P. (2006). Sources of working memory deficits in children and possibilities for remediation. In S. Pickering (Ed.), *Working memory and education* (pp. 274–307). Oxford, UK: Elsevier Press.

Neely, A. S., & Backman, L. (1993). Maintenance of gains following multifactorial and unifactorial memory training in late adulthood. *Educational Gerontology, 19*(2), 105–117.

Neely, A. S., & Backman, L. (1995). Effects of multifactorial memory training in old-age: Generalizability across tasks and individuals. *Journals of Gerontology Series B: Psychological Sciences and Social Sciences, 50*(3), 134–140.

Noble, K. G., McCandliss, B. D., & Farah, M. J. (2007). Socioeconomic gradients predict individual differences in neurocognitive abilities. *Developmental Science, 10*(4), 464–480.

Oberauer, K. (2006). Is the focus of attention in working memory expanded through practice? *Journal of Experimental Psychology: Learning, Memory, and Cognition, 32*(2), 197–214.

Owen, A. M., Hampshire, A., Grahn, J. A., Stenton, R., Dajani, S., Burns, A. S., et al. (2010). Putting brain training to the test. *Nature, 465*(7299), 775–778.

Pickering, S. (Ed.). (2006). *Working memory and education*. Oxford, UK: Elsevier Press.

Salomon, G., & Perkins, D. N. (1989). Rocky roads to transfer: Rethinking mechanisms of a neglected phenomenon. *Educational Psychologist, 24*(2), 113–142.

Schmidt, R. A., & Bjork, R. A. (1992). New conceptualizations of practice: Common principles in three paradigms suggest new concepts for training. *Psychological Science, 3*(4), 207–217.

Schmiedek, F., Lövdén, M., & Lindenberger, U. (2010). Hundred days of cognitive training enhance broad cognitive abilities in adulthood: Findings from the COGITO study. *Frontiers in Aging Neuroscience, 2*, 27.

Shah, P., & Miyake, A. (1999). Models of working memory: An introduction. In A. Miyake & P. Shah (Eds.), *Models of working memory: Mechanism of active maintenance and executive control* (pp. 1–26). New York: Cambridge University Press.

Shipstead, Z., Redick, T. S., & Engle, R. W. (2010). Does working memory training generalize? *Psychologica Belgica, 50*(3&4), 245–276.

Singley, M. K., & Anderson, J. R. (1989). *The transfer of cognitive skill*. Cambridge, MA: Harvard University Press.

St Clair-Thompson, H., Stevens, R., Hunt, A., & Bolder, E. (2010). Improving children's working memory and classroom performance. *Educational Psychology, 30*(2), 203–219.

Suter, E., Marti, B., & Gutzwiller, F. (1994). Jogging or walking: Comparison of health effects. *Annals of Epidemiology, 4*(5), 375–381.

Tallal, P., Miller, S. L., Bedi, G., Byma, G., Wang, X., Nagarajan, S. S., et al. (1996). Language comprehension in language-learning impaired children improved with acoustically modified speech. *Science, 271*(5245), 81–84.

Thorell, L. B., Lindqvist, S., Bergman Nutley, S., Bohlin, G., & Klingberg, T. (2009). Training and transfer effects of executive functions in preschool children. *Developmental Science, 12*(1), 106–113.

Thorndike, E. L. (1906). *The principles of teaching, based on psychology*. New York: Seiler.

Thorndike, E. L., & Woodworth, R. S. (1901). The influence of improvement in one mental function upon the efficiency of other functions. *Psychological Review, 8*, 247–261.

Van der Molen, M. J., Van Luit, J. E. H., Van der Molen, M. W., Klugkist, I., & Jongmans, M. J. (2010). Effectiveness of a computerised working memory training in adolescents with mild to borderline intellectual disabilities. *Journal of Intellectual Disability Research, 54*(4), 433–447.

Whisman, M. A. (1990). The efficacy of booster maintenance sessions in behavior therapy: Review and methodological critique. *Clinical Psychology Review, 10*(2), 155–170.

Willis, S. L. (2001). Methodological issues in behavioral intervention research with the elderly. In J. E. Birren & K. W. Schaie (Eds.), *Handbook of the psychology of aging* (5th ed., pp. 78–108). San Diego, CA: Academic Press.

Woltz, D. J., Gardner, M. K., & Gyll, S. P. (2000). The role of attention processes in near transfer of cognitive skills. *Learning and Individual Differences, 12*, 209–251.

Zelinski, E. M. (2009). Far transfer in cognitive training of older adults. *Restorative Neurology and Neuroscience, 27*(5), 455–471.

15

Training Working Memory

Insights from Neuroimaging

CINDY LUSTIG

Department of Psychology, University of Michigan, Ann Arbor, MI, USA

PATRICIA A. REUTER-LORENZ

Department of Psychology, University of Michigan, Ann Arbor, MI, USA

BACKGROUND INFORMATION

Insights from Neuroimaging

As noted by every chapter in this book, working memory (WM) is a major hub of human cognition. It varies widely across individuals and in the same individuals across the lifespan, and this variation in WM accounts for variance in math ability, language comprehension, intelligence, reasoning, and career success (Altshuler et al., 2007; Daneman & Merikle, 1996; Gold et al., 2002; Kyllonen and Christal, 1990). Not surprisingly, then, the training literature has taken a great interest in WM, both as an outcome measure targeted for transfer in general training programs and as a specific function to be trained with the hopes of transferring the benefits to other domains.

One major challenge in this line of research is that definitions of WM, and training programs, differ in their emphasis on storage/capacity versus executive processes. There is even disagreement about whether capacity and executive processes are separable (cf., Blair et al., 2011; Jarrold et al., 2011; Unsworth et al., 2009). Another challenge is to determine whether training should focus on improving processes—perhaps without the participants' intentional engagement of those processes—or on improving the use and efficiency of strategies. Such broader issues are discussed in the chapter by Jaeggi and Buschkuehl. Our focus here is the neuroimaging perspective, addressing both how WM training affects the brain and how neuroimaging findings may be used to create more effective training programs.

CURRENT EVIDENCE

Neuroimaging as an Outcome

Neuroimaging as an outcome measure may at first seem extraneous—isn't the goal to improve behavior? However, as we describe below, by informing us about where and how things change in the brain, neuroimaging can provide insights about underlying mechanisms of training-related change difficult to ascertain through behavior alone.

Structural brain changes.   Structural measurements have a reliability advantage when assessing training-related changes because they are less likely than behavioral or activation measures to be affected by motivation, circadian influences, and other sources of noise. Training programs that produce structural changes also have a high promise for transfer. Just as muscle bulk and cardiovascular fitness improved in the gym enhance physical performance in other settings, brain structures augmented by training could have potential benefits outside the training regimen.

Cardiovascular training increases gray and white matter volume and/or integrity, especially in older participants who were sedentary before the training program (e.g., Bugg & Head, 2011; Bullitt et al., 2009; Colcombe et al., 2006; Erickson et al., 2011). In fact, prefrontal regions strongly associated with the executive functions of working memory (see Hillman et al., 2008 for review) are among those most sensitive to cardiovascular fitness.

The use of structural measures to specifically assess WM training is still relatively rare. In one example, Lovden et al. (2010) trained young and old adults on a number of tasks including WM, episodic memory, and perceptual speed. For both age groups, training resulted in increased anterior cingulate volume and increased white-matter integrity in the anterior corpus callosum. Somewhat more common are studies examining activities that rely heavily on WM processes (e.g., juggling, piano playing, games), either in a formal training environment or using naturalistic comparison groups (e.g., musicians versus non-musicians; see Lustig et al., 2009 for a review and discussion of caveats).

Overall, structural studies indicate an increase in the size or integrity of the brain regions involved in the trained or otherwise affected (as in cardiovascular training) structures of interest. However, the evidence also suggests that training must be maintained in order for these increases to be maintained (Boyke et al., 2008; Draganski et al., 2004). A potential downside of structural outcome measures is that current methods have limited sensitivity, meaning that only relatively large changes may be detectable. Given advantages in reliability and potential generalization, this is a promising area for future development as technical advances become available.

Activation changes

Background: The CRUNCH Framework for Interpreting Activation Ups and Downs.

Activation changes and individual differences in activation levels can be difficult to interpret. Increased activations may reflect neurovascular changes (especially after cardiovascular training) or increased engagement of processes with which that region is involved. In between-subjects comparisons, it is often unclear whether greater activation is beneficial or symptomatic of an inefficient system (see Reuter-Lorenz & Lustig, 2005 and many others for review). Decreased activation may reflect either a failure to engage task-necessary processes or an increased efficiency of processing.

CRUNCH (Compensation-Related Utilization of Neural Circuits Hypothesis; Reuter-Lorenz & Cappell, 2008) provides a useful framework for resolving these ambiguities. CRUNCH is based on the well-founded assumption that activation of task-relevant regions increases with increasing task demand. In other words, activation provides an index of resource utilization. CRUNCH also assumes a resource ceiling: activation can increase up to a particular level of task demand, after which it will asymptote, or decline. Decline may be observed when task demand exceeds resource supply and performance suffers as task-related processing becomes disorganized or the individual disengages from the task. In short, CRUNCH incorporates the constraints of performance and demand level.

Figure 15.1 shows how performance and activation would vary for young and old adults in the CRUNCH framework. At low levels of task demand, the groups show equivalent performance, but older adults have higher levels of activation. As each group reaches its maximal activation point—or "crunch point"—performance declines. This pattern has been observed by several WM studies (Cappell et al., 2010; Mattay et al., 2006; Schneider-Garces et al., 2010). In the hypothetical region

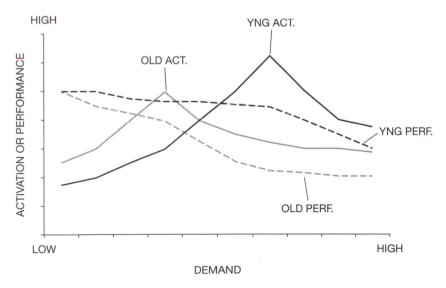

Figure 15.1   Idealized CRUNCH patterns for young and old adults

illustrated here, young adults also have a greater maximum level of activation—this may occur, for example, in prefrontal regions as a result of age-related declines in prefrontal volume and integrity.

Figure 15.2 shows CRUNCH predictions for how activation might shift after relatively short-term behavioral training that increases the efficiency of processing but does not result in substantial changes in volume or integrity of the region. As seen here, training is predicted to shift activation-demand functions to the right, increasing the dynamic range of task demand to which that region can respond. Cardiovascular or other forms of training that result in significant structural changes might also increase the maximal level of activation. Finally, CRUNCH is most simply applied at the regional level, but changes at one region may influence other regions in the task-related network. For example, as described in several studies below, training may shift processing load, and thus activation, from dorsolateral fronto-parietal regions involved in general cognitive control processes to ventrolateral or subcortical regions more specific to the processes that were the target of training.

Increases.   The CRUNCH framework predicts that increased activation of either general fronto-parietal control systems, more task-specific networks, or both (without decreases in other aspects of the task network) should be found when low baseline performance reflects inadequate recruitment of the task-necessary processes, and task-relevant processing is increased during training.

Consistent with this prediction, increases in activation after training are often found in patient groups who have inadequate or dysfunctional recruitment of front-parietal systems prior to training. For example, schizophrenia is often associated with "hypofrontality," or reduced activation of prefrontal systems compared to a

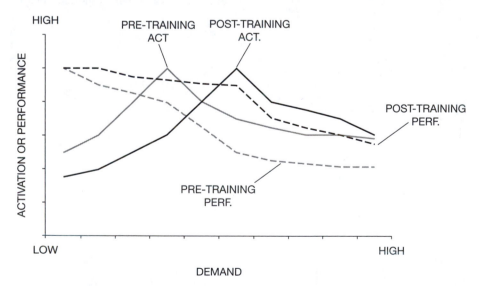

Figure 15.2   Idealized shift in CRUNCH patterns following a behavioral training intervention that does not result in large changes in brain structure

control group during tasks that make high demands on WM, especially those that tap executive-control processes (e.g., Barch et al., 2002; see review by Minzenberg et al., 2009). Several studies have shown that WM training can improve patients' performance and increase activation in prefrontal systems (Haut et al., 2010; Wexler et al., 2000; Wykes et al., 2002). In some cases (Haut et al., Wexler et al.), increases in prefrontal activation correlated with improved performance, bolstering the interpretation that increased activation reflected the increased engagement of task-beneficial processes. Importantly, Haut et al. tested both positive transfer tasks (other working memory tasks of a different format than the training procedure) and a control transfer task (lexical decision) hypothesized to have minimal overlap with the processes targeted during training. This, along with the use of active control groups consisting of participants who engaged in activities formally similar to the training program but without the WM component, allowed them to interpret the activation changes as being specifically related to improvements in WM, rather than nonspecific increases in stimulus familiarity, attention, or motivation.

Similar training-related increases in performance and prefrontal activation have been observed in individuals with attention deficit/hyperactivity disorder, which is often associated with both structural abnormalities and hypoactivation in prefrontal cortex (Seidman et al., 2004). Hoekzema et al. (2010) noted that a training program that increased response inhibition and selective attention increased activation in regions that also show activity increases in response to medication, suggesting that training helped to repair processing dysfunctions imposed by the disorder. In healthy, college-age adults, activation increases have been observed after visual working training that required acquisition of new categories or skills (Westerberg & Klingberg, 2007).

Decreases.   Decreases in activity may reflect either an increased efficiency of processing or a decreased use of the processes subserved by activated regions. As Klingberg (2010) observed, overall activity decreases are usually only seen in short, one-session training studies. This pattern likely reflects increased efficiency in the specifics of the trained task, rather than long-term training of more general WM processes. Repetition of items can also result in priming and activity reductions, but again, familiarization with materials and procedures is not typically considered to be training. In summary, simple decreases more often reflect priming or practice effects that lead to temporary facilitation, rather than the long-term benefits normally implied by the term "training."

Shifts   Working memory training most often results in shifts in activation, rather than simple increases or decreases. In most cases, training results in a reduction of activation in domain-general fronto-parietal control networks, and a concomitant increase in activation in more specialized regions. This pattern is seen both in training regimens that target WM processes per se, and those that target complex cognitive activities with a heavy WM component. For example, in a series of studies conducted by Dahlin and colleagues (see review by Dahlin et al., 2009), training the WM process of updating increased activity in subcortical regions, especially striatum, specifically associated with the updating process. In contrast, activity in more lateral fronto-parietal regions was reduced. In a study of dual-task training, Erickson and colleagues (2007a) found that a general fronto-parietal network decreased in activity for both the trained group and a matched control group, suggesting that simple practice effects made some contribution to activity reductions, but a subset of these regions showed greater decreases for the training group, indicating more specific effects. Further, only the training group showed an increase in inferior and middle frontal gyrus regions that correlated with improved performance. These results are consistent with the idea that training resulted in a reduced demand on general executive processing networks facilitated by an increased contribution of regions specifically involved in the targeted cognitive process.

Another study by this group (Erickson et al., 2007b) provides an interesting example of how brain imaging provides information about how training changes underlying cognitive processes that would be difficult to derive from behavioral data. After single- and dual-task training, young and old adults showed similar improvements in accuracy and response time. However, for the dual-task condition of interest from a WM perspective, there were large group differences in activation both at baseline and in the direction of training-related changes. That is, before training, older adults underactivated ventral prefrontal cortex (vPFC) and over-activated dorsal PFC (dPFC) relative to young adults. For young adults, training resulted in a drop in right vPFC activation and increases in bilateral dPFC activation. Older adults had a parallel drop in right vPFC activity, but increased activation in left vPFC, and decreased activation in dPFC. In sum, after training, activation levels in left vPFC and bilateral dPFC appeared to converge for the two age groups. This suggests that for both groups, training resulted in a re-balancing of general cognitive control processes versus those involved in the maintenance of the different task sets (see Badre, 2008; Dosenbach et al., 2008, for a discussion of dorsal versus ventral cognitive control processes), but in different directions. An interesting question from the CRUNCH perspective is whether the converging activation patterns for the two groups indicated that each had reached an asymptote associated with optimal performance, or whether continued training might have led their functions to diverge. Similar re-balancing interactions with baseline have also been observed in brain-damaged individuals (Chen et al., 2011).

There appears to be a common pattern of decreased activation in general cognitive-control regions accompanied by increased activation in more specialized task-related regions. This pattern may provide some clue as to why transfer effects are often frustratingly narrow: Task-specific processes are being strengthened rather than more general executive functions. Therefore, only transfer tasks that also strongly engage those specialized processes should show benefits—a point to which we return in the section on neuroimaging as a guide to training. Indeed, training programs that involve the acquisition of a new skill (e.g., hypothesis generation: Kwon et al., 2009; Grabner et al., 2009) show the reverse re-balancing pattern, increased activation in dorsal prefrontal and parietal regions and decreased activation in task-specific regions. These training programs might strengthen more general executive processes and thus produce broader transfer. Although this hypothesis has not been directly tested, it receives some support from the finding that multi-modal training programs that involve many activities are often more successful in producing broad transfer (see Chapter 14, Jaeggi & Buschkuehl). This suggests that the specific content of such multi-modal programs may matter less than the degree to which they require the acquisition of and switches between multiple new task sets.

Although cardiovascular training generally leads to positive behavioral effects on executive-function tasks, the results for WM are mixed (see meta-analytic review by Smith et al., 2010). The work of Kramer and colleagues has suggested greater fronto-parietal activation during executive-demanding tasks for individuals who are more cardiovascularly fit (Colcombe et al., 2004b), but randomized control trials are rare and have conflicting results (Colcombe et al., 2004a; Voelcker-Rehage et al., 2011). Colcombe et al. found that older adults in a walking intervention had increased activity in fronto-parietal regions and decreased activity in anterior cingulate, whereas Voelcker-Rehage et al. used a very similar paradigm and found general decreases in activity. In their study, older adults received cardiovascular, coordination, or relaxation/stretching training for a year. Cardiovascular and coordination training resulted in similar performance improvements compared to the relaxation group, but different patterns of activation during a flanker task used to assess executive functions. Cardiovascular training resulted in decreased activity throughout the brain, whereas coordination training resulted in a re-balancing pattern of reduced activation in several fronto-parietal regions and increased activation in regions associated with visuospatial attention. The authors suggest that the decreases in fronto-parietal activity in cardiovascular training may have reflected increased physiological efficiency of those regions, whereas superficially similar decreases observed after coordination training resulted from a reduced load on those regions due to strengthened visuospatial processing. Although not tested in that study, an interesting corollary of this conclusion is that cardiovascular training should result in improved performance across a range of executive transfer tasks, whereas the benefits for coordination training might be restricted to those transfer tasks that place demands on visuospatial attention.

Training WM processes may also result in shifts in the timing or dynamics of activation. For example, Kelley and Yantis (2010) found that training reduced behavioral vulnerability to both trained and untrained distracters, coupled with prefrontal activation changes that differed according to distracter type. Distracters used in training resulted in a reduced middle frontal gyrus response, ascribed to filtering at earlier stages of processing. In contrast, new distracters resulted in an enhanced response after training, potentially reflecting training-related increases in distracter suppression. In another set of studies, Braver and colleagues (2009) demonstrated that the executive-control deficits of several populations (e.g., older adults, schizophrenic patients) are characterized by a late-stage (reactive) engagement of cognitive control, rather than the early-stage, preparatory engagement of control typically displayed by healthy young adults. This pattern can be reversed by training, and in schizophrenics this reversal predicts improvements in clinical symptoms of disorganized behavior (Braver et al., 2009; Edwards et al., 2010; Paxton et al., 2006).

Other changes   Our literature search did not find reports of changes in functional connectivity or resting-state activity associated specifically with working memory training. However, results from training in related domains (e.g., cardiovascular training, attention training, motor skills training) suggest this as a promising area of research. Likewise, there has been little systematic use of pattern-classification methods to assess the brain outcomes of WM training, but recent evidence suggests that such methods may be useful for distinguishing between different types of cognitive control (Esterman et al., 2009) or the integrity of the representations being manipulated as part of a WM task (e.g., Lewis-Peacock & Postle, 2008; Stokes et al., 2009). The CRUNCH framework is applicable to multivariate analyses of imaging results from WM tasks (Carp et al., 2010), and might be extended to connectivity measures to the extent that connectivity provides an index of resource utilization.

We also found only a few studies using EEG/ERP methods to assess training outcomes specifically in WM. Berry et al. (2010) found that decreased occipital EEG measures (N1 amplitude) following perceptual-discrimination training in older adults predicted performance improvements on a WM task with perceptually demanding stimuli (moving-dot kinetograms), suggesting that an increased efficiency of bottom-up processing was the source of behavioral improvement. In a study targeting executive-control functions, Horowitz-Kraus & Breznitz (2009) found that training WM skills increased the amplitude of the error-related negativity, and that this increase predicted reduced errors on WM tasks. Particularly interesting from the CRUNCH perspective, Neubauer et al. (2004) found that individuals with high scores on intelligence tests had greater values on several EEG measures of fronto-parietal activation at their first exposure to a reasoning test, and greater decreases in such activations after training. This suggests that these individuals engaged high levels of control at early learning stages (similar to proactive control as proposed by Braver and colleagues (2009)), but were able to become more efficient with training. Finally, neurofeedback techniques that allow participants to observe their own brain activity online may help individuals optimize both performance and brain function during training (e.g., Vernon et al., 2003; Zoefel et al., 2011).

FUTURE DIRECTIONS

Neuroimaging as a Guide

We have described how neuroimaging can provide insights about how training improves performance—for example, by increasing specific control processes or enhancing perceptual efficiency. Work by Dahlin and colleagues (2008) illustrates how neuroimaging may also be used to predict which tasks and populations (or individuals) are likely to show transfer effects. As described above, for young adults, training in the updating processes of WM decreased fronto-parietal activation and increased striatal activation. An untrained WM task (n-back), hypothesized to require updating, also led to striatal activation before training and showed positive transfer effects, whereas another task (Stroop) that activates fronto-parietal but not striatal systems did not benefit from training. In other words, only the task that recruited the region whose activity increased by training showed training-related improvements. In contrast, older adults failed to show striatal activation in any task before training, and while both their performance and striatal activation increased for the trained task, they did not show any transfer effects.

These findings suggest that shared neural substrates, which we refer to as neural overlap (Lustig et al., 2009), may constrain the transfer of training to new tasks. Further, the interactions of group and individual differences with task (and activation) must be taken into account. In combination with the CRUNCH framework, neural overlap points to an important and unexplored direction for integrating neuroimaging and training research: the use of neuroimaging to tailor training programs for maximum benefits. Consider, for example, two older adults, both with lower WM performance than an average young adult. Now imagine that one of these individuals shows less fronto-parietal activation than young adults during WM tasks, whereas the other shows more. For the first individual, a training program to increase the *engagement* of executive control processes might be most successful, whereas a program to increase the *efficiency* of those processes (or reduce burden on them) might be more useful for the second.

CONCLUSIONS

The harnessing of neural plasticity to improve human performance is still in the early stages, with neuroimaging as a potentially valuable guide in identifying targets for training, assessing program effectiveness, and designing individualized interventions. Working memory should remain a high priority in training research both because of its central role in human cognition and because it is an ideal domain for deepening our understanding of how training changes the brain. As CRUNCH makes explicit, an increase or decrease in activation cannot be interpreted in isolation. Activation levels must be considered across a range of task demands in order to differentiate, for example, an underengaged system from one that is inefficient and operating beyond its capacity. Working memory tasks allow parametric manipulations of load, and measuring the neural responses across a range of loads before and after training provides a more complete characterization of what limits performance before training, and what training-induced neural changes underlie performance gains. From the CRUNCH perspective, the goal is to shift the activation-task demand function to the right, increasing the capacity of the system to respond to higher levels of task demand. According to the neural overlap principle, these gains should transfer to other tasks that share critical neural substrates with those that have been trained.

REFERENCES

Altshuler, L., J. Tekell, et al. (2007). "Executive function and employment status among veterans with bipolar disorder." *Psychiatric Services* **58**(11): 1441–1447.

Badre, D. (2008). "Cognitive control, hierarchy, and the rostro-caudal organization of the frontal lobes." *Trends in Cognitive Sciences* **12**(5): 193–200.

Barch, D. M., J. G. Csernansky, et al. (2002). "Working and long-term memory deficits in Schizophrenia: Is there a common prefrontal mechanism?" *Journal of Abnormal Psychology* **111**(3): 478–494.

Berry, A. S., T. P. Zanto, et al. (2010). "The influence of perceptual training on working memory in older adults." *PLoS ONE* **5**(7). Article Number: e11537. DOI: 10.1371/journal.pone.0011537.

Blair, M., K. K. Vadaga, et al. (2011). "The role of age and inhibitory efficiency in working memory processing and storage components." *Quarterly Journal of Experimental Psychology* **64**(6): 1157–1172.

Boyke, J., J. Driemeyer, et al. (2008). "Training-induced brain structure changes in the elderly." *Journal of Neuroscience* **28**(28): 7031–7035.

Braver, T. S., J. L. Paxton, et al. (2009). "Flexible neural mechanisms of cognitive control within human prefrontal cortex." *Proceedings of the National Academy of Sciences of the United States of America* **106**(18): 7351–7356.

Bugg, J. M. and D. Head (2011). "Exercise moderates age-related atrophy of the medial temporal lobe." *Neurobiology of Aging* **32**(3): 506–514.

Bullitt, E., F. N. Rahman, et al. (2009). "The effect of exercise on the cerebral vasculature of healthy aged subjects as visualized by MR angiography." *American Journal of Neuroradiology* **30**(10): 1857–1863.

Cappell, K. A., L. Gmeindl, et al. (2010). "Age differences in prefrontal recruitment during verbal working memory maintenance depend on memory load." *Cortex* **46**(4): 462–473.

Carp, J. C. J., L. Gmeindl, et al. (2010). "Age differences in the neural representation of working memory revealed by multi-voxel pattern analysis." *Frontiers in Human Neuroscience* **4**.

Chen, A. J. W., T. Novakovic-Agopian, et al. (2011). "Training of goal-directed attention regulation enhances control over neural processing for individuals with brain injury." *Brain* **134**: 1541–1554.

Colcombe, S. J., K. I. Erickson, et al. (2006). "Aerobic exercise training increases brain volume in aging humans." *Journals of Gerontology Series A: Biological Sciences and Medical Sciences* **61**(11): 1166–1170.

Colcombe, S. J., A. F. Kramer, et al. (2004a). "Cardiovascular fitness, cortical plasticity, and aging." *Proceedings of the National Academy of Sciences of the United States of America* **101**(9): 3316–3321.

Colcombe, S. J., A. F. Kramer, et al. (2004b). "Neurocognitive aging and cardiovascular fitness: Recent findings and future directions." *Journal of Molecular Neuroscience* **24**(1): 9–14.

Dahlin, E., L. Backman, et al. (2009). "Training of the executive component of working memory: Subcortical areas mediate transfer effects." *Restorative Neurology and Neuroscience* **27**(5): 405–419.

Dahlin, E., A. S. Neely, et al. (2008). "Transfer of learning after updating training mediated by the striatum." *Science* **320**(5882): 1510–1512.

Daneman, M. and P. M. Merikle (1996). "Working memory and language comprehension: A meta-analysis." *Psychonomic Bulletin and Review* **3**(4): 422–433.

Dosenbach, N. U. F., D. A. Fair, et al. (2008). "A dual-networks architecture of top-down control." *Trends in Cognitive Sciences* **12**(3): 99–105.

Draganski, B., C. Gaser, et al. (2004). "Neuroplasticity: Changes in grey matter induced by training—Newly honed juggling skills show up as a transient feature on a brain-imaging scan." *Nature* **427**(6972): 311–312.

Edwards, B. G., D. M. Barch, et al. (2010). "Improving prefrontal cortex function in schizophrenia through focused training of cognitive control." *Frontiers in Human Neuroscience* **4**. Article Number: 32. DOI: 10.3389/fnhum.2010.00032.

Erickson, K. I., S. J. Colcombe, et al. (2007a). "Training-induced functional activation changes in dual-task processing: An fMRI study." *Cerebral Cortex* **17**(1): 192–204.

Erickson, K. I., S. J. Colcombe, et al. (2007b). "Training-induced plasticity in older adults: Effects of training on hemispheric asymmetry." *Neurobiology of Aging* **28**(2): 272–283.

Erickson, K. I., M. W. Voss, et al. (2011). "Exercise training increases size of hippocampus and improves memory." *Proceedings of the National Academy of Sciences of the United States of America* **108**(7): 3017–3022.

Esterman, M., Y. C. Chiu, et al. (2009). "Decoding cognitive control in human parietal cortex." *Proceedings of the National Academy of Sciences of the United States of America* **106**(42): 17974–17979.

Gold, J. M., R. W. Goldberg, et al. (2002). "Cognitive correlates of job tenure among patients with severe mental illness." *American Journal of Psychiatry* **159**(8): 1395–1402.

Grabner, R. H., A. Ischebeck, et al. (2009). "Fact learning in complex arithmetic and figural-spatial tasks: The role of the angular gyrus and its relation to mathematical competence." *Human Brain Mapping* **30**(9): 2936–2952.

Haut, K. M., K. O. Lim, et al. (2010). "Prefrontal cortical changes following cognitive training in patients with chronic schizophrenia: Effects of practice, generalization, and specificity." *Neuropsychopharmacology* **35**(9): 1850–1859.

Hillman, C. H., K. I. Erickson, et al. (2008). "Be smart, exercise your heart: Exercise effects on brain and cognition." *Nature Reviews Neuroscience* **9**(1): 58–65.

Hoekzema, E., S. Carmona, et al. (2010). "Enhanced neural activity in frontal and cerebellar circuits after cognitive training in children with Attention-Deficit/Hyperactivity Disorder." *Human Brain Mapping* **31**(12): 1942–1950.

Horowitz-Kraus, T. and Z. Breznitz (2009). "Can the error detection mechanism benefit from training the working memory? A comparison between dyslexics and controls: An ERP study." *PLoS ONE* **4**(9). Article Number: e7141. DOI: 10.1371/journal.pone.0007141.

Jarrold, C., H. Tam, et al. (2011). "How does processing affect storage in working memory tasks? Evidence for both domain-general and domain-specific effects." *Journal of Experimental Psychology: Learning, Memory and Cognition* **37**(3): 688–705.

Kelley, T. A. and S. Yantis (2010). "Neural correlates of learning to attend." *Frontiers in Human Neuroscience* **4**. Article Number: 216. DOI: 10.3389/fnhum.2010.00216.

Klingberg, T. (2010). "Training and plasticity of working memory." *Trends in Cognitive Sciences* **14**(7): 317–324.

Kwon, Y. J., J. K. Lee, et al. (2009). "Changes in brain activation induced by the training of hypothesis generation skills: An fMRI study." *Brain and Cognition* **69**(2): 391–397.

Kyllonen, P. C. and R. E. Christal (1990). "Reasoning ability is (little more than) working-memory capacity." *Intelligence* **14**(4): 389–433.

Lewis-Peacock, J. A. and B. R. Postle (2008). "Temporary activation of long-term memory supports working memory." *Journal of Neuroscience* **28**(35): 8765–8771.

Lovden, M., N. C. Bodammer, et al. (2010). "Experience-dependent plasticity of white-matter microstructure extends into old age." *Neuropsychologia* **48**(13): 3878–3883.

Lustig, C., P. Shah, et al. (2009). "Aging, training, and the brain: A review and future directions." *Neuropsychology Review* **19**(4): 504–522.

Mattay, V. S., F. Fera, et al. (2006). "Neurophysiological correlates of age-related changes in working memory capacity." *Neuroscience Letters* **392**(1–2): 32–37.

Minzenberg, M. J., A. R. Laird, et al. (2009). "Meta-analysis of 41 functional neuroimaging studies of executive function in schizophrenia." *Archives of General Psychiatry* **66**(8): 811–822.

Neubauer, A. C., R. H. Grabner, et al. (2004). "Intelligence and individual differences in becoming neurally efficient." *Acta Psychologica* **116**(1): 55–74.

Paxton, J. L., D. M. Barch, et al. (2006). "Effects of environmental support and strategy training on older adults' use of context." *Psychology and Aging* **21**(3): 499–509.

Reuter-Lorenz, P. A. and K. A. Cappell (2008). "Neurocognitive aging and the compensation hypothesis." *Current Directions in Psychological Science* **17**(3): 177–182.

Reuter-Lorenz, P. A. and C. Lustig (2005). "Brain aging: Reorganizing discoveries about the aging mind." *Current Opinion in Neurobiology* **15**(2): 245–251.

Schneider-Garces, N. J., B. A. Gordon, et al. (2010). "Span, CRUNCH, and beyond: Working memory capacity and the aging brain." *Journal of Cognitive Neuroscience* **22**(4): 655–669.

Seidman, L. J., E. M. Valera, et al. (2004). "Brain function and structure in adults with attention-deficit/hyperactivity disorder." *Psychiatric Clinics of North America* **27**(2): 323–347.

Smith, P. J., J. A. Blumenthal, et al. (2010). "Aerobic exercise and neurocognitive performance: A meta-analytic review of randomized controlled trials." *Psychosomatic Medicine* **72**(3): 239–252.

Stokes, M., R. Thompson, et al. (2009). "Top-down activation of shape-specific population codes in visual cortex during mental imagery." *Journal of Neuroscience* **29**(5): 1565–1572.

Unsworth, N., T. S. Redick, et al. (2009). "Complex working memory span tasks and higher-order cognition: A latent-variable analysis of the relationship between processing and storage." *Memory* **17**(6): 635–654.

Vernon, D., T. Egner, et al. (2003). "The effect of training distinct neurofeedback protocols on aspects of cognitive performance." *International Journal of Psychophysiology* **47**(1): 75–85.

Voelcker-Rehage, C., B. Godde, et al. (2011). "Cardiovascular and coordination training differentially improve cognitive performance and neural processing in older adults." *Frontiers in Human Neuroscience* **5**. Article Number: 26. DOI: 10.3389/fnhum.2011. 00026.

Westerberg, H. and T. Klingberg (2007). "Changes in cortical activity after training of working memory: A single-subject analysis." *Physiology and Behavior* **92**(1–2): 186–192.

Wexler, B. E., M. Anderson, et al. (2000). "Preliminary evidence of improved verbal working memory performance and normalization of task-related frontal lobe activation in schizophrenia following cognitive exercises." *American Journal of Psychiatry* **157**(10): 1694–1697.

Wykes, T., M. Brammer, et al. (2002). "Effects on the brain of a psychological treatment: cognitive remediation therapy – Functional magnetic resonance imaging in schizophrenia." *British Journal of Psychiatry* **181**: 144–152.

Zoefel, B., R. J. Huster, et al. (2011). "Neurofeedback training of the upper alpha frequency band in EEG improves cognitive performance." *Neuroimage* **54**(2): 1427–1431.

Index